D0341287

THE PROMISE

Friedman, Rachelle,
The promise : a tragic
accident, a paralyzed br
[2014]
33305231481585
sa   02/19/15

THE PROMISE

A Tragic Accident, a Paralyzed Bride,
and the Power of Love, Loyalty, and Friendship

RACHELLE FRIEDMAN

Guilford, Connecticut
An imprint of Globe Pequot Press

To buy books in quantity for corporate use
or incentives, call **(800) 962-0973**
or e-mail **premiums@GlobePequot.com**.

skirt!® is an attitude . . . spirited, independent, outspoken, serious, playful and irreverent, sometimes controversial, always passionate.

Copyright © 2014 by Disability Possibilities, Inc.

ALL RIGHTS RESERVED. No part of this book may be reproduced or transmitted in any form by any means, electronic or mechanical, including photocopying and recording, or by any information storage and retrieval system, except as may be expressly permitted in writing from the publisher. Requests for permission should be addressed to Globe Pequot Press, Attn: Rights and Permissions Department, PO Box 480, Guilford, CT 06437.

skirt!® is an imprint of Globe Pequot Press.
skirt!® is a registered trademark of Morris Publishing Group, LLC, and is used with express permission.

All photos courtesy of the author unless otherwise indicated.

Project Editor: Lauren Brancato
Layout Artist: Kirsten Livingston

Library of Congress Cataloging-in-Publication Data is available on file.

ISBN 978-0-7627-9294-8

Printed in the United States of America

10 9 8 7 6 5 4 3 2 1

To anyone dealing with a spinal cord injury
and to all of those fighting tirelessly for a cure,
this book is for you.

To my alma mater,
East Carolina University, and the Pirate nation
for all of your support.
Once a Pirate, always a Pirate.

CONTENTS

Contents

When a soul is sent down from heaven it contains both male and female characteristics. The male elements enter the baby boy; the female elements enter the baby girl; and if they be worthy, God reunites them in marriage.

—THE ZOHAR

The names of all of the women by the pool the night of my accident, and of some of my friends, have been changed to protect their privacy. Some details about their identities have been slightly altered.

Prologue

My head hit the bottom of the pool and I heard an excruciatingly loud crack. Whether it was my neck snapping or my head hitting the concrete floor, I'm not really sure. I just remember that sound above all else in that moment. My eyes were open underwater, but I couldn't process what was happening. I simply floated, suspended in time. In those few seconds I didn't see a flash before my eyes. I didn't see a rush of memories. I felt frozen, as if someone had hit a pause button. I couldn't figure out anything. That crack was the only thing I heard.

When you're underwater it's usually so quiet and peaceful. But this moment didn't feel peaceful—it simply felt stuck. I felt no panic or even fear. No gasping for air and taking in water. Just my frozen mind. My body froze, too. I knew I was in water, but I couldn't feel the wetness of it; that was the strangest thing. My mind—knowing I was immersed—and my body weren't syncing up. I couldn't feel anything. I was just floating, still and nearly lifeless, toward the surface.

I had no idea when I crawled out of bed that morning that it would be the last time I'd be able to do it on my own, without help from another person. My world was about to change, as was that of my fiancé and parents.

There was another life that would unexpectedly be robbed of its joy, its ability to laugh, and it would be rocked to the core, maybe more so than mine.

CHAPTER 1

Meeting the One

OUR PLAN WAS TO HAVE EVERYTHING WE EVER WANTED: THE perfect house, a rich and happy marriage, a baby boy and a baby girl. We saw the house as the foundation of our goals and dreams. In the summer of 2009, Chris and I bought it together; it's where we were going to live our wonderfully and carefully planned life, in Knightdale, North Carolina, a small town three hours from where I grew up in Virginia Beach.

It was the Friday of my bachelorette weekend, a month before my wedding. We were home in the morning before work, scrambling to take off for fun but separate celebratory weekends. Chris was packing for his guys' camping trip. He was loading his fishing gear and clothing into the car: rods and reels, tents, all of the things you need to camp. It was all neutral colors—browns, beiges, and greens; we certainly couldn't have been packing for two more opposite events. I was preparing for a seriously girlie weekend, and he was getting ready for an ultra-guy weekend of roughing it.

My friend Britney and I had gone shopping days beforehand for a fun white dress I'd wear the next evening, and I was carefully packing my dress, curling iron, makeup, and all that I'd need to primp and party the next night. I was so worried I'd forget something, I kept reviewing what I had laid out. I was so consumed by all of the little details that were a big deal to me at the time and seemed so important. None of it turned out to be all that important in the days that followed.

Chris left before me that morning and made a point to kiss me good-bye. He was leaving for his camping trip straight from work, so I wouldn't see him until that Sunday night.

"I love you. Be safe," he said.

"I love you, too," I responded.

He went to work and so did I.

I was completely unaware it would be my last day of work ever. I was a program coordinator at an active seniors facility, and I had planned a Senior Prom for the members of the center. I dressed up in a satin polka dot dress that flared out when I twirled. I had the residents line dancing and slow dancing, and I remember dancing so hard myself. It was a fun morning. One of the couples was celebrating their fiftieth anniversary. We played a special love song for them and had them take the floor like it was their first dance. I remember looking at them and thinking, "I can't wait for this to be Chris and me." I imagined our first dance at our wedding and years of growing old together. It was a magical vision.

When I arrived home later that day, I changed out of the polka dot dress and threw on some yoga clothes for the long car ride back to my hometown. Britney picked me up that afternoon. When I left our beautiful home on May 21, 2010, I left a few dishes in the sink, the bed unmade, and a bunch of outfits on the floor that I had torn out of my closet to pack and never put back. I figured I'd clean up when I returned home. I was too excited to waste time. I had set my bag right at the door, so I could just zip in and grab it after work.

Britney and I headed to my grandma's house for our big Saturday. It's the place I always go when I head to my hometown. It's easier there. My room at my mom and dad's had been turned into a storage office, but my grandma had a real room for me still, so I liked it there. I was celebrating with my girls; Chris was celebrating with his dad. Soon, we'd be husband and wife, a day I'd waited for my entire life.

Chris and I met at East Carolina University in Greenville at a party in 2004, during my freshman year. It was October, and Halloween was a serious weeklong affair there. In fact, it's apparently one of the biggest Hallows' Eve celebrations in the country, almost like a mini Mardi Gras. This was a Friday night, October 29. But two days later, on Halloween night, all the streets would be full of people shoulder to shoulder.

It was an outdoor party, part of the festivities that we'd heard about through the grapevine. None of my dorm mates in Tyler Hall knew the guys hosting it, but we had heard it would be fun. We all got ready together, trying on a bunch of different outfits, clothes scattered everywhere. I settled on light capri jeans, a brown silky halter top, and some dangly turquoise earrings. I had my hair pulled sort of halfway back, so that you could see my jewelry.

My roommate, two other girls, and I set out in the early evening to find the place, which was all the way across campus, but we made a stop along the way. The main part of campus was designed like a square, with everything essentially no more than one mile away. I lived on College Hill, across from the main campus. We stopped at a guy friend's place first, and we began playing beer pong. With a few more people in our crowd, we headed to the party, located close to downtown Greenville. We knew we were getting close as we walked, because we could hear the din of the party blocks away. It was one loud constant noise. We walked around to the backyard, which was full of people—every square inch covered. This was by far the biggest party I'd ever attended.

My friends and I edged our way through the crowd and found our way into the house; we bought vodka and orange juice drinks before heading back outside. I saw this guy Mike that my roommate had already met, and we were all introduced to his two roommates, Chris and Tom. I thought Mike was really cute when I saw him standing there. My roommate Mary was interested in Mike, too.

I kind of flirted with all three of them that night. I was a flirtatious girl then, and it was fun to have that attention. We were all chatting and laughing over drinks. Mike, it turned out, was Chris's cousin and roommate, and as we were all standing there talking, I couldn't stop thinking about how cute he was. I didn't notice Chris as much, because I was so drawn to Mike initially. I was talking to the group of them really, not just one person. We talked for a while, getting bumped around by passing partygoers. Mike headed through the crowds with my roommate, so they could chat with some other people. I wound up sort of isolated, alone with just Chris at that point. Since the music was playing and I loved randomly teaching people to salsa dance, I grabbed Chris's hand.

"C'mon, let's dance. I'll show you how."

He was totally up for it. It was crowded, so we were moving in a tiny space as we danced.

"Where are you from?" I asked.

"Virginia Beach," he said.

"Me, too!"

I had been drinking and, after a couple of songs, took a break. I turned to him and said, "So, where are you from?"

He answered again. We laugh about this, but I asked him twice more that night. He finally said, "The same place you are from!"

Chris and Tom and I all left the party together at the end of the night. Although our other friends headed straight back to Mike's place, we went to Alfredo's to get pizza. There was a standing joke in Greenville that the pizza was edible at this place only if you had been drinking. We waited for what seemed like an hour for our pizza, then headed back to Mike's to hang out for a few more hours, all of us just talking and laughing about the night. This was my freshman year, and looking back I realize that it was the most important night of my life.

Like many of those college crushes, my roommate was over Mike by sunrise. He must have done something to turn her off. Back in our dorm I asked her, "Do you mind if I go for Mike?"

"Go for it," she said.

We hung out again on Halloween, two nights later. Mike and I were flirting with each other and even holding hands, but it didn't go anywhere beyond that night.

But by December that year, Chris and I were buddies. I had a lot of guy friends then, so I didn't think much of it. We were both going home for the holidays, and he offered to give me a ride. He picked me up in his Buick Le Sabre. We lived about two and a half hours away from school, both from the same town (as we'd by now laughed about many times). We talked about a lot of things on that drive, but honestly, since I wasn't even remotely thinking about him romantically, I don't remember much of the discussion.

To me, it was just a ride home. But I do recall that he implied he was having problems with his girlfriend, that things hadn't really been the same with the two of them. I wasn't in a place to give advice, since I hadn't ever been in a serious relationship in my life. He said that he was looking forward to a week apart from her to think things through. The term "breakup" wasn't a part of our conversation, but he suggested they'd assess things when they returned to school in the New Year. I may not have known much about relationships, but I could tell he wasn't happy. As his friend, happiness was all I wanted for him.

While I didn't have those kinds of special feelings about Chris, I was struck immediately by the fact that he was a really awesome, stand-up guy. It was something you could just tell, especially as we rode together that day and I listened to him talk. It sounds so corny and general, but it became obvious to me that Chris was a crazily honest and extremely genuine person. I could tell from the very beginning that he would never intentionally hurt someone, or purposely lie or be mean. He was just always so nice.

He took me to my house, and that's when we figured out how close we lived to each other. I knew he was in Virginia Beach, but I had never bothered to ask him where exactly. So when I gave him directions to my grandmother's house, we were shocked that his home was literally in the same neighborhood, and we could have walked to each other's houses. We did learn that our paths had crossed before college. We had the same dentist—my uncle. Chris had been to my dad's army-navy surplus store, too. Basically, he'd met several members of my family before ever meeting me. I used to go to the pool in the community when I was little, in the summers, and he said he was there every day for years, as was I, starting at age three. Chris was four years older than me, a big difference then. We're not sure if we played together, but we might have. Virginia Beach is not a small place. It's not a big city, but it's spread out, so to discover we'd been in the same neighborhood was pretty crazy.

He helped me bring my stuff inside and met my grandma for the first time, and she'll tell you to this day that she never saw me look at a guy like that before, that she saw our future right there. She saw it well before I did. I didn't see that at all.

CHAPTER 2

From Friend to Soul Mate

I JUMPED OUT OF BED THE NEXT MORNING, SO EXCITED THINKING about the bachelorette day ahead. My friend Britney had stayed overnight with me at my grandma's house in Virginia Beach. It was like a sleepover. We stayed in one room, and my grandma made us my favorite breakfast that morning: pancakes and scrambled eggs.

There was so much to do. My day was jam-packed with plans and appointments and last-minute shopping. I was getting my final fitting for my wedding dress; having lunch with my mom, Bubbie (my dad's mom), and Britney; and then heading off to celebrate my pending wedding with my other friends. Lauren was still making her way to town, and the other girls were busy prepping and planning the night ahead, so they didn't join us for lunch. It was my bachelorette party. I was going to marry my Prince Charming, the man of my dreams: Chris Chapman. This day was all part of the celebration leading up to that.

I was excited to hang out with this group of girls because we would all be going out together for the first time. They knew of each other, but we hadn't spent too much time together as a group before. Lauren, Samantha, Carly, and Britney—all from different periods of my life—would finally really get to know each other and spend time together to celebrate with me. Just the five of us. But before the evening's festivities, the group from lunch went to the bridal shop, so that I could try on my wedding dress for the very last fitting.

I had gone shopping for my wedding dress two weeks after I got engaged. All the girls were there, and each one went and grabbed a dress off the rack. Lauren pulled the one I ultimately chose. It was just beautiful. I tried on only four, but I fell in love with that one immediately. It was a strapless dress, corseted at the top and laced down the back. The skirt flowed from there, and it had an incredible train. My mom had seen it when I first picked it out, but when she looked at me in it all fitted and ready to wear, she was overjoyed. She said it looked like it was made just for me. She had wanted to buy it for me and I accepted, knowing how happy it made her to do that, even though she'd have to work very hard to do so. Everyone thought it was beautiful.

The bridal shop finished some of the alterations, and then we all headed out for a quick lunch at Applebee's in town. I brought my veil and some flowers with me. After lunch we went to a local hair salon for a trial on how I'd wear my hair on my wedding day. We tried updos and all down, but in the end, we decided that curls, with half pulled up along the sides, would be best. I left with that look, which was great because I'd wear it out for the party that evening.

The biggest stress of the day was finding the right shoes for the bachelorette night. I wanted the perfect white high heels, or else I felt like the entire outfit would be ruined. I was sort of frantic that I wouldn't find what I had in mind: really high stilettos, strappy and white, of course. I wound up finding the perfect pair, not knowing that even the ideal shoes couldn't change the outcome of the night.

—◆—

Chris and I had made it through the entire spring semester in 2005 without dating, but our friendship had grown really deep. He had become my very best friend. His relationship with his girlfriend had withered by then, and by April they'd broken up. He and I spent a lot of time together, but I didn't think anything of it beyond us being friends.

In early June of that year, he invited me to his family's vacation house on Lake Gaston by myself. We were just friends, but I knew at this point that he liked me. It was a little awkward, but I wanted to go because I thought it would be fun, and it was not too weird because we had been hanging out all of the time. I remember it was really hot around that time. I was wearing a little red bikini, sunbathing on the dock, which was down a hill a bit from the house. It was over water, connecting the house to the boathouse. The main house was a rustic place—wood, painted brown, not stained. It was on a street called Happy Valley, which was fitting because it was a really happy place. It was one of the original houses built on the lake. Chris's grandfather had built it with his bare hands, and Chris's dad had grown up spending summers at the lake house.

They had two rules at the house: You could have anything you wanted, but you had to get it yourself, and there was no skinny-dipping before ten o'clock at night. It was sweet because this house, which had sort of a main section and then some other newer additions, was a throwback surrounded by other large modern houses that were built later. It sat on a little cove, overlooking the main lake. The streets were eventually all paved, but leading up to the house was a long, straight gravel drive. You could smell the water and hear the ripples lapping up against the dock. I later learned that as I lay there that day, listening to the peaceful sound of the water, Chris was checking me out from the back deck as I caught some sun in my little bikini. I wasn't trying to taunt him, but I guess I should have known that wearing a red string bikini in front of a guy with a crush wasn't entirely innocent.

I was still wearing that same bikini when we went out on their boat that afternoon, and that's when Chris shifted his approach from staring from afar to pursuing me. We were on the boat on the lake, and he let me drive. He sat behind me and helped me steer. I'd never driven a boat before, and it was calming to have him guiding me. It felt protective and sweet. He was getting closer to me than maybe he ever had before, and then he set his hand on my thigh. It wasn't completely smooth or subtle, but it wasn't overt, either; he wasn't rubbing it in a sexual way, but it was for sure not the way a friend would touch another friend. I didn't know how to react. It was how a boy touched a girl, and I felt panicked. He left his hand on my leg for a long time; that's how I knew. It was clearly flirtatious, but all new to me.

A couple of weekends later, a group of us went to the lake, including his cousin and some of our other friends. He decided to take me for a walk around the streets in the lake neighborhood, just the two of us, and I remember him holding my hand. It was completely foreign to me, and I was so nervous. I had held a guy's hand before, but not like this, not so tenderly, and definitely not in a situation like this one that was brewing with feelings. I didn't know what it meant or what to do about it, other than to simply hold it back. I liked it, I guess. It felt natural and fun to be holding his hand.

I was wearing a bathing suit, board shorts, and a T-shirt. I hadn't gotten extra dolled up or anything; I was just wearing what I normally wore in the summer. I grew up at the beach, so I was always wearing bikinis. The walk was definitely awkward, but I think I picked up on his motives and panicked just a bit again.

"Everyone we know is in a relationship that sucks, don't you think?" I blurted out for no reason other than nerves. I was thinking things and just saying them without censoring myself at all.

"I guess," he said.

"It scares me. I don't really see many relationships going so well. And then when these people all break up, what's left? They can't even be friends anymore. It makes you really think, you know?"

"Yeah," he said.

This guy had basically taken me on a walk to ask me out, and here I was talking about these horrible relationships and how I was scared of them.

We were nearly ending our walk and almost back at his house when he finally found the courage to ask me the question he'd been saving. We stopped halfway up the driveway, and he asked, "Do you see yourself in a relationship ever?"

I was honest. I said, "Yeah." That's it. That's all I said.

Then he grew a little braver and asked, "Do you see yourself in a relationship with me?" He said it like it was an official question that he'd been working on for a while. He didn't ask me out exactly, just inquired about our potential future.

I said, "Yes." I paused for just a second and said, "But I'm really scared." By then my head was spinning. We continued walking at that point, and my head swirled with fear. We were roommates at college for the summer and we were best friends. I didn't want to give up either of those things. I kept thinking, *What if it doesn't work out?* When we walked around the house on the deck, everyone was hanging out, and I knew we needed more time to talk.

We stole a few more minutes away from the crowd by continuing past them all and slipping onto the back part of the deck for privacy. I tried to explain myself, but I just started talking in circles. I told him I was confused, and he said he could tell. I then took my second "yes" back in a way. I could feel myself breaking his heart, but I couldn't stop rambling about my fears.

"I don't know right now. But that doesn't mean never," I said. "I'm just scared right now."

He didn't say anything. He leaned down and kissed my forehead.

I spent the rest of the evening wishing I could take back all of my babbling. What Chris had done, what he had said, was the sweetest gesture ever. But there were so many people around, and I was too afraid of everything happening so quickly.

That night, we actually shared a bed. We didn't cuddle or do anything at all; the house was so full of people, and it seemed the obvious plan that we would bunk together. All night I thought about what he had said and the kiss on my forehead.

We wound up being separated that next week, so my fear and what he had said just lingered, unresolved. I returned to Greenville, and he went to Raleigh to see his cousin Mike. While Chris was there Mike called and told me that he had a friend that he thought would really hit it off with me, that we would be a good match. Worse, there was another girl at the house with them that Mike wanted to set Chris up with. I thought, *I've blown it all with Chris.*

It was an awful week. I was afraid of moving forward with Chris, but then I was suddenly scared of losing him, too. And I was jealous at the same time, which really surprised me. That was a big realization for me. It didn't change the terror of being nineteen years old and realizing that maybe I was falling for my future husband, or worrying that I'd fallen for my best friend but would lose both him and his friendship in the end. It was a weird pull, balancing commitment with potential for loss. It was an indescribable tug of war inside of me.

At some point midweek I took Tom aside in his room to help me sort things out in my head. He was also our summer roommate, and so he'd seen the progression of things.

"I don't know what to do," I said.

"I think you should just do it, go for it," he said.

"I know. I'm nervous, though."

"Chris could be your future husband," he said. He was half joking, I think.

"Don't say that. You're freaking me out!"

"He could be, though," he said.

"I know. But it scares me."

Ultimately, when I thought it through, I realized it was almost inevitable we'd at least give it a go and try to be together, mainly because besides fear, I couldn't make the argument for not being with Chris. He was a perfect guy. He was honest and genuine, we got along, and we both liked the same things—going out, outdoor stuff, and travel. We were both ECU Pirates fans, which was important. We had everything in common, but I had never had a boyfriend, I didn't know how this was all supposed to work, and I didn't want the good stuff to end if the romance fizzled.

The bigger fear, of course, was that I'd messed it all up and it was too late. That I'd let this great guy slip on by.

CHAPTER 3

The Bachelorette Party

AFTER MY HAIR WAS SET AND MY PERFECT SHOES PURCHASED, Britney and I headed over to Carly's house for the evening festivities, but I had to wait in the car for a few minutes because apparently the girls were still decorating outside. I was thrilled to be having a bachelorette party in my honor. This was one of those things we all thought about as a teen—part of the entire wedding celebration—and it was with friends I really enjoyed being around.

It was early, around five o'clock or so, and the weather was perfect, with that late spring smell in the air, when you know summer and all its excitement are fast approaching. I was wearing the casual clothes I'd had lunch in, but I had the great dress with me to change into for later that night—white, like the one I'd wear on my wedding day. But this one was fun, cute, and short. I was giddy. The four girls—Carly, Lauren, Britney, and Samantha—were going to wear a shade of purple, just like they'd wear for the wedding. Purple was one of my school colors and my favorite color, too.

All of these girls were from such different walks of my life. Lauren was my oldest friend. We'd met when we were two years old, when our brothers were in Boy Scouts together. She was the sister I never had. She lived in Charlotte now, but she was the kind of friend where no matter how much time had passed, it didn't matter; we picked up right where we had left off. We used to make videos together of us dancing and acting silly. Her mom had a whole stack of VHS tapes of us. We took acting lessons together and used to make big plans to live on a farm with a bunch of horses.

Carly and I met in middle school when I was twelve. She ended up going to a different high school, but we stayed friends. We loved to sing together. Carly was a phenomenal musician, great at both piano and guitar. We loved showing off by putting shows on for our friends.

I met Samantha through Carly in freshman year of high school, when Carly brought me to a birthday party. Samantha and I didn't get along right away. She thought I was a dork, and I thought she was a snob. We both judged too quickly. We slowly warmed up to each other and grew closer over the summer. I got to know her really well when we worked together at the beach. We used to have so much fun. Our one job was basically to sit there, a little ways apart from each other on the beach, and wait for people to come and rent stuff from us. We each had our own station, and although we stayed extremely busy, it was still boring work. Sometimes we would sneak away and go bodyboarding for a few minutes in the middle of our shift to break up the monotony. Of course, we'd return to shambles—people using umbrellas they hadn't paid for and such—and we'd have to backtrack to make up for the time. To liven it all up, we made a book. We were just far enough apart that we couldn't sit and talk to each other. So we made this book and we'd write funny things in it—well, things that we thought were funny—and then we'd run it back and forth across the sand. That's how we communicated all day.

We would write things like how cute some of the beach boys were. We talked about going dancing. We were both dancing queens and we'd turned eighteen around the same time, so we could finally go dancing at the clubs downtown at night. Our senior year we went out all the time together on weekends.

So all of the other lifeguards knew about the book and they wanted it. I remember one asking, "What's in the book?"

As he was asking I wrote his name in it, big so he could see. Then he kept asking if he could see it. It was fun. It kept us entertained as we sat under an umbrella in a beach chair all day.

Britney and I met in 2009. Her boyfriend and Chris had played ball at the university together. We were in the clubhouse playing pool one night right after college, both living in the same apartment complex. She and her boyfriend had recently graduated, too. It was practically the first week out of school for all of us. Chris and her boyfriend bumped into each other and introduced us. It was a quick encounter and I didn't think much of it at the time, nor did she obviously, as we didn't say much more than hello to each other. A week later, I saw a girl washing "Go ECU!" paint off the side of her car. Drawn to a fellow Pirate fan, I approached, hoping to make a new friend. I began talking and then a minute in, I realized it was Britney. After that we kept bumping into each other. We'd go to each other's apartments and out in downtown Raleigh frequently. It was so nice to have a girlfriend close by.

Britney wasn't in the bridal party, but she was joining our celebration. There were a few more girls who were supposed to come out with us, but they wound up not being able to make it that night, so it was just the five of us. At the time, Britney wasn't a bridesmaid because another friend of mine, Sandra, was in the wedding. But that friend and I had drifted apart, and I wished I could have had Britney in my wedding party because we'd grown so close. Unfortunately, we couldn't get another dress to match, and I couldn't very well ask the other friend to step aside and give up her dress for no reason.

When they finally let me in that night at Carly's, I felt so happy to be with them. They had hung pink banners everywhere and decorated outside beautifully. They were excited to surprise me with the decorations. The patio looked nice, all done up. We sat under an umbrella around a table catching up, enjoying the weather. We grilled some burgers and hot dogs and had a little bit of champagne to kick off the night. The limo would arrive much later to take us dancing. The girls had set up games on the deck, some of them too racy to mention, but ultimately we never played any of them, because we all talked too much.

Britney had us in hysterics. She was telling us all how she couldn't go to the bathroom anywhere other than at home, no matter where she was—it was a genuine phobia. She relayed a story about how she went on vacation with her boyfriend for the first time to his family's house, and it was small and she just couldn't relieve herself. She was afraid of people hearing it. She's always had to jump through hoops to avoid using public restrooms, so she often made us laugh with her extraordinary stories.

At some point in the evening, just for a few minutes, my parents stopped by to give me a hug and say hello. It was a very significant hug, though none of us had any idea how significant. It would be the last time they'd see me stand . . . or give me a hug at eye level.

After dinner I was sitting on Lauren's lap, reminiscing.

"How crazy is it that we were just Girl Scouts, like yesterday, playing softball and basketball together, and now we're getting married within a month of each other?" she asked.

"I know. Soon, we'll both be married old ladies," I replied.

"But it's cool how our lives have always been parallel for so long. We even used to have joint birthday parties together! Now basically weddings, too."

As we toasted, clinking glasses, I thought about how lucky I was to have such awesome friends to celebrate with, and I was really looking forward to the rest of the evening. We all got along that night, and it was one of those rare times when everyone just became fast friends. It was almost an instant connection. I had no way of knowing as we talked exactly how important and significant that group friendship was about to become. We discussed the fact that it was actually kind of unusual that we all got along so well, with only me as the common thread. Someone made the point that everyone was so welcoming and how rare that was these days. In an eerie way, even before an unspoken bond was formed, the promise of continued friendship was apparent. This was a good group of people, period.

In 2002, in tenth grade at my private school, I joined the varsity cheerleading squad. The girls on the team did not like me because I wasn't Miss Popular. They would leave me out of everything, including dinners before games. I'd remain at school the entire time in between practice and the start of a game, because I couldn't drive yet. I remember feeling restricted and stuck. Rarely did someone step up and be mean to my face, but behind my back they were awful. The other cheerleaders were always whispering about me, which made it hard for me to defend myself. Looking back now, I really wish I had stood up to them. I did prevail in a sense, though, because that year I was awarded MVP cheerleader, and man, were they pissed. No one said congrats. When I heard my name announced, I felt that all of the tears they'd caused me were worth it. I wasn't brave enough to stand up for myself back then.

That was the same summer I started working at the beach with some friends, renting out umbrellas. We were such beach bums and would go bodyboarding for hours. We partied with the lifeguards every week, but the most I ever drank was three or four Mike's Hard Lemonades. That was when I first tried alcohol. I was actually kind of a goody-goody, and I think it annoyed my friends at school, but these girls didn't care.

I really came out of my shell around then. I'm not sure what changed, but for the first time I felt beautiful, sexy, fun, and popular. I wished I could have felt like that at school, but around the girls there I never really did. It took meeting people like Carly and Samantha to remind me of how friendships were supposed to be, how people were supposed to treat each other. By senior year I had decided to change high schools and graduate elsewhere, because I didn't want to deal with the drama anymore at the private school.

After dinner and a lot of laughter, we all dolled ourselves up, ready to hit the clubs. It was about eight o'clock, and we were excited to go out dancing. I felt like I was in my college dorm room, all of us in one bathroom, giggling and applying our makeup, cracking jokes about how nicely we had cleaned up. I wore my white satin dress, and they all slipped on their various shades of purple and matching black belts. My favorite dance music was Britney Spears, so as a treat Samantha created a really cool mix of all of her songs, which we planned to blare in the limo.

After about an hour we started taking pictures. Carly's mom took pictures of the group of us, and we laughed the entire time. The limo was picking us up at ten. Just before we were leaving, we went down to the kitchen and mixed up this crazy red drink concoction to take with us while we headed from club to club. A black stretch limo pulled up in front of the house, and we jumped in with our red drinks, ready for a fun night. At one point while we were driving around, I managed to spill the red drink on my white dress. Of course, I was the only one spilling and the only one in white, so it couldn't have felt more disastrous at the time. As I sat there soaked down the front and about to freak out, Lauren yelled up to the driver, "Stop at the next Rite Aid you see."

Within a couple of minutes, he pulled over. Britney and Lauren ran inside, bought five bleach pens, and went to town on the dress. After about ten minutes of intense scrubbing and rubbing, we all looked down and agreed the cleanup had worked. Tragedy had been averted. Later, looking at the dress in the light, I could see that it was still totally stained. I had a pink sash on that said

"Bachelorette," so maybe that hid it or helped it blend a little. And ultimately it didn't matter at all.

We went to clubs all over town, and it was so cool pulling up in a limo. We stepped out like we were total rock stars. It was an incredible feeling, being treated to such a decadent night with such great people. But I wasn't quite graceful enough to live up to my pretend status. At the second club everyone poured out of the car. We headed up to the second floor, making our way to the upper deck. We reached the top, and everyone looked our way to acknowledge that a bachelorette party had arrived. Right in that moment, the heel of my shoe got stuck between the wooden deck boards. My shoe stayed, I didn't, and I fell almost facedown, sprawled out in front of everyone in line. We all thought it was the most hilarious thing that ever could have happened, and we laughed about it as they helped me up. I cheered loudly with them to play it off as cool as possible.

We danced all night, and at one o'clock in the morning, we climbed into the limo to head back home. We had to carry our shoes at this point, because our feet were so sore from the high heels. We had been drinking, but we weren't really drunk. We were sober enough to know when to go home. I've thought a lot about the timing of this night and wondered how it could have gone differently. If I *had* gotten drunk, would I have gone right to sleep when I got back to Carly's house? If we'd gone to one more club, would we have been too tired for the next series of events? I've thought about how and when we decided to call the night and head home and how that timing determined the outcome of the rest of my life.

CHAPTER 4

The Accident

LAUREN AND I USED TO DREAM OF BEING MERMAIDS WHEN WE were little and argue over who got to be Ariel. Every Sunday, my dad, Larry, used to take me to a cafeteria for breakfast where they had a fountain. I'd always ask for two pennies to make a wish. I'd use one to wish I was a mermaid, but because I felt that was a selfish wish, I always used the second penny to wish for world peace.

Once we were all danced out, Lauren suggested we take a swim when we returned to Carly's house. We all raced out of the limo and ran upstairs to change into our bathing suits. The night had been so much fun. We had talked a lot about Chris and our future and boys they liked, too. These girls had heard it all before, but part of the fun of the night was getting all the attention as a bride-to-be, and we talked about not only how Chris and I ultimately got together after all my crazy fears but also how we almost didn't.

During that week when Chris and I were apart, before we became a couple, all I could think about was how I wanted to take back everything I had said. I wanted to replace "No, I don't want to date you" with "Oh, I've changed my mind because there is this new girl coming along for you and I don't want to miss out on the greatest thing ever." But I just couldn't yet.

The girl and the guy that Mike had planned for us both did visit, but nothing came of it for either me or Chris. Thankfully. Finally, after that week of being apart, we both wound up at Virginia Beach, and that entire time I could think of nothing else but Chris and our future together. I even had trouble sleeping. I was obsessed with figuring out what my feelings meant and why I had him on my mind.

I would think over and over again in my head, *What do I do? What do I do?* I couldn't focus on anything else. That's when it became obvious that we had to remain good friends *and* become a couple. Both were allowed. Both could work. It took me some time to figure out that we could do both, but when I did I knew I'd had a life-altering epiphany. Embracing one didn't mean giving up the other. I think I knew, or at least hoped, that it was going to work out and that ultimately I wouldn't have to sacrifice friendship for love, because we would survive on both levels. I felt it in my gut, and the decision felt peaceful and right.

We arranged to meet, and he picked me up at midnight and then we drove to the oceanfront. We wound up at 65th Street, and we sat on the beach cuddling. I was kind of clingy with him because I hadn't seen him, and I remember thinking, *I am just going to have to ask him because he's definitely not going to re-ask me.*

We were sitting there alone, with a bright moon lighting up the beach, and I said, "We need to talk."

I am pretty sure a guy never wants to hear those words, but I said them anyway. He looked worried, that much I could tell.

Still, I looked at him and said, "I thought about it a lot this week, and I'm ready for us to move forward. I want to be with you."

"Are you sure?" he asked.

I nodded and said, "Yes."

We didn't even kiss—we just lay there hugging, embracing, and sitting intertwined on the beach all night long. It might sound like a made-for-the-movies scene from a fairy tale love story, but we saw the sunrise together. It was just awesome.

At the crack of dawn, we were still laughing and talking. We hadn't slept at all, and we were giddy. We got up when it became light, and we ran around a bit on the beach. He picked me up and spun me around, and I remember thinking it was the greatest moment. It had been a perfect night. That night we named the street leading to the spot on the beach *our street.*

I had never dated anyone, and I was glad we had eliminated all the pressure of a date, not knowing what each of us was feeling. There were no games or manipulation. We just decided to be each other's. We wanted to belong to each other, and we said so without any hesitation. I don't know what it feels like to meet a guy with the hope and intention that it turns into something; to be friends and already know each other on that level, and to have it gradually develop, felt natural. I had this feeling right then, as we were watching the sun and horsing around, that once we committed to each other it would never end. I was a good judge of character, and after knowing Chris for eight months, it seemed like he was flawless and we meshed so well together. I felt I was giving in to a perfect connection that no one I knew had ever had, and it seemed like I was starting my forever.

The summer we started dating was the best summer ever because he didn't have a job and I quit my job at a camping and

cycling store. I was really good at ringing people up, but I didn't know any details about road bikes, and it was hard to learn. Once I gave my notice, then Chris and I could do whatever we wanted. Fortunately, I had a little financial help from my parents, though my expenses totaled less than two hundred dollars per month. Still, that freedom made it possible for us to have a blast. We would stay up until five in the morning talking and just being together. We would sleep in, get up and eat, and then go out at night with our friends. We'd go to the lake all the time and ride around on the boat and go wakeboarding. We had this one Rascal Flatts CD, and it was the anthem of the summer. During the week in Greenville, we would always go out in big groups, but Chris and I would slip away on the weekends and go sunbathing and swimming and just be together. It was unbreakable, our bond. I think that bond made what happened by the pool that night, knowing we were together forever, manageable.

—◆—

I went outside to the pool with the girls, but I was being kind of a wimp about going in because of the temperature. It had cooled off slightly, and in a bathing suit, I was making a little noise about going in the water. It was dark, with only the moon lighting the deck and the water. We were all in a really good mood and still laughing as much as we had been when the night first began.

No one else had even gone in the water yet. The voices—who was saying what, who was giggling, who was standing where—all blurred together.

Suddenly, I felt two cold hands on my back, and then a little playful push sent me into the water.

Two feet to the right, and I would have been in the deep end.

Two feet to the right, and I would still be walking.

Two feet changed the course of my life forever.

That's it. Two feet.

I don't know why, but when I felt the hands on my back giving me a light, fun shove, instead of just falling, my reflex was to dive in. Head first instead of feet first. But my arms weren't locked out enough, so they weakened, and I hit my head on the bottom of the pool. In a split second everything froze. My mind, my body. I was in complete shock. I floated up to the top, facedown in the water, like a lifeless body, bobbing. Suddenly, I was on my back, my face out of the water, allowing me to gasp once for air and then yell, "Help." I thought I had floated onto my back myself, but since I couldn't feel anything, I didn't know someone had turned me over in the water after jumping in to get me. I looked up and said, "This isn't a joke—y'all need to call 911." Ironically, almost all of us had worked as lifeguards. A couple of other people jumped in as well, and I remember Samantha tried to do the correct thing by stabilizing me in the water until EMS arrived. I was so cold and scared that I just looked at her and said, "Get me the fuck out of the water." I later learned it wasn't the impact as much as the angle that caused my injury. It really could have been much worse. My arms may not have locked, but ultimately, my hands protected my head when it hit. There could have been substantially more damage had this not been the case.

I was a lifeguard, too, and I should have known better than to tell them to get me out of the water. Ultimately, I'm not sure if it made a difference or not. They all helped pull me out and put me on the side of the pool, with my lower legs dangling in the water.

My first moment of true fear was looking down at my legs, seeing them in the water but not being able to feel all of the sensations associated with water. I couldn't feel anything.

I knew it was serious as I lay there.

Before help arrived someone was holding my hand. I was just staring into her eyes as we waited.

"I can't feel my legs. Something isn't right," I said.

"It's probably just some kind of nerve damage; don't worry," someone said calmly. "It's not serious, I'm sure."

Everything was sort of foggy at this point. My friends remained by my side. What I remember clearly was the reaction of my friend who had playfully pushed me. She kept apologizing. In that moment I knew she would carry a huge amount of guilt, and I didn't want her to live with that. I told her right there, as I was waiting for EMS to arrive, that it would be okay. I comforted her even though I was scared myself. Even in that moment, I knew it was important to do so.

It was right then under the moonlight, after my wonderful bachelorette party, that a silent pact was formed, though in the coming months it would become formalized. It was a chilling event that changed all of our lives: the innocence we were experiencing that night at the pool, and then robbed of, and the moments of scramble to save me. It was there as I was lying at the side of the pool that instantly we all bonded. Despite the reason for our bond, it became the strongest force in my life, next to my love for Chris. If I hadn't met this group of girls, and had instead been surrounded by some of the mean ones I went to high school with, I'm not sure I'd have survived the hurdles I dealt with in the wake of that night. These friendships saved me. Most girls are competitive with each other. Not this group. We redefined friendship that night and built a support system so strong even tragedy couldn't break it.

None of us has ever revealed the name of the girl who playfully pushed me that night, and none of us ever will. Protecting her has always been too important, her feelings too important, the situation too fragile and fraught with potential pain. Besides, it could have been any one of us. Any one of our lives could have been impacted by one playful gesture. Any one of us could have lived with that guilt forever. Any one of us could have been pulled motionless from the chilly water. I think as we waited for help, we all knew the tables easily could have been turned. We'd all played by the pool before and we all knew that what happened to me, what happened to her, could have happened to any of us. For that reason, the name of that one girl who maybe suffered most in all of this remained at the side of the pool that night. That secret will stay with all of us forever.

CHAPTER 5

Paralyzed

THE EMERGENCY MEDICAL WORKERS ARRIVED AND CHECKED MY vitals, then prepared to hustle me into the ambulance.

"What's wrong?" I asked.

"You likely have a broken neck," one said.

I thought, *Holy crap, I just broke my neck and lived.* Then I said, "Whoa, I'm a badass."

Despite my joking, I was concerned my condition was most likely permanent. I looked at one of the EMS workers and asked, "How many people in your experience have walked away from something like this?"

She didn't answer right away. They both just kept working. I said, "Don't beat around the bush. Tell me."

The EMS worker said, "In my thirty years on the job, only one person has walked away."

I looked at her and said, "Well, I'll be the second." Maybe it was false hope I was grasping on to, but hey, it got me through those next few hours.

They placed me in the back of the ambulance; the trip from the pool to the vehicle was a blur. Lauren ran alongside as they moved me and jumped into the front seat of the ambulance to make the trip to the hospital. She told me later that the driver was a guy she went to church with as a child and hadn't seen since then. In all the hustle, they didn't notice until they were driving away toward the hospital.

Before I knew it I was on my back on a metal table in the hospital in Virginia Beach with my neck being stabilized. The room was small and bright. Saying it was *like a dream* sounds cliché, but it felt unreal, like it couldn't possibly be happening to me. I felt like I was witnessing someone else's horror, not experiencing my own. It took all of my energy to remain calm.

I asked anyone who came in, "What's happening?" and "What are you not telling me?" I couldn't really get any answers. Every nurse and doctor who came in said, "Let's wait for your neurologist." Until he arrived, no one was telling me anything.

The girls were in the waiting room, and my parents had been called. They got to the hospital before I did and were with me the entire time. My grandparents and Chris's mom, Susan, all arrived at some point, but Chris wasn't there. He was out of town on his camping trip and couldn't be reached right away. He was camping with his dad at Eno River State Park in Durham, about three hours away. He told me later that the park rangers found them and said only that there was a big family emergency. They both thought Chris's ninety-year-old grandmother, who had been suffering from Alzheimer's, had passed away. They finally found a point with cell reception, and his dad called home. Chris heard him say, "I understand." Then he hung up the phone.

He said to Chris, "Are you settled and okay?"

Chris said, "Yes."

His dad said, "Well, you're not about to be."

His dad drove him back to our house in Knightdale, and he raced in to grab clothes and dump the camping gear. His father told him only that there had been an accident and that I had been hurt. They both knew it was bad, but not exactly how bad. He said later that he took a very quick shower because they had been roughing it, and he cried so hard in the shower that he could hardly see.

My parents never left my side in the examining room, trying to be comforting, stroking my hair as we waited. I think it was tough on the people working there, because I was young and otherwise vibrant. Someone told me later that my makeup was basically still on, that it looked almost perfect, and that my hair had dried in pretty blond waves. I think that image of a young girl made it even harder on them. I learned later that one of the EMS volunteers who had taken me to the hospital made mine her last call because it was just too upsetting for her to process, and she didn't want to encounter anything so tragic again.

I was calm, I really was. Maybe calmer than everyone else who was there. But I guess I knew things were dire by their demeanors and worried looks, and I just wanted the facts, not the pity. Everyone's fears were evident. My one panic was Chris. I desperately wanted to talk to him, to tell him I was going to be okay. I was certain he was beside himself without details. All I knew, after a few hours, was that they'd finally located him and his father.

I had to have CAT scans and MRIs and no one was allowed to accompany me, but since my mom's brother Steve worked at the hospital, he was able to be with me and actually perform the scans. It was nice to have him there while everyone waited.

Eventually, after the tests were completed and my parents had rejoined me, the neurologist came in. It was his first time in the ER.

"Why does he look so scared?" I asked. The nurse made up a reason about something else happening in the hospital. He was touching me all over.

"Can you feel that?" he asked.

"Can you feel that?" Again.

"That?"

I couldn't feel any of it. And he was just asking, not giving me any information. It was excruciating for us all as he did the test.

After a few minutes he stopped the test and said plainly, "You will never walk again."

My parents were the only other people in the room at the time, and they broke down crying and held each other.

"What are the chances that she might?" my dad asked.

"Maybe five percent?" the doctor replied.

My parents sobbed. It was heartbreaking to hear them in tears and in such pain. I felt worse for them, actually, than I did for me. I was in shock, I guess, but the implications of what it meant for me just felt far less than what it meant for everyone else I loved. I watched them cry, and my heart sank. I kept thinking over and over in my head, *You will get through this. Stay strong. It's going to be okay.* One at a time, they went out to make phone calls to tell relatives. My mother was working desperately to get Chris on the phone, I was told. I needed so badly to hear his voice, to calm him down. I felt calm and he needed to hear that from me.

The wait felt like forever. After about five hours someone walked into the room with the phone, my mother maybe, and held it to my ear. It was Chris. He had just begun the three-hour drive to the hospital.

I wasn't crying when I spoke to him.

"I'm okay." I wanted him to know I was dealing with it. "I'm handling this, but do you know exactly what's going on? What have you been told?" I asked.

"I don't know much. Explain it to me," he said. He sounded in shock. I knew he knew what had happened, but he wanted it in my words, as though maybe my answer would be different than what he had been told, like I held the truth and it wasn't as bad as he thought.

"I'm not going to walk again. I broke my neck." I just wanted him to have the information. I didn't want to sugarcoat it for him.

He said "Okay" a couple of times but not much else. He wasn't crying either, but I could hear the shock in his voice. He didn't know how to react and suddenly became a man of few words, which was completely out of character for him. I knew he was rattled, so I just wanted to put him at ease and let him know I wasn't a mess, that I was coping. I wanted so badly for him to hear that message from me because I knew he was upset. We said good-bye and I started counting the minutes until he arrived.

It became clearer that I needed to have surgery, but we had to wait about eleven hours for some special machine to arrive. My C6 vertebra was completely shattered and the fragments had to be removed. My C5 and C7 had to be stabilized with a rod. The wait for the tools was excruciating for all of us, more so for me because I hoped Chris would get there before I went into surgery.

Oddly, my parents had gotten bad news about me once before, ironically about me walking. When I was born in Norfolk, Virginia, on October 2, 1985, the doctors weren't sure whether I would ever walk. Isn't that crazy? It was like some kind of bizarre foreshadowing. They thought I might have had spina bifida. That wasn't my only issue; I also was born with a vision impairment called nystagmus. The doctors thought even if I learned to walk, I wouldn't be able to play sports like tennis, because I wouldn't be able to see a tiny ball. I showed them on both fronts. I started playing when I was two, and I never stopped.

My parents and the doctor went out of the room at some point and told everyone in the waiting room about the surgery. A crowd of twenty-seven had gathered, apparently just for me; no other big groups were waiting for news on a loved one. All the girls from the party were still wet from the pool. The nurses brought them some blankets, and they huddled together, waiting. Some of their parents had arrived, too. The update included the information that I'd never walk again, that the damage was permanent. That was jarring news for them, as in the chaos of the accident, they had held strong to the notion that it was just a quick nerve issue that would resolve itself. This was the kind of thing that happened only to other people. That's what everyone had thought, which was why there was so much disbelief about the severity of it all. I was told everyone lost it out there—all of my girls were crying. One girl ran out, and my mom had to chase her down and hug her.

Eventually Chris arrived. He said the waiting room was absolutely quiet; he could hear people crying, but no one was talking. I had already gone into surgery, so Chris took a seat like everyone else and waited for more information. Everyone told me later that the surgery took forever. When I came out of it and people gradually came in to see me, there were tubes protruding from all over me and monitors everywhere. Most people were tall enough to sort of bend over the tubes, but my mom wasn't. They put a stool down for my mom eventually. We called it the kissing stool, because she would stand on it and could then reach in and kiss me.

I've tried to recall the first time I finally saw Chris after my surgery. There were so many drugs in my system by that point that a lot of my memories are foggy. But I do vividly remember wanting to hold his hand when I first saw him walk into my room. I was desperate for that. I couldn't ask him at the time; I couldn't speak because of the respirator down my throat. But instinctively, he did it. He reached out and grabbed my hand. I thought I'd willed him to do it. I couldn't feel him, but that didn't matter. I could feel the warmth of his hand and the pressure of it when he placed it on mine. It didn't feel the same since I couldn't hold it back, but it was comforting. I'd been craving the comfort he provides me the entire time and was so happy to have finally received it.

My bridal shower was supposed to be the next day. Needless to say, that didn't happen.

CHAPTER 6

Barely Breathing

THREE DAYS AFTER THE ACCIDENT MY HEART STOPPED, AND FOR a brief moment I was dead.

It happened, of course, in the only fifteen-minute span during which my mother left my side. From the second she arrived at the hospital, my mother, Carol, had remained awake and with me—the entire three days. She was so worried about me that she didn't want me to spend one minute alone. My blood pressure had been falling; throughout those first few days it would drop and someone would have to rush out to get the nurses.

Of course, the one time she did leave to take a small break, all hell broke loose. I was going in for what the doctors said would be a routine surgery, so she decided to take a few minutes to run home. She waited until they were wheeling me out of my room, and then she zipped out.

I don't remember anything because I'd been drugged, but basically, my heart stopped. I had to be given CPR. It was apparently extremely scary and caused major panic among the healthcare team, and it took some quick thinking to revive me. My mother was called immediately after it happened, so soon after she'd left that she hadn't even made it home. She turned right around and came back to the hospital.

My mom has always been my best friend. When I was little we had girls' nights out that my dad didn't know about. We didn't actually go out. Most nights, she'd tuck me into bed, read me a book, and rub my back while she counted to one hundred. But on some nights she would whisper "Girls' Night Out," then go to bed herself, and when my dad fell asleep, she'd sneak back into my room and grab me, and we'd put pillows and blankets down in the living room and watch Disney movies and eat popcorn late into the night. It was a really special time for me, for us both, I think. We also did so much together as I grew up. We camped and shopped and rafted and tubed. She was always a kid herself to an extent. We were a team growing up, and I knew that the aftermath of my accident was as tough on her as it was on me, maybe even more so. I was unaware then of what an enormous sacrifice she'd eventually be making for me.

I knew when I woke up in my room that my ribs seemed to really hurt and that they were bruised. I don't know how exactly, but I could feel inside of myself, like somehow my insides and my stomach could still register pressure. A day or two later, I began to wonder why my chest was still hurting. It was an odd feeling, and I noticed then that there was sort of a line between where sensation ended and where it gradually picked up again. The discomfort intensified and the pressure had increased. It began to feel like I'd been punched in the chest.

I still had a tube in my throat when a doctor came in one afternoon while I was alone, which was only because my parents and other visitors had to leave the room during a shift change for the nurses. Within that gap this doctor flat out told me my heart had stopped. I had no memory of going into cardiac arrest. There was no explanation, no comforting; he was very short and to the point about it, and then he left. I couldn't communicate or ask questions because of the tube. I was terrified. I didn't know what that meant exactly for my health or my future or anything. It was a truly awful moment. My mom and dad came in and asked me what was wrong, as my eyes were as wide as they could get. If the blow had been delivered by my family or a little more softly, perhaps I could have processed it better or easier and then moved on. Instead, that weird moment stuck with me for a while. But from then on my parents refused to leave me alone in the room even for a minute. My mom scolded the doctor later for telling me something like that without my being able to communicate.

They were supposed to put an umbrella stint into my leg to prevent blood clots. When I was in the elevator heading down for that procedure, my heart stopped.

This, of course, made me more upset. I was frustrated, mostly, that no one had told me. I didn't want to be protected like that. I wanted all of the information I could get my hands on. Information was helping me cope and process the situation. I had been strong up until then, so I didn't want anyone to think I was too fragile to know or hear about what was happening to me and what exactly I was dealing with. Information, as hard as it was to hear, was reassuring. Being informed was comforting.

After that some days went well and some days were really terrifying. Everyone would describe it as a roller coaster. There were random things happening all the time to my body while I was in the hospital. My lung collapsed while I was in the ICU, for example. I didn't have the ability to cough and I wasn't moving around, so mucous and congestion entered into my system and had the potential to cause pneumonia. The stickiness of the mucous essentially made the two sides of my lung walls stick together, and when that occurs no air can go in. I couldn't breathe. I remember one day that suddenly I couldn't get enough air, and I felt panicked.

The resolution to that problem, which happened often, was pretty horrific, too. The nurses would suck the mucous out with a tube that had suction. On days when it became really bad, they'd put the tube up my nose and down my nasal passage, into my throat, while I was completely awake, and it would suck all the mucous out from my lungs while I was sitting up. It was the most horrible feeling ever, but at the end of it I knew I would be able to breathe. They had a screen that showed what was going on in my lungs, and they could see exactly how much congestion had built up. If there was more and they needed to go in, I'd say, "Just do it again, just go for it and get it over with." The mucous made me feel like I was going to puke and gag, so the procedure became the easy part. The doctors told me no one had ever asked for them to go back in. I realized then I was pretty brave.

One of the most traumatizing experiences of my entire injury was in the ICU. When the tube that cleared my lungs wasn't doing it well enough, the doctors had to perform an even more intricate procedure. Once, before the procedure began, I was lying on my side and they were missing a part to this machine that they were assembling. I was sitting there with one lung, barely able to breathe, and I didn't want to freak out, because it would only make me breathe harder. But it was so hard to be calm, watching these people put together the machine. Then, as soon as they figured it out, there was no warning, just, "Let's do this." It happened so fast. I went from nothing—from sitting and watching them for what felt like forever—to being drugged (but not drugged correctly) to undergoing a traumatic procedure. I was trying not to overanalyze anything because I was trying not to scare myself. I *was* scared, but I was literally talking to myself in my head, saying, *Chill out. This is a procedure that I want to have, and everything will feel so much better when it is over.*

Ideally, if the procedure goes according to plan, the doctors put you half asleep, not in full anesthesia, but they give you just enough drugs to knock you out. Then they take a big scope, which is much bigger than you'd think, and put it down your throat to suck the mucous out. This time when they started the procedure, they didn't give me enough drugs, maybe because of the rush to get started after the delay in assembling the machine. But I was too awake. I began to freak out, so they gave me more drugs, and it knocked me into this weird semisleep; I was kind of awake and not awake at the same time. All the drugs were making me hallucinate, so I remember that—this was scary and traumatizing—I had a dream in which there was a barbaric war and people were putting a sword down my throat. I vividly remember the pain. This was the worst thing I ever felt, because it was not only physically but also mentally scary. It was the weirdest thing, being drugged up but awake enough to know that what was happening to me was bad. When I fully woke up, I don't think anyone was aware of what I had just endured.

After the surgery they threw me on a hard metal plate in order to take an X-ray of my chest to see what they had accomplished, and because my body had experienced a lot of physical trauma just days before, lying on a hard surface was extremely painful. So I awoke from this horrible dream only to be thrown onto a metal table, and I felt like no one was listening to me, but I could barely speak. It was a bad experience. I was trying to tell them how much pain I was in, but it was just a lot of chaos and noise; there were too many people, and I couldn't explain what had happened. The nostril suction was almost a daily occurrence initially. The sword procedure happened twice, and only the second time was it a horror show. But I never cried.

CHAPTER 7

One Day at a Time

SOMEONE MADE A BOARD FOR ME ON A GIANT ORANGE PIECE OF poster paper, writing the entire alphabet on it so I could spell out what I wanted to say, letter by letter. Visitors would touch a letter with their finger and I would nod when they got it correct. It took a little time getting used to communicating like this, which was rough, but once we had a system in place for pointing to letters, I could at least be understood. The first name I spelled out was that of the friend I knew would be having the hardest time with the accident. I wanted to know if she was okay. I would point out one name at a time, but almost daily, I returned to asking about her. No one had really asked me about who pushed me, even though the families all knew. No one outside of the core group was told. It was one topic that was left alone, maybe out of respect for us both. Everyone just knew not to talk about it.

I was able to communicate through this board that I wasn't angry. And I wasn't. Not at my friend or any of the girls there that night, not at myself, and not at what had happened. I didn't cry and I wasn't angry. We had a lot of laughs along the way as I tried to communicate all of this, but I was able to at least acknowledge how I was feeling, try to console everyone who was upset, and thank them for being there for me. I told them I was there for them, too. I wanted them to be okay. Even later when I could talk, I informed them over and over again, "I am totally fine." I think they suspected I was more hurt than I was portraying, which is half true, half not true, but they were just trying to protect me. I was processing information pretty darn well in spite of everything.

After the whirlwind at the very beginning, where there was an urgency to my treatment, after everyone caught their breath and the initial shock began to subside, deeper conversations with the girls really began. Step one was obviously getting myself stabilized and knowing the physical challenges that were ahead of me. That was the most important element of recovery. Next, of course, was the mental aspect of it. Everyone by the pool had had some time to really process, at least to a certain extent, exactly what had happened.

We had a couple of group discussions. The girls wanted to be certain there was no anger. Once I could speak, I was clearer about this: I wasn't holding back. I wasn't angry at all. I think because I hadn't really shown a lot of emotion, they thought I was repressing my feelings. Even at this point, when I was getting stronger, they were still crying. I'd heard they cried together in the ICU. They were extremely upset and traumatized. I had to help them, and this was the first time I realized it was up to me to be the spine for the group. Even though they were still quite emotional, they were there for me, really there. They visited a lot, they talked, they helped, and they were committed. It was a nice feeling to experience that kind of love from friends.

One of the girls told me she'd initially been worried that Chris might leave me, but after seeing us together, and witnessing how he had responded and cared for me, she wasn't worried anymore. She saw our love firsthand and realized we were both strong individually and our love was strong, too.

I don't think anyone doubted my strength beforehand, but it was never really put to the test until this accident, so it was never questioned. I never had anyone ask me to think about what would happen if my life took this kind of turn. Who thinks of those things? In this case, there was nothing that had happened to even compare it to. It was a bizarre situation. I couldn't say how anyone else would handle it. Every day was one day at a time.

Whenever I felt my mind going into a negative place, I literally told myself to stop. I didn't want negative thoughts to send me spiraling downward into a depression or rage. I never allowed it to get to that point, and it wasn't just for all of my friends and family; it was for me, too. It was simply a fight-or-flight response for me, a coping mechanism, as if my brain told me not to cry because crying would be bad. Crying wouldn't do me any good. I didn't want to feel like crying or being close to tears, and so I would tell a joke or request that my friends come in and then talk to them constantly. I was never alone with my thoughts.

Looking back, sure, that might have been avoidance. Maybe. But at the time it still got me through it.

The tears eventually fell, but not exactly because of my situation as a whole. I cried about incidents that occurred but not where life had taken me. One time, I thought my fingers moved. I was always trying to move them, and I could have sworn that one finally did, and I remember telling my dad that it was the one thing that I wanted back. I had been in a hospital bed in the ICU for six days, and my dad was in the room. I moved my wrist, and it appeared as if my finger had moved. I said, "Dad, my finger moved!" I cried out of happiness then. If my wrist moved even slightly, it made it look like my finger moved. I saw what looked like a twitch for the very first time, and I gasped quietly with happiness because I thought movement and function were returning in my fingers.

Having movement in my fingers would have meant a lot, because small twitches like that are significant. From what I'd heard it would have been a good indication that I'd recover finger movement someday. I'd heard that if you started feeling your digits five or six days after breaking your neck, that was good. In the big picture it would have meant touch, and an ability to do my own hair, or to hold Chris's hand back when he held mine, or a million other small things we take for granted each day.

It's funny how even then everyone was saying, "She can't walk." Walk, walk, walk, walk. I wasn't even thinking about my legs. In the beginning I didn't even know what was moving and what was not. But by the sixth or the seventh day, I was trying to pick up things and use my hands, and I realized, *All I want is my hands back.* I began to understand how much regaining finger function would mean to my life and how drastic an impact it had on my day-to-day functioning. It was one of those things I hadn't given any thought to before: my fingers and the importance they play in my life. Suddenly, they'd become almost everything, monumental.

A woman from physical therapy came in for an evaluation, and she held my hand to see if I had any twitches or flickers of the muscle. She felt something, too, and it reinforced the idea that I had in fact made my finger move. I got really excited, but I think I knew deep down that my fingers weren't exactly working.

Sadly, she was wrong and I was right. I waited for my fingers to work again, desperately searching for a sign they would, but eventually I realized they weren't doing anything at all. There were no more twitches. There really hadn't ever been any. I learned about my wrist and how it was making my fingers appear to move. I was slowly relearning my body and realizing that there were muscles I hadn't even thought about that weren't receiving the signal from my brain to move. It wasn't one heartbreaking moment or day. I just eventually realized over time that my fingers weren't going to move.

It's a toss-up between feeling sex and moving my fingers, but I think fingers would be all I would ask to have back if I could, more than anything else.

CHAPTER 8

Support from Friends

As soon as I regained my voice a few days into my hospital stay, I was cracking jokes. There was one extremely happy and hilarious moment when Samantha brought my first McDonald's meal during my stay—it was such a treat. It's funny that having that burger and fries is one of my greatest memories, but it thrilled me to no end and I was grateful she had smuggled it in. It's so memorable because we laughed pretty hard about how excited I was about fast food.

There were a lot of little laughs, mostly because I didn't want to live in a somber, stressful environment. I know my upbeat attitude and ability to laugh off a lot of things was a concern for some people, because they thought I was burying my pain. But when I said I wasn't hiding anything, I wasn't. It wasn't as if I sat there thinking, *I'm not going to share my feelings with anyone.* I truly wasn't able to cry and I was finding humor in my day-to-day, even in the hospital. Crying is what people expect, I guess—the reaction that reveals to others what's in your head. Maybe I didn't process it all, but I didn't have the ability to cry or scream out; that hadn't come to me yet in those early hospital days. I just didn't have the urge to do that. I was obviously scared and sad, but when you're in that kind of situation, you're simply not thinking about five or six months down the road; you're in the hospital and you're just sick. I was in that moment, trying to get through that day. I wasn't thinking about not being able to walk; I was just trying to cope with the challenges of that particular day.

I was told that there were never fewer than fifteen people in the waiting room at any given time. The girls fastened together little pieces of purple and gold ribbon and handed them out to my visitors to pin onto themselves and wear as they arrived. My grandparents came with doughnuts every morning, and on some days other people brought food, too. I couldn't join in, but the Monday after my accident, everyone tailgated out in back of the hospital, consuming all the food they'd had ready for my bridal shower. They got in trouble from security for lighting up a barbecue grill in the parking lot. It was nice, having all these friends. Everyone popped into my room that day and read notes to me, and the support made me feel really good.

Although it was lovely to have so many people around me and to notice improvement daily, I had grown increasingly aware that there would be no wedding anytime soon. I knew, of course, there would be one eventually, but not for a long time.

People slowly started spreading the word that our big day was postponed until further notice. Each relative took the time to contact the people they knew who were invited to let them know what was happening and advise them to cancel their travel plans. On CaringBridge.com, my mom and Samantha posted updates on my recovery and said that the wedding was on hold. My paternal grandmother, Bubbie, and grandfather, Zadie, were paying for the wedding originally, so she ended up cancelling a lot of the food orders and other arrangements. While many brides might have sobbed at the thought of their wedding being postponed, I was just so focused on getting through my injuries and figuring out where my life was going to end up that the wedding wasn't even a blip. I was excited about it, but I knew it would happen anyway someday. I focused more on healing and rehabbing.

Understandably, all of the energy and concern was directed toward me. Chris, my parents and relatives, everyone put their vibes toward my healing, sometimes at the expense of their own. No one put his or her own health aside more than my mother. Her friend Margie had fortunately come to town to provide my mom with some needed support. One night at midnight the two of them dashed out to get some items they needed at Kmart (and probably Margie wanted to give her a break from the hospital), and they jumped on the carousel there as a release. She said they barely fit, but it was nice to laugh and enjoy a bit of a distraction during an intense time.

Despite tiny reprieves like that, the stress of constantly being on-call for me took its toll. One day, toward the end of my stay in the ICU, my mom left to take a quick shower in Margie's hotel near the hospital. Out of nowhere, half of my mom's left eye went dark. She said later she thought it was because her own blood pressure had increased (she'd been monitoring mine). But it wasn't; it was because of exhaustion, and she wound up being admitted to the hospital for three days herself. She was in a wheelchair, but at the time I had no idea. She'd get wheeled to my room from her room, which I didn't even know existed, and she'd stand up outside and then come into my room as if nothing had happened. She would leave at a certain time to return to her room, and although I never asked why I knew she didn't want me to see her sick like that. She didn't want anyone to worry about her, not me and not friends who had been coming and going during my stay in the ICU.

At around the ten-day mark, my dad asked the doctors often how long I'd be in the hospital. We never were given a solid idea of just how long it would be, and my parents and Chris began discussing rehab and trying to figure out where I'd go next. They were trying to develop a plan for that. The woman at the hospital who handled the rehab process came rushing in one day when only my mother was there with me and said a spot had opened up at a facility in Greenville. She said if we didn't take that spot, it would be given to someone else. We literally had thirty minutes to figure this all out, and my mother was the only one available to decide. It was incredibly stressful for her, and we were frustrated that we had gotten so few answers on all the days we had asked, then all of a sudden it was, "Take this, or who knows." We took the spot in Greenville, unsure if we were making the right decision. The next day, I was whisked off.

CHAPTER 9

Rockin' Rehab

MY GIRLS REALLY MADE MY ROOM IN REHAB ROCK. IT BECAME a cool place to hang out. They hung up a small whiteboard to replace the alphabet board from the hospital, and they decorated the room to make it fun as well. The white message board became the focal point of my friends' and my recovery. I didn't need it to communicate because I could talk by this point, but the board symbolized a lot. People wrote some fun and crazy messages on it. One of the girls drew a palm tree and a beach scene for me, so I could be at my favorite place. "Go Pirates" was also a regular message. People wrote words of love and inspiration and even jokes on this whiteboard. It was a place for everyone to share his or her feelings. Of course, "Let It Be" was a daily mantra. It was written up there and never erased.

The original alphabet board survived the hospital and became part of the rehab decor. One of the girls wrote "You a Badass" at the bottom of the letter board they'd created in the hospital and hung it up as well. She remembered me saying I was badass when the ambulance workers arrived. They even hung an ECU Pirates flag over my bed, and the football and basketball coaches sent me autographed balls. I had an ECU throw, too. Lauren's sister-in-law was a Redskins cheerleader, so she arranged for an autographed squad photo to be sent my way. The girls made it so much fun and so lively in a place that usually isn't colorful in any way. This was such a troubling circumstance to be in, but we still all managed to laugh and have a good time with the cards that had been dealt.

The matter of who had pushed me hadn't really surfaced up to this point. We all felt concern for that friend, and we kept the dialogue very open about the status of my health and how everyone was feeling. But at this point in my recovery, no really serious issues had emerged from that girl. She seemed, on the surface, to be dealing with any guilt constructively, showing up like everyone else. I thought she had gotten through it okay. Maybe in my heart I worried just a little that it would all boil up at some point, but I wasn't sure.

Despite the gravity of my situation, we tried to have fun and find peace in rehab. It was actually a really fun time, as odd as that might sound. Some of the laughs we had there were the best laughs we'd ever had.

Sometimes, we'd have so much fun that we'd get into trouble. A couple of us figured out where they kept the power wheelchairs. I would get into one, and one or two of my friends would get into one, and we'd go to this really big hallway at the main hospital section of where I was in rehab. It was really straight, and it went on forever. Each chair had two buttons for speed. One had a picture of a rabbit, obviously for fast, and one had a picture of a turtle, for slower movement. I thought that was hilarious. So we'd get in the chairs, and we'd race up and down the hallway. I'd win the most, as I recall. Once we were really moving and this grumpy front desk woman came out and started yelling at us to stop. We stopped briefly, but once she left, we went right back at it. What were they going to do, kick me out?

We participated in calmer activities that made me equally happy. I had grown up singing and was afraid I'd never be able to sing again without a strong diaphragm and core muscles. I hadn't lost my voice, but I couldn't yell or scream or even speak very loudly. It was twenty times harder to find the strength to sing, but while I was in the rehab I did sing again; I worked hard to get to that point. One day, Carly and I went into the all-purpose room where they had a piano, and we began to sing as we often did before my injury. I wasn't thinking about my injury but about how happy singing made me feel. It became something we did together during rehab. People would stop in the halls and listen to us. Our bond was strong, as it was with all of my friends from that night. It always had been, but it was more so following the accident.

Samantha, Lauren, Britney, and Carly had different schedules and lived in different cities, so they coordinated their visits so that at least one of them came to rehab most days. Carly was around a lot, maybe the most after the accident. All four of them were there, but she had a flexible work schedule that allowed her to visit more often. She even slept there sometimes. Now, when something like this happens, you get pretty used to things you might otherwise be bothered by. Carly did two really big things for me that showed me how much she loved me.

Since I couldn't use my fingers and my nose was full of, well, junk, I was often uncomfortable. Carly went the extra mile and early on would actually pick my nose. I mean, Chris had to do that, too, and I love him for it, but a girlfriend? It was unbelievable what a good sport she was about that.

Also, I got used to people seeing me naked. Carly was with me in the hospital one day when a nurse was inserting a catheter into me. The nurse was explaining to my mom how it would have to be done and when. I was concerned because in addition to everything else, my mom and Chris were going to have to deal with this after I left rehab. There were just so many things they were going to have to do for me because of my lack of dexterity. Carly jumped right in.

"Would it be helpful if I learned how to do that?" she asked my mom.

"Sure," she said. "It would be a big help whenever you come to visit."

I laughed. "Carly, would you really do that? You're prepared to get all up in my business down there to help?"

"Sure. We're close, aren't we?" she asked.

The nurse began explaining right then and there. Carly learned to insert a catheter into my urethra, so I could go to the bathroom. I think the nurse was even moved. That's friendship. That's love. I think we women, as a group, underestimate our power. Our collective power. I think we all know the power of love between a couple. That's completely different and significant. But the power of friendship and love between female friends? It's amazing, and it was something as simple as a catheter insertion that had a profound impact on me and my realization of this power we can all harness by sticking together.

CHAPTER 10

The Proposal

CHRIS'S PROPOSAL HAPPENED WHEN I WAS LEAST EXPECTING IT. It was July 11, 2009. It took a minute or less, which is funny, since I had spent my entire life waiting for that minute.

Before it happened, things were really shaping up in our lives. I had finally landed an amazing job working for the parks and recreation department part time that summer, and we'd bought our first home together. We had adopted a sweet yellow Lab, and Chris had finished his first year of teaching. It felt like it was really the perfect time to take that next step with one another, and I was ready for a ring. Really ready. I patiently waited, day after day, expecting on every occasion he would pull out a ring. I was reading into his every thought and movement all summer to try to guess when it would happen. On our four-year anniversary, we went to the 65th Street spot, *our street,* where we had first started dating. It was so romantic. We talked for hours on the beach, then made love under the stars, and it was amazing. At the end of the night, I was basically shocked that Chris hadn't pulled out a ring. It was a setup made for a marriage proposal. Like a Hollywood movie setup. Yet he didn't ask me.

Then on the Fourth of July we took his parents' boat out on the lake to watch the local fireworks. As we cuddled at the front of the boat, he grabbed me and kissed me softly. I couldn't even focus, because my thoughts were so preoccupied with this possible proposal. The fireworks ended, and we began to head back to the house. Another opportunity lost. I realized I needed to stop being such a girl and just let it happen. So I put my proposal obsession aside and went about my summer. I think he wanted to catch me off guard, and he really did.

We were at a fancy restaurant one night called Freemason Abbey, and after we finished our drinks, he got out of his seat. At first I barely noticed what was happening. He stood up abruptly without saying anything, and I was thinking, *Where is he going?* Then he got down on one knee.

"Will you be my wife?" he asked.

I exclaimed, "Yes!" I was startled. I think I said it ten times over and over again.

He pulled out a ring and said, "This is my grandmother's ring. I will buy you your own when we can afford it."

It was a princess-cut diamond in a yellow gold setting, and it was beautiful. He'd spoken to his mom and told her that he couldn't afford a ring but that he wanted to propose. She had some family jewels, so they sorted through them and chose this one. He stood up and announced to the restaurant, "This is Rachelle, and she just agreed to be my wife!" Everyone clapped. Then we kissed.

Then Chris started to lead me upstairs right away. The restaurant had enormously high ceilings, flanked with wood paneling and a huge rustic chandelier hanging low. It had this zigzag staircase that led up to the balcony seating. I was so confused as to why we were on the move like this, leaving our table, but I was so giddy, filled with joy, surprised, and excited, that I didn't ask any questions. I looked up and I realized both of our entire families were there! I hadn't even seen them, but they had watched the entire proposal, and we were all able to have dinner and celebrate together. Some were waiting on the stairs, and we all hugged. It was such a perfect night. He took my breath away.

— ⁓ —

Sadly, many people asked if Chris and I would still be together after the accident, but even in the hospital that doubt never crossed our minds. We were deeply in love, and the accident didn't change that. In fact, I felt sorry for the people who asked because it suggested to me that they didn't know true love. It was essentially the most asked question. It was crazy. Honestly, if given the opportunity to walk again, but having to do so without him, I wouldn't do it. Our love proved to be far more powerful than this accident.

I believed in love and soul mates, and I knew through Chris that dreams came true. But I didn't believe everything happened for a reason. I didn't believe that if I simply worked hard, I'd walk again. I hated when people said things like that. It implied that everyone in a chair wasn't trying hard enough. That they just didn't want it bad enough. People also said that I was so positive that surely I would walk again. Positivity doesn't make you stand up. It's like telling an amputee that if he's positive and tries hard enough, his leg will grow back. My spinal cord was an actual thing that broke, soft like a banana, easy to snap. I didn't have a disease I was fighting through. I had damaged my spinal cord. If you unplug a lamp, no matter how hard you try, or how positive you are, it will not turn on. I believed in science, and since I was still young, maybe when I was fifty someone would develop something that would allow me to walk again one day—even if it was only for twenty or thirty years of my life.

All along I knew Chris and I were supposed to be together, not meant to be. That was the only place I got confused about pre-destiny a bit, when I pondered why all of this happened, knowing there was no good answer. Chris and I were *supposed to be* because we were the right fit for each other, the perfect match, but I'm not sure if we were *predestined,* though the differentiation con-fused me when I thought about it. I didn't believe I was *meant to be* injured, or predestined to spend my life unable to walk. That's why it confused me a bit when it came to our love; it was the only thing that I couldn't square because otherwise our relationship was so perfect, it felt like we were soul mates. I felt like I'd die without him; I couldn't breathe were he not there. I realized it was hypocritical to say you believe in soul mates but you don't believe in fate. It's kind of convenient: Some good things are meant to be and bad things are not, and maybe fate steps in sometimes. There is a passage in the Zohar, a set of books on Jewish mysti-cism, that says that one soul comes down to earth but it's split into two. One part goes to a baby boy and the other part to a baby girl, and if they be worthy, God reunites them in marriage. So you have to be a good person to get that other part of your soul. You won't necessarily be together for sure, but your choices make you worthy of finding your soul mate or not. Maybe that's the case. Maybe it's not.

It was a dilemma I struggled with often beyond the ques-tion about love. Many people e-mailed me and commented on news stories about my accident, saying that it was "God's will" and "Everything happened for a reason." There are so many awful things that occur in our world, and I found it difficult to believe that any higher power would purposely cause people pain. I just refused to believe that. A horrific event like Sandy Hook couldn't have been God's will. Kidnapping of children can't be God's will. Terrible diseases can't be God's will. My never walking can't be God's will. I like to believe if there is a higher power, he or she wouldn't do such terrible things to people.

I was raised Jewish, and I went to Hebrew school twice a week and Sunday school once a week, but in my household I was simply raised with morals and taught to be a nice person. At times religious people said, "Be good, so you can go to heaven" or "Because that's what God wants," but I didn't want to be good to go to heaven; I wanted to be good because it was the right thing to do. So religion wasn't a big thing for me, though I knew it had helped a lot of people and I didn't begrudge anyone who clung to it. I didn't pray or talk to any higher power or base my decision on any religion or higher power. I just went about my life as a moral person.

Honestly, more than a church, Chris and I had a place on the beach that was our place to reflect, and it was meaningful for us. It was the 65th Street spot. That night we started our relationship, we didn't kiss, but the next day we went on a date to a restaurant called the Duck Inn. The restaurant was a Virginia Beach staple. I had had my prom there and lifeguard banquets there. It was just one of those places with a lot of history. We ate seafood, and when the bill came he paid, a courtesy I wasn't used to at all. After dinner we went to our spot on the beach, the one where we had just stayed up all night talking. We put down a blanket, and I remember him leaning into me, and we kissed with the sound of waves crashing, the smell of the ocean making me so happy.

In rehab I looked back on those days, and I was so proud that I knew how good I had it. I believed, even then, that we, as humans, have the power to make something positive of a bad situation. While I don't believe that "everything happens for a reason," I believe we can give anything a purpose, even a negative situation. Good things came from my injury because I made the decision for that to happen, not because it was predestined to happen.

With Chris, I just felt like I had to have him, every moment. If we weren't together, I wouldn't be the same person. If that was taken away from me, I wouldn't be able to breathe. I felt that a soul mate was a person who made you the best that you could be, made you happy, made you want to live life and wake up.

During my time in the hospital and rehab, everyone marveled at how Chris knew, almost instinctively, how to make me comfortable. He knew me so well. My dad said later he was impressed by how quickly Chris fell into that routine as the person to defer to, and even the doctors turned to him to ask questions. He was my other half for better or worse. He knew.

CHAPTER 11

The Big Day, Take One

INSTEAD OF SPENDING JUNE GETTING READY TO MARRY CHRIS, I'd spent it trying to survive and then learning about how life would be at rehab. I had sat in a wheelchair for the first time on June 5 instead of organizing who was sitting where at the wedding. I was learning how to feed myself and how to use the remaining strength in my arms to push my wheelchair instead of making last-minute floral arrangements or talking to the DJ about the music.

Since the accident Chris and my mom had gotten into a pattern of switching off, making sure each night one person stayed with me. There was a tiny chair that pulled out into a poor excuse for a bed. One night Chris and I were lying there in the dark, and we were talking. We both were aware our wedding date was approaching, just days away.

We should have been sleeping or trying to fall asleep, but Chris was talking through some feelings of guilt I hadn't realized he had.

"I hate seeing you like this," he said. "I was supposed to protect you, and I wasn't there to do it."

I didn't say anything. My heart broke for him. I knew he was suffering badly and it was bubbling up to the surface at that moment.

Then he broke down and said, "I just wish I had danced with you more. I'm really sorry, because now we can't."

All I could say was, "It's okay, sweetie."

He doesn't cry often. We just cried together and hugged that night. There was nothing that could be said. I could see the sadness in him that night, and I didn't want that for him. I didn't want him to feel regret or any kind of guilt at all. But it was the saddest moment of my stay. At that moment I wanted out. I didn't want to be in rehab anymore. I didn't want to be in this situation. I wanted to be dancing at my wedding. His tears were too much for me to hold it together.

⸻

June 27, 2010, arrived, the day that would have been my wedding. I didn't wake up with butterflies in my stomach and anticipation like I should have, and while I was disappointed, I wasn't sad. I knew we'd get there, but I had to get well first. It was hard to imagine during those days how different my June had become.

Still, we had a huge party at the rehab facility to mark the day. We'd briefly discussed getting married right then and there in the garden at the facility, but I was concerned that would mean the accident would have taken the dream wedding idea away from me. I wanted the real deal regardless, so ultimately we decided to wait.

I obviously couldn't get dolled up clothing-wise that day, but everyone was casual for our little celebration. It was a jeans and T-shirt party for sure. Samantha was excellent at hair and makeup; on most visits she'd fix me up. So on this day, my would-be wedding, she styled my hair and applied my makeup in my room before everyone arrived.

As we got ready that day, she said, "You look so pretty."

"Thanks," I said, "even in my bum clothes!"

"Yes. And you'll look even prettier on your actual wedding day. We're all holding on for that and can't wait."

"I'm excited about that day happening," I said.

"We all are, too," Samantha said.

My aunt and uncle, my parents, Chris, all the rest of the girls, and Chris's family were there—everyone brought great food, and we took over the multipurpose room to celebrate. My mom brought Funfetti cupcakes, which are my absolute favorite. There was watermelon, too. There's a really great place in Greenville called Parker's BBQ and someone brought food from there, which was a nice break from the food I'd been eating for the past four weeks. It was like we had a big backyard BBQ celebration, but in this little rehab room with Wi-Fi and a big-screen TV instead of at someone's house. It was just as fun.

At some point while we were eating, we heard some commotion coming from the hallway. We all quieted our chatting to have a listen, and all of a sudden some senior citizens that I had taught cheerleading to came busting into the room. I had taken them on when I was the activities coordinator at their center. They represented our town at the Senior Games. They were in uniform and everything, cheering "L-E-T-S G-O, let's go, let's go, L-E-T-S G-O! Gooooo RACHELLE!" As I sat there watching, I realized that these women, even though they were forty years older than me, were my friends. My heart warmed at the thought.

Everyone clapped, and I was completely moved. It was so nice of them to do this. The entire thing was a true celebration with lots of laughs, and not a tear was shed. We were all happy to be together, all my closest family and friends. Chris and I stayed together that night. We spent the night holding each other and talking about our future plans and how much we loved each other. I will say, in the morning when I woke up, I felt a little sad. I should have been on my honeymoon trip to the Bahamas. I should have been running up and down on the beach in a bikini with my new husband. I should have been married. That was when reality hit me.

CHAPTER 12

Finding Peace

ABOUT A MONTH INTO REHAB, AROUND THE END OF JUNE, I TOOK my first trip out of the hospital. We went to a park I used to go to for fun and concerts. It felt nice to be outside while I was still recovering. I was turning a corner mentally and physically, and I was aware of that.

My parents, Chris, and my friend Rebecca came along, and they wheeled me to the park. We sat there and enjoyed a concert. I hadn't been outside since my injury, so I was taking it all in. I felt a little nostalgic and maybe a little bit sad. It was my first time back in that park in a while, and I couldn't help but look around and think back to when I had *walked* around the grounds. It was situated next to the river my mom and I had gone kayaking on when she came to visit me when I was in college there. Rehab and my college were in the same town, so I was surrounded by history. Walking history. Able-bodied history. I tried to explain how I was feeling to everyone.

"It's so weird to be here, because I have so many good memories from this place," I said.

My dad said, "Well, now you'll make new memories."

It was a simple yet profound statement.

He said, "It's actually a really good and important philosophy to make new memories every single day, especially now that you are healing. We shouldn't live for old ones. We should live for new ones."

Those were some smart and powerful words, and I decided to make a daily effort during my recovery to live by them. It became my approach to all of this change. Later, my friend Rebecca, after pondering what my dad had said, wrote me an e-mail saying that she'd thought a lot about the statement and that it was true—there was so much more ahead of me. It was really nice to hear from her, knowing she'd given it as much thought as I had. That she was as moved by this simple concept: Life goes on and we make new memories every day, regardless of our situation or the hand we've been dealt. The note she sent made me realize something else, too: that my life and this accident had an impact on everyone around me.

Arriving at the understanding that all would be okay happened there in rehab, but it was a gradual process. It didn't mean I was okay with my injury—obviously, given the chance to change it, of course I would have. But the reality was that I couldn't, so I found peace instead of beating myself up over my situation. It wasn't about complacency; it was about dealing with what I had to deal with and knowing that making peace helped.

I can't pinpoint the exact moment it occurred, but in rehab I just realized, "It is what it is." I said that to myself a lot. I had to manage myself because no one was going to do that for me. I had to *let it be*. There was never a time when I was angry, but there were definitely spurts of sadness. I would always make jokes with the therapist, and then I would break down a little bit at night, when it was quiet and I was alone and wasn't being kept busy.

And that was natural to me. Of course I'd break down. Of course I was sad, but overall I realized there was nothing I could do to change what had happened. I couldn't go backward; I couldn't stay where I was, so I had to move forward. I simply didn't want to be a depressed, negative person; I wanted to be myself. So I went forward with the same personality that I'd always had for the sake of my own mental health and for the sake of Chris. It wouldn't have been fair for him to not only part with me physically but also lose me as a person. I knew my physical condition would not be the end of us and that he deserved to have the woman he set out to marry originally.

Another woman, Frances, really defined friendship for me. She was in rehab and helped me through a lot of tough moments. She was a volunteer and a quadriplegic herself, and she would visit me often. I had a lot in common with her. She was hurt in her twenties like me and was also very active. We had both taught aerobics. We had similar functions. She gave me some pointers on how to apply makeup. I learned through Frances that I was able to do a lot with my arms. I realized that there was no horizontal line cutting off my feeling and function, but that my biceps, wrists, and shoulders had a lot of strength and could compensate for my lack of triceps, so with time, I would gain mobility. For example, when applying foundation, I learned to pour it onto the palm of my hand and wipe it on my face. I had enough strength to lift my arms to do that. With eyeliner, I squeezed the stick together with two hands and could apply it.

Frances explained to me that I could ultimately do a lot with the strength in my wrist, like feed myself and eventually drive. She had a caregiver who helped her in the mornings and evenings, but Frances did many things on her own. She cleaned her own pool at home, washed her own car, and gardened. It was so motivating and enlightening. She kept me positive in general and was someone to laugh with and even ask the personal questions that no medical professionals could really answer.

Frances had a huge part in my recovery. I wouldn't have been as positive without her as my mentor and my friend. She was there every single day, and we spoke for hours. I asked her hundreds and hundreds of questions over the two and a half months I was there.

Laughter helped, too. Samantha had a little Chihuahua named Marley. I don't usually like that kind of dog, but I was really missing my Lab. One day, she showed up and opened her purse.

I said, "Oh my God, you brought your dog!"

She said, "Yeah, why not? No one will care."

I explained we had to keep it on the down-low.

She had smuggled little Marley into rehab, past everyone who might have tossed her and the doggie out. All to cheer me up. You can't have animals in hospitals unless they're certified therapy dogs, so this was really breaking the rules.

We had to involve the nurse on duty because she was in the room a lot. But we knew she wouldn't tell on us. We also needed to keep the door closed and instituted a password for entry. I'm not sure why, but I decided the code word was "chicken leg." So family and the nurse would be coming in and out, and that day they had to say "chicken leg" every single time they knocked. Sam and I laughed so hard that we cried. It was one fun afternoon for sure.

CHAPTER 13

Love and Sex

PART OF REHAB WAS GETTING USED TO REAL LIFE AFTER THE hospital. And for me, that meant sex. So one day in late July during rehab, Chris and I were given the opportunity to stay together in a room within the hospital that was set up like a small apartment. The idea was that we were on our own that night to practice what it would be like when I went home. The nurses were a phone call away, just in case. Frances had given me a lot of information on how sex was going to be following the accident, and it was helpful for me to have my expectations in order.

We were finally alone for the first time in two months in this tiny room that looked like a nice hotel room, complete with floral comforter and small TV. I was simply happy to lie beside him, wrapped up in his arms. I can't describe how painful it was to have to endure months without being able to lie in bed cuddling and embracing the one you love, but instead having to be in a hospital bed alone. We hadn't been intimate in months, and we were previously an extremely sexual couple. I longed to share that with him again, but I knew it would be different. I could no longer feel below my chest, so I wasn't sure this was even going to be enjoyable. But I quickly realized that it wasn't about having an orgasm.

It was about being with him. Before, sex was all about the final result, and now it was more intimate, more personal, passionate, and loving. This time, we didn't totally know what we were doing. It was a lot like losing my virginity again.

It was my first time sleeping in a real bed since the accident. I still wore a neck brace, which wasn't very sexy, but we worked with it. I was no longer able to move all around, but I laid flat on my back and I was able to wrap my arms around him. I was told that the parts of your body that you can feel, particularly your neck, become more sensitive, and it was true. I learned where I was sensitive and where I hadn't acknowledged being sensitive before. That night was incredibly intense, more intense than the physical sex we'd had before the accident. This time it was emotional; it was making love. It certainly wasn't better than the physical relationship we'd shared, which I was sad to have lost, but at least I knew there was hope and that we would still be able to find a way to remain physically connected.

Chris was my first and only. We dated for a few months, and in October 2005 I lost my virginity to him. It was an emotional experience for me, because I had waited a long time to find the right person. It was my sophomore year of college, about a week after my twentieth birthday, and it was one of those things that was perfectly set up. By now I had moved into a house with two of my friends and they weren't going to be there; it was our only opportunity to be by ourselves, so it had to be that night. We both knew it was going to happen, so I was very nervous. I was thinking, *I am not going to be a virgin anymore.* How many twenty-year-olds do you know who are virgins? The poor guy had a lot of pressure on him. But I had no expectations at the time—I just wanted to be with the man I had fallen in love with.

I felt at that moment in time that Chris really was the one. With the lights out we made love and he told me he loved me. It was beautiful. It was great, being with him and knowing he'd be the only man I'd ever sleep with. I didn't cry, but I got misty-eyed sharing that moment with him.

The first time Chris told me he loved me was two weeks after we'd started dating. We had made out on my grandma's couch. He whispered something in my ear. I wasn't sure if I'd heard correctly, that he'd said, "I love you," so I couldn't say it back. But then I sat up and looked at him and asked, "Did you just say 'I love you'?" He nodded. I said, "I love you, too."

My mother and father weren't strict with me at all, but there was always a mutual respect and an open line of communication. My mother always said, "Don't have sex until you find someone who is worth it. Wait until you meet someone you care for and who cares for you." I listened to that. I believed she was sharing the best advice with me, and I was glad I listened. I had waited until I found someone who loved me, and I wouldn't have wanted it any other way.

⚊⚊

Obviously sex had become different for me after the accident, and it was also one of the things that I had taken for granted. We were a sexual couple before the accident; we connected deeply in that sense, and to have an orgasm taken away from me was incredibly hard, but we compensated. It just wasn't natural to not be able to do that. Honestly, I still enjoyed sex and I still got excited. Even though I couldn't feel sex, my brain still received signals of pleasure. I got a tingling feeling all over, but it wasn't like a peak and a finish. It was not an orgasm, followed by the type of release an able-bodied person might feel. But at times I felt my body and mind were more relaxed when we'd finished.

Rehab at the hospital was a really important element to my recovery—sex was only one aspect of that recovery. There were so many layers to getting better. I knew I wouldn't walk, but that's not the only thing to recover. I didn't want my spirit broken, too. I didn't want to be a different person than I was before the accident. I wasn't Superwoman, and I certainly still had my low moments, but rehab gave me some time to gradually grow more and more at peace with what I was dealing with. Also, I made a promise to myself that I was going to be fine.

I felt obligated to make sure everyone else was okay. I could see how the injury was affecting everyone around me. I wanted to lift them up in the same way I was working to lift myself up. Like a group project, almost, that I would lead. I convinced myself that it would all be fine. In going through that process in my head, I definitely put on a happy face for everyone else, I think because I needed to sort through it all. By being happy all the time, by telling jokes and laughing with other people, it helped me convince myself. It made it okay to believe because life felt normal. I think I had more support than many people have, but I also learned I was the most important support I'd need. I needed to know I could survive. I needed to know I was strong enough to get through. I needed to figure out in my head that, yes, this would all be okay.

In rehab Chris and I would always talk about how awesome my friends were and how lucky I was to have them in my life. We discussed how friends sometimes leave your side in these kinds of situations because they simply don't know how to handle them, and you often find out exactly who your real friends are. This was the case for me—it became clear to me what friendship stood for and what it meant. Suddenly, I knew I had true friends. There was no doubt in my mind that they would be there for me. Without them during those long months, it would have been harder to make it through. But they wouldn't have made it without me either; they told me that many times. We comforted each other and learned to be there for each other, and we started to really understand the impact that night had had on us as a group.

I had to heal. That was clear. But even more, I had to step up. I had to really be there for this girl, this friend who had pushed me in a simple, playful gesture. We laughed a lot, but I could see through our laughter. She hadn't even reached the low point of her despair during my rehab stint, though my friends and I didn't know this at the time. It was just an unspoken promise at this point that we all protected her instinctually. We acknowledged that the accident at the pool had happened but almost pretended that the push itself hadn't. Maybe we were in denial; maybe we weren't ready to open that can of worms just yet. It wasn't spoken, but it wasn't too far out of all of our minds. We focused on the recovery for sure. As I think back, it's almost like we refused to confront it. Whenever the thought of how I got where I was entered my mind, I'd push it out. If I didn't think about how the accident happened, then I didn't have to worry that our friendship would be different. But still waters run deep, and denial wasn't enough.

CHAPTER 14

Getting Through

ABOUT TWO MONTHS AFTER THE ACCIDENT, I HAD MY FIRST intense conversation with that friend we were all so worried about. Everyone had been quietly thinking about her, hoping the worst had passed and she'd healed from what had happened. My brother had come out from Virginia Beach to stay with our family, and I learned that in the wake of the accident he had made a point to take her aside and tell her that I asked about her often and that I loved her. He wanted to make sure she was okay. We all did. I'd hoped it had been enough, laughing with her and having her see me in rehab really doing well.

There was a little garden area at the rehab center. It was always so freezing cold inside that I'd spend as much time as I could sitting out in this garden. It was hot out, around 100 degrees. I used to make people sit out there and stay with me, even though for them, it would have been more comfortable inside. My body had lost the ability to regulate its temperature, so I always felt cold. Some days, I simply could not stand being inside.

One afternoon, this friend was visiting. I had never brought up the incident because I didn't want to upset her. I knew she'd come talk to me when she was ready. And that day finally came.

Her face wasn't so much sad as it was very serious. We had made our way to the garden and she said, "I'm really sorry this happened." I think she just wanted to hear that I had forgiven her.

For me, it wasn't even about forgiveness. I'd have had to have thought that she did something really wrong to forgive her. She hadn't. It could have happened to anyone, and I didn't blame her.

She said, "I feel really bad about this. I'm so sorry."

I said, "Don't be and don't feel bad. I'm okay. I'm honestly at peace with it. You should be, too."

I had made peace with it in a very short amount of time. During this conversation I knew she had not yet found peace in the same way I had, but I thought she would soon. I was naive as to just how much she was hurting and how bad it was at that moment. I assumed that since I was okay, she'd be okay—that she just needed to hear me say I was all right.

She nodded. She was holding it together. "Are we okay?" she asked.

"Of course. I love you. You're one of my best friends. I don't blame you for this."

I thought, or maybe I hoped, that that would be enough. She didn't cry or break down, but deep down I guess she was putting on a good front. She was being strong for me, but she must have been hurting inside.

"When you're upset, talk to me. Call me. I will talk about this with you anytime," I said. I told her she didn't need to pay anyone to help her sort through her feelings, that I was there whenever she needed to speak, day or night. Maybe that was a mistake, but not really knowing how deeply affected she was, I suppose I believed she could shake it off. The problem was that we were accepting two different realities. We were both badly hurt that day, but in two completely different ways. I could work hard to make the best of my situation. She really couldn't. There was no upside to living with that hurt. There was no finding a way to put a bad situation to good use. It was just a tragic event that could have happened to any of us that night. I've had my share of horseplay in the water, that's for sure. Everyone has.

She thanked me that day, and I thought all was sorted out and we'd both be okay, leaning on each other for strength. Sadly, the worst was yet to come for her. She'd have to face this all later when the media circus began, which none of us saw coming.

CHAPTER 15

My Competitive Spirit

I WAS PRETTY ACTIVE AS A KID. WHEN I WAS GROWING UP, MY dad never just let me win a game. He allowed me to lose, and I wanted it that way. I was really good at board games, and I could usually win, even against my dad. Once though, he beat me at Pretty, Pretty Princess and he had to wear the crown and beads.

I loved sports and often played with my dad. He took me to basketball games as soon as I could walk. I liked to keep score, hug the mascots, and talk up the cheerleaders. We used to collect trading cards, too. Once, we were at a summer league game where prospective pros were scouted. My dad pointed out a player, Joe Smith, and told me he was going to be the number one draft pick. I was four years old at the time.

I said, "I want his autograph."

Instead of going to get it for me, my dad handed me a pen and a paper and said, "Go ask."

Of course I got it, but I was a little bummed not to have been treated like one of the guys by this player. He called me cute.

I think I always wanted to be one of the guys because I so loved hanging around my dad. During recess in fourth grade, I walked up to the boys and asked if I could shoot some hoops.

One said, "Girls can't play basketball." I made them give me the ball, took one shot, and swished it. After that I was always invited to play with them.

I worked with kids when I graduated from college, and we didn't even keep score until they were eight years old, because we didn't want the kids to get upset about losing. The thing is, if kids haven't ever lost until they are eight, how are they going to handle losing later in life? They will inevitably lose something. I knew when I had won. I knew when I had earned it. And I think that just made me more competitive. Not only that, I enjoyed working toward something. I really did. I enjoyed an accomplishment, however big or small.

Basketball was where my dad and I really bonded. On the court the winner won. He didn't allow me to get a free shot in, nothing. He made me work for everything, and I think I drew on that for strength after my accident. That was real life. You won some, you lost some. How you handled the ups and downs revealed your true character. Even when I was really little, my dad would never throw a game. People never believe me when I tell them that.

My dad and I would play the game Horse all the time, from when I was four until I was in high school. It was one of our things. We had a basketball hoop in the backyard and, as in everything else, he'd never let me win. He wouldn't go all pro player on me—he wasn't mean about it—but he played for real. I might get a few letters on him, but if I started catching up, then he'd up his effort and I'd lose. He'd just never *let me* win Horse. Never. Once when I was a teenager, I actually beat him at Horse—it was the one and only time. But it felt like the biggest accomplishment ever because it took me ten years to do it. The funny thing wasn't just my reaction, but his. He didn't like to be beaten, but he was so proud of me. He said, "You finally did it!" Of course, I couldn't help but shove it in his face and celebrate my sweet victory by talking some smack, but boy was I proud.

We were a sporty family, and we used to do a lot of activities together. We also played catch and football; I was kind of a tomboy when it came to that stuff. My dad worked sixty hours a week usually. But Sunday was our day. When spring hit we were outside on Sunday afternoons, playing sports.

Right after the accident, I was fighting as hard as I had fought in sports or games. I drew on that. I didn't want to break; I didn't want to lose the new battle. I guess I saw it as being weak, and I didn't like to be weak. Of course, no one would have blamed me for being crazy and breaking down and crying. But I saw it as a game I was trying to win, like I was trying to be the best at recovery. To have the best attitude.

This injury was almost like the Horse victory that was ten years in the making. I knew there were going to be little moments where I was going to have to suck it up and fight and beat those challenges. And I was determined to win.

Every time I lost at Horse, I didn't feel defeated. It made me feel more determined. I understood that it would be a miracle if I ever beat my dad at a game. I never expected to beat him, to be honest, but I always tried my hardest regardless. Being competitive at sports made me competitive at life, and this injury, well, I wanted to win. As I prepared to leave rehab, I drew on that inner fight and spirit my dad had spent a lifetime instilling in me.

Toward the end of rehab, my mom and I were in full prankster mode. I had a roommate in rehab, a lady who had worked at ECU. She had gone on a bike ride, fallen off the bike, and actually been stung by a bunch of bees. She broke her neck in the fall but ended up walking by the time she was out of treatment; she was an incomplete injury. It was so weird to see someone as paralyzed as I was, and then right before my eyes, see her walking. I think that happens a lot in rehab. I was definitely the most screwed-up one there at the time.

Anyway, her husband walked into the room one day, and my mom was in bum clothes, with no bra, so when she heard him coming, she opened the closet door to hide. It was like a dorm closet, a big cubbyhole with a door, so she opened the closet door very fast and fell into the closet and was basically sitting down. We were laughing so hard over the fact that she could fit into the closet, so I said, "Mom, stay in the closet." We called the nurse, Tammy. She came in and I said, "Tammy, I've got this beautiful dress, and I want to wear it out." (I was able to go on day trips once I was cleared, and my family could transfer me into a car. So I had been out in public by this time.) I told Tammy, "Look in my closet and get the dress out." She opened the door to find my mom just sitting there. Tammy screamed and threw a pillow at her, and we laughed hysterically.

Since Mom could sit in the closet, I wondered if I could, too. My mother checked. It was big enough to get a chair into, just a plastic chair. So this time we got Tammy on our side to scare the doctor. Tammy happily got in on our scheme and a couple of therapists did, too. The night before our prank, I practiced how I would fit, and it totally worked. And then the next day we scared some more people. We spent the day, my last day at the rehab hospital, using this trick. I remained in the closet while Tammy or a therapist brought someone by. Tammy was so funny because she'd have to create elaborate lies to get people to open the closet. She told my caseworker I was hoarding catheters. She told the supply guy that I'd stolen a box of medical gloves. She even told the doctors I was stashing medication in that closet.

That was the day I left and got to go home. Everyone had made such a significant impression on me and my life during my time there. They were such wonderful people. I guess I'm glad the closet gag gave me the chance to leave an impression on them . . . and maybe let them know I'd be okay once I left their care because I had a good sense of humor and was surrounded by a lot of love.

CHAPTER 16

On My Own

I LEFT REHAB ON AUGUST 13, 2010. I HAD SO MANY MIXED FEELINGS about leaving. I knew I was ready to go, and I remember around the time I was being released thinking that if I had to stay there one more minute, I would snap. There were so many people there with lower-level injuries who had more function than I did, people recovering quickly, and they complained often; sometimes the negative energy took the wind out of me. I had reached the point where I simply couldn't take it anymore. I felt for everyone and didn't mean to judge. Not everyone had a great network of friends or a committed family, and I understood that. But sometimes the negative energy consumed the space in there. An exciting world still existed out there, and I was more eager to tackle the new challenges than to dwell on what I couldn't do. I wanted to learn and grow and take it on. Also, I missed my dog PeeDee very much. I missed my house and my old life, which I knew was going to be at home waiting for me.

Of course, that's what terrified me, too. Just because I was okay with challenges didn't mean they weren't scary. My old life was just that: my old life. Nothing was the same except my love for Chris and my family and friends. I knew I wouldn't be able to get up to the second floor to my bedroom. The house was my home, but it was no longer what it had once been to me. I had been there only as an able-bodied person. There would be a lot of change ahead of me. All of my care would be up to us, and lots of little things could go wrong.

One of the most significant changes in my life was that my mother would have to live with us. Chris had to go to work, and my mother had to get me out of bed. I was thrilled, but I realized it would be a tremendous hardship for her, leaving her job and her husband. We all thought about me moving in with them, but that would have kept me from both Chris and rehab. We discussed briefly both of my parents moving to Knightdale, but my dad had an army-navy surplus store in Norfolk and couldn't leave it. We knew eventually he'd sell it and retire, but until then my mother decided to spend five days a week with me and weekends with my dad.

It was hard for her, but she moved in without complaining. We knew we all had to change our lives drastically, and I appreciated that she agreed to change hers as well. I knew when I returned home from rehab that I'd continue to see my friends, go to ECU football games eventually, and eat at the restaurant that I always went to. I was able to come back to my house and be in my own environment with the people I cared about. So, in a sense, I did return to my life, but she couldn't. We decided as I left rehab that hopefully one year or so would be enough to get me settled.

I knew then that I could manage only halfway on my own. If I wanted to wear sweatpants and a T-shirt every day, I could put that on myself. I hadn't learned to transfer from my bed to my chair and wasn't sure if I ever would, so my mom would have to get me out of bed and up every day. I knew having her there would make things feel as normal as possible for me, and I was grateful for her sacrifice and willingness to play my unsung hero. I learned the true meaning of friendship from my mother. She was my best friend growing up, and she set the tone for all of my other relationships.

I realized quickly that caring for me was emotionally draining for her. In addition to needing help moving, there were serious medical complications that plagued me, and seeing me struggle upset my mother terribly. She had to always be on high alert, because we realized quickly that my blood pressure dropped so low that there were days when I had a hard time keeping my head up without passing out.

I also suffered from severe nerve pain, which was an unexpected yet overwhelming side effect. On a normal day I would spend a good hour getting out of bed, because I had to wait for the nerve pain to go away. This pain doesn't happen to everyone, and there's no explanation as to why it happens in some with spinal cord injuries and not in others. Mine in particular was pretty debilitating, occurring mostly when I woke up but lessening during the day. In the early morning movement was impossible. Nerve pain feels like fire, it feels like needles, it feels like beatings all over, or even like a thousand bees stinging me all at once. Basically, wherever I had no normal feeling is where I would have this nerve pain, everywhere from my chest down. My brain would try to connect with my body. When it was unable to, it would send a signal back in the form of pain.

The nerve pain was one of the harshest realities of my injury, and I was told I would likely live with it forever. It gradually became a part of my life, increasing bit by bit each day. It became worse when the weather deteriorated, and some days it grew unbearable. If I had known how bad it was going to be, and how overwhelming the pain, I never would have survived this experience. Initially, I felt upset because I learned it was a rarity—very few people with a spinal cord injury experience my level of pain. Whenever I mentioned it to other friends in a chair, they all told me it was something they'd gotten used to, which indicated to me that we were not talking about the same pain. This was not a tingling "sensation." It was absolute torture. If you asked me, "Would you rather walk again, but live with the nerve pain, or stay in the wheelchair and be pain free?" I would choose the latter.

I remember the first few times it happened, I was screaming as I was awakened by the pain. I could hear my mother sobbing in the other room, upset that I was suffering. I felt so badly for her. I tried multiple pain-relieving meds, but none seemed to work. It was frightening because the main one I took would essentially destroy my life over time, which made me realize it would have been nice not to be on any meds at all; I couldn't be sure that they were even helping me or having a positive impact.

My mother and I dealt with logistical issues, too, once home. Once, on a really hot day, my mother was trying to get me into the car, and I fell on the hot pavement in the driveway. She couldn't lift me because I was too heavy. I was in shorts, lying there, and she started to panic. She thought my legs would burn on the hot asphalt. I said to her, "This is not the time to panic. I'm okay." She ran into the garage, found a very low-rise lawn chair, and managed to get me into it. I had some scrapes on my knees but really nothing major.

The other issue we knew we'd face out of rehab, which was a major concern, was that if we had any kind of problem medically, and we did occasionally, we'd have to go to a doctor or hospital. There was no longer a nurse's button to press for help. There wasn't all this great equipment, or fast diagnoses, or people checking up on me all the time. It was on us. Period.

Very few local places had experts on spinal cord injuries. A couple of months after I returned home, I had an incident that sent me to the emergency room. When I was in the hospital recovering, at least I knew there were people around to help. But when I was home, it was scary when something went wrong. In order to go to the bathroom, I had to insert a catheter, and one day when I did that, there was all this blood. I had no idea what was going on. I was dizzy, and my body was reacting badly. My mother and I were alone, and we didn't know what to do. Normally, at the hospital, we'd call a nurse in, but we were on our own, and I couldn't even sit up enough to get into the car and go to the hospital. We had to call an ambulance. So I had to have EMS come to the house and put me on a stretcher, because I was so dizzy. I had an infection, and my body had to tell me in a different way than another person's body would tell her. I was extremely lightheaded, and my blood pressure was sky-high. It was a traumatic moment. I was thinking, *This is not supposed to be my life. I am not supposed to have EMS coming to my house and getting me.* It was a moment when I had to suck it up and fight through it.

It turned out it was a really bad bladder infection. For an uninjured woman it would hurt like crap, and she would know something was wrong early on and of course go to the doctor, get some medication, and clear it up. But for me it was different because I couldn't feel anything. An infection wouldn't alert me with pain. My body had to react in a different way. I got clammy and sweaty, had goose bumps, and felt dizzy. They were all signs that something was wrong with my body.

These were symptoms of autonomic dysreflexia, which affects people with spinal cord injuries like mine. Because I was hurt at a higher level of injury, my autonomic nervous system was also affected. If I had been hurt below a T-7, which is someone paralyzed only from the rib-cage area down, then my autonomic nervous system would have been intact. My blood pressure would have been normal, I would have sweated regularly, and so on. But when there was pain in my body and something went wrong, my nervous system reacted and my blood pressure shot up. I got goose bumps, felt sort of clammy, and had the shakes. I could die if I didn't figure out what was wrong quickly. I could wind up dying from a urinary tract infection because my blood pressure increased so dramatically.

I was lucky that I experienced it only twice. Some people get it all the time. If I was wearing pants with a zipper on them and they were poking into me, I'd become really dizzy and I'd have to look at my body and try to determine what was wrong. It was scary because I couldn't feel anything from my chest down, so numerous things could be the cause—it was a large area!

One weekend, Lauren came to visit and stay with me. My mom was like a second mom to her, so we all hung out together all weekend. She caught a real glimpse into the reality of my injury. Chris was still carrying me up the stairs on his back at that point, as the house hadn't been updated yet, and since I was cold all the time, I had to sit near the heater. She'd heard all about this from the other girls, but seeing it was different. We had a really fun Saturday, all of us, going out to eat and laughing, but on Sunday, before Lauren even woke up, my mother and I had to go to the hospital because I had another UTI. Lauren called us when she woke up, and it seemed like we were going to be at the emergency room for hours and hours, so she headed back to Charlotte.

I think it was an eye-opener for her, seeing the day-to-day. She did get to see me play quad rugby, which was cool, and we did hang out, but the reality of it all wasn't lost on her. She even told me later that her life's mindset was different after that, that her perspective on life and enjoying it was so altered—she appreciated everything she had so much more. And her love of our other friends was strong and genuine. She told me she was speaking to one of the other girls once, and that girl said she was going to run, to use her legs as much as possible, to honor me. I thought that was pretty cool. I know each of the girls handled and processed the accident differently.

CHAPTER 17

Adjusting at Home

THE PROCESS OF GETTING OUT OF BED EVERY MORNING TOOK ABOUT an hour once I refined it. It took up to two hours when I first got home, but we managed to figure out how to make it quicker. The pain and dizziness slowed things down considerably, but on a good day, when my mom dressed me in the morning, we'd get that part down to ten minutes. Since I have some arm use, I could have slid a top on fairly quickly, but pants would have taken me about forty-five minutes to get into. My mother sped that up considerably, so it made sense for her to start helping me dress.

Sleeping was a big challenge, which I hadn't expected. Like anyone, if I were up all night, which happened with great frequency, the morning would be rough. I couldn't roll over or change positions. When I first returned home, my mother and Chris would turn me over in the middle of the night. There was initial concern I'd get bedsores from not being able to move. Chris would go to work wiped out from not getting continuous rest, so they eventually switched off and let him turn me only on weekends. After a few months they weaned me off of this process and I didn't get pressure sores at all. I missed being able to roll over and wrap myself around Chris. I compensated for that by cherishing his touch. Sometimes, when I was awake at night, I'd look down to see his hand on my hip. It made me feel safe seeing it, knowing he was embracing me, even if I couldn't feel it.

The entire situation was exhausting for everyone, especially my mom. We had to figure out how to dress me, book and keep track of appointments, and transport me to those appointments. It was an enormous undertaking, and we didn't know what we were doing. One morning, after my mother helped me out of bed, dressed me, and everything else, at a time when we were still getting our routine down, she was styling my hair for me. I asked her to spray hairspray on me, and she was so tired and frazzled that she sprayed Pine-Sol on my hair instead. She had my hair perfect, too. She was so distracted that she soaked it in cleaning supplies. We had to redo it, but we laughed so hard at what had happened, we cried.

It was difficult to keep up with the clutter, too. I loved a clean house, and I was frustrated at first with all the medical supplies stacked up in my bedroom. I think that impacted my sleeping a little.

My friends were so amazing during this time. They all wanted to help and give my mother a reprieve. Carly used to make it over twice a month to hang out and keep me company. While she was there she helped take some of the responsibility off of my mom by cathing me. It had to be done four times a day. I threw the bag away as it filled. This duty had the potential to be upsetting, but it was mostly humorous when she took the first couple of shots at it. We laughed about it a lot, about how we couldn't imagine two years ago that one of us would be seeing me from this angle. She also knew how to transfer me, lifting me up onto my chair. She was great company and gave my mother some much-needed relief.

My brother, Aaron, was a big help as well. For the first six months, he moved from Virginia Beach to North Carolina to live with me. He was able to pick me up and put me on the couch, and it relieved my mom a bit from having to do everything.

We wound up actually making a crazy connection through some serious talks, which became fairly deep. Once when we were sitting up at night on the couch, he said, "I thought the world was kind of a cruel place. I thought it was filled with only self-ish people. I have a different outlook now, after seeing so many people who care about you, stepping up."

He saw my friends, my parents, Chris, even strangers who donated time and energy and goods and money that changed my life, and he was moved. He hadn't realized people could be like that. He was jaded before I was injured. The accident had actually restored his faith in people. When I heard things like that, it made the injury feel easier, as if there was an upside to it. I had pain and suffering, sure, but I grabbed hold of moments like this with my brother, these little enlightening revelations, and it kept me going.

Aaron stayed with us until we managed to restore a sense of order, and then he moved in with our friend Tom, who was close by. It was really nice to have Aaron near us. One time he was over at the house hanging out, and my mom stepped out for a little while. I was still in bed. I can't remember what I dropped, but whatever it was it must have made him think I had fallen out of bed. Three seconds later, he threw open the door.

Startled, I said, "Well, hello there."

He said, "That was so loud I thought you fell."

We laughed so hard. He must have hit only three steps of the full staircase, he moved so quickly.

I felt like I didn't really know him very well before the accident. Maybe my entire life. He was eight years older, so we never hung out. But after the accident we became extremely close. He lived down the street and came over for dinner, and I saw him much more than when we were young. I was grateful for renewing that connection. It was awesome just to be able to chill with him in a way that I hadn't expected.

CHAPTER 18

The Ugly Reality

Unfortunately, while I was getting used to things inside of my home, factors I couldn't control outside of my home painted an unexpected picture of how people with spinal cord injuries are sometimes treated. Ugly truths began to reveal themselves to me, and I was shocked by some of my experiences.

I'd never really given parking much thought, but when my mother started driving me around, we soon realized that accessible spaces were scarce and that few people respected the law. I even began to think about the name *handicap parking* and why it was still socially acceptable. The term *handicap* originated in a time when people who were in wheelchairs and couldn't work would have to put a hat out for money, or a "handi-cap." Many people don't know that history, and when they say that word, they don't mean anything by it.

My first run-in with the issue was when I still had a neck brace on, and at that point I had no idea that people abuse handicap parking spots the way they do. A guy on a motorcycle had parked between the lines of two handicap spots; usually that space is reserved for a ramp to come out. Regardless, I don't know why anyone would park there; obviously someone could come out of their car in a wheelchair, and anyone thinking logically would know that they needed space to do so.

I was in my mother's car, and I had to be slide-boarded out of it. My mom had to get in front of me to slide me out of the car. The guy had parked so close. Now, I was a confident person, but I did not want to be dragged out of a car like a ragdoll with a neck brace right in front of some idiot because he was too stubborn to move. It just was not a comfortable situation. I remember my mom asking him very nicely to move. He said, "All right," and then all he did was bring his leg around to the other side of his motorcycle. This guy didn't even look me in the eye, didn't make any space for me to get out. He was such an asshole. He just sat there, right next to our car—one foot away from my wheelchair. A waitress came out, and he sat there flirting with her while I was struggling with my mom to get out of the car and into my chair. I said to my mother out loud, "Is this really happening?" We were boiling mad, since it was so soon after the accident and we hadn't encountered anyone quite so obnoxious and selfish. I should have said more. I wasn't afraid of him or even nervous, but until that point, I just had not known people acted like that. He could clearly see I was sitting in the car with a neck brace and a wheelchair, and he needed to get out of the way and he wouldn't. I thought, *Just get out of the way. Period.* It boggled my mind. Of course, just as I was out and in the chair, he took off, revving up the bike really loudly and speeding away. He couldn't even walk his motorcycle out four feet. He had to start it next to us like that.

The next time that happened, I had more smarts and awareness. We went back to the same restaurant, which attracts a lot of sporty people and people with motorcycles. A man had parked his motorcycle *on the lines of* the handicap spot. So I waited. I knew I couldn't walk away from everyone who abused these things; otherwise I was not doing anything to better the situation. If I spoke up, maybe an able-bodied driver wouldn't do it again, and maybe the next injured person wouldn't have a hard time coming out of his or her car. I realized that the more people I could educate, the fewer injured people would face what I was facing right then.

So we waited and waited for this one guy; it was a frustrating experience. I eventually called the cops this time, and the cop was totally on my side. The guy finally emerged from the restaurant, and he noticed the cop by his motorcycle.

He said, "I was only there for one minute." That's everyone's excuse, by the way.

I said, "That's not true. I called the cops twenty minutes ago."
The cop said I was right.

So the cop made the guy come over and apologize to me, but then the cop apologized to me because he couldn't write the guy a ticket. The guy wasn't technically *in* the handicap spot. He was in the wide space between the two painted lines that separated it from another parking space, the space to create room for people in wheelchairs to get out between the cars. I tried to argue that parking on the line made the handicap spot inaccessible and invalid, essentially. The lines are part of the spot and illegal to park on. I was happy the cop wanted to stand up for me, but clearly he didn't understand the law. The cop said to me, "I will get him for something else." And he did. The guy didn't have the correct helmet and so he couldn't ride off. He was livid and had to walk his bike home. Still, it wasn't enough.

CHAPTER 19

The Pact

IN NOVEMBER CHRIS AND I GRADUALLY BEGAN RECEIVING A LOT OF press about our love story and the accident. While some incredible things emerged from that exposure, it was a doubled-edged sword. It exposed the friend who had playfully pushed me to some unexpected nastiness and brought all of the feelings from that night bubbling up to the surface. The unexpected bad part happened over the use of one word, really rocking her world. It was a report that used the word *prank*. This headline changed everything for my friend: WORST BRIDESMAID PRANK EVER LEAVES BRIDE PARAPLEGIC AND UNMARRIED. It almost seemed as if some outlets were only interested in overdramatizing my story and not concerned about getting the facts straight. It's not as if the story required any more drama. In the same news broadcast that called it a prank, they said the pool was two feet deep. They had even called to clarify with me before airing the story, and I had told them the shallow end was four feet deep. By making it worse than it already was, it just gave people more negative things to say about her and the entire situation. Some stories even said I was thrown in. What a big difference one word made.

She had come to watch me play at a quad rugby tournament, along with two other girls from the pool that night. After the match they were in my hotel room, and we knew the story would be on, so we watched on the computer. That was the start of her really having to confront what had happened that night. She couldn't deny her feelings anymore because everything about that night was now public knowledge, and she was a central character in the entire ordeal. The denial she was perhaps using to cope ultimately only masked her true heartache, which none of us had seen fully up to that point.

As soon as she heard it, I knew immediately that the word *prank* would bother her. It was a terrible, dumb word, but I didn't know what kind of impact it would have. It was a really poor choice that left me feeling rubbed the wrong way. I was unaware how much it would dig into her. We talked about it. She told me that the moment she heard it, she was upset, and that the next day she still couldn't shake it. She said, "They called it a prank. It wasn't a prank." She was extremely upset. She obviously had lost sleep over this report. We all knew this was going to be a problem for her and that it was going to snowball from there.

I received a hard lesson in the importance of language. After hearing *prank*, which I never would have said myself, I was much more aware of my word choice and how what I said would be portrayed. I made it a point then to start using the term *playfully pushed,* and some of the media actually caught on.

Unfortunately, others began doing stories and the word *prank* gathered momentum. It became the more frequently used word to describe the night. My friend broke down. That word crushed her. She tried to hold on, but once the national media latched on to the story, her pain escalated.

Just as the story started to spread, she came to me. It was like she was falling off a cliff in front of me, and I couldn't stop her.

"I can see that you're hurting," she said. "I feel like I don't deserve to be happy and I don't deserve to have a good life." The floodgates had been holding back all of her emotion, but that one word opened them up, and it all rushed out in front of us at once. I was saddened and surprised she'd been holding on to the guilt and anxiety.

I begged her to really understand that I wasn't hurting. I was having bad days and good ones, sure, but a bad event didn't take over my life, and I was making more than the most of it. I was rising above the challenge, and I was strong and happy as a result.

All of the girls from that night by the pool were athletic. They ran, played sports, swam. That was part of our bond. She said, "When I'm out doing something active, using my legs, I feel guilty."

I told her not to even think about it, just to enjoy it, that it was okay. I told her, "Be active for me." I wanted all of my friends to live life like it was their last day. Most tried, but with her it just wouldn't sink in, and that word wouldn't go away. *Prank*. It was the most evil trigger for her.

The media attention that followed overwhelmed me and became a part of my everyday life. In all of this, I was never really angry about my situation, but one thing did infuriate me: the way people spoke of my poor friend. It was awful and unrelenting. People would comment on stories, saying horrible things. Nonstop.

Forget how insulting it was to me; my friend was devastated because the word *prank* made it sound like she had planned the push and it was on purpose, and that really wasn't how it happened at all. Notice that whoever wrote the original headline and story didn't even get the simple facts correct—I'm a quadriplegic, not a paraplegic.

Then there were the thousands of comments in the thread of that particular story. People said terrible things about Chris and sometimes about me, such as, "Don't have children with her because you'll have to raise them yourself." But we let it slide. My friend couldn't let it go so easily. One person commented, "I'm sure the friend feels terrible and she should. She crippled this woman because she didn't think." Aside from the fact that the word *crippled* was incredibly offensive and demonstrated tremendous ignorance, the writer of such scathing statements had no idea how my friend or any of us felt.

I wanted to scream, really, at the stupidity of it all. It could have happened to absolutely anyone. It's not uncommon to put a light hand on someone and give them a tender shove into the pool. I've done it. The people writing these comments, they must have led some seriously perfect lives and had really good luck. There were of course multiple supportive comments, but they didn't even cause a blip on my friend's radar. They were eclipsed by the nasty, evil ones that had so much impact.

The accident just happened. It was scary and random, but to write that she should be crippled, too? It was just plain insanity and judgmental, and I hoped none of these people ever had to deal with this situation, because that was no way to find peace. No one is immune to an accident. All of us have done things in our lives that could have caused injury.

People asked me all of the time if I was angry about the accident. The only time I felt anger about this accident was when I read crap like this. It was never-ending. I knew I shouldn't read it all, but I couldn't help myself.

My friend started reading it all, too, more and more. I don't know why. But then she began believing it. Even after I was long out of the hospital and on the road to figuring out my life, she kept getting stuck on the negativity, and with every story she felt worse and worse. People wrote that she should hurt herself, or she should be paralyzed, too, and indebted to me. They got inside her head. These evil, rotten people really messed with her.

Early on she was so consumed by it all, worried that people would figure out who she was, that she stopped using Facebook and shut down in other ways, too. We all sort of closed out of Facebook for a while. She decided if she posted anything to me, she was giving it away that she'd pushed me, even by posting a picture. She didn't want anyone to know anything. I respected that fear and never talked about it at all, not a word.

At one point *In Touch* magazine became really aggressive, trying to figure out who was there that night and who had pushed me into the pool. They actually went so far as to contact about one hundred people on Facebook who were friends with me, trying to put the pieces together. I had casually spoken with the other girls all along about how protective we needed to be of our friend's feelings. We all agreed that had the situation been reversed, it would be painful to feel responsible, and in an unspoken way, we all respected and protected that. But the *In Touch* situation was upsetting. It meant it was time to draw a line in the sand. We had to formalize things. I phoned each girl individually and said, "That's it. We aren't going to talk about it." No one argued, that's for sure, and we made a promise to protect ourselves as a group and to protect our friend who had been the most emotionally devastated by the traumatic event. It was a pivotal moment. The pact had been unspoken until that point, but we knew we were stronger as a whole than we were on our own, so we all agreed it was us against them. I called her, too, and told her that we promised this secret would never get out.

After that, my friend who was having a hard time with the accident began to call me daily, and during our talks she would always apologize profusely. The media blitz intensified, and she appeared to sink deeply during the day. During every call I'd tell her about all the great things that were happening. By the time we hung up, it felt like she was hearing it and it was sinking in. I soon realized that the lift was always temporary, and that by the next day, her despair would reemerge. I felt so sad for her and was deeply concerned. I could tell that a one-second event had really bled into her being. I think she distracted herself at work, but in quiet moments it was harder on her. I could relate; it was like that for me in rehab.

Eventually, I began to worry our friendship might never be the same. I did not want the accident to get in the way of what would have been a fun-filled girly visit, like the ones we had shared before the accident, but it did. The accident loomed large. Up until then I really thought each and every day she'd turned the corner. One afternoon, seeing me in the wheelchair at my home really upset her. It was before we had had the place remodeled and was the first time she'd visited me there, when it was more difficult for me to get around. Someone had carried me upstairs before her arrival, but I had no way to get down on my own. That meant that she and I would have to stay up there together for the entire day. She hadn't seen how limited I was before that day. She had to experience what I was living, and she really felt it.

At first we tried to make casual conversation, but it was strained. It was awkward and forced. I wouldn't say the visit was fun; it was uncomfortable. Not that I was uncomfortable being around her—it just felt sucky being with a great friend with this accident looming there between us. She was hiding what she was feeling, I think for both our sakes. She didn't want me to feel bad for her, and she didn't want to face all that was happening. I feared she hadn't even admitted to herself how much pain she was in. She was a pretty strong-willed person; she and I were alike in that sense. She was putting on a brave face for me, but there had been a lot of denial. I think she just pushed it all down at the beginning. I knew she had guilt, but I thought she could manage it. Maybe she even ignored the stress of what it was doing to her and just thought it would go away.

So at the end of this long, weird day, Chris, my mom, his parents, my friend, and I were going to a restaurant for dinner. It was the Lone Star Steakhouse near my house. It was my favorite restaurant, and I was excited we were all going. I loved steak, and their rolls were so good. But that night, I became so cold from the air-conditioning that I began shivering, and it actually made me feel dizzy. I felt so awful that I had to leave before dinner was over. Chris put me in my friend's car and went back in to finish eating, and my friend and I sat there for a while so I could feel better. Then we decided to go to Burger King. She didn't say much. She just experienced it with me but didn't really know what to do. I remember feeling so bad at the time that she had to see how it all played out. I didn't want to show her the weakness of the injury. I didn't want her to see it in my everyday life. But I knew it had hurt her.

One very intense conversation between us was laced with both positive and negative. *Today* had been great about getting my story out there, and *Headline News* had, too. After my appearances on these programs, some wonderful things were sent in that really helped me. People sent money through a special-needs trust I had set up, and it was enough to pay for a monthly insurance premium for a year or two. A team from the show *George to the Rescue* remodeled my home, making it wheelchair friendly, and Lulus.com donated some clothes to help me feel beautiful. But there was a flip side to the publicity.

"What do these people really want from me?" my friend asked about the media outlets that seemed to sensationalize the accident in their reports.

"Ignore them. We are. We're never letting them in," I tried to assure her.

She said, "I hope you know, I'm happy for all the good that is coming of this and all the great things you're doing as a result."

"Thank you. I know you are," I said. "There's a lot of cool stuff going on, and I'm psyched."

Then we got back to the undercurrent of it all. "Why are they coming after me? Do you think they'll figure it out?"

"We won't let them, I promise."

"I'm afraid of what people will do and say if they find out it was me," she said.

By the end of it that day, as with most days we spoke, she seemed fine. She seemed upbeat, and she could see I was invigorated by the positive elements of my story being told and all the nice letters and words I was receiving from people. She left that night, and I thought she was going to be okay. But then the next day, and then many of the following days and weeks, we'd talk and it was strained. There was a lot of "How are you?" but not much else. It felt as if our friendship was a shadow of what it used to be like. We wanted to talk more, I knew that much. We wanted to be genuine, but we were trying to avoid getting into the discussion of my injury. So it was always weird, and while generally it ended with her feeling better, the next day the negative feelings crept back in.

I never told her, but as she bottomed out right after that first *Today* interview, I became really concerned. The shift in her stress was visible. I was worried that if her name was revealed, she might do something bad to herself, like commit suicide. It just felt like it was that overwhelming to her, and she was that worried about it all. The requests for interviews and evil comments with her name in them would have been too much. She was good at putting on a smile, but I could see through her. She didn't want me to hear her cry, but the spunk was out of her voice. It was timid. She was not at all her usual strong-willed, vibrant self. That's why I continued and will always continue to protect her. I knew the stakes were high.

CHAPTER 20

Turning Down Oprah

OBVIOUSLY, THE ACCIDENT HAD BEEN DIFFICULT FOR MY FRIEND to deal with. It was tough for all of us. The other girls were always reminded and their lives changed, too. Mine had radically changed, but so much good was coming from it all that I was getting carried along by the momentum. I thought, eventually, she would simply figure it all out in her head and find peace. But with so many people trying to interject and get her story, and all the horrible comments that she couldn't help but read, it just became unbearable for her. She was terrified of the online bullying that would likely occur if they found her out. It had been bad enough without her name out there.

I remember sitting at home one afternoon in January and receiving an e-mail from a producer for Oprah Winfrey. I was so excited. I was a little mystified, too. Oprah Winfrey? I mean, I knew my story was interesting to people, but I was surprised it was *that* interesting. I'd watched Oprah almost every day. She was my idol. I knew this was something I needed to share with my friend, so I gave her a call. I thought that good news for me would make her feel good, too, that she'd see these really cool things happening for me and be relieved in a way. But I also knew the attention on my story made her nervous.

"Oprah wants to talk to me!" I said.

"That's cool," she said. I could tell she was a little anxious. "Are they going to want to talk about me?" she asked sheepishly.

"Of course not. Oprah would never ask that." I thought Oprah wanted to hear about my love story and have Chris and me appear on the show together. "Don't even give it a thought. I can't imagine that's what they want, but it doesn't matter because even if they do, I wouldn't do anything to hurt you. So don't worry about it."

I finally did speak to a producer and my heart just sank. A few people had wanted the story, but I had been clear that I wasn't going to say anything about my friend. *Oprah* was really the last outlet I thought would ask because that information had been more of a quest of the tabloids and gossip magazines up to this point.

"We're doing a show on forgiveness. . . . " That was all I needed to hear. I explained to her that I don't look at it like something I need to forgive. If someone had hurt me intentionally, then forgiveness would be in order. But there was no ill intent. I would have had to have been angry in order to forgive, and I wasn't. There was no blame, so nothing to forgive. I didn't even consider asking my friend to participate. The thought never even occurred to me.

I said, "I can't do that to her. She can't talk about it. She doesn't talk to anyone about what happened. It hurts too much."

It turned out the producer wanted us both to come on the show. She told me it would happen only if I brought my friend along. I think she was stunned we'd turn down Oprah—that anyone would turn down Oprah. She called back twice, asking me to appear with my friend, trying to convince me, pressing harder each time. Twice more I said no. I offered to come alone, but they weren't interested. I explained that my friend was having serious anxiety attacks and that it would be too much for me even to ask her.

A lot of people have asked me and the other girls there that night why we were so protective. Seriously? Releasing her identity would have been equivalent to releasing the hounds, so to speak. We would have been an accessory to her pain. What human being would do that to another person? I know her better than anyone, I think. I know it would break her if I didn't continue to protect her and hide her identity. If people hadn't been so evil and mean with comments and seeking out her name, we might never have needed to work so hard to shield her. We might have been able to go on *Oprah* and discuss our friendship. It was unfortunately made apparent early on that we had to step in and form our protective pact; people were suggesting online some seriously inhumane things. We couldn't stand for that.

The *Oprah* folks acted like an appearance on the show would help her heal, but I felt they didn't have our best interests at heart. It would have ruined all of us, and we all knew that. What if her name was out there and people could message her directly, before she'd had a chance to heal? We knew the risk was too great. That's what bothered me the most about Oprah's people. How could someone who had no idea who I was or who she was try to convince me this was good for us? Believe me, it was Oprah, and I was starry-eyed. But not stupid. I was offended that they tried to coax me like I was an idiot. I felt disillusioned. I idolized Oprah. I grew up watching her. I thought Oprah would do the same thing for her friend, too. I thought Oprah would have been proud of how I was taking a stand for a friend's life and well-being. I think had she actually known that, she herself would have understood. She is famous for being a tremendous friend. I was being a pillar of strength at my weakest moment to help someone in a worse predicament. I knew Oprah would have appreciated that act. At least, I hope.

I wound up having the same conversation over and over with my friend with great frequency after that. It appeared to hit her hardest right then. I remember my words, on the phone or if she'd come to visit. It was always the same.

"You don't deserve to feel anything from this," I'd explain.

I'd say, "I've pushed you in the pool so many times; you've pushed me in. It's just this one time I got hurt. It doesn't make me better, and it doesn't make you a bad person that this happened this time. We've messed around near the water before."

She would call when she was anxious, but the calls started to dwindle a bit. She would feel better when we hung up, that I could tell, but it seemed it would all creep back in overnight and she'd wake up the next day stressed again. She never told me she was going to kill herself, but it became a growing fear of mine as the media barrage escalated and the risk of her name getting out grew. I felt like it would be a very long road to her finding happiness, if that even happened. I felt like I'd lose my control of the situation if her name got out there. I don't think I would have been able to pull her back from the damage that would have done.

I knew she was trying to stay busy with her work. She had a great job, and all of us were there for her. I comforted her the most, I thought, because when she could see I was okay, then she felt okay. "I'm at peace. You should be, too." I told her again and again, "Don't waste your money paying to talk to someone you don't know." It seemed like it was the right thing. A therapist would cost so much money, and even though she had insurance and had toyed with the idea, I thought I could help her more, that I'd get the words right, that I'd comfort her because it had happened to us, not a stranger. I worried that once-a-week sessions wouldn't be enough, and that she'd maybe shift away from talking to me. I didn't want to manage the situation in a control-freak kind of way, but I wanted to offer some sort of control for her. I knew it would take her so long to develop trust with a stranger but that we already had deep trust between us. Even as I told her I could be her support again and again, maybe at that point she should have spoken to someone. Maybe it was too much for her and I wasn't equipped. She fell into such a blue place. Maybe a therapist could have helped her. That was one regret I did have as months went by and she didn't appear to feel better.

CHAPTER 21

Laughter and Tears

CARLY AND SAMANTHA WERE SERIOUSLY FUNNY GIRLS. ONE DAY, about a year after the accident, they'd come with me to my rugby tournament. It was my first season of rugby, and as we went to the gym Carly was wheeling me through double open doors. As we were approaching, I said, "Hey, you see that thing in the middle where the doors close? Watch out for that."

Carly said, "Okay."

She must have thought my wheelchair could go over it, but my footplate was too low, and so when she went head on into it, the chair stopped but I didn't. I fell out of the chair and flew through the air. Both girls tried to reach down and catch me by my sweatshirt, but that didn't work; they couldn't get a grip at all. It happened in slow motion. Well, I was lying there on the floor, not hurt, and none of us could stop laughing. That kind of situation always made me laugh. It reminded me a bit of life before the accident, because it was the kind of crazy stuff we used to laugh about back then, too. It was a cool moment because there was always stress about the accident and me being in a wheelchair, but this was just a good old-fashioned laugh, and it felt great. It wasn't scary. People fall out of their chairs all the time.

Something else fell out another time shortly after that, but it wasn't my entire body. It was my boob. One night, Samantha, Carly, and I went to dinner. It was the first time I'd gone out without Chris or my mother to help with the transition out of a car. We pulled up to the valet parking guy, which was our only option, and began the process of getting me out. We were laughing hysterically because it took both of them to slide me out of the car to go into the restaurant. The valet guy just stood at first, but when he saw them struggling, he tried to get in there and help. But one of my boobs had popped out of my dress, so of course we were laughing even harder at this point, and there was chaos because they were trying to get him to go away while they stuffed my boob back in the dress. They worked hard not to drop me on the ground. We caused quite a scene before they got me into my chair to go eat.

With no plans yet to set a wedding date and the media coverage continuing, there seemed to be little improvement for my one friend in getting beyond the accident. In one of our daily calls, she said, "It's really hard to see you like this. I don't want this to cause distance between us just because it's hard for me. Please don't let this happen. Call me every day."

"I won't let us slip," I said. "I'm here for you."

"I'm afraid I'll put myself somewhere away from you," she admitted. I knew seeing me was a constant reminder of her agony. Both of us knew we didn't want to lose a friend. Sometimes it is human nature to run away from what scares you, to distance yourself from something that might unleash bad memories.

I think she had the urge to push herself away from me to feel better, but she was asking me to help her stay strong. In part, she felt like she didn't deserve to be my friend anymore, but she wanted to. She wanted to heal. I know that.

I missed talking about boys and going out and life. Our conversations were always the same now, so repetitive. I wanted so badly for my words to stick.

"I don't have any nerve pain today," I'd tell her. Or, "I had a really good day today," or "I got a great letter today." I would relate anything positive that happened. You could hear her breathing change either in person or on the phone. Literally. It was that important to make her feel better.

She would get it. She would get that I was happy. She would get that I had moved on. Everyone else had. The family had. We drew on the great things that had happened. We wanted to grab her and shake her and pull her in on all of the joy we felt.

She had become severely depressed. She kept saying that if people knew it was her, they would have been calling for interviews and she wasn't ready to talk about it. I honestly felt she would have been viciously slandered in the media, and she didn't deserve that. People were so judgmental, as if they'd never made a mistake: never taken their eyes off the road for a split second to change the radio station, never accidentally run a red light, never been part of horseplay or fooled around. Something bad had happened as the result of an innocent gesture, and that one moment did not, and should not, define her as a person.

I knew she wanted to be reassured that I was happy and doing well. The comments people blogged and e-mailed made her feel awful, and she took them to heart. Online, I argued that the people who had negative things to say had no life. I defended her.

They sat behind their computers judging others when, in reality, I didn't think they were happy with their own lives. It was a form of bullying. People could say whatever they wanted to online without anyone knowing who they were. They could say something hurtful and mean and then go about their day. It infuriated me.

I told her that these people must have never had a true friend and that was sad. We were lucky to have each other, and I still would rather have her as my friend than the use of my legs. People writing hate weren't worth her time or her tears; we talked a lot about that.

From our conversations it became clear she had started to believe what people were writing about her. I told her all the time that she was not stupid, evil, or reckless, as everyone implied, and that she didn't deserve her guilt. People actually wrote that she deserved to be miserable. These were comments on blogs and following online media stories. I told her that the people judging her had most likely done something in their lives that could have caused someone injury, but they were lucky to have sidestepped that fate. People didn't realize how easily a spinal cord injury could occur.

Helping her heal became my mission: Her happiness would be the final piece to mine. I wasn't healed until she was.

From there it just poured out. She told me she had major anxiety attacks and that she watched that night play out in her head, frame by frame. Every single day. She told me she was worried that someday I'd hate her, but I think she knew deep down I wouldn't. She apologized for bringing it up because I think it had actually sunk in that I wanted her to be happy. I think she knew I was okay with it all, but she felt despair inside. It wasn't that she didn't believe me. She did. It was like a waterfall of emotion that she'd carried inside for six months, and the word *prank* broke her internal dam. It just shattered her, and she was reeling.

I couldn't believe what I was hearing. I was worried about her. I was even more worried than I had been before. I knew it was really bad, and I knew I would have to help her. The irony was that, honestly, I *was* happy. I was happy to be alive, grateful to be in love, and thankful that I had so many great friends and family members. Sure, I was scared, and some days rather terrified, but I was happy inside. I knew she wasn't. I knew I had to focus on putting aside my own issues, and I decided to take on hers.

One day I said to her, "I have physical pain. You have emotional pain. But they are so different. Don't carry this sadness forever. I don't intend to."

I decided during that conversation that I would be her pillar of strength forever, and I told her that. I felt like our friendship was so strong that our shared experience would get us through this together. I told her she could always talk to me. I became her spine. I channeled optimism for her. I wanted to save her. I knew I would be fine, but I didn't know if she ever would be.

CHAPTER 22

Wedding Plans

THE FEBRUARY AFTER I RETURNED HOME, CHRIS AND I DECIDED to go ahead and pick a wedding day. We chose July 22, 2011. Part of our decision to lock in the date was due to 1-800-Registry kindly coming forward, offering to give us our dream wedding. They'd seen the story on *Headline News* and called for my information. I knew it would be wonderful but very different than the wedding originally planned. I was nervous about being wheeled down the aisle, not walking, and I was pretty terrified that our first dance wouldn't be what I'd always dreamt it should be. But I knew who my bridesmaids would be, and that gave me a lot of comfort.

Along with all the media attention came a couple of generous and interesting offers. In addition to 1-800-Registry, *Today* offered to pay for my wedding and cover it live. And *George to the Rescue*'s remodel of my home had made our bedroom a real oasis. It was suddenly green, with hardwood floors, and it had a roll-in shower and a low sink and granite counter I could roll under. The decor was beautiful, and they installed an elevator that saved me. The wedding was shaping up to be just as spectacular.

All of the girls of course knew they'd be in my wedding, even Britney, who hadn't been a part of the original party. The good fortune of having the wedding sponsored meant I could include Britney, which I'd told her the night of my bachelorette party I wanted to do but couldn't since we had nothing coordinating for her to wear. I was thrilled to have a second chance to include her. She had become such a good friend to me, and we had confided in each other a lot during my recovery. Our friendship had become so deep. Plus, the accident had made her part of the group. I wanted her to stand with the rest of the girls when I said my vows.

※

Originally, I was to have someone other than Britney standing up there with me: my friend Sandra. She hadn't been able to make it to the bachelorette party, and that surprisingly had some heavy implications for our friendship. It all resulted in a terrible friendship-ending e-mail exchange. We had gone to college together and were really close, especially in senior year. I used to think of her as my Pirate-in-crime. After college she moved to Raleigh, and we drifted apart a bit. I guess when you grow up you start to become more aware of differences that in college you wouldn't have noticed. Sandra and I discovered we had political differences. It wasn't a huge thing, but we weren't on the same page and we wound up not seeing each other as much as we once did.

Sandra had a birthday party one night and I decided to leave early, and she got kind of pissed off about it. A silent tension existed between us, and so the wedding came around and she didn't attend my bachelorette party. She was visiting her cousin, who was going off to war the next day. It was understandable so I was okay with her absence, obviously.

By this point I'd actually been wishing Britney could be in the wedding, but I'd already ordered the dresses for the bridesmaids, and I couldn't find one to match for her. I even checked eBay. I couldn't ask for the dress back from Sandra, and I couldn't ask for everyone to buy new dresses.

Then the accident happened. I was growing so close to these other girls, but Sandra and I were getting further apart. She lived fifteen minutes away and never really came to visit, and for whatever reason, that upset me deeply. Believe me, I appreciated that people had busy lives, but a friend is a friend and I had an expectation she'd show up when I needed her. She said I should have invited her, that she wouldn't just appear, but it felt a little weird to ask someone to visit me at home. Mostly, people called and asked if they could stop by. They asked how they could help or if I needed something specific picked up. Sandra kept saying, "I'm going to stop by," but never ever did. At one point I said, "Stop saying it if you're not coming." In her defense, we had already drifted apart. I thought that maybe she didn't feel comfortable coming over. She supported me in the way she knew how. She did visit the hospital a couple of times and, after the accident, she threw a small fundraiser for me and I was grateful for both gestures. I just needed more friendship from her and she from me. There were some lonely days when I first returned home, and I needed a lot of support.

The tension broke, and it sounds so immature but we had a Facebook fight, and she said something that threw me completely off guard. She said that she was frustrated in the hospital that she had to wait so long to see me. She meant the night I broke my neck. My own family had to wait to see me; the girls who were actually there, who had to experience that traumatic event, hadn't even seen me, and she was frustrated and had the nerve to tell me that. In retrospect, I think our argument got out of hand and we both reacted poorly. This happens to a lot of friendships. Our relationship just wasn't strong enough to override the hurtful words we had both said.

Once we both cooled a bit, I wondered if it was simply too weird for her to see me in my new environment. The hospital actually might have been more comfortable in some ways. It wasn't a new reality, just a stopover. It was possibly my first realization that people who had known me once as an able-bodied person might feel uncomfortable around me. Maybe she also held some guilt for fighting with me or not attending the party that night, which is crazy. But the strangest part is that I think she saw the five of us together, who were all at the pool, and she felt left out of that bond. It would have been hard to break through it; we had a shared experience. The stronger my friendship became with the girls by the pool, the more difficult it was to maintain the flimsier ones. The girls by the pool became the gold standard, and not just in how they treated me, but in how they treated each other. It was really unbelievable and admirable to have witnessed the growth of our relationship.

Then on the other hand I had Sandra actually saying things in an e-mail like, "You don't know how singled out I felt, to be the one who wasn't there." Maybe I would have felt left out in the same situation, but she should have been happy that she wasn't part of that event. I've learned that I really don't know how other people feel or how they should react. It has all been a good lesson in empathy. You just don't really know what people are actually thinking inside. Maybe the four who were there filled up so much room in a positive way that my friendship with Sandra was one of the casualties of this accident.

It turned out she did feel guilty, which she later revealed. She wrote, "I don't wish I was at that party. I did at first because I thought, if I was there could I have done something to prevent it? I felt guilty for not being there . . . but I felt like I should have been there. I thought, if I had been there what would have been different?" In her final note to me, she wrote something that startled me. She said, "You have no idea what it feels like to be the one person who wasn't there to witness what happened, who you don't even speak to anymore. I'm sure you've called all the girls who were there, but you haven't called me at all." It shook me up and we never spoke again after that. I wasn't sure if the bond with the other girls had grown so large that maybe it blocked up space for other people to enter that circle. Either way, Sandra sadly wasn't included in the new wedding plans.

I called the girls individually to make sure the date was okay with them and explained that, since it was being paid for, we'd get new dresses, too. That, of course, was very exciting to them. They didn't love the original dresses.

As we made plans to wed, I also scheduled surgery to have what's called a suprapubic catheter put in—a permanent tube that was to be inserted into my bladder and attached to a bag strapped to my leg. I was told it would be convenient because I could open it up myself and go to the bathroom by myself. There was still a bag attached and it would be a 24/7, like a ball and chain, but I was excited at the forward momentum of everything.

New dresses aside, everyone was ecstatic that we were finally going to have the wedding, but there was one concern among all of us. We'd navigated the murky waters of the press, careful to keep our promise not to reveal exactly what had happened that day. We had done a good job in protection mode as a team. But a televised wedding meant more coverage and more discussion. It meant all of our faces would be on TV. Of course, one girl in particular felt panicked at this prospect.

Today and 1-800-Registry decided to team up in a joint effort, and it was incredible that they'd both donate so much, but as we got into the planning, we learned that *Today* could air only a five-minute ceremony. Sadly, I realized that wasn't for me. That was to be the most exciting part of the wedding, and I wanted to cherish it, not rush it for five minutes start to finish. I'd waited so long for it. I hated to miss the opportunity, but I would have rather had the wedding in the backyard than compromise the ceremony like that, despite how grateful I was for the show's generosity. For me, the most important part was our vows. I didn't want to be rushed for commercial break. A meaningful ceremony was far more important than being on television.

It also alleviated another concern—no faces live on TV. I told the girls of my decision and heard a collective sigh of relief.

I was sincerely appreciative of everything *Today* had done for my cause. They were the most wonderful people. And I was eternally grateful and happy that 1-800-Registry was still on board even if *Today* wasn't part of the wedding anymore. So 1-800-Registry handled everything, and I was able to choose all of the details.

The planning began. Again.

CHAPTER 23

One Year Later

On the first anniversary of my accident, I was on the way back from an Abilities Expo in New Jersey. I had met the people at Colours Wheelchair, who had sponsored me and agreed to donate a really amazing wheelchair to me. I had attended the event to meet Rick Hayden, who ran the company and whom everyone called Big Daddy. I was going to choose the details for my chair. He was nice and hilarious and was the one who had asked me to be part of Team Colours originally, months earlier. I selected a blinged-out chair with spinners and suspension and was fitted, because anyone with an injury like mine needs a customized chair. They're quite expensive, and I was honored to receive such a lovely gift. Also, I had hoped it would give me confidence because it was so pretty, with Aztec designs and bright blue colors, but the experience with the other girls I met on that trip tapped into some insecurities I hadn't realized existed yet.

I was feeling a little shyer than usual meeting these beautiful Colours Girls. They were all paraplegics, and it was hard being the only quad among the little group. I remember feeling self-conscious, because I needed so much more help than all of them. I was fascinated by what they were able to do: They could easily transfer in and out of their chairs; they could lean over and just grab something off of the ground; they'd go to the bathroom together like any other group of girls. Their bodies didn't even look paralyzed. They just looked like able-bodied people sitting down. They had no quad pooch, which I had developed; my belly protruded due to inactivity, and it made me look pregnant. And obviously their hands weren't balled up like mine were.

What made me most self-conscious was that their hair and makeup were perfect. Mine used to always be perfect. I knew that if I could do my own hair, I could look just as nice. I knew how to do my hair better than anyone, obviously, because it was my hair. So while it was a great experience, it was also just a reminder of how disabled I really was. We all went out to dinner the last night, and I felt so *not* cute. My mom was there and she tried hard to help me get through it, but that night I was probably more sensitive than usual, and even though my hair did look nice, I felt insecure. These girls all looked hot. I wanted the use of my hands so I could look just as hot.

We came back from Jersey, and I was relieved that I was going to be able to see some of my friends. My mom brought back a giant cannoli from a New York–style deli, and we celebrated her birthday. Admittedly, there was a bit of sadness and negative energy in the room as we celebrated her birthday, but as I had hoped, the new chair eventually gave me a lot of confidence.

Looking back at the year that had passed, I knew a lot had changed and taken its toll on all of us, but through it all, I was certain my love for my family and friends had grown. Chris and I became more aware of what we had as well. We'd always been affectionate, but in the wake of the accident, after a year of being in it together as a team, we'd learned to be so grateful for each other and our love. After we returned home from rehab, Chris got into the habit of hugging me as soon as he walked in the door, a gesture I greatly anticipated each afternoon. We'd mindlessly done it before, but after the accident we did it with intent. At night, as we lay in bed, he would say, "I love you, sweetheart" and then I would rub his back gently until he started snoring. Each morning, he made my day by saying, "Good morning, beautiful." We never left each other without a kiss and an "I love you" exchange. None of that routine was lip service either, and I knew in my heart it would always be our way. The year that brought us so much tragedy had also enriched our lives. We never let one day pass without our special moments. We'd become painfully aware of how quickly and drastically life could change. No one knew what the next day would bring, so neither of us wasted time not loving one another fully or taking our love for granted.

Chris and I reaffirmed our love for each other. I was amazed by how many people found this difficult to believe. It made me think that many people, those who questioned whether he would stay with me, just don't know love. Love clearly wasn't as common as I thought it was. It was hard for me to imagine that just because of a physical problem, a perfect relationship between two people who loved each other wouldn't work. I only wished more people had that love for each other and could understand what we had. If you asked someone who has lost a spouse to cancer or some other terrible disease if they'd take their deceased loved one back if they were in a wheelchair, they'd say yes without question.

I never set out looking for our love to be tested, but I was glad—and not remotely surprised—that it survived. I never expected my strength in general would be tested or that I'd be forced to push the limits of that strength, but I was given no choice. I was always a careful girl, and I thought I was doing everything right. I was safe, or I tried to be. I really didn't have to think about strength before, whether I was or I wasn't strong. If you'd asked me as a twenty-four-year-old, "Hey, how would you manage being a quadriplegic?" I'd have said, "I wouldn't want to know. I don't think I'd handle it well." You just don't know until you need to know.

CHAPTER 24

The Rehearsal

JULY FINALLY ARRIVED, AND THE THURSDAY BEFORE MY WEDDING was the most hectic day. Mom and I were rushing around, and I was kind of stressed out. We had a lot to accomplish before we left town for the rehearsal and the wedding. I had to worry about my hair and my tan. I had had an opportunity to have hair extensions put on for free, but because of timing, I missed the window. So I was freaking out a bit, like any other bride, because I wanted my hair to be perfect. I had the actual hair extensions but no one to attach them. I found one guy who said he could do it for three hundred dollars, but that was way out of my price range. I didn't expect it to be so challenging. Finally, after many frantic calls, I found someone who was available and who gave me a really great price.

For me, the wedding was not about the flowers, the food, or any of that. It came down to two things: One, I needed to look great. Before I got hurt I used to say all the time that I wanted to look good. I wanted it to be the same after the accident. I wanted to look as good as any other bride, knowing I would be upset if I didn't. It wasn't about having the perfect wedding day, but look-ing good still mattered. I wanted to look good enough that no one saw the wheelchair, that all anyone would say was, "What a beautiful bride." Two, I needed Chris to be there. That was the bottom line.

Part of looking great meant that the tan and hair were integral parts of that equation. I had solved the hair problem, but the challenge of the tan was full of additional obstacles. I used to get spray tans all the time where you stand up and get sprayed. But that was when I was able-bodied. Luckily, I found a woman who would come to my home since we'd have to adjust the methodology a bit to get it done.

"Normally, we set up a tent so your home doesn't get spray tanned, too," she explained. "You'd stand up and I'd spray you."

I laughed. "Obviously, I can't stand up in the tent. We'll have to figure something else out."

She was so nice and not weirded out at all, which made me happy.

"I've seen a ton of people naked," she said. "We'll figure something out."

We brainstormed a bit and decided to do it in my bedroom on the bed, with me lying down. It was a production and it took about an hour, because we had to spray and dry, spray and dry. I was flipped around, and at one point my mom had to hold up my legs one at a time so we could spray those.

In the middle of it all, Chris came home and had no idea that I was getting a spray, and no idea that there was a random person at my house in our room. He came in the bedroom and opened the door. He made the funniest face and said, "All right," and closed the door and went downstairs.

After all of that, the tan was overly dark and I had to do a little scrubbing to lighten it up.

We had an intimate bridal shower at the wedding site, which was so nice. The wedding was being held on a dairy farm in Pittsboro, North Carolina, with a hotel on the grounds called the Fearrington House and community called Fearrington Village. There were cows in the field behind us while we got married, so you can imagine the setting. It was really country, which was what I wanted.

My shower was originally planned for the day after the bachelorette party. So I'd never had one. I wore a flowing maxi dress that was very casual. With all my extensions in, my hair was long and straight, very hippielike. The shower was in a beautiful room, set up on a terrace with windows all the way around. It was an open and elegant space with a Victorian look to the furniture. It had a big floral carpet with a large wooden table in the middle that held all the food. My mom brought a cupcake holder, and we had these hilarious drinking cups with noses drawn on the side of them. They were just plastic cups, but when you took a drink, it looked like your nose; some had mustaches, some had nose rings, and some were really big. We played a few games, such as "Who Knows the Bride Better?" and we all laughed when my mom guessed my eye color incorrectly. My eyes are hazel, and my mom wrote green. Lauren won the game. Britney was late and could come only for the rehearsal, but Samantha and Carly drove up together and made it to the lunch.

Coincidentally, all the girls matched. Lauren and Samantha were both wearing coral dresses, and Carly wore a tan dress with a coral flower in her hair, and a fifth bridesmaid I had added—a woman named Mayra who worked with Chris and had become friends with us—wore floral, too. By the time the rehearsal took place, it was a typical hot and steamy July evening.

During the rehearsal we all had a good laugh because Chris and I practiced our kiss, which I hadn't really expected to be any kind of problem, since we'd kissed a million times before. It turned out to be the funniest part of the evening. I had no core muscles, so I couldn't lean forward and kiss him or I'd fall right out of my chair. Carly wound up having to sort of block the chair so it wouldn't roll backward at that very important moment. At the same time Chris had to hold my wrist to pull me toward him. He had to hold on firmly so I wouldn't fall. I fell over a couple of times until we got the right balance. Chris caught me. Next we had to practice putting on the rings because I didn't have finger function. He obviously put a ring on me, but I wanted to put his ring on him, too. We thought about it for a long time, trying to ensure it was meaningful. We finally came up with the solution to put his ring at the tip of my finger, then he'd connect his fingertip to mine and I'd slide it on—like a fake push from me, and he did the rest. Chris's uncle Ron came up with that one. He was the minister performing the ceremony the next day.

After all the laughs and the rehearsal, I said goodnight to Chris. He kissed me and said, "I love you."

I said, "I love you, too."

He said, "I can't wait to marry you. I'll see you tomorrow."

I remember thinking, *Wow, this is finally happening.* We were ready to be married. We had waited so long, and it was so exciting. It was fun getting his friends and my friends together and having this wonderful time that we'd never been able to have. I was thrilled that it was the last time I was going to see Chris before I could finally call him my husband.

That night, Carly, Samantha, and I all stayed together in one room. It was like a slumber party, and we had so much fun. Every time we were sort of drifting off to sleep, someone said something, like when you're fourteen and having a sleepover with friends and someone keeps talking. It was the greatest night.

CHAPTER 25

The Perfect Wedding

WHEN I WOKE UP ON JULY 22, I WAS NOT JITTERY AT ALL, BUT I had happy anxiety. It was my day, with my girls by my side. I was excited about my hair and my dress, and I was overjoyed that they were all there for me and were all going to be part of it. I had so many happy thoughts. We had people who had donated their time to fix our hair and makeup. One of the makeup artists was actually the wife of a local radio celebrity named Mike Morse. Chris listened to his show every morning and was a big fan. Our wedding planner knew him, and Mike offered to MC the wedding at the last minute. We'd already lined up a band and DJ, and now we'd also have Mike as our MC. It was a huge surprise for Chris. We didn't tell him that Mike would be MCing our wedding and that his wife, Lindsay, did our makeup. She is highly requested around our area for makeup and he's often requested for parties, so we felt like celebrities.

I have two *really* vivid memories of my group of girls. One, of course, was the night of the accident—that's seared in all of our heads. But the other, the bookend of my thoughts of them, was on my wedding day in the early morning. Those girls were as important to that day as Chris.

We were all getting ready together in this really pretty little room. Lauren, Carly, Britney, Samantha, and I were all having our makeup and hair done, just like we had before we headed out dancing the night of the bachelorette party. We needed three hairstylists to keep things moving.

I had to get into my dress, and we knew ahead of time that might prove to be a challenge. I wanted to keep my wedding dress—the one I had bought originally, before the accident. It was definitely one of those "This is the dress" moments that I had with it, so changing it was not even remotely an option. Even if 1-800-Registry wanted to buy me the fanciest dress on the planet, I wouldn't have been able to accept it. I had fallen in love with mine. My mom really wanted to buy my dress, and she had worked so hard to make the payments on it. We couldn't afford it all at once, and she had made the final payment right before the wedding. I was in love with the dress, and it was so meaningful to me.

So 1-800-Registry paid for the seamstress to fix my original dress. She had to take it in a bit, but it required a much larger alteration. The back had a corset that laced down and then exploded into a train. The train had to be removed, because I certainly couldn't sit on top of that crazy pile of fabric. It would have filled my chair. We laughed really hard when we tried to put it on a couple of months before the wedding, before the alteration. We pulled it over my head, but you couldn't see me. It wouldn't go down over my head, so it looked like a person with no head and long legs. Everyone laughed as I sat there covered in dress, and someone said, "Nope, nope, this won't work." Which of course made us all laugh harder.

Essentially, after much thought, we decided to have the dress sliced open up the back, so that when you unlaced it in the back, it literally folded open. I had to do this so I could get into it. There was simply no other way for me to put it on. We tried. It was hard enough to put on a wedding dress while standing up with help. Putting it over my head with me sitting wasn't an option. So that day, we had to lay it down on the bed, spread it out, and open it up, almost like a wrap you would make a sandwich with. After much deliberation I had to lie facedown on the bed and get my boobs lined up, and then someone had to lace me up while I was there facedown. It was pretty hysterical, I have to say. They had to keep moving me around and shifting body parts to line things up. Obviously, I was totally over being naked in front of people—you lose that shyness after an injury like mine.

We were all laughing and giggling, and the moment felt perfect. It was eight in the morning. I didn't normally drink coffee, but I was tired so I had a cup and it actually tasted really good. It was probably because I loaded it up with cream and sugar. I remember at one point looking around and feeling like this was the start of something better, the beginning of a new chapter. I felt like some healing would occur because the wedding was no longer something that had been taken away. It was given back to me, and I was overwhelmed with happiness. It was given back to my friends, too, especially the one who had pushed me and suffered so much for that act. I was so grateful they were all there. These girls were more than just bridesmaids to me. In fact, I had not one but four best friends who were all like sisters. My wedding wouldn't have been my wedding without them. But my favorite part about that morning as we got ready was that no one mentioned the accident, the wheelchair, or the reason we were glued together for life. I am sure no one even thought about it. It was just a happy day. A beautiful, happy day.

It was so hot that day—102 degrees. Everyone was laughingly complaining about the heat. Out of the blue Carly began to put baby powder between her thighs.

Of course ridiculous laughter erupted.

"What the heck are you doing?" I asked.

"Well, I don't want my thighs sticking together from all the sweat!"

We shared ten minutes of real laughter. Everyone was throwing the bottle of powder back and forth, and it was hilarious. They all looked so dignified and dainty all done up, but they were still acting like their goofy selves, and it felt so normal and good. I didn't sweat anymore because of my injury—most C-level injuries don't sweat because the part of the nervous system that controls that function no longer works. I was also always freezing, so the heat didn't bother me at all. But we were laughing hysterically about the baby powder. All of them were hiking up their dresses and trying to delicately put powder on their thighs without getting it on the dresses. They'd gotten these new beautiful, flowing J. Crew dresses in turquoise, which went really well with the country setting and the sunflowers they would be carrying. They loved the new dresses, too.

Every moment of the wedding was amazing. I had always dreamed of a country wedding—something very Southern. I just thought I would like something rustic. I had really wanted to get married in a setting with a barn. I had Googled "North Carolina barn" and "North Carolina barn wedding," and one of the results that came up was this perfect place. I originally thought it was more of a casual setting, but it turned out to be extremely fancy. On the grounds of this dairy farm was a beautiful five-star hotel, and it had appeared in many magazines. The barn was not just a barn; it was like a reception hall, quite elegant with chandeliers

© MARTHA MANNING PHOTOGRAPHY

everywhere. I didn't expect all that, but of course when I saw it, I thought, *Oh, definitely.*

I could see the ceremony beginning outside. I watched each bridesmaid make her way down to where she would start her walk. I think they were more nervous than I was because they were being videotaped, but not by any TV cameras, just our own cameras. Plus, I was a center-stage kind of person. I didn't mind being in front of big crowds, but the bridesmaids were worried about tripping down the aisle. At least I no longer had to worry about stumbling down the aisle in heels.

I know it must have been hard for my friend who pushed me, because it was only one year after the accident, but that night by the pool was completely off limits. This was not a day to reflect on the incident by the pool, and everyone knew that. I was grateful for that unspoken silence. We were all looking forward to my wedding day, even though she hadn't healed. Still, I took great pleasure in looking down the aisle, knowing she was happy and she seemed to be getting caught up in the moment with us all, having a good time. I'm sure it was hard for her, but it would have been sad if she hadn't been there, sad for me. I think she knew that. Plus, I knew that seeing me marry the love of my life would give her a little bit of inner peace.

It all felt real when I watched my bridesmaids walking down the aisle, and I thought to myself, *Wow! They're going and then it is my turn!* As my dad pushed me in my wheelchair, I was looking at the crowd to see who was there, instead of looking at Chris, and then suddenly I was at the front beside him and my dad kissed me on the cheek.

It felt to me (and my mother said this, too) that the wedding day wasn't only the day I'd committed to Chris, but it was my finish line. It marked the end of the ordeal, the end of the interruption from the accident. It felt like things had come full circle.

The setting was perfect. The only rough part was that Chris and I had to sit a little farther apart than I would have liked. My chair and the chair he sat in facing me couldn't really fit any closer together. But we held onto each other and it was all okay. Better than okay.

Our vows were incredibly special. I remember them vividly. We said the same thing to one another. I said, "I, Rachelle, take you, Chris, to be no other than yourself. Loving what I know of you and trusting what I do not yet know, with faith in your love for me, through all of our years, and in all that life may bring us. I promise to be ever open to you and above all to do everything in my power to permit you to become the person you are yet to be. I give you my love." I was smiling as I said that, though I thought I was going to cry. I was just so happy to be there that I didn't stumble over the words at all. We each repeated them after his uncle said them for us, a few words at a time. We kissed after that, and then, in Jewish tradition, Chris stomped on a glass. Carly was holding my bouquet. I turned to go back down the aisle without taking it. She said, "Rachelle, don't forget this." I turned and looked, and really loudly I said, "Oh, crap." Everyone laughed.

After the vows we had a special moment to ourselves. We went in this little room, and even though everyone wanted to congratulate us, we took five minutes to be alone together. There was no conversation. Chris just hugged me tightly and kissed me. And we looked at each other with this amazing shared excitement.

What I cherished most about my wedding day was my first dance as Chris's wife. The entire day felt like a movie in my head being played second by second, but one beautiful moment, my favorite, was the first dance. Chris and the guys wore dark grey striped tuxedos with turquoise ties to match the girls' dresses. Chris wore white on white—white tie, white shirt—and a sunflower boutonniere. I took a moment to absorb how he looked as we were getting ready to dance. We hadn't practiced it before our wedding day, and I was nervous even though I figured it couldn't be that difficult. Who would have ever thought my dance would be done from a chair and that still it would be the most memorable, heartwarming part of my day? We danced to "Won't Let Go" by Rascal Flatts. The chorus fit perfectly; it's all about never letting go of the person you love and being there no matter what. I had actually switched the song to something

© MARTHA MANNING PHOTOGRAPHY

by Corey Smith, but the DJ hadn't made that change, so Rascal
Flatts came on. It was funny and yet so perfect. I'm glad it got
chosen for us like that.

There wasn't a dry eye in the house. We did twirls all over
the floor and everyone thought it was rehearsed, but really it just

came naturally and was totally spontaneous. It wasn't being able to stand up that I missed during that dance, but I wished I could have used my hands so that I was able to hold Chris's hand during our dance. He held my hands, but I would have loved to hold on in return. I wished we could have been able to embrace one another. As someone who loved dancing, I never thought I'd be wheeling around the dance floor with my new husband. But it was still an amazing moment that I will never forget.

My maid of honor read something at my reception that had meaning to a lot of people. It was a quote from Bruce Lee: "Love is a friendship caught on fire. In the beginning a flame, very pretty, often hot and fierce, but still only light and flickering. As love grows older, our hearts mature and our love becomes as coals, deep-burning and unquenchable."

I know people find this hard to believe, but there was never a moment where I felt sad about being in the chair that day. I really, truly didn't. I had a dream wedding. I had had a dream bachelorette party before the accident, too. The wedding wasn't about walking. It was about love. It was about the man I loved and my family and my friends being there for us, together. Walking wasn't a requirement for celebrating. I don't think anyone else had any sad feelings, either. In fact, it might have been more meaningful to everyone. It might have been more significant and a reason to celebrate because I'd survived. It was just a bride and a groom and a great ending to a terrible ordeal. It was as sweet as everyone else's wedding. I had all the trimmings and fun and an awesome husband—more than everything I'd dreamed of.

After that, at the reception, a Southern band played and we cut the cake. The photographer and videographer zoomed in on the knife. We were trying to cut our Funfetti cake, my favorite, with the knife upside down. I blamed Chris. I had no grip, so he was holding it. We included all the fun traditions like throwing my garter, which was an ECU Pirates garter purchased for the original wedding, and tossing my bouquet, which I did as Beyoncé's "Single Ladies" played in the background. My brother was dating a really cool girl named Becca, whom he had met at one of my rugby tournaments. She was also a quad due to a birth defect. He flew her up from Florida for the wedding. She caught my bouquet. A guy from my rugby team, Ronnie, also a quad, caught the garter. So that was pretty cool and kind of fitting.

We gave everyone blue bracelets for spinal cord awareness and we made a donation to the Miami Project, whose goal is to cure paralysis, in the names of everyone who had been invited to the wedding.

BraunAbility had loaned me a van while I planned my wedding, but I never imagined that they'd actually give me one. At the end of my wedding reception, everyone lined up outside to throw yellow rose petals and blow bubbles as Chris and I made our exit. We rolled down the middle of a long row with everyone on either side. We turned a bit as there was sort of a bend in the crowd, and there it was: this big van covered in a white tarp with a bow. They pulled it off to reveal a sporty Toyota Sienna that didn't look like a soccer mom van. I was in love. Later, a local company called Van Products installed hand controls, which didn't require hand function, but just the strength in my arms to maneuver, and a transfer chair. The driver's chair moved back and turned with the press of a button, so that I could transfer in from my wheelchair.

Chris and I did not consummate our marriage that night. Everything had been romantic and sweet, but we were too tired. I

was playing with my little nephew after the wedding. We were trying to throw a football in the room, and I was lying on the bed. He
wrapped my hand around the ball for me. He was really good with
the injury. He asked if we could watch a movie, which made Chris
realize it would be a long night, so Chris and his best man went to
get ice cream. I thought they were coming right back, but they were
gone for a long time because Chris thought I was hanging with my
family. It was funny. He finally returned, and we ate some leftover
food from the wedding. We were exhausted by that point, so instead
of having some passionate night as man and wife, we just crashed.

Chris was like Prince Charming sometimes. When he was
feeling romantic, he'd hold my face and rub my cheek and look
into my eyes, and he often said the sweetest and most genuine
things. On this night, as we were falling asleep after the most
wonderful day, he turned to me and said, "Rachelle, I could never
live without you. I'm so excited we are starting our life together.
You were so beautiful today."

I said, "Thank you." We kissed. "I loved our dance together."

"Everything was perfect. The dance was perfect," he said. "The
whole wedding."

"I wouldn't change a thing about the day," I said. "Nothing
went wrong, either," I said laughingly.

He grew serious again, looked me straight in the eyes, and
said, "I wouldn't want to spend the rest of my life with any other
person. Just you. Forever."

I always felt we were two halves of one whole, but that night,
it was official. I was his other half and he mine—and it was forever. We'd beaten all of the odds and skeptics because we knew
love. We had true love. Our souls had connected.

CHAPTER 26

The Finish Line

SOMETHING UNEXPECTED HAPPENED FOLLOWING MY WEDDING that I heard about only afterward. My girls—who wouldn't have met had it not been for me, and who wouldn't have bonded as strongly if they had not had a shared experience by the pool that night—went out after the reception and had the greatest time, the four of them and their dates, plus Chris's best man and Mayra.

I was told later they had been worried initially about the one friend who had suffered, but after spending time with her that day, they could see that she was really happy to be a part of it all. That night, after Chris and I left, they talked about their new perspective on life, and how much they cherished it. They said the wedding ceremony itself was closure for all of us, so they danced and partied their butts off afterward and had the best time ever. It was their night, too, I think. In fact, some of them weren't even going to stick around that night, but this crazy party erupted among them. I actually felt a little sad that I missed it, but I was glad that they found peace in their own way, too, together. Apparently, they all just let loose and had a blast for the first time together since the bachelorette party.

I think this marked a nice ending for my troubled friend. I wanted her to have a good time, and it sounds like she did. It was a really big deal for her that day. It was important to her that I got married and had that milestone. It was probably the real start to her healing—to see me happy and to know that love had not been taken away from me, that the one thing I wanted had only been postponed, not stolen completely. It was as important to her for me to say "I do" as it was for me. It was good for her to have these girls around her. They all protected each other, and that came out collectively on the dance floor as they burned off one year of steam.

CHAPTER 27

Paradise

We left in the morning and had our first night in Vegas. It was so much fun gambling for the first time, but we wound up losing, of course. We got tickets to see *The Lion King*, courtesy of 1-800-Registry. I'd never seen anything like it before—it was amazing. We stayed at the Mirage Hotel. I thought the lights and the strip were the coolest thing ever.

After the night in Vegas, we headed off to Fiji, which had always been my dream destination. I never thought in my wildest dreams I'd be able to travel there. We flew in and had to take a helicopter ride to our destination, which was called Tokoriki Island. It was breathtaking. We had a large bungalow at the Tokoriki Island Resort with a huge bed and white linens, and we could open the windows and the back door and it felt like we were outside even when we were inside. It was just a ceiling, and the walls were basically open. The shower was outdoors and had blue tile.

Everything was blue. The water was blue, crystal blue as far as you could see. There was an infinity pool that Chris would float in; we could sort of see the edge of it, but then it would blend in with the ocean. There were palm trees everywhere. It was gorgeous.

Of course all of the food was amazing, but my favorite dish was at breakfast. Pancakes covered in powdered sugar—so good I couldn't get enough. We ate every meal on tables outside, looking at the ocean. It was truly paradise. At dinner the waiters would play music. Once, our waiter came around to us and asked if we wanted a love song or an upbeat song. I said both. They started playing Jason Mraz's "I'm Yours." I couldn't help but sing along.

Chris learned to scuba dive while we were there. That was something I used to do and always wanted him to learn. They allowed me to go on the boat with him even though it was rough. I just sat there and held on tight. The workers were so nice, all native Fijians from the local village. They carried me on and off the boat. We took two trips over to the local village, which was our favorite part of the trip. It wasn't exactly wheelchair accessible, so Chris had to lean my chair back and wheelie me over a lot of the terrain. It seemed like none of the kids on the island had ever seen a wheelchair. I let them touch it and spin the spinners. The inside piece actually spins, kind of like a pimped-out car you might see, except I spin these manually. They loved it.

Some other kids approached me on the trip and wanted to know what had happened to me, so our guide, Vili, told them in their native language. He knew my story, as we had become good friends while we were on the island.

Chris did a lot to help on that trip, even going so far as to put waves in my hair with a wave-making iron I had brought along. It turned out he was very particular about wanting to make my hair look good. He'd talk me through it, saying, "Hold still. Wait a minute. Almost done." It was pretty darn funny. One day, we plugged the iron in and it totally fried. We just stared at it in disbelief. We had a good laugh about that.

While we were away, absorbed in luxury and sunshine, the media had apparently gone absolutely crazy because the wedding stirred up the story again. We did get some time on the Internet there, so we read all these crazy stories and the comments. I was amazed the world had taken such interest. We were scheduled to fly to New York when we returned from Fiji for appearances on *Today*, HLN, MSNBC, and *Inside Edition*. It was exciting and exhausting all at once.

Of course, when we first arrived in Fiji, we were very tired. That kind of travel was something I'd certainly never experienced. Plus I was jet-lagged. But after we caught up on our sleep and overcame the exhaustion of our wedding and the trip, we finally consummated our marriage. It was really wonderful. I wrapped my arms around him and he kissed my neck, and it was passionate and loving. A moment I'll never forget.

CHAPTER 28

My New Reality

WHEN WE RETURNED FROM FIJI, WITH THE WEDDING BEHIND US, it was time to start moving forward and figuring out what I would do with my time. The wedding and my healing had taken up a lot of my efforts, and the media appearances surrounding it all had been a whirlwind.

I started to find that my days weren't very interesting. I wanted to work, of course, but the nerve pain made me an unreliable employee, sometimes taking over my body for hours in the morning and often into the afternoon. Still, in the months that followed our wedding, I began to grow increasingly aware that the fast-paced, media-infused life I'd been leading wasn't real, and with the wedding planned and done, well, suddenly, everything stopped. That's when I was confronted with really understanding my injury and learning to handle it. I knew I had to do something to fill my days and figure out what my next steps in life would be.

That meant my friends became that much more important to me. Those girls by the pool were suddenly everything. I had Chris to look forward to at the end of each day, and I loved seeing him and eating dinner with him, but I found myself relying more and more on them. In fact, there had been a dramatic shift: I had been their strength, especially for one of them, but now I needed them badly to help me figure it all out.

I found that all of them helped. Samantha suddenly had such a calming way with words and situations; that was her gift to me. Britney was always there to talk and kept me company, as some days stretched on and felt endless. Lauren was always that friend who responded to texts in the middle of the night, no matter how much time had passed, and Carly was the one who provided me with the most random laugh over the most absurd thing, always right when I needed it.

That support helped me make some big decisions. I decided to return to doing what I loved before I was hurt: coaching the Wake Shakers, the seniors cheerleading team. They participate in local and state senior games that lead to the Senior Olympics, with all different events, including sports but also acting, singing, and cheerleading. Right after college, I was working with kids in an afterschool program, and these seniors were using the back room of the same facility. I had to set it up for them before I left, and I overheard them talking about needing a coach.

I jumped into their conversation and said, "I'm here anyway, so if you want help, I'm available."

They took me on. I felt bad because I'd taught them all of their cheers, but then I got hurt. I was supposed to add dance lessons, but I wasn't able to. They had to scramble to find someone to help right after the accident. Still, I was able to return, and they were excited to have me. It was really nice to know they missed me, and they said that they'd never let me go again.

Since we had a specialized van, I needed to learn to use it. So that became another project for after the wedding. At first it was really helpful for my mother to get me around in it. A small car was challenging. The first time my mom drove me in my van, I was strapped in, but somehow I shifted and tilted and eventually fell back flat. We laughed our heads off. I called moments like that "quad moments."

Eventually, I had to take steps to learn to drive myself, so in July 2012 I decided to get started. I needed to get used to just getting into the van. The way the van was set up made it possible for me to drive alone, but it was a physical undertaking at the same time. I had to use all of my strength to push my wheelchair up the ramp and into the van, and then getting into the driver's seat meant using every available muscle in my arms, as well as a slide board. I didn't have the strength to lift myself, so I learned to slide myself. I had to get used to steering once I was inside, too—and it also required more arm than hand strength. To turn the wheel I kept my right hand wedged between triangulated pins surrounding my wrist, and to apply brakes or gas I kept my left hand on the hand controls. It was completely different than anything I'd ever done. Just sitting there the first time I got in was really scary, and I knew I'd be afraid on the open road. It was nerve-wracking. Add to all of this that I had never driven anything larger than a Honda Accord before the accident, so driving a van felt like driving a spaceship. I knew it was going to be a challenge.

Like everyone else, before I really even got going, I had to struggle my way through the DMV. It was a huge ordeal, and I had to argue with them to obtain my permit. I needed a permit so I could learn to drive with an occupational therapist first, but they repeatedly told me a road test was in order. I made arrangements to meet with the therapist, but I never took that road test.

I couldn't. My car would not be fully adapted until after I trained with the occupational therapist. The therapist evaluated me to see what I needed. I finally made the DMV workers understand.

There was another hurdle, though. I trained with the occupational therapist in her car and it took some getting used to. I had two hours of fiddling around, and then this woman made me drive on the busiest interstate in my region. It was trial by fire, but I pulled it off. After just four hours of one-on-one training, I took and passed a driving test.

I realized quickly that I liked the independence. I would take an occasional trip to T.J.Maxx just to go look at clothes and be girly, but it always took a lot out of me energy-wise. One afternoon, I took a trip to the mall, and while there I rolled by a kid who was clearly intrigued by my chair. I heard him say something to his mom about it.

I stopped and went back and said, "Wanna see something cool?"

He said yes.

I spun my spinners for him, and his eyes lit up.

He asked, "Can I try?"

I said yes, of course, and he loved it. He didn't want to stop. He finally did and I started to roll away.

He yelled, "Wait."

I did and he came up and gave me a huge hug and a kiss on the cheek. It was a great moment, and I hope it changed that kid's view of people in wheelchairs or of anyone who might be different. I loved that his mom hadn't pulled him away. I had started to notice that some parents yanked their kids away from me so quickly. I tried that afternoon to teach at least one kid that we are all the same. I hope, in some small way, I helped to eliminate the ignorance so often instilled.

So I took small trips on occasion, but driving to one place took four transfers, which I learned was exhausting. It meant I had better *really* want to go somewhere badly to make the trip. Nevertheless, because being so dependent on others was frustrating, getting my driver's license helped somewhat. It allowed me to more easily visit my girls and some days to just take a ride to get out of the house.

When I first started learning, there was a huge debate between my driving trainer and me. She insisted I should get rid of my manual chair and get into a power chair. I had been adamant about staying in a manual, so it was sort of frustrating and took away from the excitement of the situation. Yes, it's easier to get up the ramp and to roll yourself in and drive from your chair. But there are basic freedoms taken away when you choose a power chair. I'd never be able to ride in my friends' cars, because they couldn't transport the chair, and Chris wouldn't be able to pop me up and down stairs. I wouldn't be able to simply be wheeled out onto the beach. So even though transferring to the driver's seat is more difficult and time consuming in a manual chair, I was never afraid of hard work. I could push, so I wanted to push.

Driving made me feel normal. Cleaning my house did, too, and so after we were married I made an effort to be a typical wife and to provide my husband with a nice home to return to at the end of each workday. Unlike some people, I hated cooking, and that never changed. But I found that after the wedding, and as the media attention died down, I liked the peacefulness of cleaning, so I tried more and more to do things like laundry by myself.

CHAPTER 29

Let It Be

THREE WORDS SUMMED UP MY LIFE BEFORE THE ACCIDENT: LET IT Be. My dad used to sing to me when I was little. He didn't sing lullabies; he sang songs by the Beatles. I knew "Hey Jude" and "Imagine" by the time I was five years old. One of the songs I loved most as a kid was "Let It Be." The song had an early impact on my life, and the lyrics were words to live by for all of us—my family, friends, and me. When my friend Carly and I sang in the hospital, we sang that song often. Of course, when I was out of rehab, "Let It Be" lingered in my mind, well beyond the whiteboard it was written on that had made it our group mantra. It grew to be my mantra and our way of coping. It was a term that defined how we came to realize our bond without actually saying much about what had happened, and it was critically important to me and to the group. It gave us all strength.

I was being interviewed on the news about the accident, and I mentioned that I wanted to get a tattoo on my neck. Shortly after, I received a phone call from this really cool guy at the Blue Flame Tattoo shop. He'd seen the story and he said he wanted to give me a tattoo for free. I was excited but also a little bit afraid.

But with such a nice offer, I couldn't say no. I had to go through with it. I made the appointment.

I called my brother to share the news. He already had so many tattoos and he'd done so much to help me out that I wanted him there to share the experience with me. The day of, we grabbed my mother and headed out to the shop. I decided to have it done on the back of my neck. I'd thought about that area for a tattoo before the accident, but not for any reason as meaningful as this one.

Breaking your neck at the C6 level affects movement and feeling from the chest down, as well as triceps and finger function. The neck doesn't actually experience paralysis until you reach the C1 or C2 level, which are the very first bones at the top of your spine. Many people think, "Oh, you broke your neck, so you are paralyzed from the neck down," but that's not the case. *Quadriplegic* just means impairment in four limbs, not necessarily full paralysis. So I felt pain in my neck, which I guess made the tattoo more significant and ironic at the same time.

Just saying *pain* doesn't really describe it. It hurt. The tattoo was applied right where the bone was on the neck, so I think that was why it hurt as badly as it did. Still, hair pulled back, leaning forward with my neck exposed, we got down to business. It was excruciating. I don't know how many words in, I yelled, "Stop! I can't take the pain anymore."

My brother said, "You're barely halfway finished; you can't stop now."

I thought about it for a while, then took a deep breath and said, "Okay, let's keep going." In case I might forget just how horrifically painful it was, my brother snapped a ton of pictures of my miserable face wincing from the needling.

Another problem also slowed things down. Whenever my body experienced pain or infection, it often responded with muscle contractions or spasms. This was the case during the tattooing. We had to take a lot of little breaks to deal with my body's reaction.

But at the end of it all, I was set to remember, for life, those three special words that have been my guiding light. I had *Let It Be* and a peace sign inked onto the back of my neck in the exact spot of my injury. Chris and I have talked a lot about getting a couple's tattoo to ink our bond, but I wanted this one first. I wanted a permanent reminder that I had made peace with my situation, that it was what it was, and that, simply, the only way to get through life is to just let it all be. Having it in ink on my neck gave me secret strength. Knowing it was there powered me, and those words both literally and figuratively became a part of me.

CHAPTER 30

Buckets of Love

CHRIS AND I HAD AGREED WE WOULD SPEND THE REST OF OUR LIVES celebrating our love and never letting an opportunity to make a memory together pass us by. We had gone to visit his family in Ohio over Christmas break, and while we were lying in bed, we starting talking about how we enjoyed celebrating love and doing things for one another. We of course already made a big deal of Hanukkah, Christmas, Valentine's Day, and our anniversary, but between it all, we had a five-month gap with nothing to celebrate. We decided as we were lying there to make our own day, for only us to enjoy. Later that day, we hopped on the computer and started searching holidays for that time period in the gap, looking for something random and funny that we could celebrate. There's a day for everything, but when we saw My Bucket Got a Hole in It Day, we knew it was ours, and it was timed perfectly in May. It was random and goofy, but we marked our calendars, both excited to celebrate.

When the first one came around that next year, I bought Chris a subscription to *Bassmaster Magazine*. His dream was always to have a bass-fishing boat. So I opened a savings account and put $100 into it because, hey, you can dream and you have to start somewhere. He had waited until the last minute to buy me something and got a little panicked by his decision. He had to call my mother on his way home for suggestions about the perfect gift. He settled on a pretty engraved key chain that said "Chris & Rachelle Driven by Love" on the front and "My Bucket Got a Hole in It Day" on the back. He wanted me to have a special key chain as I perfected my driving skills. Ironically, Chris's dad had a bucket with an actual hole in it. We created a tradition in which we'd put our gifts in it for the exchange. We take a picture with that bucket every year.

—◦—

Maybe I did take for granted the simple, obvious things before the accident. I hated going for runs, for example. I hated going to the gym and preferred to relax after work. I know those are normal feelings for many people, but if I had my old life back right now and the ability to walk, there are so many things that I would do. . . . I'd go for runs, rock climb, travel more, hike, and see some of the big mountains. I'd do all these things and make sure that I didn't let a week go by where I didn't do something new or awesome with my legs, something that required physical ability.

Our Bucket Day grew to become really important to me. I needed to cherish all the little things in life, because some of them were fleeting. Looking back, maybe I would have simply done more when I could walk. I worked at the senior center and as a lifeguard, and that was my life. I am not saying it wasn't a good life. I had a fun job—I loved working with seniors and I loved lifeguarding. I just didn't do enough. I didn't appreciate the ability to dance then, for example. It's unlikely we would have come up with another celebratory day for our love if I hadn't learned how important the appreciation of these things was. People need to appreciate every day. I even looked back and appreciated the ability I once had to go to the bathroom on my own. I started speaking to groups, and that was always my message: Take advantage of running or dancing or even the simplest things while you can.

CHAPTER 31

What If

FOR A LONG TIME, THE ACCIDENT AND THE WHAT-IFS WERE ALWAYS part of the conversation with the girls. Not overtly, but they were the elephant in the room. One night, as we approached the two-year anniversary of the accident, we were all hanging out at Samantha's house in the living room and something shifted. It was a mini-reunion almost, not planned as such, but we just happened to be together. We were gossiping and catching up, which was our favorite thing to do.

This particular night, with all of us hanging out, the accident didn't loom. The sadness wasn't masked with laughter. It felt gone. I don't know how else to explain that. It's as though it didn't matter to us, as a group. Individually, sure, I am certain we were all dealing with it, but as a group we'd been liberated from it somehow, and this casual, uneventful night was only about fun and laughs and friendship.

One of the girls was really nervous because she had to have her wisdom teeth removed.

"I'm freaking out about it," she said as we all sat around chatting.

"You'll be fine. It's just the dentist," someone else said.

"I'm scared," she kept saying.

I said, "Geez, I broke my neck. You can get to the dentist."

We all erupted in laughter. It was different laughter. It was like something significant had changed in a good way, especially for the friend who had so playfully and innocently pushed me. She laughed, too. Finally. We all did. It wasn't somber anymore. The accident had become fair game. It didn't own any of us. It was one of those markers, you know, those moments where it's all different, and although the pain still existed, it didn't fill up a room anymore. We could genuinely laugh. I don't think I would have made that joke a year earlier. She was just too sensitive about it then. Everyone was. It was raw, and the guilt and pain consumed them all. But I remember the shift so vividly. We could all feel it and see it and hear it. We were girlfriends again. We'd all come out of this okay.

That night, it became clear as we talked that we all felt guilt to a certain degree. It had come up over time, little by little, but it took us nearly two years to really address and solidify our feelings. We all felt it in different ways. My friend who helped me get out of the pool that night told me late in my stay at the hospital that she felt badly about the fact that maybe she injured me more on the scene by listening to me and pulling me out of the pool, instead of stabilizing me. I assured her that I really felt like the damage had been done when I hit the bottom. Another friend felt that maybe she should have caught me or done something—that she could have prevented the fall if she could have reached out and grabbed me. To me, that was so illogical and her guilt so unnecessary.

One friend told me she watched it all happen in slow motion and, looking back, believed that she could have prevented it.

Instead, she called 911. I felt guilt, too, about my split decision to dive instead of allowing myself to fall feet first. I even felt guilty that I was afraid to go into the water. *What if I had just walked into the pool at the steps, instead of hesitating or talking about it being too cold to jump in?* My friend who pushed me watched that scene in her head like a movie, frame by frame, and every time, she played the "what if" game and was then overwhelmed by anxiety. We felt guilt for all the times before as kids and adults that we had played around by a pool. I'd done it. They'd done it. Thinking of all the times before made us cringe, and nothing even happened then.

If only one little thing had been different or we'd been standing in different places. They all wondered if it could have been one of them who got pushed instead of me. I wondered what would have happened if *I* had pushed someone that night, which of course could have been the case. I am sure they all would have rather not been there given what happened, but no one ever actually said that to me.

For all of us, it was a loop in our heads, and we were finally at a point where we could share our feelings on the matter, which to me meant the healing perhaps had really begun.

What if I didn't push her?

What if I didn't complain about the cold and had just gone in on my own?

What if I hadn't made it downstairs because I was still inside?

What if I had been able to catch her?

What if I had not made us go swimming in the first place?

What if we'd stayed out longer?

What if we'd gotten drunk and were too drunk to go swimming?

What if it had been the next night instead?

Airing our feelings like that opened a door for us all. A month or so later, a bunch of us got together for Samantha's birthday and we had the most amazing time, in part because it was fun and we were all together, but in part because no one said a word about the accident again, something that had been slowly happening with increasing frequency. It was becoming a pattern. There wasn't really any kind of deep conversation at all, just pure fun like we used to have back in the day.

The night began at Samantha's house. Before we left Chris stood behind me and helped me look like I was standing up with my girls, and we took an old-fashioned group picture like the night of my bachelorette party. Chris was the designated driver, so it was his job to chauffeur us to the club. My van has a nice amount of space, and along the top it has an outline of blue light. We blasted the music, and for one night it was more like a pimped-out party van instead of a wheelchair van. We were all dressed up, too, and we went to a rooftop club.

I felt a real change that night: It didn't feel unique or special or out of the ordinary. It just felt completely normal. Can you imagine striving for normal? Not spectacular or anything insane. I was just so relieved we were back to 100 percent regular, raw fun. We'd had so many nights together where the sadness filled the space. They made the rest of the talking feel forced. But not this night. This night, it was just plain real and normal. And I cherish that night when nothing else was with us but friendship and love. It took a long time to reach that moment, but I think once we did, a lot changed forever. We couldn't roll backward in any way because the healing had begun.

CHAPTER 32

Keeping My Head in the Game

AFTER THE ACCIDENT I HAD TO WORK REALLY HARD TO TACKLE the mental aspect of my life—which grew to be the more challenging part. Life sometimes felt kind of lonely, though I've always hated the negativity that stems from that word. Since the accident I hadn't figured out how to connect with my old friends, other than my core group of girls. I missed college, but I hadn't figured out a way to connect with many of my college friends, mostly because it had become clear that going out was a challenge for me. Crowds were difficult to navigate and I always got so cold.

So I figured I'd bring the crowds to me. I decided I would hold a party at my house, for the first time since my accident. It was going to be a college party, though no one was actually in college anymore. I put together a list of people, ordered a keg, and set a date. I was really excited that most of the girls could make it, that we could be together again. It almost happened, but at the last minute Lauren said she couldn't come.

Samantha and Carly came early to help set up, although we were laughing that there wasn't much to put out besides the beer. We bought a keg, but college parties don't have real food, so this one didn't either. They'd driven down together and were staying the night. Once the essentials were in place, they had to quickly do their hair.

Britney came, too, with her new husband. They'd gone out to watch the ECU game for a bit at a restaurant and then stopped by. She was the person I attacked with joy when ECU claimed its first basketball championship in the CIT. The Pirates won on a three-point shot at the buzzer, no less. The entire crowd went crazy.

I invited a bunch of people—the guy friends I had in college, people I hadn't seen in forever, and people who lived in the area. When I was in college, I had the perfect party house. It was up on stilts because it was close to a river, so I could have people over and everyone would just hang out underneath the house. I didn't have to let anyone inside, so no mess. We had parties all the time, and I really missed that. And, to be honest, I had so many good friends from back then that I hadn't seen since before I got hurt, and I wanted to see them.

Before the accident it was so much easier to go out, so it was nice to have people come to me and be in my environment.

It was really hard to make new friends, being injured and no longer being around people as often. In college it was so easy, because you had neighbors and you had dorm mates. People my age found friends through work or some group they were in, but I couldn't work. So the way adults typically made friends was difficult for me.

I had friends who were nice and we were Facebook friends, but I think we would have been really close if I were able-bodied. It would have been easier for me to just drop by and visit them. I wasn't in a position to grab lunch at a restaurant or meet up with girlfriends, which they probably did more on a whim. So it was hard. I was growing more independent, but I hadn't developed enough confidence yet to drive on my own and just go meet up with someone. I guess that's why my friends from before the accident were so valuable to me.

About twenty of my tight friends came to this party, and they were the ones who had been in my life for a long time. Sometimes I felt a little awkward around new people. I had become less confident because I knew people were sometimes uncomfortable with the chair. I'd met some cool people, but I got a little self-conscious about things like not being able to shake someone's hand. I didn't have a grip, and shaking hands was just what people did. I was sure it was noticeable and put people off sometimes. I didn't blame people for being uncomfortable. When people meet a quadriplegic for the first time and don't have a history with them, I think it's really hard for them to see past the chair, and then it's hard for me to get past the point where they're not awkward. So it was nice, if only for one night, to feel like I was living back in the old ECU days, with crowds and a keg and a bunch of friends around me.

Carly and Samantha came into my room in their pajamas after everyone had left, at two in the morning, and we sat up talking until five. Chris just snored away in the bed; he can sleep through anything. We began talking about how we really wanted to see more of each other, saying that we should try to get together at least once a month. I needed them in my life. They brought me joy. The past was the past, and college was awesome, but these girls had kept my head screwed on straight and had become my present.

I had to come to terms with not walking, but that took a lot of mental exercise, too. I had accepted the overall situation, but I struggled a lot with body image issues, just like most women do. Mine were the same as most people's, with some differences, like the quad pooch. I tried on tighter shirts that I used to wear, and all I could see was my belly. Since I taught aerobics before, I had a pretty good body, but my core muscles deteriorated, and I started to feel really sad when I looked in a mirror.

I actually grew jealous of lower-level injuries as well. Many paraplegics have function in their core, so they get to keep their abs. Of course their arms and hands have full function, too. I met so many paras during the first year of my injury who were so down on life because of their situation, and all I could think was, *Come on! Your hands work! You were independent within a year of your injury.*

Two girls I met right after my injury were paraplegics after each was in a car accident. They had been dancers before being injured but continued to participate in wheelchair dancing. I wanted nothing more than to be able to do that. To move my arms like I used to and to gracefully use my hands. They would do spins in their chairs while popping wheelies. It was actually pretty awesome what they could do. As someone who had danced regularly, it was hard to watch, as beautiful as it was. They gave me advice once.

"Once a dancer, always a dancer," one of them said when we were talking about it. This was true in my heart but not my reality. Sure, I was able to go on the dance floor and jam a little to the beat, but I will never do any choreographed dancing. I'm not talking about messing around. I missed dancing so much. It was my favorite thing to do, and I wished it hadn't been taken away from me. It was the one activity I wanted back.

I was always the dancer in my relationship with Chris. I took ballroom dancing before the accident, and I loved Latin and salsa. Chris would occasionally agree to dance with me, but generally he didn't really dance. He had two left feet, in fact. I always used to have to try to drag him out on the dance floor and say, "Come dance with me," and I teased him by saying, "If you're not going to, I'll dance with someone else." I never did. Even though he was a bad dancer, I loved dancing with him. Every once in a while when I was out with my girls, there would be a guy on the dance floor who really knew how to Latin dance, and I would dance with him. I never wanted to turn down something fun like that, although I would have rather danced poorly with Chris than well with a stranger any day.

There were people who had it worse—some higher-level injuries than me who would give anything to have the arm strength that I still had. Some quadriplegics would give anything just to breathe on their own. High-level quads want to be low-level quads. Low-level quads want to be paras. And high-level paras want to be low-level paras. I realized independence was the most significant measure, and that every hardship is relative in this world.

I had to work on not getting frustrated by how people behaved in front of me. I noticed some were extremely uncomfortable, but others were okay. I realized educating people was my job, and I started to work on landing more and more speaking engagements to help enlighten people.

I was thrilled that from the second I was injured, my friends treated me like just another one of the girls. That was always important. Some people, mostly when I met them for the first time, would bend down to get to eye level to speak to me. It wasn't insulting if someone couldn't hear me, but otherwise it sometimes seemed demeaning. Strangers thought that since I was in the chair, they needed to treat me like a child. Some patted me on the head and others who were my age called me sweetheart or honey, which I didn't think they would have done if I were able-bodied. I hated being treated like a dog or a kid.

My friends never scrambled to help me with things I could do myself, even when they saw I was having a hard time. They waited to be asked, which was cool. When you help someone without asking them, it takes away the only independence they have left. If I could push myself across the sidewalk, that's something I needed to do. Picking things up off of the ground, driving, and putting on my shirt were now all things that I didn't take for granted. I didn't want people taking the few things I could do for myself away from me. I had lost enough.

CHAPTER 33

Marriage

BRITNEY GOT MARRIED ON MARCH 22, 2013, AND I WAS REALLY excited to go to her wedding. When I got engaged, I'd known Britney for maybe eight months. We were more "going out friends" than anything else at the time, but I knew I liked her a lot. I was glad she'd come into my life. This whole new level of our friendship grew in such an unexpected way.

She'd go for a run and just swing by my house and sit on the couch for a talk. It was easy for us to spend time together, and we would go downtown and have lots of laughs. And more than the other girls, we had face-to-face time, for talking about everything, and that was really nice. It still is.

I was with Britney before her wedding. We were getting ready together.

"Are you having fun?" I asked.

"Yeah, for sure. It's so cool to have all of these people here for us," she said.

I agreed.

"Do you remember the night before your bachelorette party?" she asked.

I didn't really. I remember a lot of stuff, but of course the night itself had been more memorable.

"Not really," I said.

"We stayed up really late. You don't remember?"

"No," I said.

"We talked about ghosts and spirits. We were up all night."

I loved that she had this crazy memory of that time. I loved that she remembered some really fun stuff that had nothing to do with the accident. Ghosts and spirits had been the topic of conversation, not anything else about my party.

With Britney wed, that meant she joined Lauren and me in commiserating about the ups and downs of being married. Despite the hugeness of our love story, Chris and I have had some tense moments, like any other couple.

Lauren had gotten married four weeks before my accident. Our birthdays were so close together, and then we were almost married around the same time, too. We also had similar relationships. Their relationship was easy, like ours. I connected with her on that level. I was supposed to be born on her birthday, she on mine. I was glad I was paralyzed *after* her wedding because it would have ruined her day. She was the person who had always been in my life, like family, since I was two. I don't even remember meeting her; she was just always there.

One night, Chris and I made the three-hour drive up to visit Lauren and her husband; we all went to hang out at a sports bar near their house in Charlotte. Lauren told me that night that she'd cried at work, in front of her boss, the Monday after the accident. We also talked about how the accident had really tested my strength.

I remember sitting there during our dinner and thinking that I was actually glad the injury hadn't happened to anyone else. I handled it. I'm a patient person. I don't mean this offensively, but Chris is a stresser. I'm not sure he would have been as easy about having someone take care of him as I have been. He overanalyzes things, too. I thought about that as we sat there, how his traits, or anyone else's, might have impacted their ability to deal with this situation. I'm calmer, I think.

Chris and I never really argued. Neither of us were fighters. But he misdirected his frustration sometimes, and I knew that. We had disagreements, of course, every couple does, but we weren't the type of people to raise our voices. We never yelled at each other. Some people wondered if he controlled himself because of the injury. It was not that. He didn't cut me any slack. There was a time when we butted heads over what I was actually doing for myself and not doing for myself. He wanted me to be as independent as possible. It was the kind of head-butting that only came out if he'd had a stressful day at work. In year two of my injury, when I was better able to handle the nerve pain but had also figured out how to do a lot for myself, I'd get lazy. He'd come home and we'd be watching TV, and I'd say, "Can you get me a glass of water?" And some days he'd get it, but on some days, he would say, "You are able to get it yourself." He was pushing me. He'd say, "You want to be independent. I want you to live as full a life as you can." He was right. It took me longer to get a glass of water, but I could get my own water. Absolutely.

When my body was on fire and I was in pain, it was hard. It was hard to be motivated when I felt that way. There were days when I was struggling and he'd come at me wrong. But it was a good period in time to learn, about each other and about myself.

Sometimes I actually was so drained and felt so guilty about the situation that I cried. At the end of each day during this little rough patch, we'd sort it out. We never went to bed angry.

Communication helped us survive all of this. Neither of us ever held back on sharing our feelings with each other. We understood that both of our feelings were valid and that everything we felt was always okay. I believed nothing got fixed if you avoided talking about it. We resolved a lot, and I felt stronger for it. You don't know a lot about yourself until you are tested.

CHAPTER 34

The Big Shift

It took two and a half years, but the day finally arrived: My friend and I talked about anything but the accident. In a group setting there were so many laughs, and in private we had them, too. But there was a long stretch of time during the media blitz when not one phone call or online chat or get-together transpired without her saying she was sorry that this had happened. Think about that: I saw or spoke to her hundreds of times, and every single time she was sorry, and every time I swore to her it was okay. And then, suddenly, we turned this amazing corner, and we were just girlfriends again. Even after the shift, of course I knew the accident would always be there, but I finally felt like she looked at me and didn't just see the accident, but *me* again. We had finally recovered something that we used to have.

Someone once asked me if I'd rather bear her burden or mine. I gave that a lot of thought over the years. I think she suffered far more than I ever did in the beginning. The accident, fooling around by the pool—it changed her as a person. She eventually gained her footing and came back down to earth, but before that it was something that was constantly in her head. She could never escape her guilt. For someone in my situation, there were support groups, resources, and sports. I had so many people to turn to for help to guide me through my life. There wasn't exactly an "I accidentally hurt my friend" support group. So when I thought of that question, I knew it was a lonely feeling for her, realizing that there might be no one out there who could relate to how she felt. I guess the only difference was that it was also easier for her to hide from her situation and demons than it was for me. When she was able to shut herself off from anything that reminded her of the accident, she operated fine.

Physically, she was still able to do things, whereas physical limitations were always going to be a part of my life. She probably didn't pass a day without thinking about the accident. But I hoped it didn't bleed into every aspect of her life like it did mine. At least it would be possible for her to have normal days, and I would never have another "normal" day, not my old normal anyway. I never resented her for that, even though I knew it was hard for her to be around me, even though I had to be her support group and we both knew I was the only one who could help ease her pain. Unfortunately, it was a double-edged sword, because she had to see me and remember why I was in my wheelchair. Every day was like reopening a wound. That's why when our friendship turned a corner, I was ecstatic. It was no longer all about that night. The impact evened out, but we suffered differently, and we accepted that finally.

I think about how the roles could have been reversed and wonder how I'd handle her situation, because honestly, it could have been any one of us pushed in the pool that night. It was so innocent and playful and random. But when I imagine suffering through my pain or her pain, I honestly think that in the end, I would choose my own situation—maybe because I know only what these shoes feel like.

It's not new or scary for her or me anymore. I think that makes it easier for her. One time I was sitting on the bed, and she could see I was hurting a bit and uncomfortable. I tried never to let her see this side of things. But this time I was dizzy, so there was no hiding it. I could hardly move. I could see the look on her face, and I said, "I know this looks bad, but it's really not."

We erupted into laughter. It actually *was* bad—I was feeling awful and struggling. But by just saying it, I guess it finally became okay to laugh about it with her. Humor had been one of the main things that had helped us endure this ordeal. Then we returned to talking about girl stuff. And the elephant in the room just disappeared.

Neither of us thinks it will ever be gone from our lives completely; that's naive. But just to have days when we're together and it's not part of the equation, or stuck in the back of either of our heads, is a huge step forward. Even actually being able to talk about that night at all, without it being scary or sad, is a relief. Things are just more logical now.

I don't want to suggest that her healing didn't come from inside, because it did. It had to. You can't get past this kind of horrific event without your own strength, but I feel proud that I played a part in saving her and protecting her. I know what revealing her identity would do to her, and I want to protect her forever. Her secret is forever. She shouldn't even have to hide it as a secret. She did nothing wrong. But people can be cruel, so we have all decided that no one else needs to know. This unbreakable friendship, it's a real thing between us all.

There's no doubt that we all survived because we worked as a team, worked together to stay strong and hold each other up.

We all had moments of weakness, sure. But we had to weave our way through the jungle—the night, the hospital, the media, *Oprah*, the cruel comments. Beating those experiences was a team effort.

In the early days after the accident, I could feel her pain without her saying a word. I began to notice a shift in her aura finally. She just looked happier, and I noticed it without her telling me. She'd shed a skin almost. I don't think she'll ever forgive herself completely, and if she could go back, she'd change it all in a heartbeat. At least she learned and finally believed she didn't do anything wrong; it was an accident, and we're able to laugh again. The laughter has replaced the angst.

Something else happened, too—something really significant with her, and it had to do with the press. People were saying that I had shared my financial struggles with the public to gain sympathy and get donations. Of course, that was ridiculous. For starters, it was part of my story. It was part of the discussion. Being in need of different medical attentions meant I was very familiar with the shortcomings of healthcare, and those shortcomings are usually about money. I was grateful for all that people had done—remodeling my house, giving me the equipment and training I needed to drive again—but accepting these wonderful things didn't make me a bad person. Neither did enjoying a dream wedding and honeymoon; I was happy with the ceremony I had originally planned and would have had it in my backyard if need be. Plus, I had no idea any of this would happen. How could I? It happened quickly, and I didn't seek out the attention at all. People were just kindhearted and helped. I would have done the same if the tables were turned and I was able.

But all of that aside, I'm not the only person suffering or living with this financial problem. I shared my shortcomings in relation to healthcare and insurance to shine a spotlight on a critical issue. I was fighting the fight and hoped my efforts and the attention I received helped others, too. My accident and recovery made me no more special than anyone else with a disability.

Shortly before the three-year anniversary of my accident, I was doing a catch-up session with the online discussion site Reddit in a section called "Ask Me Anything." I received more than a thousand questions. *Today* did a follow-up online in response, titling the post "Bride Stays Positive in Spite of Financial Struggles." People of course piled on and judged me based on that. There were so many mean comments. I called my friend who had once been haunted by these kinds of words. I couldn't hide how upset I was, and I told her what had happened.

"You've done so many positive things from this injury. Ignore the haters!" she said. She was giving me the same advice I'd given her so many times before. I had slipped. I was allowing myself to be emotionally affected by the ignorance of these people, all for my honesty. It made me so angry. It didn't make me feel bad about myself, but I felt bad for society. People were judging me for no reason. She stood up for me. She supported me. The tables had turned. I had felt comfortable enough to share, and she had become strong enough to help. It was a powerful moment.

CHAPTER 35

Being Heard

I STILL HAD ONE THING TO CONQUER THAT I HADN'T SINCE THE accident: I wanted to sing again in front of people. In my efforts to remain really busy and meet new people whenever I could, and to not let this wheelchair ever get in the way, I worked hard to find new things to do. I loved my wheelchair rugby team, and I had always wanted to try something crazy, like skydiving, but sometimes I checked out the website Meetup.com to find activities in the area that might be fun for just a night.

Since I loved singing so much—it was always my passion; I loved entertaining people—I was immediately struck when I saw a karaoke night for twenty- to thirty-year-olds listed on the Meetup website. I was excited, but I was also really scared. I used to belt it out all the time before the accident, and Carly and I had done lots of singing in rehab—but I hadn't really tried to sing much after that. Especially not in front of other people. I'd met some cool people through this site, so I decided I would sing and try something bold.

I was just going to wing it. Tom was there and Chris and Mike, too (another friend, not cousin Mike). I was wearing a burgundy mini-dress and brown leather boots. The event was at a pretty cool place in downtown Raleigh, right by NC State, a rival of ECU, and I think the drama school was there; they were belting out amazing tunes that night.

I had to coax myself a little in my head. I kept thinking, *You've been singing all of your life. You feel pretty right now, which is important. You're dressed nicely. You can do it. You can do it.* I kept saying this in my head as I watched other people get up to sing.

When I was little, I was always performing. My friends and I would make up skits and shows, and we'd sing for our families all the time. I loved it. When I was in high school, every year I did the talent show. I always chose a Shania Twain song. One of them was "Honey, I'm Home." I thought back to high school and remembered that people really got into that country music. I decided as I flipped through the book to channel high school and stick with a crowd-pleaser. So I did.

Chris helped me get up there and get set up. I wasn't even nervous because I really never got nervous on stage. I was more worried because I knew I lost my breath so easily now, and I could actually get dizzy from exerting myself. So that was one concern for sure. But I had practiced at home to make sure these new issues wouldn't slow me down. I had speakers in the walls at home and a karaoke system, and I practiced often.

But this came up on a whim and was my actual debut, and as I looked out at the crowd I had this crazy adrenaline kick. I just started singing my heart out. I don't even remember if I thought about it. It just came so naturally and was so much fun. The crowd was totally into it; they sang along and cheered a lot at the end.

I felt really proud that people liked my performance. When I looked back at the video, which we put on YouTube, it actually looked like I was nervous. I had to hold my arm across my stomach and push on it to keep the blood pressure up—it kept me from getting dizzy. So to someone who didn't know better, it looked like I was holding in my butterflies. But I wasn't. It was a really meaningful night for me for sure. It had been on my list of things to do since the accident, and I felt happy to have accomplished it.

CHAPTER 36

The Positive

I THINK WHAT BOTH SURPRISED AND INSPIRED ME THE MOST SINCE my accident was the attention my story received. I had no idea when I was released from the hospital that it would reach anyone. Then, suddenly, I was in the news. What I appreciated most as I watched was that my determination, my character, and my personality somehow got through to people, and that really gave me confidence; it made me feel good. I felt like I did beat this injury, turned something negative into something positive by reaching out and impacting people. It was like a light switch went on, and I was forced on a new mission in life determined by circumstance, not fate.

The realization followed my first appearance on *Today*. People donated a lot of money, which was amazing, but they also sent letter after letter to my Facebook inbox and my e-mail. I read and responded to every single one, or at least I tried to. I did it because it made me feel great and I knew people wanted to hear back from me. People wanted to relate to me and wrote things like, "My son had this happen to him," or "I am married to a quadriplegic." They were trying to connect, and I quickly learned I had the strength to help them. I had spent a lot of time dwelling on the hurtful comments, but eventually I found purpose from my accident in the positive comments and the people seeking help.

I realized I could connect with people and let them know they shouldn't just *think* about changing their lives when they read my story, but that they really needed to *live* that change. I knew that, in many instances, my story would air and then I'd be out of sight, out of mind in a sense. But when I heard stories about real changes people had made, that's when I knew I'd made a difference and done something amazing in the years following the accident. It was easy for me to say, of course; I had a constant reminder. I lived in this chair.

So I set out to do what so many had done for me: help a recently injured patient. One in particular was fifty-three when he had a motorcycle accident. (The driver of a van had failed to yield.) I visited him in the hospital often and began giving him and his wife advice. It was so hard to look in their eyes and see the sheer fear and shock when it was all so fresh. But I told them that I was there for them day and night.

I was given a new job following the accident: Fight for the cause I lived, work hard for a cure, raise awareness, and be strong for others. As I sat by this man's bedside for the first time, I knew I had a mission for life.

—◦—

One night, as the third anniversary of the accident approached, the girls and I had a conversation. We were all sitting on the couch at Samantha's house in our sweatpants. I remember we were playing the board game Apples to Apples, where someone draws a card with an adjective on it while everyone else puts down a card with a noun that they think best represents that adjective. Most people don't play the game realistically but instead put down cards they think will be humorous. It was a silly, mindless game, but fun, and we liked that. I had recently visited my high school to give a speech, so I guess the accident was on my mind.

We had the frankest discussion that night about how they had all changed. Someone said, "It was the worst night of my life." I think I was surprised by how horrified and terrified they all still were when we put it on the table. It will never be forgotten. They all admitted that they think about the accident regularly.

It is a cliché, but we were all made newly aware of life in a very different way. We were so happy-go-lucky before. We never woke up thinking, *Tonight something terrible is going to happen to one of my best friends.* But when it did, everything changed. However, we realized it wasn't all negative; the one good thing that came out of it was gaining a greater appreciation for each other and our lives. Maybe if our friendship overcame my accident, it could overcome anything.

I had two sides to my life. I didn't have the perfect life without problems before the accident. I had ups and downs like anyone. But I did have everything going for me; all of us girls did. We certainly didn't think something like this would get in the way of our lives, and we realized we're not immune to tragedy. Even though something like this happened to me, it doesn't mean it can't happen again to someone in our group in a different way. Realizing that wasn't negative, either. We became healthy and grateful but not immune to reality anymore.

We're mostly grateful for each other.

CHAPTER 37

My Mother's Birthday

ON MAY 23, 2013, MY THIRD QUADAVERSARY, I RECEIVED AN incredible gift. My friend called me.

I'd grown a little lazy about calling her. I was getting ready to take my mom out for her birthday, when my phone rang.

"Hi," she said.

"Hi, how are you?" I asked.

"I'm okay. I was thinking about you today, obviously."

"How are you feeling today?" I asked.

"Well, I want to tell you that the last three years on this day, I would just sit and look at pictures from the past. I'd feel so sad. I used to have a really hard time with this day. All I could think about was you being in this chair."

"I know," I said. "It's been rough for you. I'm sorry you've had such a hard time."

"Well, I wanted you to know that I can look back at that day now and think of all of the really amazing things you've done from your chair and how many people's lives you've impacted. I just wanted you to know I'm really proud of you."

"I'm proud of you, too," I said.

I knew this moment didn't mean she was all right forever or that she was over what had happened. But it was such a powerful snapshot in time for us both—a considerable step toward healing. It meant to me, at least, that sadness hadn't consumed her, that maybe she was on the way to really feeling better. That's all I'd ever wanted for her and for all of us. I was so happy to talk to her and hear her voice. We'd both grown and we'd both healed, and we did it together.

Everyone always used to ask me what I planned to do on the anniversary of my accident. The first anniversary was tough, there was no denying that. But I had never wanted to see the day the same way many others in my situation might have. I didn't want it to be negative for me. It was a bad day, don't get me wrong. But May 23 was really no different than May 24 or May 25. The days that followed the accident were just as crappy for me as the actual date, so I didn't feel there was a difference on that day.

I think the majority of people attached their anniversary to a specific date, and I was unique in that I'd chosen not to. I decided I would acknowledge it briefly, in my head, but I wasn't going to be sadder on that day. I didn't dwell on that date because I live with this injury every single day.

Some people in chairs who acknowledged their anniversaries grew depressed and anxious. Other people had parties. I thought about doing something to celebrate life. People get killed in accidents every day. I survived. I could have died that day. Instead, I hit at a bad angle, and it wasn't catastrophic. That's a reason to celebrate, and I like celebrations.

I thought of May 22 as the day I'd had my bachelorette party. It's funny because I remembered it as a really awesome bachelorette party, and I think that surprised some people. We had talked about having another bachelorette party before the wedding, but we just didn't. I had had one already, and it was amazing—the best bachelorette party I could have ever asked for. It was the next day, technically, that I was pushed in the pool—May 23—and, oddly, I didn't mix the two up in my head as one event. Maybe for self-preservation or to maintain my sanity, I kept them separate. I remembered the one event as wonderful, and all I'd hoped it would ever be, and the other as not so great, but as something I had triumphed over.

For my friend, because she struggled with pushing me, it was never going to be a day for celebration. I knew that. It had been a sad day for her. Since May 23 was actually my mom's birthday, I wanted it to always be more about that—a special day to celebrate her. I wanted that for my mom, and I didn't want it to be anything negative.

On my third anniversary, I made a wish for the future: I hope someday May 23 will just come and go and the accident, for both of us, will escape our radar for good. I hope, too, that something wonderful happens on this day for my friend, something that eclipses the accident for her forever.

Epilogue

I was submerged again, but this time it was peaceful, even though the force of the waves in the ocean was tossing me around. I couldn't swim because I couldn't move, and yet I felt really calm. I'd been offered a life jacket, but I declined. Having grown up in the ocean, I knew how to hold my breath while I was underwater. With my eyes closed, a few feet under, motionless, I thought back to the accident. It was the floating upward toward the surface that reminded me of that day. I was underwater for what felt to be about the same amount of time—ten seconds. I knew if I had to wait more than five more seconds for someone to grab me, I would have serious problems. I felt confident someone would be there. I had a smile on my face this time. I wasn't remotely afraid. I had that one-second inkling of a thought: *Do they know where I am in this big ocean?* I'd overcome a lot during the past three years, but this experience was a major win for me.

I was underwater, deep in the ocean, because I'd been thrown from my bright green surfboard after riding a wave. I got the opportunity to surf from an organization called Life Rolls On, run by Jesse Billauer. He was a pro surfer, and years ago he went headfirst into a sandbar and broke his neck. He sold me my board and all the equipment to make it adaptive for my injury, such as the straps normally used for kiteboarding. I was able to break it in that day. The Life Rolls On team was all around me, so I felt safe. Before we left the sand, they taught me how to lie on my stomach, propped up on my elbows, which were tucked into a pocket on the board. They showed me how to lean with my body to control the board. Then they helped me get on the board and out into the ocean, where the waves would take over. I had two safety measures offered: I could wear a life jacket and I could have someone ride with me. If I were able-bodied and trying to surf for the first time, I wouldn't have accepted either one. So for my first ride on a surfboard, I ignored my injury and declined both.

Part of the reason I said no to the life jacket was that it was a little more awkward and bulky, but also because of image. It was much less badass. I didn't want to be covered in floating devices. I'm an ocean girl, born and raised. Even this injury wasn't going to put me into a life jacket in my playground. Not a chance. I was going for it. I trusted that the team would come and swoop me up as promised, and in the meantime I'd let the water safeguard me while I held my breath.

There I was, propped up on my new board, with six or seven people around me in the water, on a surfboard for the first time in my life. They had to help me get over the waves. Able-bodied surfers dip their heads under the waves as they make their way out. These guys helped pull me up and over each approaching one. The water splashed in my face and I loved it.

I got out just past the break, and the waves were coming in pretty hard. I was excited but not afraid. The team turned me around, had me facing the shore, and then some of them swam away, back to shore. Just before they pushed me onto a wave, they said, "Okay, ready?" Then one person on either side of me gave me

a push. I tried not to fall off, but I did. I didn't quite have the hang of the board; it was an advanced board, which required some getting used to. I realized my error and figured out the proper way to balance myself once I got back on, by sitting a little higher up on my elbows, with my head up to take a bit of the weight off.

They asked again, "Okay, ready?" I said, "Yup." And they shoved me off and I caught that wave. It was an amazing feeling. I can't remember how long I rode it before getting overturned, but I felt so happy. The water splashed, and I was moving pretty darn fast because I could feel it on my face.

I am determined to overcome the accident. That's a certainty. But I want to be clear that there is an enormous difference between showing positivity and being content with my injury. Just because I work hard and live a full life doesn't mean it's okay with me. I often get concerned that my outlook masks the hardship people like me face all the time and also potentially diminishes any urgency for finding a cure. We can be happy and independent despite our injuries, but this is by no means the life any of us would have chosen for ourselves.

This kind of disability is portrayed very differently than something like cancer, which has more urgency for a cure. I want a cure for this, too, right now. Choosing to be strong and triumphant may make us appear as though we've outsmarted our injury and battled it with a great outlook, but behind closed doors we suffer terribly. Our fight is 24/7 and will be for the rest of our lives. We're a force, too. According to the United Spinal Association, a spinal cord injury (SCI) happens in the United States every forty-one minutes. That adds up to about 12,000 new injuries per year. There are 1.2 million people in the world who currently suffer from an SCI.

I've heard people on a certain reality show that highlights people in wheelchairs say they love life in their wheelchair and they wouldn't go back. While I love what that show does for the community and how it breaks stereotypes, I don't agree with that sentiment. I'd go back if I could. I'd give anything to go back. I hate that my body has turned against me, and that the nerve pain soaks up a lot of my time every day. Mentally, you can be strong to survive an accident; you have to be. You can laugh at all the antics and challenges, and you can have love and support. But at the end of the day, the basic facts of this injury can't be willed away with positive thinking and a great outlook. An injury like this is expensive. To be clear, a newly injured quadriplegic requires between $400,000 and $700,000 in healthcare and treatment. After the initial hospital and rehab work, the follow-up costs are about $100,000. I can't afford this, and I know most people in my position can't. Insurance covers some things, but the 20 percent I have to pay is still beyond my means.

I've always been a fairly liberal-minded person, and I cared about politics even when things didn't affect me directly. I was concerned about human rights and education, but I wasn't really aware of the crisis we face as a nation with regard to healthcare. I'd been young and healthy up until the point of my accident. My parents are young and healthy. Chris and my friends, too. We faced a very expensive crisis after the accident.

The hospital was expensive, and the bills are still stacked up and waiting to be paid. They're not from my original stay so much but from my continuing doctors visits. It's so difficult and overwhelming trying to keep up with everything. Rehab, which I really need, is out of reach. I can't afford to go; just paying the premium on healthcare for us is all we can afford. I was watching the Democratic and Republican national conventions, right around the time I was working on bolstering my Twitter numbers, and I started having conversations with people online, arguing about healthcare. Suddenly my life and my well-being are totally affected by politics.

I'm not eligible for Medicaid. If I were, I'd get a caregiver to help me. That's because I made about $28,000 at my job, so I now earn 60 percent of that through long-term disability. That tiny income combined with Chris's state teaching income would make the monthly deductible around $1,000. We don't have that much money. We can't afford that. I've been fortunate to have had some great organizations pay for stints of care. Walking with Anthony, for example, sent me to this really great place called Project Walk in Carlsbad, California. Medicaid would provide regular rehab, which I can't afford. If the healthcare situation were different in this country, my mom could move back home with my dad and still have her job, and I could get the treatment I need.

Originally, following the accident, I had inpatient rehab at the hospital, which was covered through insurance. After that I received only twenty days of rehab a year. Once those twenty days were up, I didn't get anything additional. I was trying to relearn every aspect of my life, and I had the same coverage as someone who had torn their knee. Rehab costs about $400 an hour until I meet my $3,000 deductible. There's no way I can afford that—not many people can.

Chris teaches middle school, so we're on the state health plan. The cost to cover me alone is $625 per month. That's just for the premium, before the deductible or out-of-pocket expenses. When we were on TV before we got married, the misconception was that we were scheming the system, trying to qualify for Medicaid, and that's why the wedding was on hold. It wasn't a scheme. We were researching our care options; it was sad, of course, that we had to consider our union in terms of how it might affect health coverage.

One of the worst comments I ever read related to the healthcare drama was that I was a "parasite." Someone read my story of love, loyalty, and overcoming adversity and that's what he decided. This person thought that if I married, I wouldn't qualify for Medicaid and it was all part of a big master plan to milk the system.

I was just out of college, without enough work experience to qualify for Social Security Disability Insurance, and the deductible to receive Medicaid would have been much higher than my insurance premium of $625 a month. The irony was that I didn't qualify deductible-free, even as a single woman. I couldn't afford what I would have had to pay. But people were writing nasty comments all over the Internet, saying that I was attempting to abuse the system by putting the wedding on hold. It's as if people assumed that being disqualified from benefits meant that we were perfectly financially capable of going on with our lives without them. But it wasn't like healthcare treatment was some sort of luxury item. Did they think I'd rather be milking the system or able-bodied, working a full-time job, walking, and never needing a doctor? Well, the answer is obvious. And please, who knows any middle school teachers with disabled wives who are getting rich off all that government healthcare?

Six months after breaking my neck, someone even called me "lazy" for not working. Six months! I hadn't even received my fitted wheelchair yet. We were scrambling for some semblance of order, making it up day by day as we went along, but they would see me on TV and think, "She should get to work." I hadn't even figured out how to go to the bathroom, and apparently I was lazy. Before I was injured, I was anything but lazy. I went to college because I wanted a career. I worked fourteen hours a day before the accident and would give anything to do so again. I paid for college. I am still paying for college.

But even more recently, people have uttered horrible comments about the fact that we shouldn't be allowed to have children. We are doing what all parents-to-be do. We're assessing our finances, planning for our child's future, and making sure we can afford to have a baby. We are lining up the support system of our family, which we are grateful to have, and we're going to make our dream come true. The child will be paid for and cared for by us, so it's really no one else's business. Just because I'm in a wheelchair doesn't mean I'm going to be a bad mother. I'm going to be a great mother, just like many women in wheelchairs already are.

The bottom line is that in this country healthcare is a mess. We shouldn't have to think so hard about whether to go to the doctor because we can't afford it. Everyone I have to see is a specialist. I'm a spinal cord injury patient. Every healthcare decision I make is financially motivated.

But what I can do from all of this is defend people who are disabled. I read these comments and respond because I feel like it's my job to stand up to the ignorance and mean-spirited words people write. If they are saying I shouldn't have kids, I'm defending myself on behalf of everyone in my situation because I have the platform to do so. I take it personally and am offended for all of us—the entire society in my situation and the situation with healthcare itself. The ignorance keeps people down. And that really pisses me off.

I don't cry about it, but I become very angry. I wish people would have the guts to say things to my face, so I could more specifically shut them down. But sitting behind a computer, commenting on a thread, is weak. They think I have no voice there, but I do here.

I have developed another voice, too, in all of this, but it's not a good one. It's my own and it's the one that talks to me alone. I know we all judge ourselves. I did even when I was extremely fit, but there's been a lot I have had to accept with this new body of mine, and it's been difficult. I am a new person now. Realizing that has been the ultimate challenge, but I have done it as best as I can. I went from being a lifeguard to being watched over like a child with floaties. I used to teach aerobics and light weightlifting to seniors, and now here I am struggling with two-pound weights, a shadow of the active and athletic girl I once was.

When I was in college, I took a class called inclusive recreation. We had to complete volunteer hours that were relevant to the course, so I chose to assist with the annual adapted sports day at ECU. It was a program that allowed people with all kinds of disabilities to try out different adapted sports and activities. I vividly remember trying out wheelchair tennis. I couldn't wait until it was my turn to get into the wheelchair and hit some balls with a wheelchair user. I don't think many people can say that they've done that kind of class and then ended up a quad.

I've almost taken on a new identity. I used to define myself by that active part of my life, and suddenly it has all disappeared. My grace and ability to dance dissolved in the water. I am like a rag doll moving to music—no more hip-hop classes, no more ballroom dancing lessons. My hands are balled up, and my legs have atrophied.

It has been difficult to accept a deteriorated appearance, too, not just deteriorated function. I didn't expect so much atrophy. It's happened to not only the muscles in my legs, but also the muscles in my chest—and that means my boobs. I've gone from having a solid B-cup to buying bras in the kids' section. My feet swell up like balloons, too. My hair used to fall out in chunks and sometimes I had to wear wigs. I have to hide a lot with leggings and tunics and boots. A lot of sexiness was taken away, but I work on making sexy a state of mind. I work with what I have, and I try to make myself feel good about things. Sometimes just a little eyeliner and lip gloss change my day.

I can't say I love this new body because I'd be lying. That's a happy universe that I have not reached, and in reality I may never get there. I will say that I have made a huge effort to define my love for myself based on what's on the inside. I think once you start really loving who you are, your confidence and positive vibes will be apparent to those around you. And you know what's really sexy? Confidence. I was kind of a sexpot before my injury, so it has really been about getting my sexy back and reclaiming that confidence that I believe allows me to show my inner vixen again. That's not specific to women who are injured. It's something women in general should remember.

That's why I want to tell people who complain about superficial things to cut themselves a little break. I was fit, but I picked myself apart and focused on the negative things about my body, not the positive. We always judge ourselves, whether we're a supermodel or not. If I knew then how awesome and flat my stomach was, I would have gone easier on myself. I've had to accept, too, that without the use of my hands, I can't do my own hair. That is at the top of the list of things I wish I could do. Britney still comes over sometimes to help me with my hair. She lives close enough that she can do that, and I love that she'll stop by if I need her. I have figured out with the bending of my wrist how to grip cosmetics enough to actually do my own makeup. It wasn't easy to master, and some days I didn't look exactly like I wanted to, but now I'd say I do a pretty darn good job.

There are so many girl things that are impacted by this chair, such as my desire to be a mother. I face a lot of hurdles, such as weaning myself off certain meds. I have to do that gradually to get ready to have a baby, so that's hard. I am on pain meds that I don't want to be on when I am pregnant, but my main concern is the medication that keeps my blood pressure up. It constricts the veins, which isn't good when blood is trying to get to your baby.

© REVOLUTION STUDIOS OF NORTH CAROLINA

© REVOLUTION STUDIOS OF NORTH CAROLINA

© REVOLUTION STUDIOS OF NORTH CAROLINA

In the first two months of pregnancy, the veins need to open up even more. I already have low blood pressure, so imagine taking that medicine away. What might happen in those two months when my veins are open even more? It will be a major challenge. It's not this difficult with most spinal cord injuries. I have added health issues, and therefore I have to find doctors who specialize in my situation. Even though I am struggling with doctors' bills, I know my family and Chris's family will not let anything get in the way, because they want us to have this baby. They'll support us financially as best they can. Ideally, if I had $80,000, I could have someone else carry it. This would be the best option for me, and I so wish I had the finances to do it, but I don't. And I would never ask a friend to be our carrier. I don't want anyone to offer out of guilt. It's not something anyone I know would be interested in, and I would never put them on the spot like that.

I am afraid of getting pregnant: It's not bad for the baby, but it's bad for me. I think my lifestyle change will be dramatic. I won't move for months. I may be in bed for months, because I likely won't be able to sit up due to my low blood pressure. When I'm lying down my blood pressure is higher. Sometimes I can't sit up or I'll feel like I'm going to pass out. It happens to me now. I have that feeling, and then I just take my meds and lie down and wait for them to kick in. Then I'm usually okay. If I'm not on the medication, as long as I'm lying down, I won't pass out. Still, even though it would be nine months of hell, this is something I really, really want and something Chris wants, too. I'm not willing to give that up just to avoid being bedridden for a few months out of my entire life.

The hurdle right now isn't the fear of being in bed; it's the fear of getting off of my medication. I want a baby now. I wanted it yesterday. But I have to get over that mental block and get off the meds. I've had an initial conversation with the doctor and I'm on prenatal pills, which I need to take for six months. So we're prepping. We're a year away from trying.

I used to want one boy and one girl, but I'll probably be able to have only one child. I think pregnancy will be hard on my body, so one will be it for me. And that's okay. Financially, it will likely be out of reach for us to have more than one. Everyone in my family knows how important this is for us, and they're going to do everything in their power to help us through.

My girlfriends are so excited. They have told me they are ready to be aunts and to help spoil my child. I think they're not quite ready to be mothers themselves, so this will be fun for them, too. They've all expressed a lot of concern over the way in which I'll have to exist during the pregnancy, the pain and being stationary, but I think that with them around, I'll get through it. I know they're excited because they pretty regularly say, "What's the status of our niece or nephew?"

Lauren comes from a big family and we've talked a lot about kids, but she's just not ready yet to have a baby. I'm thinking I'll be the first one of our little group. I'm ready to get started. But she will eventually have children, and we both know it will be fun when we can share that experience. I hope our kids are close friends the way she and I are. I hope all of our kids maintain the bond we all have with each other.

It was an exhilarating feeling being pushed by the ocean like that. I felt free and strong as the wave caught me and carried me to shore. I had never surfed before the accident, just bodyboarded.

The feeling was similar. But this time, it felt like more of an accomplishment for me.

People ask me all the time if I'm afraid to go swimming or if I'm afraid of pools or the water in general. I get cold so easily now, so the water has to be really warm for me to go in, like the ocean on a hot summer day, or a therapy pool. But afraid? I'm not afraid at all. There's really nothing to be afraid of. I'm not afraid of what lies ahead for my life. I carry no grudges and no blame. I have no fear or anger toward the pool. It's not the pool's fault or the water's fault or her fault. It's one of those things that was no one's fault. I don't blame the water or the floor of the pool, and I certainly don't blame her. It's also pretty clearly not going to happen again. So, despite it all, I still love the water. I grew up by the water.

I can still feel water on my shoulders and my face when I'm submerged, and there's a space on the inside of my arms where I can feel it, too. Instead of dwelling on what I can't feel, I concentrate on what I can feel, the places where I do feel the touch of water. It's not weird to me anymore, the way it was that night in the pool or when I first showered in rehab, where the water was dripping down from a shower but I couldn't feel it. I'm so aware and appreciative of the little things that I can feel—the water on my neck, or my wet hair. I love the feeling of the water, the ocean, and the sand. I love it all, still.

Surfing was a dream come true for me. Life got harder for me, but my life is not over. Still, I'd rather surf standing up. I have a list of things I dream of doing one day if a cure ever becomes a reality in my lifetime, things I probably took for granted before the accident. Chris once said it was hard to remember back to when we just walked out and got into the car. I'd give anything to do that again. That, and a lot of other things, too. They aren't extravagant adventures, but everyday things I barely thought about before the accident. I want to do a cartwheel again, throw a football, and play tennis. I want to bodysurf, dance in my husband's arms, and climb a tree. Someday, I hope to walk my dog, style my own hair, and do sit-ups.

Mostly, I dream that one day when Chris holds my hand, I will be able to hold his right back.

Acknowledgments

Putting it all out there in this book has been both cathartic and challenging. I thank you all for reading my story, here and throughout the years in the news following my accident. So many of you reached out with kindness, without which I would never have gotten through this, so thank you for all of the letters, e-mails, encouragement, and generous donations.

I'd like to thank my agent, Maura Teitelbaum, for believing in my story; my editor, Lara Asher at GPP, for the care she put into weaving it together; and my project editor, Lauren Brancato, for her final manuscript fixes.

Thank you to Stephanie Krikorian for helping me get the words out of my head and onto the page. I appreciate greatly the time and effort you spent on my life story.

From the bottom of my heart, I want to thank my mom, Carol Friedman. Without hesitation, you left your life to help me live mine in the most normal way possible. Thank you for being my best friend. A huge thank you to my dad, Larry Friedman. You've always worked your butt off for this family. Thanks for teaching me to be a fighter.

And to Chris's parents, Susan and Bob Chapman, who have helped us stay afloat in hard times on more than one occasion: You have been a second set of parents to me, and I'm so grateful to have you both as my in-laws.

To my brother, Aaron Friedman: You have been such a big help, and I love you very much.

To Tom Vrnak: You've been such a good friend to me and Chris. Thank you for staying with me in the ICU so my mom and Chris could sleep that one night, for being our best man, and for being a night owl like me, so I have someone to talk to when I can't sleep.

If I haven't said it enough, to you four girls who shared that night by the pool with me, I love you and will always. You all stuck with me through hard times when many people walked away. The love, support, and loyalty that was always a part of our friendships was solidified on that spring night.

I'd like to thank all of my sponsors and supporters and those organizations that have donated their services, products, and time so that I can live a happier, more independent life. They include BraunAbility, 1-800-Registry, Colours Wheelchair, Van Products, Toyota, *George to the Rescue,* Lulus.com, Home Builders Association of Raleigh-Wake County, *Today,* Martha Manning Photography, Erin McLean Events, Morse Entertainment, Made-Up Special Events, New Mobility Resource, PhotoAbility, Crossfit APx, Drive Medical, Ocean Cure, and Walking with Anthony.

Of course, the love of my life, Chris Chapman, we have something so special that no one can ever break. I can't wait to celebrate My Bucket Got a Hole in It Day year in and year out for the rest of our lives. I'll continue to rub your back every night before bed as long as you keep calling me your sweetheart.

To my alma mater, East Carolina University, and to the Pirate nation for all of your support, and of course, for being the place at which I met my man. Once a Pirate, always a Pirate.

Reading Group Guide

1. What do you think of the Prologue and the way Rachelle describes the feeling of being stuck? How do you think the analogy of the "pause button" does or does not have relevance in her life after the accident?

2. In the first paragraph of Chapter 1, Rachelle talks about how carefully she and Chris planned out their future. How does this foreshadow the events to come? In what ways do they achieve or not achieve their goals?

3. What do you think of how Rachelle and Chris met? Do you think their initial friendship is what ultimately made their relationship so strong? Is your significant other also your best friend?

4. It can be fun to get all dolled up and find that perfect pair of shoes for a special occasion. On page 9, before her bachelorette party, Rachelle says, "I wanted the perfect white high heels, or else I felt like the entire outfit would be ruined." Does this statement seem insignificant now? Have you ever had a time in your life when you worried about something somewhat superficial only to later realize how unimportant it was?

5. The night of the accident the girls form a silent pact, an unbreakable bond, among them. Do you have a group of friends that you have this type of powerful bond with? Have you experienced any moments of tragedy in which you have helped one another survive, either physically or emotionally?

6. What are some of the things we take for granted in our day-to-day lives? After Rachelle's accident she can no longer hold Chris's hand or do her own hair. Are there ways to feel more gratitude for the seemingly little things in life?

7. In Chapter 8 Rachelle talks about how she wasn't able to cry and was finding humor in her day-to-day moments. What do you think about others' expectations of how we should react in moments of challenge or tragedy? Do you find it strange that she didn't cry or get angry? Do you think it's interesting that her honest, true reaction was so different from what others assumed it would be? What can you learn from this?

8. In Chapter 9, when Rachelle chronicles her experiences in rehab, she talks about how her friend Carly even learned to insert her catheter. On page 57 she says, "I think we women, as a group, underestimate our power." Do you agree? Can you share any memories you have of the collective power of women?

9. In Chapter 10, on page 60, Rachelle mentions that many people asked if she and Chris would still be together after the accident; she feels sorry for them because they must not know true love. Do you think their question is a valid one? If you were in a similar situation, would you have to think about it or would it never even cross your mind?

10. Do you believe everything happens for a reason? In Chapter 10 Rachelle talks about this statement and the idea that other people had that positive thinking could lead to her walking again. Do you think this belief is more harmful or helpful to people? Are there times when it's appropriate and times when it isn't?

11. In Chapter 12 Rachelle takes her first trip outside of the hospital and visits a park where she has an "able-bodied" history. Can you imagine how that would be difficult? Have you ever been in a situation where you return to a place that is full of memories of another time? Her father makes the profound statement, "It's actually a really good and important philosophy to make new memories every single day, especially now that you are healing. We shouldn't live for old ones. We should live for new ones." What do you think of this? Why is it important? How can you apply it to your own life?

12. In Chapter 13 Rachelle describes having sex with Chris for the first time after the accident. Do you think the intimacy between them has grown? How does Rachelle find other ways to feel connected to Chris? What do you find more important, physical or emotional intimacy?

13. How do you think Rachelle's competitive spirit helps her to recover from the accident? How does seeing her rehab as a game help her to get through it? How much does attitude have to do with it? She talks about the difference between her father, who never simply let her win, and kids today, who are more coddled in that respect. Do you think that it means more when you have to work for something? Are we doing a disservice to today's kids by giving them all trophies? Does hard work build resilience in the long run?

14. When Rachelle comes home from rehab, her mother has to move in with her to help care for her. How would you feel if your mother moved in with you? Would it be difficult? How might it change the nature of your bond?

15. What do you think about some of the issues Rachelle now faces, such as parking? Are you surprised by how thoughtless people can be? Are there ways we can change this behavior by enforcing stricter laws and/or higher fines?

16. What do you think of the pact that the five friends made? In today's world of posting everything on Facebook and Twitter, do you think it shows a strong sense of character that these women were able to keep this important secret? What do you think of the word *prank?* Was it mean of the media to use such a word? Does the Internet provide a forum where people can more easily hide behind their cruelty?

17. In Chapter 20 Rachelle talks about turning down Oprah and how her concern grew for the friend who had playfully pushed her. She tells the friend not to waste her money paying someone for help because Rachelle will always be there to listen. What do you think of this? Would you have suggested that your friend see a professional therapist?

18. What do you think of Rachelle's friend Sandra? Do you think it would be hard to be left out of the group that made the pact after the accident, or do you think in some ways she's lucky she wasn't there? Were her reaction and behavior immature? Do you think you can have a real friendship with someone who doesn't make the effort to spend time with you during a challenging time? Have you had any moments in your life where you feel as if you found out who your true friends were?

19. Do you think that Rachelle and Chris's wedding was more meaningful in some ways because of everything they had been through? Was it a milestone for everyone? Did it provide a sense of closure after such a terrible tragedy?

20. In Chapter 34 Rachelle talks about whether she'd rather bear her friend's burden or her own. Which do you think would be harder?

21. What do you think of the water imagery in the Epilogue? Are you surprised that Rachelle still has no fear of the water and in fact loves it? Are you impressed by her courage to try surfing?

22. What do you think of Rachelle's comments in the Epilogue about how women are always judging themselves and picking themselves apart? Do you find yourself doing that, too? After reading her story, can you better accept your physical appearance and appreciate all that your body can do for you?

About the Author

Rachelle Friedman, once a program assistant at a seniors activity center who taught aerobics and line dancing in North Carolina, is still recovering from an accident on the night of her bachelorette party that left her paralyzed from the chest down. She spends her time as an advocate for others with spinal cord injuries and is hoping to pursue a new career one day soon. She makes daily efforts through speaking engagements and social media to inspire people with her optimism and her bright and vibrant spirit. Rachelle grew up loving the ocean, cheerleading in high school, and playing sports. Although she tackles physical activities a little differently now, Rachelle still surfs, plays rugby on an otherwise all-male team, and loves the outdoors. She recently learned to drive on her own and is working at perfecting her skills on the road. Rachelle has appeared on most major news outlets in the United States and has been and is still being written about in thousands of publications worldwide. Rachelle graduated from East Carolina University, majoring in sports recreation. She and her husband, Chris Chapman, live in Knightdale, North Carolina, with their two dogs. Visit her at rachellefriedman.com.

NATIONAL UNIVERSITY
LIBRARY FRESNO

Sexual Involvement With Therapists

PATIENT ASSESSMENT, SUBSEQUENT THERAPY, FORENSICS

Kenneth S. Pope

AMERICAN PSYCHOLOGICAL ASSOCIATION
WASHINGTON, DC

YTISABVINU JANOITAN

Copyright © 1994 by the American Psychological Association. All rights reserved. Except as permitted under the United States Copyright Act of 1976, no part of this publication may be reproduced or distributed in any form or by any means, or stored in a database or retrieval system, without the prior written permission of the publisher.

First printing June 1994
Second printing December 1994

Published by the
American Psychological Association
750 First Street, NE
Washington, DC 20002

Copies may be ordered from
APA Order Department
P.O. Box 2710
Hyattsville, MD 20784

In the United Kingdom and Europe, copies may be ordered from
American Psychological Association
3 Henrietta Street
Covent Garden, London
WC2E 8LU England

Typeset in Palatino by Techna Type, Inc., York, PA

Printer: Princeton Academic Press, Inc., Lawrenceville, NJ
Cover designer: Berg Design, Albany, NY
Technical/Production editor: Susan Bedford

Library of Congress Cataloging-in-Publication Data
Pope, Kenneth S.
   Sexual involvement with therapists : patient assessment, subsequent therapy, forensics / Kenneth S. Pope.
       p.   cm.
   Includes bibliographical references and index.
   ISBN 1-55798-248-1
   1. Sex between psychotherapist and patient.   2. Sexually abused patients.   I. Title.
RC489.S47P67   1994
616.89'023—dc20   94-11534
                                                                                    CIP

British Library Cataloguing in Publication Data
A CIP record is available from the British Library.

Printed in the United States of America

Contents

Foreword

Sexual dual-role relationships, intimacies between psychotherapists and their clients, are all too common. We know that such cases account for the bulk of malpractice judgments and the resulting financial damage awards against psychologists and other mental health professionals (Bennett, Bryant, VandenBos, & Greenwood, 1990). We can only imagine the emotional costs in terms of anxiety, depression, feelings of betrayal, guilt, and other stresses and symptoms that are experienced by the patients in the aftermath of these relationships. We also know that, depending on which particular survey or estimate is being cited, 1% to 12% of male psychotherapists and 2% to 3% of their female counterparts have at some time been sexually intimate with a client. No one will deny that this is a significant clinical and professional problem, yet there has been little effort to train psychotherapists to deal with the impact of the problem aside from cautioning them to avoid it.

Data presented early in this volume advise us that fully half of all practicing mental health clinicians will assume the role of subsequent treating therapist to people who have been sexually mistreated by a psychotherapist. We also know that sexual feelings in the course of psychotherapy, both transferential and countertransferential, are commonly experienced yet inadequately addressed in our current training programs for mental health practitioners. In one respected survey (Pope, Tabachnick, & Keith-Spiegel, 1987), 87% of psychotherapists reported experiencing sexual attraction toward a client at some point in their careers. (One suspects that the other 13% were lying or repressing!) The majority of these therapists reported feeling "guilty or confused" by these sexual urges, and, even though they never acted on these urges, a significant percentage of those surveyed never even told their own supervisors, colleagues, or therapists of such feelings. Only 9% of survey respondents believed that their training to deal with such feelings was adequate.

How can the extant population of psychotherapists be expected to adequately address the needs of patients who have been sexually misused by a previous therapist if we pay so little attention to training in these matters? We are not well trained at dealing with the indiscretions of our colleagues or with sexual matters in the context of treatment generally. Aside from the fact that the topic is a sensitive one to begin with, a likely reason that it is inadequately addressed is the lack of good teaching materials and clinical guides. In that respect, this book is especially welcome.

It is easy to editorialize, but far more difficult to document one's rationale with solid clinical evidence. In addition, this is a field marked by too much "attitude" and political posturing. That is, many vocal practitioners and patient advocates espouse attitudes and political positions that do not necessarily focus on the best interests of the client–victim or that present formulas for treatment that are based more on personal opinion than on a solid research base or theoretical foundation. Some have called for mandatory reporting of such relationships to district attorneys, whether or not the client–victim agrees. Others have argued that a therapist ought to tell each new client at the outset of treatment of all possible inappropriate sexual acts or innuendos that might give the client a future basis for suit (e.g., "If I leer at you or make an off-color remark, you have the right to. . ."). One must look beyond outrage and personal discomfort to what is known about psychotherapeutic principles and the needs of clients whose prior therapists have exercised a poor sense of professional boundaries. For all of these reasons, readers will find this book refreshing and valuable. Pope has brought the full weight of his considerable clinical expertise, encyclopedic scholarship, and lucid writing style to bear on this project. This book is rich with facts, principles, and treatment strategies. It helps readers to recognize the special needs of this unique client population and to anticipate the fears and concerns that these patients bring to treatment. Pope thereby helps to inform our treatment planning in the clients' best interests.

In his usual self-effacing manner, it is unlikely that Pope will advise readers that he has waived all royalties from the sale of this book so as to lower its cost and make it more readily available to students and the professional community. This further potentiates the true value and significance of the effort that has put this writing in your hands.

GERALD P. KOOCHER, PHD
Harvard Medical School

Acknowledgments

Many friends and colleagues were extremely generous with their time, reading drafts of this manuscript, offering critiques, and suggesting improvements. I would especially like to thank the following individuals: Nancy Adel, Esq., Christine A. Courtois, PhD, Philip Erdberg, PhD, Thomas S. O'Connor, Joe George, PhD, Esq., Gerald P. Koocher, PhD, Joan Madsen, PhD, Sheila Namir, PhD, Katherine Pope, PhD, Mark Roohk, Esq., Joyce Seelen, Esq., Judith R. Seligman, Esq., Jerome L. Singer, PhD, and Janet L. Sonne, PhD.

I would also like to give special thanks to Kate Allen, PhD, Kurt Bachmann, MD, Don Bersoff, PhD, Esq., Bruce Bongar, PhD, Debra Borys, PhD, Aldo Carotenuto, PhD, Temi Firsten, MSW, Monika Becker-Fischer, PhD, Ann Bernsen, MSW, Jacqueline Bouhoutsos, MSW, PhD, Hans Brenner, MD, Jim Butcher, PhD, Brandt Caudill, Esq., Shirley Feldman-Summers, PhD, Gottfried Fischer, PhD, Rena Folman, PhD, Lyse Frenette, PhD, Erika Fromm, PhD, Glen Gabbard, MD, Rosa Garcia-Peltoniemi, PhD, Nanette Gartrell, MD, Jesse Geller, PhD, Mike Gottlieb, PhD, Diane Grodney, DSW, Tom Gutheil, MD, Rachel Hare-Mustin, PhD, Don Hiroto, PhD, Jean Holroyd, PhD, Larke Nahme Huang, PhD, Linda Jorgenson, Esq., Andrew Kane, PhD, Henry Keidan, Patricia Keith-Spiegel, PhD, Doryann Lebe, MD, the late Helen Block Lewis, PhD, Michele Licht, Esq., Georges-Guy Maruani, MD, Michael O. Miller, PhD, Esq., Carol Nadelson, MD, Elizabeth T. Ortiz, DSW, Fritz Redlich, MD, Bruce Sales, PhD, JD, Gary Sampley, JD, Barbara Seaman, David Shapiro, PhD, Joan Sieber, PhD, Lynnette Sim, MSW, Robert Simon, MD, David Summers, Esq., Barbara Tabachnick, PhD, Melba Vasquez, PhD, Lesbia Martinez Villalta, Lenore Walker, EdD, Michael White, Esq., and Leland Wilkinson, PhD, who provided information, books, reprints and preprints, legal and clinical documents, advice, and other forms of help and support. Many of the ideas for this book were first discussed with two close friends, Laura Brown, PhD, and the late Alan

K. Malyon, PhD, whose kindness, wisdom, and warmth have benefited me more than they will ever know. Many of the approaches embodied in Appendix B were drawn from the original work of Drs. Brown and Malyon.

I would like to thank Oxford University Press for permission to use copyrighted material; the Division of Psychotherapy (Division 29) of the American Psychological Association (APA) and Donald Freedheim, PhD, editor of *Psychotherapy*, for permission to reproduce tables and other copyrighted material from articles published in that journal; and Karen Thomas of the APA Permissions Office for helping to secure permission to reprint copyrighted material from APA journals and books.

I also owe an enormous debt of gratitude to Theodore J. Baroody, Susan Bedford, Ralph Eubanks, and Julia Frank-McNeil of APA Books, Devona Marinich of Marketing Services, and Gary R. VandenBos, PhD, of the APA's Office of Publications and Communications for their wonderful support, skill, generosity, knowledge, understanding, and hard work.

Introduction: Encountering Patients Who Have Experienced Therapist–Patient Sex

This book was written to help clinicians respond knowledgeably, competently, and effectively when they encounter patients who have been involved in therapist–patient sex. The reader will find here a brief summary of major issues, reminders of relevant research, and suggested approaches to clinical and forensic responsibilities.

When patients report sexual activity with a prior therapist, subsequent therapists[1] encounter complex challenges. Patients may be unaware that therapist–patient sex is prohibited. They may expect, want, or fear sexual involvement with subsequent therapists. They may feel that they are powerless to prevent a recurrence with the former or current therapist. They may feel guilty or suicidal because they failed to prevent the sexual behavior. They may find it so painful or terrifying to be with another therapist that they seek safety within a set of impenetrable boundaries, making therapy impossible. Or they may find separation from the therapist so painful or terrifying that

---

[1]For brevity and convenience, the term *therapist* is used inclusively in this book. It is meant to refer not only to therapists but also to counselors, behaviorists, and others who provide mental health, clinical, or similar services. Unless context indicates otherwise, *therapist* is also meant to include those who conduct assessments—forensic or otherwise—of an individual when therapist–patient sex is at issue, even though some who conduct such assessments are not themselves therapists.

they seek a boundaryless relationship of enmeshment or merging with the subsequent therapist. They may be convinced that the subsequent therapist is contemptuous of, disgusted with, or overwhelmed by them because they are too sexual, too angry, too depressed, or too intense. They may believe that no one could ever empathize with, care about, understand, or help them because of what they have been through.

The use of the word *may* in the previous paragraph is crucial. Every patient is unique. Some effects of therapist–patient sex are extremely common; others are virtually unheard of. None of the reactions mentioned in the previous paragraph is especially rare. Each of these feelings, beliefs, impulses, and so on—regardless of whether it is effective or adaptive—may be understood as a patient's normal and understandable response to a therapist's decision to engage in sexual behaviors with the patient.

However common such reactions may be, they are not universal. When patients report sexual involvement with a prior therapist, subsequent therapists can never accurately assume that the patients inevitably behaved, reacted, or suffered in a particular way. Nor can they reflexively assume that an allegation must inevitably be true. In each case and without exception, subsequent therapists must respect the uniqueness of the individual patient.

Subsequent therapists must maintain awareness of the evolving scientific and professional literature in this area to avoid practicing outside their areas of competence. Formal research and clinical case studies help practitioners to understand the nature and effects of therapist–patient sex. Awareness of typical scenarios, common reactions, and recurrent patterns can help guide and inform inquiries and treatment plans. Clinicians who have worked on these issues with more than a few patients also have their personal experience as a resource. Both the literature and personal experience form an important part of— never a substitute for—a careful, open, sensitive process of inquiry. If a particular patient does not fit a specific profile, it is the profile—whether drawn from a general collection or from professional literature focusing more specifically on therapist– patient sex—rather than the characteristics of the patient or the particulars of his or her situation that needs to be adjusted or set aside in this instance. Profiles, however firmly they rest on empirical research, are conceptualizations that aid rather than preempt or determine the assessment of the individual patient.

In light of such complex issues, subsequent therapists bear crucial responsibilities. Their work may be pivotal in helping patients to survive devastating consequences of prolonged sexual abuse, to make sense of a chaotic and confusing experience, and to decide whether to file formal complaints. As the following chapters will explore, subsequent therapists often experience powerful feelings. These emotional reactions should not be surprising; the clinician is encountering and attempting to respond to patients who, in the words of the Menninger Clinic's Glen Gabbard (1989a), "have courageously come forth and have spoken up about the unspeakable" (p. xiv). Harvard professor Judith Herman (1992) described how the volatile dynamics of the unspeakable may stir intense feelings in clinicians as well as patients:

> The ordinary response to atrocities is to banish them from consciousness. Certain violations of the social compact are too terrible to utter aloud: this is the meaning of the word unspeakable.
>
> Atrocities, however, refuse to be buried. Equally as powerful as the desire to deny atrocities is the conviction that denial does not work. . . .
>
> The conflict between the will to deny horrible events and the will to proclaim them aloud is the central dialectic of psychological trauma. People who have survived atrocities often tell their stories in a highly emotional, contradictory, and fragmented manner which undermines their credibility and thereby serves the twin imperatives of truth-telling and secrecy. But far too often secrecy prevails, and the story of the traumatic event surfaces not as a verbal narrative but as a symptom. (p. 1)

The intense feelings that many clinicians experience when encountering patients who describe sexual involvement with a previous therapist (see chapter 4) are *not* abnormal or harmful per se. But if unrecognized, unacknowledged, or unaddressed, they can prompt subsequent therapists to act contrary to their clinical and forensic responsibilities. Upon first hearing a patient's allegations, for example, subsequent therapists may—on the basis of their own needs, unexamined assumptions, and biases—reflexively conclude that the allegations must be true, forego any genuine assessment, and remain oblivious to any contrary evidence. As another example, subsequent therapists, upon learning that the alleged perpetrator is a respected colleague, may hastily conclude that the colleague could never exploit anyone, that the patient must be dishonest or delusional, and that therapy must focus on helping the patient to acknowledge that the allegations are false (e.g., see Noel & Watterson, 1992).

The impulse that many therapists feel to avoid the difficult and sometimes painful work of exploring patients' allegations of therapist–patient sex is understandable when viewed in light of the devastating consequences often associated with such activities. The following passages summarize the findings of two pioneers who studied the effects of therapist–patient sex.

> [M]any of the women described being humiliated and frustrated by their therapists' emotional and sexual coldness or ineptitude. . . . [O]ne woman tried to kill herself; two others lapsed into a severe depression; a fourth woman's *husband*, who was also in treatment with the same therapist, killed himself shortly *after* if not *because*, he found out about the affair. This particular therapist's rather sadistic and grandiose attempt to cure this woman's "frigidity" one night resulted in her developing a "headache" that wouldn't subside for a year. His behavior was depressingly typical.[2] (Chesler, 1972, pp. 146–147; emphasis in the original)

> In my research, there were many reports of suicide attempts, severe depressions . . . , mental hospitalizations, shock treat-

---

[2]This therapist systematically had sex with as many of his female patients as he could. He also employed them as babysitters, secretaries, cooks, errand runners, chauffeurs, and so on. [This footnote was in Chesler's original passage.]

ment, and separations or divorces from husbands who just could not understand or be supportive. Women reported being fired from or having to leave their jobs because of pressure and ineffectual working habits caused by their depression, crying spells, anger, and anxiety. One woman who participated in my study eventually did commit suicide. (Durré, 1980, p. 242)

Two major prospects can make careful, extensive exploration of patient allegations daunting to therapists: One, that a colleague has chosen to place a vulnerable patient at risk for such extensive harm or, two, that a patient is making false but damaging allegations against a colleague. Subsequent therapists must face these complex challenges and responsibilities within social and professional contexts that are sometimes problematic. Chapter 2 focuses on these contexts.

Because therapist–patient sex can cause devastating consequences for patients and complications in the subsequent therapy, it is distressing that so many patients seeking therapy appear to have experienced sex with a prior therapist. The studies summarized in Table 1 show that about 44% to 65% of the therapists surveyed reported having encountered at least one patient who had been sexually involved with a previous therapist. These studies, taken as a whole, suggest that the probability that a therapist will provide clinical services to a patient who has been sexually involved with a previous therapist approaches or exceeds 50%.

That so many therapists will encounter sexually exploited patients[3] is also cause for concern from another perspective: National survey results suggest that therapists do not tend to describe themselves as highly competent to provide services to this population (Pope & Feldman-Summers, 1992; see also Feld-

---

[3]The terms *patient (or client) who has been sexually involved with a therapist, exploited patient, sexually exploited patient, abused patient,* and *sexually abused patient* are used interchangeably in this book. The mental health professions have established a clear prohibition against sexual involvement with a patient as an abuse of power, position, and patient and similarly the exploitation of power, position, and patient.

Table 1

Percentages of Therapists Surveyed Who Encountered Patients Who Were Sexually Involved With a Previous Therapist

Survey Source	Profession surveyed	Geographic area	Return rate	% Encountering patients[a]	Male patients[b]	Female patients[c]
Bouhoutsos et al. (1983)	psychology	California	16%	45%	6%	94%
Gartrell et al. (1987)[d]	psychiatry	national	26%	65%	9%	91%
Pope & Vetter (1991)	psychology	national	50%	50%	13%	87%
Stake & Oliver (1991)	psychology	Missouri	31%	44%	—	—

Note. Adapted from Pope, 1993, p. 376, by permission.

[a]Percentage of respondents who reported encountering at least one patient who had been sexually involved with a previous therapist

[b]Of all patients reported as having been sexually involved with a previous therapist, the percentage who were male

[c]Of all patients reported as having been sexually involved with a previous therapist, the percentage who were female

[d]See also Gartrell et al. 1986, 1989, 1992

man-Summers & Pope, 1994). Lack of competence may be related both to the contextual factors described in chapter 2 and to the relative neglect of this topic in graduate school and internship training programs (see Foreword). When therapists rated the degree to which their training programs (including internships) covered this topic (providing services to patients who had been sexually involved with a therapist), the modal rating assigned by both male and female therapists was "very poor; e.g., little or no attention devoted to the topic" (Pope & Feldman-Summers, 1992, pp. 356–357).

This book seeks to focus awareness on context and other factors that have made it difficult for the professions and their training institutions to address this topic effectively and for the individual professional to provide effective clinical and forensic services. The book rests on five basic premises.

1. *Therapist–patient sex is never an ethically or clinically acceptable act.*[4]

2. *It is the therapist who bears responsibility for refraining from sexual involvement with a patient.* Sexually exploitive therapists often rationalize that the patient agreed to, consented to, invited, or even demanded the sexual involvement. Finkelhor (1984), however, outlined one factor accounting for the professions' rejection of this attempt to justify therapist–patient sexual involvement and to shift responsibility for the exploitation to the patient. Comparing therapist–patient sexual involvement to incest and other forms of child abuse, he focused on "the fundamental asymmetry of the relationship. A patient . . . cannot freely consent to sex with a therapist. The main consideration here is that, in the context of a therapeutic relationship, a patient is not really free to say yes or no" (Finkelhor, 1984, p. 18). To the degree that a patient cannot give genuine informed and voluntary consent, such involvement, according to Masters and Johnson (1976), bears significant parallels to rape.

---

[4]Coleman (1988) conducted "a comparative analysis of the approach" (p. 577) of various countries (e.g., Latin American countries, Middle East countries, European countries) and concluded: "Virtually universal condemnation exists for sexual contact between therapist and patient" (p. 605).

They observed that a patient's "consent" is meaningless under such circumstances and stated that

> when sexual seduction of patients can be firmly established by due legal process, regardless of whether the seduction was initiated by the patient or the therapist, the therapist should be sued for rape . . . i.e., the legal process should be criminal[5]. . . . Few psychotherapists would be willing to appear in court on behalf of a colleague and testify that the . . . patient's facility for decision making could be considered normally objective when he or she accepts sexual submission after developing extreme emotional dependence on the therapist. (p. 3372)

The possibility that "the seduction was initiated by the patient," acknowledged by Masters and Johnson, was examined in more detail by Gutheil and Gabbard (1992):

> Clinicians knowledgeable in this area are well aware that a significant fraction of sexual misconduct instances are initiated by the patient. Such initiation empirically encompasses the full realm of human interaction from innuendo to overt requests, demands, threats, and blackmail, even to the threat of suicide. . . . Subject to no code, patients are free to demand, request, and threaten as they wish. These behaviors are suitable for therapeutic exploration; the therapist alone bears the blame for acting on these behaviors, since axiomatically only the therapist can be blameworthy. (p. 518)

---

[5]An increasing number of states have begun to criminalize therapist–patient sex. Judicial review of the constitutionality of such a law in Colorado held that "the state has a legitimate interest not only in protecting persons undergoing psychotherapy from being sexually exploited by the treating therapist but also in regulating and maintaining the integrity of the mental health profession. It is equally obvious to us that the legislative decision to criminally proscribe a psychotherapist's knowing infliction of sexual penetration on a psychotherapy client is reasonably related to these legitimate governmental interests. Section 18-3-405.5, therefore, comports with due process of law" (*Ferguson v. People of the State of Colorado*, 1992, p. 810). Morton Rapp, M.D., of Ontario's Whitby Psychiatric Clinic, in reviewing the advantages of defining sexual misconduct with patients as rape, emphasized that "It would underline society's abhorrence of the act" (1987, p. 194).

A spokesperson for the American Psychiatric Association stated, "There is no such thing as consensual sex between a therapist and patient. The power balance is too uneven" (Blamphin, cited in English, 1992, p. 41). Similarly, Lebe and Namir (1993) wrote, "The power in this asymmetrical relationship is often underestimated, or in more grandiose [therapists], mistaken as mutuality, i.e., that the patient's view of the [therapist] is not influenced by the asymmetrical power granted to the [therapist] and his or her qualities" (p. 14). Some court decisions reflect the professions' rejection of the rationale that the patient "consented" to sexual involvement. According to the National Register of Health Service Providers in Psychology's *The Psychologist's Legal Handbook* (Stromberg et al., 1988), for example,

> As a defense to the charge of battery or malpractice, practitioners have claimed that the patient consented to the sexual relationship and that the sex did not affect the therapeutic relationship. The courts have rejected such arguments. They have found that the consent was not voluntary or informed because it was affected by the powerful transference created by the therapy, or that as a matter of public policy, a patient cannot consent to a professionally irresponsible form of treatment. (p. 461)

Similarly, Mann and Winer (1991) wrote,

> The therapist alone has the duty to safeguard the therapeutic relationship, and given the disparity in power, the fiduciary relationship, the client's vulnerability, and the client's diminished capacity, public policy requires that there be no comparative negligence as a matter of law. In these circumstances, [the patient's] responsibility to exercise self-care is encompassed or subsumed by the therapist's duty. . . . [L]iability may be imposed regardless of whether the client started or wanted the sexual involvement with the therapist. (p. 351)

Perpetrators' attempts to use consent to justify sexual involvement—some even asking their patients to sign forms indicating their agreement to have sex with the therapist, to keep the sex secret, to be responsible for any harm that comes from the involvement, and to never file a formal complaint or law suit—is a cynical abuse of an otherwise (i.e., in other contexts) valid and important concept. Attempts to use informed consent in a context in which it not only is not beneficial but may add insult to injury are similar in some respects to the general practice by which "an attendant will . . . swab the 'patient's' arm with alcohol before inserting the needle" in order to prevent infection when a condemned prisoner is being executed by lethal injection (Prejean, 1993, pp. 217–218). In both cases, an otherwise valuable concept is applied in a context in which it makes no sense but seems to mask the nature of a destructive act.

That the professions have rejected the notion that patients can consent to and are therefore responsible for instances in which therapists sexually abuse them—and some courts, as Stromberg et al. (1988) and Mann and Winer (1991) noted, have accepted the professions' stance by rejecting the notion of contributory negligence in such cases—does not, of course, mean that the issue can be ignored. For example, a court recently held a plaintiff to be 4% contributorily negligent for sexual interactions with a counselor; the counseling occurred during the years in which the client was 9 to 14 years old (*Debose v. Wolfe*, 1994); at the time of the writing of this book, this case was under appeal. The availability of contributory negligence and consent as defenses in civil litigation resulting from therapist–patient sex varies from state to state, even from court to court within individual states. Absent a clear mandate from the highest court in any given state, individual judges determine whether the defenses are given to the jury for their consideration. Expert witnesses must be able to provide informed and illuminating testimony on the topic, and attorneys must be able to address the relevant issues through such means as jury instructions (see, e.g., Mann & Winer, 1991). Chapter 2 provides additional discussion of consent issues.

3. *Each patient is unique, and reflexive conclusions must be avoided.* The research and clinical literature have revealed consequences and patterns that occur frequently, increase understanding about the phenomenon of therapist–patient sex and the healing

process, and help clinicians to ensure that inquiries are not incomplete (see chapter 5). But such frequently occurring consequences and patterns must never be mistaken for a "one size fits all" response that characterizes all patients in all circumstances. Every patient experiences therapist–patient sex and its aftermath "in his or her own way in the context of his or her unique life. Therapist–patient sexual intimacy is a deeply personal experience" (Pope & Bouhoutsos, 1986, p. 21).

4. *There is no fixed or standard therapy for patients who have been sexually involved with a prior therapist.* Just as therapist–patient sex causes no "one size fits all" set of consequences, there is no unvarying set of components or steps to a subsequent therapy. The therapy must be tailored to the uniqueness of the patient, the patient's experience of therapist–patient sex, his or her needs, and the current situation. Subsequent therapy must also be consistent with the theoretical orientation and competencies of the therapist. This book attempts to present approaches that will be useful to clinicians across a wide range of theoretical orientations.

5. *Although there is no unvarying sequence of therapeutic interventions for patients who have been sexually involved with a previous therapist, there are important issues that the subsequent therapist must be aware of and address.* This book identifies some of the most crucial of these issues—particularly those that seem to be most easily overlooked or that pose the most serious difficulties— and presents them in a concise format useful to therapists who provide clinical services or forensic testimony.

Therapists' sexual exploitation of patients and clinicians' clinical or forensic services for exploited patients never occur in a vacuum. They are never free of historical, cultural, professional, and other contexts. These contexts can help practitioner and patient alike to understand the nature, meaning, and effects of instances in which therapists exploit their patients and place them at risk for serious and lasting harm as well as the ways in which subsequent clinicians may provide help to these patients. These contexts are fundamental to the preparation of the subsequent practitioner and the creation of a genuinely helpful working relationship between subsequent therapist and patient; hence, they will form the focus of chapter 2.

2

Contexts

This chapter explores contexts significant for understanding therapist–patient sex and for working with sexually exploited patients. The professions and society in general have often found it extremely difficult to address or even acknowledge such contexts. The contexts—particularly when unacknowledged and unaddressed—tend to shape perceptions of and responses to the sexual abuse of patients. Taking account of such contexts and their effects encourages a rethinking of issues that have seemed settled, suggesting that routinely discounted factors may be significant and prompting questions that have all too often seemed off limits.

The responses of individual therapists to sexually exploited patients often reflect these historical, cultural, professional, and other contexts. Awareness of these contexts is an essential component of competence in responding to the needs of such patients. Assessments that view characteristics, intentions, behaviors, and consequences out of context are almost certain to be misleading if not completely invalid. Even the most simple, accepted, and well-meaning interventions can cause serious problems when important contextual factors are ignored. The specific strategies and approaches described in chapters 4, 5, and 6 make real sense for the patient only when they are understood in adequate context. Only when subsequent clinicians are adequately informed by, attentive to, and prepared to consider questions about the potential effects of significant contexts are they able to understand the exploited patient in adequate context and to provide a helpful response.

Gender

Research findings published in peer-reviewed scientific and professional journals reveal a striking aspect: They suggest an extreme gender incidence imbalance among the therapists and patients who become sexually involved.[6] For example, Table 1, presented in the previous chapter, summarizes studies suggesting that female patients are far more likely than male patients to be sexually involved with a therapist. Table 2 summarizes national self-report studies of therapists published in peer-reviewed scientific and professional journals. It is important to note that when the base rate is very low, the gender differences are not always significant for the sample size. However, in *no* study does the obtained percentage of female therapists who report a sexual relationship with a patient equal or exceed the percentage of male therapists who report such a relationship. In fact, the ratio of male percentages to female percentages ranges from 1.5 to 9 (i.e., in the latter case, the percentage of male therapists reporting sexual involvement is nine times as large as the percentage of female therapists reporting such involvement).

---

[6]Perpetrators may attempt to undermine the prohibition against therapist–patient sex and support their sense of entitlement to return to practice by portraying arguments in favor of protecting patients from abuse and removing perpetrators from practice as efforts to grant "special" protection to "weak" women. (Their view seems to assume that freedom from sex abuse in the therapeutic situation is a "special" perk to be granted by beneficent therapists.) These efforts, they maintain, are insulting and discriminatory. However, the efforts to protect patients and remove perpetrators from practice have as a goal not special status for female patients but rather equal status to that of male patients and equal protection from abuse. Both female and male patients are vulnerable to abuse by an unscrupulous therapist; currently, however, the research indicates that women suffer a disproportionate share of sexual abuse by therapists. Thus, as Holroyd (1983) observed, they do not have equal access to nonabusive therapy.

Taken as a whole, peer-reviewed published findings from these two kinds of surveys—those based on therapists' self-reports about their own sexual involvements with patients and those based on reports by subsequent therapists working with patients who have been sexually involved with a previous therapist—constitute substantial evidence that therapists who become sexually involved with patients are overwhelmingly, although not exclusively, male, and that patients who become sexually involved with therapists are overwhelmingly, although not exclusively, female. For example, Jacqueline Bouhoutsos, who at the time of the study was professor of psychology at the University of California, Los Angeles (UCLA), and her colleagues reported a landmark study in which it was found that sexual involvement between a male therapist and a female patient constituted 92% of the instances in which a subsequent therapist reported that a patient had been sexually involved with a previous therapist (Bouhoutsos, Holroyd, Lerman, Forer, & Greenberg, 1983). Nanette Gartrell, who at the time of the study was professor of psychiatry at Harvard University (and is now in independent practice and on the faculty of the University of California, San Francisco Medical School), and her colleagues reported findings from the first national self-report study of sexual involvement between psychiatrists and their patients. They found that 88% of the "contacts for which both the psychiatrist's and the patient's gender were specified occurred between male psychiatrists and female patients" (Gartrell, Herman, Olarte, Feldstein, & Localio, 1986, p. 1128). Data based on the anonymous self-reports of patients supplement the data based on therapists' anonymous self-reports and reports by subsequent therapists. In one study, about 2.19% of the men and about 4.58% of the women reported having engaged in sex with their own therapists (Pope & Feldman-Summers, 1992).

A fourth source of data (in addition to those provided through reports by subsequent therapists, therapists' anonymous self-reports, and patients' anonymous self-reports) supports the hypothesis that sexually involved therapists are overwhelmingly (although not exclusively) male and that sexually involved patients are overwhelmingly (although not exclusively) female.

Table 2

Percentage of Therapists Who Had Sex With Clients, According to National Self-Report Studies[a]

Source	Discipline	Sample size	Return rate	% Reporting Sex with Clients	
				Male	Female
Holroyd & Brodsky (1977)[b]	psychologists	1,000	70.0%	12.1%	2.6%
Pope et al. (1979)	psychologists	1,000	48.0%	12.0%	3.0%
Pope et al. (1986)	psychologists	1,000	58.5%	9.4%	2.5%
Gartrell et al. (1986)[c]	psychiatrists	5,574	26.0%	7.1%	3.1%
Pope et al. (1987)[d]	psychologists	1,000	46.0%	3.6%	0.4%
Akamatsu (1988)[e]	psychologists	1,000	39.5%	3.5%	2.3%
Borys & Pope (1989)[f]	psychiatrists, psychologists, and social workers[g]	4,800	56.5%	0.9%	0.2%
Bernsen, Tabachnick, & Pope (in press)	social workers	1,000	43.0%	3.6%	0.5%

Note. Adapted from Pope, in press, by permission. Footnote 28 on pages 113–114 presents statistical analysis of these eight studies.

[a]This table presents only national surveys that have been published in peer-reviewed scientific and professional journals. Exceptional caution is warranted in comparing the data from these various surveys. For example, the frequently cited percentages of 12.1 and 2.6, reported by Holroyd and Brodsky (1977), exclude same-sex involvements. Moreover, when surveys included separate items to assess post-termination sexual involvement, these data are reported in footnotes to this table. Finally, some published articles did not provide sufficiently detailed data for this table (e.g., aggregate percentages); the investigators supplied the data needed for the table.

[b]Although the gender percentages presented in the table for the other seven studies represent responses to one basic survey item in each survey, the percentages presented for Holroyd and Brodsky (1977) span several items. The study's senior author confirmed through personal communication that the study's findings were that 12.1% of the male and 2.6% of the female participants reported having engaged in erotic contact (whether or not it included intercourse) with at least one opposite-sex patient; that about 4% of the male and 1% of the female participants reported engaging in erotic contact with at least one same-sex patient; and that, in response to a separate survey item, 7.2% of the male and 0.6% of the female psychologists reported that they had "had intercourse with a patient within three months after terminating therapy" (p. 846).

[c]"Respondents were asked to specify the number of male and female patients with whom they had been sexually involved" (p. 1127); they were also asked "to restrict their answers to adult patients" (p. 1127).

[d]The survey also included a question about "becoming sexually involved with a former client" (p. 996). Gender percentages about sex with current or former clients did not appear in the article but were provided by an author; 14% of the male and 8% of the female respondents reported having had sex with a former client.

[e]The original article also noted that 14.2% of male and 4.7% of female psychologists reported that they had "been involved in an intimate relationship with a former client" (p. 454).

[f]The original article also asked if respondents had "engaged in sexual activity with a client after termination" (p. 288); 6% of the male and 2% of the female therapists reported engaging in this activity.

[g]Survey sample comprised 1,600 psychiatrists, 1,600 psychologists, and 1,600 social workers.

Data from licensing disciplinary actions suggest that about 86% of the therapist–patient cases are those in which the therapist is male and the patient is female (Pope, 1993).

Why therapist–patient sex so often involves a male therapist and a female patient is not clearly understood. Psychologists Jean Holroyd and Annette Brodsky (1977) concluded the first national study of therapist–patient sex by identifying the major issues that had not yet been resolved. "[T]hree professional issues remain to be addressed: (a) that male therapists are most often involved, (b) that female patients are most often the objects, and (c) that therapists who disregard the sexual boundary once are likely to repeat" (p. 849). Holroyd, the study's principal author and professor of psychology at UCLA, suggested that the gender imbalance tended to reflect sex role stereotyping and bias. She concluded that in regard to the vast majority of cases in which a male therapist engaged in sexual involvement with a female patient, "sexual contact between therapist and patient is perhaps the quintessence of sex-biased therapeutic practice" (Holroyd, 1983, p. 285). Holroyd and Brodsky's (1977) groundbreaking research prompted a second national study focusing on not only therapist–patient but also professor–student sexual relationships. The results of these and other studies[7] suggested that the gender issues that Holroyd discussed were often linked to role-power and role-vulnerability:

> When sexual contact occurs in the context of psychology training or psychotherapy, the predominant pattern is quite clear and simple: An older higher status man becomes sexually active with a younger, subordinate woman. In each of the higher status professional roles (teacher, supervisor, administrator, therapist), a much higher percentage of men than women engage in sex with those students or clients for whom they have assumed professional responsibility. In the lower status role of student, a far greater proportion of

[7]For research data on student–teacher sex in mental health training programs, see Carr, Robinson, Stewart, and Kussin, 1991; Glaser and Thorpe, 1986; Pope, 1989b; Pope, Levenson, and Schover, 1979; Pope and Vetter, 1992; and Robinson and Reid, 1985.

women than men are sexually active with their teachers, administrators, and clinical supervisors. (Pope, Levenson, & Schover, 1979, p. 687; see also Pope, 1990c)

A clear, comprehensive, and useful understanding of the nature, meaning, and effects of therapist–patient sex and of ways to help exploited patients cannot emerge from denial of this obvious, marked gender imbalance and the context that it creates. Endeavors to understand how therapists could place those who have come to them for help at risk for severe and lasting harm, the consequences for patients, and the response of an individual therapist or of the society of therapists more generally to this phenomenon must take into account this gender imbalance.

Minorities Masked by the Majority

One unfortunate consequence of this stark gender pattern is that it has contributed to the smothering of adequate attention to the *relatively* small minority[8] that involve other dyads (such as female–female or male–male), triads, or larger groups. Benowitz (1991), for example, noted that many early research reports tended to use exclusively the pronoun *he* for sexually involved therapists, as if a female therapist would never sexually exploit a patient (p. 2). She also observed that until relatively recently, "sexual abuse of women clients by women psychotherapists was largely invisible publicly" (p. 3). Attempts to acknowledge, attend to, and understand how the predominant male therapist/female patient gender pattern influences professional responses to therapist–patient sex must lead to an increased awareness of instances for which this predominant pattern does not hold and must not lead to a denial, discounting, or trivialization of these less frequent types.

---

[8]A minority that is small only in the sense of relative to the large majority of therapist–patient sexual involvements that the research suggests involves male therapists and female patients.

To acknowledge and attempt to address the significant gender differences that have consistently emerged from the diverse national studies of dual relationships does not, of course, imply that men are the only perpetrators, that women are the only victims/survivors, or that victimization of male clients is somehow less damaging or important. As with the phenomenon of incest to which certain dual relationships have often been compared in terms of nature, dynamics, and consequences (Chesler, 1972; Gabbard, 1989; Marmor, 1961; Pope, 1989; Pope & Bouhoutsos, 1986; Siassi & Thomas, 1973), women may take advantage of a more powerful role, engage in rationalization, and cross boundaries serving to protect those who are vulnerable, and men may be harmed. But to affirm one obvious point—that unethical behavior needs to be recognized and prevented, regardless of gender—need not mask another obvious point: that a higher proportion of male than female psychologists engage in sexual and nonsexual dual relationships of the sort that are expressly prohibited by the Ethical Principles (APA, 1981) and that a significantly disproportionate number of female clients and students are harmed and exploited. (Borys & Pope, 1989, pp. 290–291)

Gender incidence imbalance is a factor that can shape the clinician's response to sexually exploited patients in ways other than helping to create a tendency to deny or overlook the minority of incidents that do not fit the predominant male therapist/female patient paradigm. Gender influences often blend with other factors that, when ignored or discounted, tend to distort or block helpful and effective responses. The following sections note some of these contexts.

Parallels to Incest and Rape

Chapter 1 cited statements comparing therapist–patient sex to incest and rape. Such comparisons are neither recent nor rare. The citations that follow suggest the extent to which an extremely broad and diverse range of researchers and clinicians have noted substantial ways (e.g., in regard to dynamics, uses

of power, lack of freely given consent, characteristics of perpetrators, and consequences for victim/survivors) in which
therapist–patient sex is similar to rape and incest: Bailey (1978);
Barnhouse (1978); Bates and Brodsky (1989); Benowitz (1991);
Borys (1988); Brown (1984); Burgess (1981); Chesler (1972); Connel and Wilson (1974); Dahlberg (1970); Davidson (1977); Finkelhor (1984); Freud (1915/1958b); Gabbard (1989a, in press);
Gilbert and Scher (1989); Herman (1992); Herman, Gartrell,
Olarte, Feldstein, and Localio (1987); Kardener (1974); Kavoussi
and Becker (1987); Keith-Spiegel (1977); Kottler (1993); Maltz
and Holman (1984); Marmor (1972); Masters and Johnson
(1976); Rapp (1987); Redlich (1977); Russell (1986); Saul (1962);
Schoener, Milgrom, Gonsiorek, Luepker, and Conroe (1989);
Searles (1959); Siassi and Thomas (1973); A. A. Stone (1990);
L. G. Stone (1980); M. Stone (1976); and Walker (1989).

One of the most helpful books for both sexually exploited
patients and clinicians who are providing services to these patients is *Sex in the Therapy Hour* (Bates & Brodsky, 1989). Psychologists Carolyn Bates and Annette Brodsky gave this compelling case study the subtitle, *A Case of Professional Incest*. Their
detailed account explores the ways in which a therapist's choice
to place a patient at risk for serious and lasting harm is similar
to the act of incest. Psychiatrist Glen Gabbard (1989a) eloquently
noted important aspects of the incestuous nature of therapist–
patient sex.

> The problem of incest has lurched into public awareness over
> the last decade or so. . . . In parallel with this increased
> interest has been a growing awareness of another form of
> incest—sexual exploitation of patients . . . by professionals.
> The victims of this form of professional incest have placed
> their trust in a person whom they assume will place their
> interests above his or her own by the very nature of the
> professional relationship. When this trust is betrayed, the
> impact is often as damaging as familial incest.
> . . . Incest victims and those who have been sexually ex-
> ploited by professionals have remarkably similar symptoms:
> shame, intense guilt associated with a feeling that they were
> somehow responsible for their victimization, feelings of iso-
> lation and enforced silence, poor self-esteem, suicidal

and/or self-destructive behavior, and denial. Reactions of friends and family—disbelief, discounting, embarrassment—are also similar in both groups. (p. xi)

A person who has been subjected to incest may have difficulty trusting any familial figure. A patient who has been subjected to therapist–patient sex may have difficulty trusting any therapist. Thus therapist–patient sex can place the patient in an excruciating dilemma. If the exploited patient is to secure therapeutic services for the original difficulties that led him or her to seek help initially or for any harmful consequences that the sexual involvement with the therapist may have caused, the patient must seek help from another therapist. Yet the patient's own experience may lead him or her to conclude that therapy is not an enterprise that offers safety or justifies trust. It is understandable for an exploited patient to view any therapist with suspicion, fear, and anxiety, and many do.

That therapist–patient sex is incestuous in nature is part of the context essential to understanding how it can affect exploited patients and how therapists—both individually and as collective members of a profession—tend to respond to the phenomenon. Therapists typically see themselves as members of a profession that provides services to those in need. Individuals typically seek help from therapists for difficulties caused by a wide variety of personal, social–environmental, or biological factors. When therapists attempt to evaluate and respond helpfully to harm caused by therapist–patient sex, however, they are evaluating and responding to harm that a fellow member of the profession has caused. The perpetrator is a colleague. Both the subsequent therapist and the profession more generally must confront this uncomfortable, little-discussed, but influential professional dynamic: Nonoffending therapists are in a position similar in many respects to that of nonoffending family members who have knowledge that other family members are incest perpetrators. Fellow professionals, like fellow family members, may need to acknowledge and understand tendencies that seem naturally to arise in such situations: tendencies to collude with perpetrators, to deny or minimize their offenses, or to enable them to continue or resume a practice that puts vulnerable individuals at risk for deep and pervasive harm. Burgess (1981), in her pioneering study of cases in which physicians sexually exploited their patients, identified and analyzed this phenomenon. She found that "except for one instance, physicians who were told of the exploitation remained loyal to their professional brother and did not side with the patient" (p. 1339). She observed,

> This type of adult sexual exploitation is similar to incest situations in which a child is repeatedly pressured for sexual activity by a family member; just as some of the women did not return to the physician, some children from incest situations leave the home. It is interesting, however, that some physicians remained loyal to the accused physician in much the same way that some mothers side with the incestuous father against the child and refuse to believe such a complaint. (Burgess, 1981, p. 1341)

If on a larger scale the profession has shown evidence of colluding, denying, minimizing, and enabling on behalf of offender colleagues and at the expense of exploited patients, on the individual level subsequent therapists have all too often, without adequate assessment, provided a "treatment plan" designed to make a patient give up the belief that a fellow therapist, particularly a prestigious one, has done anything wrong (see Noel & Watterson, 1992, for an example). In other cases, the twin factors of offender distress (or impairment) and the prospect of rehabilitation are used to protect and enable the offender; one subsequent therapist, for example, told the patient,

> "Well, he's [the perpetrator] been having a bad time, going through some tough times in his career; he's trying to rehabilitate himself." In making excuses, the second therapist had only confused the patient. Instead of saying, "What happened to you should not have happened to you; you were violated, and there is no excuse for it," he attempted to displace the abusive therapist's responsibility for his sexual misconduct. (Bates & Brodsky, 1989, pp. 99–100)

The tendency of therapists to emphasize that, as the previous passage illustrates, a colleague offended because of extenuating circumstances and, having been rehabilitated, will never do it again, is reminiscent of Molly Ivins's (1993) comment in summarizing outrageous crimes by Texas politicians: " 'Texas political ethics' is not an oxymoron. Our guys have'em. They just tend to have an overdeveloped sense of the extenuating circumstance" (p. 203).

Therapist–patient sex shares similarities not only to incest but also to rape. All three are forms of sexual abuse in which perpetrators are typically, although not exclusively, male, and in which victim/survivors are typically, although not exclusively, female. It may be useful for therapists to consider the social or cultural history of professional acknowledgment of and response to each form of abuse (Pope, 1990b). The difficulties that the profession is still struggling with in confronting therapists' sexual exploitation of patients may parallel previous professional efforts to respond to incest and rape. The sections that follow note three specific responses that the forms of abuse—in which perpetrators are typically although not exclusively male and victim/survivors are typically although not exclusively female—tend to elicit. These are (a) denying or minimizing the scope of occurrence, (b) allocating to the victim/survivor responsibility for the behavior of the perpetrator (or, in slightly modified form, relieving the perpetrator from responsibility and accountability by focusing on the character or worth of the victim/survivor), and, generally in the context of this allocation of responsibility, (c) enabling the (generally male) perpetrator to place unsuspecting other (generally female) individuals at risk for sexual exploitation.

The Scope

One of the most obvious historical parallels between professional responses to therapist–patient sex and to incest and rape is the difficulty in acknowledging the scope of the phenomenon. Only relatively recently has the profession focused attention on incest and rape as anything but extremely rare events.

Previously, both incest and rape were considered to involve only very few people (Courtois, 1988; Estrich, 1987; Herman, 1981; Russell, 1986; Walker, Bonner, & Kaufman, 1988). A scholarly text published slightly less than 40 years ago, for example, reported that incest affected only about one or two people per million U.S. citizens each year (Weinberg, 1955). About 20 years ago, the widely read and respected *Comprehensive Textbook of Psychiatry* reported that the incidence rate for incest was about 1.1 to 1.9 per million (Henderson, 1975). Like incest, rape received relatively little attention from the profession. As late as 1971, Amir reported that he could not find a single book focusing exclusively on rape. Until relatively recently, allegations of rape were usually understood to be "lies or fantasies" (Estrich, 1987, p. 43).

The profession historically tended to attribute allegations of sex abuse to a presumably innate female tendency to invent such allegations and hurl them at innocent men. This attribution may have taken firm root when Freud renounced his "seduction theory": "When girls who bring forward this event [incest] in the story of their childhood fairly regularly introduce the father as the seducer, neither the phantastic character of this accusation nor the motive actuating it can be doubted" (Freud 1924/1952, p. 379). Freud assumed that the motive was female sexuality and the female desire for an incestuous relationship with the father (p. 379).

Wigmore's (1934/1970) respected text on legal evidence illustrates how deeply the assumption that virtually all allegations of sex abuse were false, motivated by an inherent female impulse to make false complaints and to fantasize about being raped, became rooted in the legal and psychiatric professions. The following statement is taken from the 1970 edition:

> chastity may have a direct connection with veracity, viz. when a woman or young girl testifies as complainant against a man charged with a sexual crime—rape, rape under age, seduction, assault. Modern psychiatrists have amply studied . . . girls and women coming before the courts in all sorts of cases. Their psychic complexes are multifarious, distorted partly by inherent defects, partly by diseased derangements

or abnormal instincts, partly by bad social environment, partly by temporary physiological or emotional conditions. . . . The unchaste (let us call it) mentality finds incidental but direct expression in the narration of imaginary sex incidents of which the narrator is the heroine or the victim. . . . No judge should ever let a sex offense go to the jury unless the female complainant's social history and mental makeup have been examined and testified to by a qualified physician. . . . The reason I think that rape in particular belongs in this category is one well known to psychologists, namely, that fantasies of being raped are exceedingly common in women, indeed one may almost say that they are probably universal. (Wigmore, 1934/1970, pp. 745–746).

As with prior professional and forensic denial of rape and incest, the responses to therapist–patient sex tended to assume that it rarely if ever occurred and that any allegations were probably made by women who created fictional accounts of longed-for but unattainable sexual involvements. It is important to note, however, that the prohibitions against therapist–patient sex, like those against rape and incest, have a long history. The Hippocratic oath and at least one earlier code, for example, contain explicit prohibitions against sexual involvement between doctors and their patients (Brodsky, 1989). Freud similarly set forth an injunction against sex with a therapy patient. Though *explicit* mention of therapist–patient sex did not appear in professional ethics codes until the mid-1970s (one reason being that it was assumed to occur so rarely, if at all, and to be so clearly unethical that explicit mention of it was unnecessary), sexual involvement with a patient was contrary to various sections of the ethics codes, and offenders could be held in violation of the code. Pennsylvania psychologist Rachel Hare-Mustin (1974), a former chair of the American Psychological Association's (APA's) Ethics Committee, for example, published an article three years before her association's ethics code made explicit mention of therapist–patient sex. She emphasized that APA's 1963 *Ethical Standards of Psychologists* contained standards that would prohibit therapist–patient sexual involvement. She stated that in light of "a review of principles relating to competency, community standards and the client relationship that genital contact with patients is ethically unacceptable" (p. 310). Likewise, UCLA Professor Jean Holroyd, who, as was mentioned earlier, was senior author of the first national study of therapist–patient sex, testified that the 1977 code did not represent a change in the standards regarding sexual activities with patients:

Administrative Law Judge:	Was it [the 1977 ethics code] a codification of what was already the standard of practice?
Holroyd:	Yes, it was making it very explicit in the ethics code. . . .
Administrative Law Judge:	What I am asking is whether or not the standard of practice prior to the inclusion of that specific section in the [1977] ethics code, whether or not that changed the standard of practice.
Holroyd:	No, it did not change the standard of practice. The standard of practice always precluded a sexual relationship between therapist and patient.
Administrative Law Judge:	Even though it was not expressed in the ethics codes?
Holroyd:	From the beginning of the term psychotherapy with Sigmund Freud, he was very clear to prohibit it in his early publications. (*In re Howland*, 1980, pp. 49–50)

This long-standing prohibition has gained judicial recognition. Almost 20 years ago, Presiding Justice Markowitz of the New York Supreme Court noted evidence that from the time of Freud to the present, therapist–patient sex had been viewed as harmful: "Thus from [Freud] to the modern practitioner we have common agreement of the harmful effects of sensual intimacies between patient and therapist" (*Roy v. Hartogs*, 1976, p. 590).

Just as the scope of rape and incest was historically assumed to be exceedingly small—with allegations generally dismissed as manifestations of an innate female tendency to fabricate false sexual charges—so, too, was the scope of therapist–patient sex. As psychiatrist Virginia Davidson (1977) wrote, less than 20 years ago the phenomenon of therapists engaging in sex with their patients could be aptly labeled the "problem with no name."

One of the first reports of therapists' sexual transgressions to be drawn from a database containing more than 10 years of actuarial information about malpractice suits was published in the *American Psychologist* in the early 1970s. Interestingly, this report contained no mention of *any* valid allegation of therapist–patient sex. It did, however, provide an analysis of why women would file false allegations:

> the greatest number of [all malpractice] actions are brought by women who lead lives of very quiet desperation, who form close attachments to their therapists, who feel rejected or spurned when they discover that relations are maintained on a formal and professional level, and who then react with allegations of sexual improprieties. (Brownfain, 1971, p. 651)

As plaintiffs in malpractice suits involving therapist–patient sex complaints began to prevail in larger numbers and as juries began to award sexually abused patients verdicts in the multi-million dollar range (Pope & Bouhoutsos, 1986), however, it became difficult for the professions[9] to deny the scope of the

---

[9]A variety of disciplines (e.g., psychiatry, psychology, social work, marriage and family counseling) are represented by the term *professions*, as it is used in this chapter. It is important to acknowledge not only the similarities of these professions, but also the significant differences between them that may be relevant for an adequate understanding of therapist–patient sex and its implications. A study designed to compare the rates at which psychiatrists, psychologists, and social workers engaged in sex with their patients showed that the "professions did not differ among themselves in terms of . . . sexual intimacies with clients before or after termination" (Borys & Pope, 1989, p. 283; see also Bernsen, Tabachnick, & Pope, in press). Yet when professionals are expelled from an association on the basis of unethical behavior such as having been sexually intimate with patients, the steps each association takes may be viewed from the perspective of how likely it is that the decision will become known to the perpetrator's current patients and potential patients (who may be at considerable risk for abuse), colleagues in other disciplines

problem and for allegations of therapist–patient sex to be reflexively dismissed as fabrications of miserable and desperate
women. Prior to the widespread introduction of specific legislation that named therapist–patient sex explicitly as a cause
of civil action, appeals courts had begun to affirm therapist–
patient sexual involvement as legitimate grounds for malpractice or general tort actions (see, e.g., *Roy v. Hartogs,* 1976; *Zipkin
v. Freeman,* 1968). Nicholas Cummings, a former APA president, called the sexual exploitation of patients a "national dis-
grace" (Bouhoutsos, 1985).

Large financial settlements caught the attention of the professional community. For example, in the early 1980s, the jury in
Walker v. Parzen (1981; see also Shearer, 1981; Walker & Young,
1986) awarded the plaintiff $4,631,666. Cumulatively, these
cases began to drain the financial reserves that therapists had
created with their insurance premiums. According to the president of the insurance company that provided liability insurance
to APA members in the 1980s, therapist–patient sex claims came
to account for about half the costs related to malpractice suits
filed against psychologists (R. Imbert, cited in Pope, Sonne, &
Holroyd, 1993, p. 29; also see Foreword). Perr (1989), a psychiatrist and attorney, wrote in a volume published by the
American Psychiatric Association: "Complaints concerning
psychologists' sexual involvement with clients are the leading
cause of lawsuits. Sexual involvement by psychiatrists with
patients now constitutes the second leading cause of all professional practice litigation" (p. 212).

The large jury awards helped bring the issue to public attention. The expenses (e.g., jury awards, settlement figures, defense costs) increased insurance premiums to such an extent

---

(who may employ or refer patients to the perpetrator), and the public more
generally. Currently, for example, the American Psychological Association
notifies its membership through a confidential mailing when someone's membership is discontinued on the basis of a serious ethics violation. The American
Psychiatric Association reports "all expulsions by means of a press release to
the media in the area in which the member lives and [publishes this] . . .
information in *Psychiatric News*" (Sharfstein, 1993, p. 1580).

that swift action was inevitable, the most visible and far-reaching action being the elimination or capping of insurance coverage for suits involving sexual violations (Cummings & Sobel, 1985; Perr, 1989; Stromberg et al., 1988). The coverage that the American Psychological Association Insurance Trust secured for APA members, for example, in 1985 eliminated the coverage for judgments based on therapist–patient sexual involvement. Thus the "problem with no name" became the "problem with no coverage." A few years later, the American Psychological Association Insurance Trust's plan for members restored a very limited form of coverage for awards, capping them at $25,000.[10]

Eliminating or capping coverage for liability based on sexual involvement with patients may have helped—at least temporarily—to hold down expenses for individual therapists by producing savings in terms of professional liability insurance premiums. It is possible that a much more wide-reaching effect has been to discourage sexually abused patients from filing suits. Few exploited patients possess wealth adequate to enable them to bankroll all plaintiff costs associated with such litigation. The costs may include attorney fees for preparing and trying the case, deposition costs, fees or expenses for expert and fact witnesses,[11] and, should the plaintiff prevail in the initial trial, the expenses associated with an appeal process that can take years. These costs tend to be high because most trials for allegations of therapist–patient sex are extremely complex. When abused patients lack adequate wealth to advance such funds, one of their only avenues—if not the *only* avenue—to

---

[10]Depending on the policy, an insurance company may cover the cost of defending the case regardless of whether coverage of awards is excluded or capped. In some cases, however, the costs of defending the case may not be covered. The court in *Chicago Insurance Co. v. Griffin* (1993), for example, held that "based on this court's finding that . . . claims in the underlying action . . . are either excluded from coverage or not covered under the policy, no possibility of coverage exists and there is no duty to defend arising from the policy" (p. 867).

[11]Fees for fact witnesses are usually not allowed, although some costs (e.g., transportation) may be reimbursable, depending (as always) on the jurisdiction and situation.

court is for an attorney to take the case on a contingency fee basis.

Relatively few sexually exploitive therapists possess great wealth. If neither the defendant nor insurance coverage (which is nonexistent or capped) can fund the hospitalization, therapy, and other clinical needs of an exploited patient, the potential recovery for even the strongest malpractice suits is likely to be small once trial preparation and other expenses are subtracted. There may be few plaintiff attorneys in this area of litigation who have adequate financial resources to bear the costs, especially when they could hope to recover only a small share (once litigation expenses and the funds paid to the plaintiff are subtracted) of nonexistent or severely limited professional liability insurance coverage. Thus patients who have been sexually exploited by a therapist may in many circumstances have little or no access to plaintiff attorneys who are experienced and skilled in this area.[12]

A practical effect of eliminating or capping insurance coverage for therapist–patient sex malpractice suits, then, may be once again to dampen attention to the scope of the problem. Jury determinations (reflected in large awards) that sexually exploitive therapists caused great harm to patients and the sheer number of malpractice cases did much to draw attention to the scope of the problem. Actions that would reduce the size and number of cases (without addressing the occurrence of the sexual involvements that prompted them) would likely decrease attention to the scope of the problem while depriving many patients of access to the courts.

It is worth noting that in many settlements of such cases, defense attorneys employed by the professional liability insurance carrier seek "gag stipulations." In order for the plaintiff to receive a settlement, he or she must agree never to speak, write, or otherwise communicate to others about the allegations themselves or about the contents of settlement. As will be discussed in later sections, sexually exploitive therapists—like

---

[12]Plaintiff firms specializing in therapist–patient sex litigation are relatively rare.

many incest perpetrators—seek through inducements, threats, or other measures to bind the patient to secrecy about the sexual involvement. When "gag stipulations" are made part of settlements, funds from insurance premiums paid by therapists are spent, in essence, to buy the patient's silence. The patient is metaphorically gagged and prevented from telling his or her experiences to others, including other potential or actual patients who might be at risk from the perpetrator. It seems likely that imposing secrecy on patients in this manner may, like insurance policy changes that make it difficult if not impossible for some patients to find skilled representation, reduce the *apparent*—but not actual—scope of the problem at the expense of many patients' welfare.

It is interesting that the insurance coverage capping was designed to apply specifically to a form of malpractice in which the overwhelming majority of perpetrators were men and the overwhelming majority of patients were women. It is worth asking whether such a cap would ever have been imposed or tolerated if it were to have emerged outside the contexts noted in this chapter (e.g., the historical tendencies—in regard to sexual exploitation for which the perpetrators tend to be male and the victims/survivors tend to be female—to discount the abuse, to shift responsibility for the abuse to the victims or survivors, and to act in ways that collude with perpetrators, allowing them to continue or resume placing others at risk). Alan Stone (1990), former president of the American Psychiatric Association and professor of psychiatry and law at Harvard, questioned the change in coverage as not only representing unfair gender discrimination but also undermining patient welfare.

Each of us contributes by paying liability insurance to a fund that has two functions: to protect us and to compensate those who are unfortunate victims of our negligence. With this in mind, the policy decision to exclude victims of sexual exploitation, who are typically women, from participation in our victim compensation fund is difficult to defend. If we are concerned about them, why should they be "victimized" by the exclusion? (p. 25)

Whereas Stone raises the question of whether the current policy cap is good policy, fair, or ethical, there is the unresolved question: Regardless of whether it is good policy, fair, or ethical, is it legal? *American Home Assurance Co. v. Cohen* (1993) addressed two aspects of the legality. First, the court acknowledged the disparate impact of the cap on women but upheld it as not in violation of Washington law. The court quoted state statutes that do not prohibit "fair discrimination on the basis of sex . . . when bona fide statistical differences in risk or exposure have been substantiated" (p. 372). Second, however, the court refused to enforce a provision of the policy that applied the $25,000 cap to *all* claims (in the aggregate)—even those which do not involve sexual misconduct—against a therapist once sexual misconduct is alleged. The court held,

> The sublimit provision before the Court . . . has the broader effect on victims of sexual misconduct of limiting recovery for all non-sexual misconduct claims arising out of the same therapeutic relationship where sexual misconduct claims are alleged. As a result, the victims of sexual misconduct, 90% of whom are women, are also disproportionately disadvantaged in their recovery for non-sexual misconduct claims. (p. 372)

The court addressed the potential of such a cap to discourage patients from reporting valid claims of sexual misconduct:

> The present provison of American Home's Policy will discourage or preclude bona fide claims of sexual misconduct which arise out of the same or related therapeutic treatment in which non-sexual misconduct has also occurred. Because the sublimit extends to all other non-sexual misconduct claims, a victim will be reluctant to allege claims of sexual misconduct. In effect, a *toleration of sexual misconduct by licensed psychologists is encouraged* [italics added]. If a victim exercises rights under Washington law to seek injunctive relief against the therapist who has sexually abused the victim, or if the victim cooperates with others who have initiated either civil or criminal action against the therapist, insurance companies such as American Home's could then assert that

the sublimit of $25,000 would apply to the entire cause of action because of the accompanying claims or evidence of sexual misconduct. In a practical sense, victims of sexual misconduct would be worse off by the existence of a policy sublimit of this breadth than if sexual misconduct claims were excluded from the Policy altogether. Such a result is contrary to public policy. (pp. 370–371)[13]

Seattle attorney David A. Summers, who represented the psychologist's former client, notes that both rulings are now on appeal (personal communication, March 1, 1994).

Accountability, Integrity, and Trust

Historically, when professionals explicitly authorized by the state to hold special positions of trust significantly violate that trust, it has been understood that they have waived their right to resume those positions under any conditions. Therapists, however, seem to have exempted themselves from this general standard of accountability, integrity, and trust. The degree to which there is, in the words of Keith-Spiegel (1977), "sanctuary provided by the profession for those who engage in sexual intimacies with clients" (p. 2) forms an important context for

---

[13]Interestingly, the Appellate Division of the Supreme Court of New York examined a case in which a psychologist who had been sued by a client became a plaintiff in a legal action against her own insurance company. As the court summarized, "shortly after counsel was assigned to her case, plaintiff concluded that there was a conflict of interest between her and defendant since the policy provisions governing claims of sexual misconduct would make it advantageous for defendant to have all the claims against her linked to sexual misconduct so as to make them subject to the $25,000 limitation. . . ." (*Ladner v. American Assurance Company*, 1994, pp. *2–3). The appellate court held "that a potential conflict of interest does in fact exist rendering plaintiff's representation by an attorney employed by defendant improper. . . . Under these circumstances, plaintiff is entitled to a preliminary injunction pursuant to CPLR 6301 enjoining defendant [insurance company] from selecting counsel to represent her in the underlying litigation and directing defendant to pay the reasonable legal fees of counsel of her choice" (p. *5–7).

understanding the phenomenon of therapist–patient sex and responses to those who are involved in it. (See also The Therapist as Former Perpetrator, in chapter 3.)

If a judge were convicted of abusing the power and trust inherent in the position of judgeship by allowing bribes to determine the outcome of cases, numerous sanctions, both criminal and civil, might follow. However, even after the judge "paid the debt" due society by the abuse of power and trust, the judge would not be allowed to resume the bench, regardless of any "rehabilitation."[14]

Similarly, if a preschool director were discovered to have sexually abused the students, he or she would likely face both civil and criminal penalties. The director might undergo extensive rehabilitation efforts to help reduce the risk that he or she would engage in further abuse of children. However, regardless of the effectiveness of the rehabilitation efforts, the state would not issue the individual a new license to found and direct a new preschool.

---

[14]This focus on the more fundamental issue of abusing a position of power and trust illuminates one of the fallacies of the attempts to enable perpetrators to resume a limited therapy practice (e.g., mandating that a self-identified heterosexual male therapist who has sexually abused female patients can conduct therapy, but only with male patients). It is not unlike allowing a justice who has admitted accepting bribes to resume the bench but only to adjudicate cases involving litigants of modest financial means who would not be able to offer a sufficiently tempting bribe.

Harvard psychiatrists Harold Bursztajn and Tom Gutheil (1992) analyzed from a different perspective the attempts to enable perpetrators to return to a limited therapy practice. Addressing the case of *Bash v. Board of Medical Practice* (1989) concerning a licensing board prohibiting a psychiatrist from treating females, Bursztajn and Gutheil noted that such interventions "do little to address the underlying failures of self and clinical management that characterize patient–clinician sexual contact. . . . In our forensic psychiatric experience . . . , cases where such contact has occurred are also characterized by other serious breeches of the standard of care, such as the failure to focus on the development of a therapeutic alliance essential for treatment to proceed. . . . We are concerned that the clinician who cannot be considered as competent to treat women should be considered as competent to treat men" (p. 1276). (For another case in which a hearing panel recommended that a therapist—this time a psychologist—was, for a period of time, "not to treat any female patients," see *Osborn v. Board of Regents of the State of New York et al.*, 1993, p. 362.)

Neither of these two offenders would necessarily be pre-
cluded from practicing their professions. The former judge
and preschool director, once rehabilitated, might conduct
research, consult, publish, lecture, or pursue other careers
within the legal and educational fields. However, serving as
judge or as preschool director are positions that involve such
trust—by both society and the individuals subject to their
immediate power—that the violation of such an important
and clearly understood prohibition against abuse of trust
(and power) precludes the opportunity to hold such positions within the fields of law and education. (Pope & Vasquez, 1991, pp. 110–111)

However, the ease with which perpetrators are able to achieve
"rehabilitated" status and return to practice reflects a stance
that therapists have a special exemption from the standards of
integrity applicable to others—such as judges and preschool
operators—in whom society in general and vulnerable individuals in particular invest special trust (see chapter 5).[15] This exemption may be related to a variety of contextual influences of
the type noted in this chapter:

1. To some extent the contextual influences may support a
deep and chronic sense of special entitlement among therapists
(see, e.g., Gilbert & Scher, 1989): There may be a widespread
belief that therapists who sexually exploit patients are inherently entitled to resume practice. This entitlement places the
professional beyond the mechanisms of accountability and responsibility applicable to others who hold regulated (e.g.,
through governmental licensure) positions of great trust.

2. To some extent the contextual influences may lead the
profession to ignore, discount, or condone decisions to ex-
pose—in the absence of informed consent—unsuspecting patients to the risks of entering therapy with a known (but not

---

[15]Interestingly, although people who have been known to sexually abuse
children may have difficulty finding any support in efforts to become a judge
or gain a license to operate a preschool, it may be much easier for them to
find prominent professionals who will support their efforts to gain licensure
as therapists.

to the patients) offender. These very real risks are ignored, discounted, or condoned by rationalizing that everyone lives in a world of risks. (Using this twisted logic, of course, no one need be informed of any risks in research because life itself involves risk.) Perhaps the most clear and forceful articulation of this view was set forth by a member of the pesticide regulatory board charged with protecting citizens against undue risks from pesticides. Discussing the use of Chlordane, which kills termites, the regulatory board member stated, "Sure, it's going to kill a lot of people, but they may be dying of something else anyway" ("Perspectives," 1990, p. 17).

3. To some extent, mental health professionals who violate trust may be viewed as nevertheless possessing such important skills that patients just should not or cannot do without them. As one licensing board member stated about an offender: "He contributes significantly to our society . . . and we thought that resource should not be denied to patients" (cited in English, 1992, p. 41). Unless all therapists are viewed as so important and skilled that permanent license revocation is unthinkable, this approach suggests that there may be at least two different standards or mechanisms of accountability: one for those renowned for their skills, and the other for everyone else.[16]

4. To some extent, the profession may view itself as possessing such effective skills that to ask for evidence that a par-

---

[16]A search of the literature unearthed no instance in which this argument (i.e., that the professional was such a resource for patients and made such contributions that patients should not be denied) was made on behalf of a female clinician. Whether this apparent absence was due to the inadequacy of the search, random fluctuations in instances reported in the literature, or cultural gender bias is unknown.

Any tendency to portray some therapists as so important and skilled that preventing them from practicing would be unthinkable would be thwarted, at least in part, by the bill that Senator McCorquodale introduced in California legislature on February 25, 1994. Senate Bill 2039, if enacted, would require the Board of Psychology to revoke any license to practice psychology upon a decision made, in accordance with specified procedures, that contains any finding of fact that the licensee engaged in any act of sexual abuse, or sexual relations with a patient, or sexual misconduct that is substantially related to the qualifications, functions, or duties of a psychologist or psychological assistant.

ticular intervention (i.e., rehabilitation) actually works is viewed as an affront to be answered on the basis of authority and self-esteem rather than evidence (e.g., "I am just sure that rehabilitation works. I wouldn't do therapy and value myself as a therapist if I didn't believe that people can change and that I am effective at bringing about that change."). One of the major difficulties—or strengths, depending on one's point of view— of this form of self-assurance is that the forms of assessment and intervention that it supports (e.g., astrology, phrenology, past-life regression) appear to be limitless.

5. To some extent, when instances of abuse in which the perpetrators are predominantly male and the victim/survivors are predominantly female cannot be denied (e.g., abuse is attributed to a supposedly inherent female disposition to invent false accusations), there is a tendency to lessen the perpetrator's responsibility or accountability by shifting the focus toward the behaviors or characteristics of the victim/survivor. What the individual said, wore, thought, fantasized about, or otherwise did is believed to indicate that the individual caused the abuse or must share responsibility or accountability for being abused. Both the professional and popular literature provide examples of the tendency to focus on ways in which people not only consent to but also elicit, cause, or share accountability for being sexually exploited (see Pope, 1990b, for examples), but some of the least subtle examples come from the courts.

□ A judge declined to convict two adult men of raping an 8-year-old girl because she was, in the judge's opinion, "a willing participant" ("Judge Urged to Resign," 1985, p. A6).

□ A judge refused to confine an individual who pled no contest to sexual assault of a 16-year-old girl because rape, according to the judge, is a "normal" reaction to the girl's "provocative clothing"—i.e., blue jeans, a blouse over a turtle neck sweater, and tennis shoes ("A Woman's a Sex Object," 1977, p. 2).

□ A judge took a 5-year-old girl's "character" into account in discounting the responsibility of the 24-year-old man who sexually assaulted her. According to the judge, she was "an unusually sexually promiscuous young lady. No

way do I believe that [the adult] initiated the sexual contact" ("Unbelievable," 1983, p. F2).

In this context, the longstanding "conspiracy of silence" (Belli
& Carlova, 1986; Brooten & Chapman, 1987) by which professionals refuse to acknowledge the harm that their colleagues
cause becomes a "conspiracy of accusation" in which the
profession focuses attacks on the person who was abused. It
is important to note that such analyses purporting to identify
ways in which a victim should be held accountable for causing
victimization seem to occur almost exclusively within the context noted at the beginning of this chapter (i.e., when perpetrators are generally male and victim/survivors are generally
female). Assume, for example, that Mr. X, a well-dressed man,
leaves his therapist's office and steps into an elevator of the
therapist's office building; at the next floor, a large man gets
on the elevator and robs him of $200 cash. It is unlikely that
clinicians, society more generally, or the courts will seek to
hold him accountable for the crime for reasons such as the
following:

☐ To be well dressed is to let potential robbers know that
you are unlikely to be poor and thus may have money
with you (i.e., the man is "asking for it").

☐ To enter an empty elevator is to assume responsibility for
placing yourself at risk for robbery or worse; Mr. X could
obviously have prevented the robbery by not placing himself in such a vulnerable position and thus must be held
accountable for the robbery (in fact, to go anywhere alone
is to invite trouble).

☐ To carry such a large amount of cash in these days of
credit cards, travelers checks, and so forth, is to do the
robber's work for him or her (i.e., take cash to where the
robber can get at it).

☐ Mr. X reached into his pocket, pulled out the $200, and
handed it over to the robber, thereby presumably consenting to the transaction.

☐ Mr. X had rented a number of action movies containing
scenes of robberies and other crimes, suggesting that he
may have been obsessed with being robbed, may have
had unconscious fantasies about being robbed, and may

have secretly wished to be robbed (in fact, he admitted
early developmental manifestations or "acting out" of the
theme of being robbed, having often role played as a child
a fantasy game that he called "cops and robbers").

When the contexts of the type discussed in this chapter (e.g.,
types of harm in which most perpetrators are male and most
victim/survivors are female) foster attempts to locate accountability in the victim/survivor, it may be useful to consider Is-
rael's attempts to address an epidemic of rapes. The Prime
Minister's mostly male cabinet concluded that the accountability of women for contributing to the epidemic (e.g., going out
alone and being out of the house at night) should be openly
acknowledged, explored, discussed, and used in strategies of
prevention. As a result of women's apparent contribution to
the epidemic, the cabinet decided to enact a curfew for women. Golda Meier, the Prime Minister, counteracted the contextual issues that were distorting the discussion and changed
the focus of the meeting by remarking, "Why not a curfew for
the men? They are the ones doing the raping" (Unger, 1979,
p. 427).

6. To some extent, therapists who sexually abuse patients
and those who enable them to resume practice may characterize
what offenders have done as a "mistake in judgment" due to
unhappiness, personal stress or distress, the absence of adequate support and nurturing by important others, burn-out,
financial pressures, trying to do too much, unrequited love,
difficult work conditions, role-strain, not enough positive feedback, preoccupation with family issues, poor work habits,
wanting to please too many people, unfulfilled longings, unresolved life questions, the fast pace of modern society, a bad
diet combined with not enough sleep and exercise, existential
uncertainty or angst, inadequate planning, not living up to
potential, well-intentioned bungling, or inattentiveness.

The attempt to compare decisions about whether to engage
in a prohibited activity that puts a vulnerable patient at risk for
deep and lasting harm to difficult professional judgments such
as whether a particular patient may be safely treated on an
outpatient basis, a particular couple will be better served by

individual or conjoint therapy, or a married 16-year-old would benefit more from an adult or an adolescent day-treatment program is one that involves significant distortion. The prohibition against therapist–patient sex is clear, long-standing, and absolute. Therapists do not carefully evaluate patients to arrive at a judgment about whether to engage in sex with patients and if so how and under what circumstances. Although the therapists in some of the documented cases summarized in chapter 4 make this claim, therapists do not engage in sex with their patients by mistake (in judgment or otherwise), unintentionally, or without realizing it. It is difficult to find reliable information about *any* instances of therapist–patient sex in which the therapists were either so out of touch with fundamental reality that they lacked understanding that they were engaging in sex with a patient or so lacking in voluntary motor control that they were unable to prevent themselves from engaging in the sexual act. Engaging in sex with a patient is a prohibited activity that places a patient at risk for pervasive and lasting harm, that may lead to a patient's suicide, and that is not an unintentional mistake of which the therapist was unaware.

7. In some instances, professionals, either individually or together within their associations, may attempt to enable those who offend to continue practice by attributing the commission of sexual abuse by therapists to some form of mental illness, psychiatric or psychological impairment, result of debilitating emotional wounds, and so on. According to this approach, a disorder was the necessary condition that caused the offense; once the disorder is alleviated through rehabilitative treatment, there could be no reasonable alternative to allowing the perpetrator to continue practicing. Morton Rapp, of the Whitby Psychiatric Hospital in Ontario, remarked upon the licensing board's directing some sexually exploitive therapists to "seek psychotherapy. Such an event tempts one to raise Szasz's spectre of the danger of medicalizing all abhorrent acts and of the 'therapeutic state.' . . . Whether [such therapy to rehabilitate offenders] should ever occur is an open question" (Rapp, 1987, p. 194).

It is important to note that the seemingly settled and un-questionable decision that abusive therapists, once rehabili-tated, have a justified sense of entitlement to resume practice, are too important to deprive patients of their services, and so on is a separate issue from this question: Is there *any* published evidence that any approach to rehabilitation actually works that adequately addresses such fundamental research questions as the following:

- ☐ How many systematic investigations were completed?
- ☐ For those systematic investigations that produced evi-dence that the rehabilitation approach was effective, what was the size of the sample?
- ☐ How was "success" measured?
- ☐ Was the time period covered by the research appropriate to the hypothesis?
- ☐ Did the perpetrator's previous knowledge of or experi-ence with . . . instruments used to assess rehabilita-tion . . . invalidate, qualify, or in any way raise questions about the findings?
- ☐ What level of success did the rehabilitation program dem-onstrate?
- ☐ If the rehabilitation program depended on an accurate classification of offenders (e.g., offenders are divided into different types, with each type associated with a specific rehabilitation plan and "prognosis"), what are the reli-ability and validity of the classification system, as for-mally and impartially assessed?
- ☐ Was the investigation conducted by a disinterested party? (We all share a very human trait: When we develop or endorse a particular intervention or method of classifi-cation, we are not disinterested observers of its efficacy, its intended results, or its unintentional side effects.)
- ☐ Was the research conducted in a way that meets the high-est ethical, legal, clinical, and similar applicable stan-dards? (For example, were there adequate informed con-sent forms by which future patients of therapists who were returned to practice after trial or experimental re-habilitation interventions gave their fully informed and voluntary consent to be put at risk to see how well, if at all, the rehabilitation program actually works?)

□ Was an adequately detailed report of the research published in a peer-reviewed academic, scientific, or professional journal?

□ Has the apparently low base rate of reporting been taken into account in the validation study? (If not, even completely worthless rehabilitation strategies may seem to work for all offenders. The low base rate—like other methodological issues such as validity and reliability—can be adequately addressed by appropriate research design and statistical analysis; what is crucial is that such essential research issues be addressed adequately in research planning, considered carefully in selecting appropriate statistical techniques, and reported candidly in research reports.) (Pope, Butcher, & Seelen, 1993, pp. 171–186)

It is difficult to find any published evidence meeting these fundamental criteria that shows any effectiveness of rehabilitation interventions (see O'Connor's statement in The Subsequent Therapist as Former Perpetrator, in chapter 3). The American Psychological Association Insurance Trust (1990) concluded that the "recidivism rate for sexual misconduct is substantial" (p. 3),[17] and the executive directors of the California licensing boards for psychology, social work, and marriage and family counseling concluded that for sexually exploitive therapists

---

[17]Current policies regarding returning sex offenders to licensed status may be severely suppressing licensing complaints by exploited patients. Exploited patients who file licensing complaints are providing an unpaid (i.e., licensing tribunals do not grant financial awards to the prevailing party) service to future potential victims of the therapist. It is also a service that is likely to cost them in terms of time, effort, and discomfort (e.g., through cross examination by the offender's attorney). To the extent that they see their efforts as ineffective and not worth the cost (i.e., the offender will resume practice after a trial or experimental rehabilitation), they may believe that the profession is more concerned with protecting and enabling offenders than ensuring patient safety and welfare and that filing a licensing complaint is pointless. As with insurance caps (see, e.g., *American Home Assurance Co. v. Cohen*, 1993), the effect would be to suppress the apparent rather than the actual scope of the problem as reflected in the number of licensing complaints and disciplinary actions.

"prospects for rehabilitation are minimal and it is doubtful that they should be given the opportunity to ever practice psychotherapy again" (Callanan & O'Connor, 1988, p. 11).

Contexts of the type discussed in this chapter can exert strong influences on the social and professional responses to issues of therapist–patient sex, which in turn can be reflected in the individual clinician's response to a patient who has been sexually exploited by a prior therapist. The clinician brings more to the patient, however, than the potential effects of these contexts. It is to the individual characteristics of the subsequent clinician that we turn in the next chapter.

Chapter

3

The Subsequent Therapist

Attending carefully to historical, cultural, and professional contexts—of which the previous chapter provided a few examples—can help subsequent therapists to conduct a more informed and meaningful examination of their own personal characteristics. These characteristics influence how therapists respond to patients who have been sexually exploited by a previous therapist, and whether the response is informed and helpful.

It is crucial to reemphasize this book's premise that there is no one-size-fits-all method of providing assessment, therapy, or forensic services to sexually exploited patients. Whereas there are some clinical or forensic practices that clearly cause harm to patients or others, violate professional standards, or create unnecessary risks, the uniqueness of patients, subsequent therapists, and situations call for a diversity of approaches. The purpose of surveying subsequent therapists' personal characteristics in this chapter is *not* to suggest that there is one set of characteristics (e.g., personal experiences, beliefs, tendencies, behaviors, and clinical needs) that fosters acceptable practice but rather to encourage the notion that careful attention to such characteristics—while preparing for, providing, and later reviewing clinical and forensic services to sexually exploited patients—is an important part of work in this area.

What the Therapist Does and Experiences With a Patient

The following list presents a small sample of what a therapist might do, experience, or encounter with a patient. The list focuses attention on a variety of boundary issues, physical— and specifically sexual—events, feelings, and other aspects of the therapeutic situation.

Behaviors, Experiences, and Events

- ☐ Using self-disclosure as a therapy technique
- ☐ Disclosing details of current personal stresses to a client
- ☐ Telling a client that you care about him or her
- ☐ Crying in the presence of a client
- ☐ Having clients address you by your first name
- ☐ Holding a client's hand
- ☐ Hugging a client
- ☐ Kissing a client
- ☐ Lying down next to a client
- ☐ Lying on top of or underneath a client
- ☐ Cradling or otherwise holding a client in your lap
- ☐ Giving a massage to a client
- ☐ Reassuring a client that having sexual feelings about a therapist is not uncommon
- ☐ Noticing that a client is physically attractive
- ☐ Telling a client that you find him or her physically attractive
- ☐ Suggesting that a client tell you about his or her sexual fantasies
- ☐ Telling a sexual fantasy to a client
- ☐ Engaging in sexual fantasy about a client
- ☐ Flirting with a client
- ☐ Feeling sexually attracted to a client
- ☐ Telling a client: "I am sexually attracted to you"
- ☐ Hearing a client tell you that he or she is sexually attracted to you
- ☐ Feeling sexually aroused while in the presence of a client
- ☐ Noticing that a client seems to become sexually aroused in your presence

- ☐ Noticing that a client seems to have an orgasm in your presence
- ☐ Talking with a current client about sharing a sexual relationship after termination
- ☐ Becoming friends with a client after termination
- ☐ Telling a client that you are angry at him or her
- ☐ Raising your voice at a client because you are angry at him or her
- ☐ Having fantasies that reflect your anger at a client
- ☐ Feeling hatred toward a client
- ☐ Telling a client of your disappointment in him or her
- ☐ Feeling afraid that a client may commit suicide
- ☐ Feeling afraid that a client may need clinical resources that are unavailable
- ☐ Terminating therapy if a client cannot pay
- ☐ Lending money to a client
- ☐ Inviting a client to a party or social event
- ☐ Accepting a gift that is worth over $50
- ☐ Feeling afraid because a client's condition gets suddenly or seriously worse
- ☐ Feeling afraid that your colleagues may be critical of your work with a client
- ☐ Feeling afraid that a client may file a formal complaint against you

While patient and subsequent therapist meet and work together within the larger historical, cultural, and professional contexts discussed in chapter 2, what the subsequent therapist believes (e.g., will this client become sexually aroused? be my friend after termination? file a complaint against me? commit suicide?) and, in the context of those beliefs, does (e.g., self-disclose personal stress, hold a client's hand, suggest that a patient talk about sexual fantasies), help form the more immediate context for the therapist–patient relationship. Careful attention to this list may help strengthen the therapist's ability to distinguish between those behaviors (e.g., lying down underneath or on top of the patient) that are so likely to harm a patient that they should never be used and other behaviors that may, under appropriate circumstances, be helpful. What is important is that the therapist arrive at decisions about how to shape the immediate context of the professional relationship on the basis of adequate attention to the nature, meaning, implications, and likely consequences of the relevant behaviors.

Using the preceding list might involve responding to three sets of questions in regard to each item:

1. *Has the therapist ever done, experienced, or encountered what the item describes while working with any patient?*

If not, why?

If so,

- Did it ever arise as a topic in consultation or supervision, either before or after it occurred?
- What consequences did it have?
- Was it recorded in the treatment notes or chart documentation?
- Did it seem to occur more frequently with male or with female patients?
- Did either therapist or patient comment on it?
- What did the therapist or patient learn from it?
- If the therapist engaged in any of the therapist behaviors, did the behavior represent more a carefully planned act based on thoughtful deliberation or more a spur-of-the-moment intuitive impulse?
- How, if at all, did any of the therapist behaviors seem to be based on an appropriate (or inappropriate) response to the patient's needs?
- How, if at all, did any of the therapist behaviors seem to be based on a response to the therapist's needs?

2. *Has the therapist ever done, experienced, or encountered what the item describes while working with any patient who had been sexually involved with a previous therapist?*

If not, why?

If so,

- Do the therapist's responses to any of the questions in regard to Item 1 change in any way?
- How, if at all, was it related to the patient's experience of sex with a prior therapist?

☐ If the patient has disclosed this information or if it is
   available from any other source, to what degree did the
   previous therapist do, experience, or encounter any of
   the listed items and how, if at all, did this affect the
   patient?
☐ If the patient filed a malpractice suit or other formal complaint, did the subsequent therapist's behavior in regard
   to any of the listed items ever arise as an issue in deposition, trial testimony, or other hearings?

3. *Does the subsequent therapist anticipate doing, experiencing, or
encountering what the item describes in future work with a patient
who has been sexually involved with a prior therapist?*

When considering decisions about whether to engage in the
listed therapist behaviors,

☐ Are decisions about whether to engage in any of the
   behaviors (e.g., hugging a client, suggesting that a patient describe sexual fantasies) consistent with the therapist's theoretical orientation?
☐ Have such decisions been influenced by consultation with
   colleagues?
☐ For any behaviors that the therapist has decided against
   ever engaging in, can the therapist imagine any situation
   in which such a behavior might serve a therapeutic purpose?

Readers interested in considering their own responses to these
items in light of national survey information will find relevant
data in Appendix A.

The Therapist's Clinical Needs

Therapists may confront numerous stressful prospects and
events in their work. One national study suggested that almost
all (97%) have been afraid that a client may commit suicide,
about 29% have experienced a client suicide, about 83% have
been afraid that a client would attack them, about 19% have
been physically attacked by a client, about 89% have been afraid
that a client would attack a third party, about 61% have worked

with a client who attacked a third party, about 66% have been afraid that a client would file a complaint against them, about 12% have had a client file a complaint against them, and about 53% have felt so afraid about a client that it affected their eating, sleeping, or concentration (Pope & Tabachnick, 1993).

Particularly in light of these stressful events and prospects, therapy can play an important role in the life of the therapist, and there is some evidence from a recent survey that newer therapists are making more use of this resource (Pope & Tabachnick, in press). About 81% of the therapists over 50—in contrast to 93% of the therapists under 40—have been in therapy.[18] Most (61%) reported that they had been what they would describe as clinically depressed. Over one fourth (29%) reported having felt suicidal and almost 4% reported having made at least one suicide attempt. Therapists may resist revealing certain kinds of information to their own therapists. One in five reported refusing to disclose important information to his or her therapist. The majority of these secrets involved sexual issues.[19]

From their earliest training, therapists are reminded of their ethical obligation to avoid allowing personal distress, impairment, or clinical needs to negatively affect their work with patients. As many as 60%, however, have reported having worked when too distressed to be effective (Pope et al., 1987). It is crucial that therapists working with exploited patients monitor carefully their own clinical needs to ensure that the patients do not encounter yet another destructive therapy. Subsequent therapists may find it particularly useful to review carefully The Therapist's Personal Responses to the Patient and to the Work, in chapter 4; some responses may reveal clinical needs of the therapist that can be addressed in other settings so that they do not distort the subsequent therapist's work with an exploited patient.

---

[18]More female (90%) than male (80%) therapists report having been patients in therapy.

[19]The ability of therapists to withhold important sexual information from their own therapists may have troubling implications for rehabilitation trials in which it is believed that the offender has not engaged in such withholding.

Personal Involvement With Abuse

The most immediate personal involvement in abusive or potentially abusive acts is as a victim/survivor or perpetrator. The degree to which a subsequent therapist has or has not been personally involved in abuse and how such experiences may affect the therapist's work warrant careful attention and examination.

The Subsequent Therapist as Victim/Survivor

Abuse experienced during childhood or adulthood is capable of inflicting deep, lasting harm, although, of course, such significant and extensive harm may not occur for a specific individual. Research suggests (see Table 3) that the experience of abuse is not a particularly rare event in the history of therapists. These anonymous self-report data, taken together, suggest that about two thirds (69.93%) of the female therapists and one third (32.85%) of the male therapists have experienced at least one of the listed phenomena.

The subsequent therapist's history of having suffered abuse can, in work with sexually exploited patients, serve as a resource, create vulnerabilities, or both. One of the greatest potential effects that a history of having suffered abuse can render is to ground the subsequent therapist's understanding of the nature of abuse in personal experience. The subsequent therapist knows firsthand at least some of what it can mean to be an abuse victim/survivor. This personal experience may make it a lot less likely that the subsequent therapist will reflexively dismiss or discount a patient's reports of sexual involvement with a therapist (see chapter 2), will fail to recognize common patterns of harm, or will ignore the implications of such reports for further assessment. The subsequent therapist may also have firsthand experience of what it is like to address abuse issues *as a patient* (Pope & Tabachnick, in press; see also Feldman-Summers & Pope, 1994).

Having experienced abuse firsthand, however, can also create vulnerabilities, but they are vulnerabilities that can be safely addressed in the context of responsible practice. Just as the

Table 3

Percentages of Male and Female Therapists Reporting Experience of Abuse

Type of Abuse Reported by Therapists	Male Therapists	Female Therapists
During Childhood or Adolescence		
Sexual abuse by relative	5.84	21.05
Sexual abuse by teacher	0.73	1.96
Sexual abuse by physician	0.00	1.96
Sexual abuse by therapist	0.00	0.00
Sexual abuse by nonrelative (other than those previously listed)	9.49	16.34
Nonsexual physical abuse	13.14	9.15
At least one of the above	26.28	39.22
During Adulthood		
Sexual harassment	1.46	37.91
Attempted rape	0.73	13.07
Acquaintance rape	0.00	6.54
Stranger rape	0.73	1.31
Nonsexual physical abuse by a spouse or partner	6.57	12.42
Nonsexual physical abuse by an acquaintance	0.00	2.61
Nonsexual physical abuse by a stranger	4.38	7.19
Sexual involvement with a therapist	2.19	4.58
Sexual involvement with a physician	0.00	1.96
At least one of the above	13.87	56.86

Note. Adapted from Pope and Feldman-Summers, 1992, by permission.

subsequent therapist who has never suffered abuse must ensure that this particular background does not distort clinical or forensic work with patients who describe abusive experiences (e.g., through assuming that if the therapist has been able to avoid abuse then the patient likewise should have been able to and therefore must have secretly wanted the abuse, enjoyed the abuse, caused the abuse, fabricated the abuse, etc.), the subsequent therapist who has experienced abuse must ensure that this experience does not distort clinical or forensic work.

The subsequent therapist bears a responsibility to avoid, for example, assuming that the patient's experience of abuse was identical—or even similar—to the therapist's experience, that the abuse has the same level of importance in the patient's life that it does in the therapist's life, or that the patient must address the abuse in the same way that the therapist did. It may be extremely useful for subsequent therapists to consider frequently how the specifics of their own personal experience are affecting the degree to which they identify with, empathize with, maintain effective boundaries with, and manage issues such as dependence and independence, attachment and separation, and autonomy and control, with a patient. In light of the patient's sexual involvement with a prior therapist, these issues are likely to be especially powerful.

As the findings in Table 3 suggest, the percentage of therapists who have been sexually involved with their own therapists is relatively low, probably less than 5%. Patients are unlikely to assume that subsequent therapists have been sexually involved with their own therapists. If patients have any impulses to idealize therapists, to see them as having exaggerated power or charmed lives, they may forcefully resist the idea that a subsequent therapist has been involved as a patient in therapist–patient sex. In light of these and other obvious factors, self-disclosure by a subsequent therapist that he or she has been involved as a patient in therapist–patient sex is likely to have a strong impact on a patient.

As always, subsequent therapists cannot validly and therefore should *never* reflexively assume that a patient is having a particular reaction. Some reactions to self-disclosure, however, are relatively common and it is useful to be particularly alert to these possibilities:

☐ The disclosure may shock, disconcert, and frighten some patients for whom the subsequent therapist has become symbolically associated with power and protection. Learning that the therapist, whom the patient has idealized, could be abused may leave the patient feeling suddenly exposed and vulnerable.

☐ The patient may begin to contrast the patient's and the therapist's experiences in a self-punishing and self-defeating manner. If the subsequent therapist seems, in the patient's estimation, to have suffered more, the patient may discount his or her own experience of abuse (e.g., "What I went through was really nothing compared to what my therapist and other *real* abuse survivors have gone through. I should quit my whining. I'm embarrassed that I brought it up at all."). If, on the other hand, the patient seems to have suffered more, the patient may berate himself or herself for having mishandled the experience or lacking strength to get on with it (e.g., "You went right on and became a therapist and have a happy life and all, but I let it knock me completely into the ground, I haven't gone to school or anything since it happened, and I don't know why I even pretend to go on. I just don't have what it takes.").

□ The patient may believe that the therapist will be unable to help.

□ The patient, having learned from the popular press that those who are abused tend later to turn into abusers themselves, may begin to fear that the subsequent therapist, having been involved in therapist–patient sex as a patient, will turn into a sexually exploitive therapist.

□ The patient may become so focused on the therapist's experience of abuse that the roles seem to reverse. The focus can shift from the patient's experience to the therapist's. The patient may seek to spend therapy sessions listening to, understanding, and responding to the therapist's experience. The patient's needs and treatment are forgotten. This potential dynamic can represent a reenactment of the patient's experience with the previous therapist: The clinical needs of the patient fade in importance and are overshadowed or replaced entirely by the needs and wants of the therapist.

The Subsequent Therapist as Former Perpetrator

The fact that a subsequent therapist has previously engaged in abuse presents significant difficulties and raises complex issues. In light of the high level of trust involved in psychotherapy, it might generally be assumed by potential patients, the profession, and the public that an individual with a history of abusing a patient would not be entitled to resume practice (see chapter 2). The assumption is not always valid, however.

A fundamental vantage point for considering whether therapists who have engaged in therapist–patient sex should be allowed to return to practice after rehabilitation highlights informed consent. To struggle with this issue is to take serious account of what professors Jean Holroyd and Annette Brodsky (1977) concluded was one of three major professional issues that needed to be addressed: "that therapists who disregard the sexual boundary once are likely to repeat" (p. 849). The executive officer of the California Board of Psychology brought this particular informed consent issue into focus.

> In much more trivial matters that do not threaten the safety of citizens, we would not think of proceeding with such an experiment until there is reliable evidence that a product or procedure is both safe and effective. To take the example of therapists who sexually abuse their patients, who can name even one independently conducted study published in a scientific or professional journal showing that any rehabilitation intervention has ever worked? When someone claims to have an effective treatment, drug, or intervention, we test *first* for safety and effectiveness and *then* approve it for general use. But pressures to protect abusive and dangerous licensees from accountability may have resulted in ignorance of this fundamental principle.
>
> If in fact there is no evidence based on independently conducted studies published in scientific or professional journals which establishes the effectiveness of rehabilitation programs for therapists who have sexually abused their patients, then are not all interventions currently used—both by definition and in actuality—trial interventions? Who is exposed to the harm caused by bogus or ineffective trial interventions that enable abusive therapists to return to practice? Is it not the consumers? A review [by Bates and Brodsky] of the research on consumers who are likely to be sexually victimized in therapy reveals: "The best single predictor of exploitation in therapy is a therapist who has exploited another patient in the past." Even the Insurance Trust of the American Psychological Association acknowledged that "the recidivism rate for sexual misconduct is substantial." Do those who

place consumers at risk of harm on the basis of experimental or trial diversion methods not have a responsibility to obtain informed consent of these consumers as they study and research their methods? According to the Nuremberg Code, the first principle of trying out procedures is to obtain the "voluntary consent" of those who are placed at risk. Consumers simply should not be used as guinea pigs, without their knowledge or consent, while diversion programs test as-yet-unvalidated procedures. (O'Connor, 1992, p. 4)

O'Connor not only set forth evidence and argument but also appealed to the profession's conscience: Until there is "evidence based on independently conducted studies[20] published in scientific or professional journals which establishes the effectiveness of rehabilitation programs for therapists who have sexually abused their patients," trial rehabilitation interventions must be tested "*first* for safety and effectiveness and *then* [approved] for general use." Any use of unvalidated rehabilitation interventions should, in accordance with the Nuremberg Code, inform subsequent patients of a perpetrator that they are being placed at risk for substantial harm as part of an investigation to test the "safety and effectiveness" of a rehabilitation intervention, should document clearly that they are aware of the risks and are voluntarily consenting to assume the risks and that they are aware of the means by which they are (or are not) being compensated for serving as research subjects and assuming the associated risks. In light of the contextual issues reviewed in chapter 2, however, a powerful impetus for adequate examination of complex rehabilitation issues may take the form of legal actions with their associated financial implications and publicity. Recently, for example, an article addressing a related area—the rehabilitation of priests—appeared under the headline "Center Must Pay $5.7 Million Over Abuse by Priest It Treated" (1994). The article quoted the plaintiff attorney: "They [the center] were negligent in the way they

---

[20]That is to say, studies that address the list of fundamental research questions outlined in the section "Accountability, Integrity, and Trust" in chapter 2.

treated him [the priest] . . . and they were negligent in suggesting that he was anything less that totally unfit for the priesthood. . . . They implied that he had been cured" (p. B13). Just as the large jury awards played a significant role in forcing the professions to attend more carefully to initial sexual offenses, it is possible that such awards will also play a significant role in forcing the professions to attend more carefully to rehabilitation issues. "It may be that the elimination of bogus rehabilitation efforts and of the overly hasty granting of 'rehabilitated' status to offending therapists will be facilitated by malpractice suits filed against those who are less than adequately professional, careful, thorough, and knowledgeable in assessing and rehabilitating offending therapists. Regardless of the circumstances, mental health professionals cannot in good conscience continue to enable offenders to practice in the absence of reasonably persuasive evidence of rehabilitation" (Pope, 1989a, p. 136; see also Pope, 1991; Pope, Butcher, & Seelen, 1993, pp. 177–186).

In addition to issues of informed consent, a second vantage point focuses on how a history of having perpetrated abuse might affect the subsequent therapist. Unacknowledged, unaddressed, or unresolved feelings about having engaged in abuse may find expression in countertransference or other distorted responses to the patient. These feelings may also be associated with beliefs that can profoundly bias the assessment process and other clinical endeavors. Research findings reported by UCLA professors Jean Holroyd and Jacqueline Bouhoutsos (1985), for example, suggested that therapists who had engaged in sexual involvement with at least one patient tended not to discern harmful consequences from such involvements, even when assessing patients who have been sexually involved with *other* therapists. Similarly, research findings reported by Harvard psychiatrist Judith Herman and her colleagues (1987) showed that 19% of the offenders believed that therapist–patient sex would benefit a patient and 21% believed that therapist–patient sex could be appropriate if the therapist and patient were in love.

A third vantage point presents a view of the subsequent therapist's history of abuse against the background of likely or potential forensic testimony. If the subsequent therapist has engaged in sex with a previous patient, a current patient's civil suit or other formal actions based on therapist–patient sex may be severely affected. Defense attorneys, for example, may attempt to shift the focus to the subsequent therapist's history as a perpetrator. Such attempts to shift the focus are common in civil suits, and they may have no other result than to muddy the waters and to obscure the major facts at issue. The defense may attempt to establish that because the subsequent therapist has been allowed to continue or resume practice despite having engaged in sexual relations with a patient, such a violation of professional standards is relatively trivial and not to be taken with great seriousness. The defense may attempt to establish that the subsequent therapist's history made it likely that he or she mishandled the subsequent assessment and treatment and therefore is both an unreliable source of information and a likely cause of any harm that the plaintiff may have suffered. If the subsequent therapist is appearing as an expert witness, the defense may focus on the subsequent therapist's history of engaging in therapist–patient sex abuse as relevant to potential bias in clinical judgment in light of the research reported by Holroyd and Bouhoutsos (1985), discussed previously. Whether the expert would be compelled to produce his or her own personal mental health records (e.g., assessment and treatment records about the expert's history as patient) would be decided according to the facts of the case and applicable law in that jurisdiction. To the extent that therapist–patient sex may be construed as similar to child sex abuse (see chapter 2), an appellate decision by Texas' Twelfth District Court of Appeals is interesting. *Cheatham v. Rogers* (1992) considered whether a counselor, whom the court had appointed—pursuant to a divorce decree—to provide assessment and counseling services to three children of the divorcing parents, should be compelled to turn over records of mental health services she had received. When a motion was filed to modify the decree, an attorney for one of the parents arranged to depose the counselor and served a subpoena requiring the counselor to produce "[a]ll psychological and/or psychiatric records in the custody of or subject to the control of [the counselor] . . . pertaining to the mental and/or emotional health of [the counselor] on which her examination is required" (p. 233). Contesting the subpoena, the counselor argued "that her personal mental health records are (1) confidential and not subject to disclosure . . . , (2) 'protected from discovery by [counselor's] right to privacy under the United States Constitution,' and (3) 'not relevant to any issue in dispute in this cause nor reasonably calculated to [lead] to the discovery of admissible evidence.' " (p. 233). The appellate court, however, held that the subpoena should be enforced. Justice Colley's opinion stated that applicable law "made a necessary intrusion upon the privacy rights of persons who become prospective expert witnesses in judicial proceedings involving the status, welfare, and interests of children. We are of the opinion that this vital and compelling state interest far outweighs [the counselor's] constitutional right of privacy with respect to her personal mental health records" (p. 236).

It is also worth noting research suggesting that perpetrators are *more* likely than nonperpetrators to provide clinical services to patients who have been sexually involved with other therapists. Psychiatrist Nanette Gartrell and her colleagues found that "A comparison of repeaters, one-time offenders, and non-offenders on this variable revealed highly significant differences, with repeat offenders the most likely to have treated previously involved patients and non-offenders the least" (Gartrell, Herman, Olarte, Feldstein, & Localio, 1987, p. 289).

Vulnerability to Making the Patient Responsible for the Offender's Actions

It is the therapist who *always and without exception* bears the professional responsibility to refrain from engaging in sex with a patient. Patients do not typically spend year after year in graduate school and internship during which they learn that they must never, no matter what the situation, enter into a sexual relationship with a therapist. Patients are not charged by licensing laws and regulations to avoid sexual encounters with a therapist. Patients are not usually professionals who have affirmed explicit ethical mandates to forego sexual involvement with a therapist. No laws impose criminal penalties on a patient for having sex with a therapist. No laws create a cause of civil action against a patient who becomes sexually involved with a therapist. Therapists, on the other hand, learn in graduate school and internship settings that therapist–patient sex is prohibited. A choice to engage in sex with a patient is not only a clear violation of the terms of their license, the ethics of their profession, and civil and sometimes criminal standards, but also a choice to place the patient at risk for significant harm.

The contextual factors described in chapter 2 and what has come to be called the profession's "conspiracy of silence" helped obscure the professional's fundamental responsibility to avoid engaging in sex with a patient, regardless of *any* characteristics of therapist and patient or of their situation. Psychologist Rachel Hare-Mustin (1992) wrote, "How can we understand the silence of the profession on this ethical issue? Sexual abuse . . . persists because of the professional collusion that does not hold the perpetrator accountable and allows him to continue to practice" (p. 408). As with legal defenses in rape and incest trials (see chapters 2 and 6), responsibility and accountability are, through a process of distortion, shifted blatantly or subtly away from the perpetrator and toward the victim/survivor.

Shifting blame from perpetrator to victim may be one of many ways in which context and other factors block effective responses to abuse. Considering instances in which two of Freud's colleagues perpetrated boundary violations against three patients and in which both colleagues and patients consulted Freud may suggest recurrent patterns or dynamics.

On May 30, 1909, one of Jung's patients with whom he had been intimately involved, Sabrina Spielrein, wrote to Freud asking for a consultation. Interestingly, Freud was not particularly honest with her. On June 7, he wrote Jung and assured him, "Well, after receiving your wire I wrote Miss Spielrein a letter in which I affected ignorance, pretending that her suggestion was that of an over-zealous enthusiast . . ." (cited in Bettleheim, 1983, p. 42). Persistent, she presented her information through correspondence. There are at least three major

themes to Freud's response, upon receiving additional information, to this patient who alleged that she has been involved
with her therapist: (1) the assertion that Jung could not and did
not behave improperly, (2) the idea that her feelings should be
obliterated, and (3) the idea that secrecy should prevail and no
one else should be involved. As he wrote to her on June 8,
"Dr. Jung is my friend and colleague; I think I know him in
other respects as well, and have reason to believe that he is
incapable of frivolous or ignoble behavior. . . . I would urge
you to ask yourself whether the feelings that have outlived this
close relationship are not best suppressed and eradicated, from
your own psyche I mean, and without external intervention
and the involvement of third persons" (cited in Carotenuto,
1982, p. 114). It was not until June 21 that Jung wrote to Freud
of what he had done with his patient: "I . . . deplore the sins
I have committed, for I am largely to blame. . . . Caught in my
delusion that I was the victim of the sexual wiles of my patient,
I wrote to her mother that I was not the gratifier of her daughter's sexual desires . . . my action was a piece of knavery" (cited
in Bettleheim, 1983, p. 42). Bettleheim noted that in one paragraph of this letter, "Jung refers to Spielrein both as his former
patient and as his patient in the present tense. That is, when
talking about their love affair he calls her his former patient,
but when asking Freud to write to her and convince her of his
honesty in having told Freud everything . . . , he calls her his
patient" (p. 42). Learning that his assumptions had been
wrong, Freud wrote a letter of apology to Spielrein: "I have
learned today something from Dr. Jung himself about the subject of your proposed visit to me, and now see that I had divined
some matters correctly but that I had construed others wrongly
and to your disadvantage. I must ask your forgiveness. . . . I
was wrong and . . . the lapse has to be blamed on the man
and not the woman, as my young friend himself admits. . . .
Please accept this expression of my entire sympathy for the
dignified way in which you have resolved the conflict" (cited
in Carotenuto, 1982, pp. 114–115). Professor Aldo Carotenuto
(1992) of the University of Rome noted: "Jung's letter to Freud
of July 10, 1909, expresses his 'heartfelt thanks for your friendly
help in the Spielrein affair, which was resolved so positively.'

The positive nature of the conclusion for Jung and Freud con-
sisted in their not having been damaged by the affair" (p. 187).
On October 26 of the same year (1909), Sándor Ferenczi wrote
to inform Freud that he had become intimate with one of his
patients, Gizella Pálos. He noted the possibility that it might
be a long-term relationship even though "I admitted to her . . .
having sexual desires toward other women and even re-
proached her for her age" (cited in Brabent, Falzeder, & Giampieri-Deutsch, 1993, p. 88). When Ms. Pálos consulted Freud
about the relationship in December, 1911, Freud assured her
in a letter that "When I . . . became acquainted with you, I
quickly learned to esteem you. . . . Since then, not a word or
a gesture has issued from me that could have weakened his
attachment to you" (pp. 319–320). On July 14, 1911, Ferenczi
had informed Freud that he had now taken Ms. Pálos' daughter,
Elma, as a patient, and by December 18, he wrote Freud that
"[his own] marriage with Elma seems to be decided. . . . Frau
G. [Gizella Pálos] . . . the other, more severely ill patient . . .
is suffering greatly" (pp. 321–322). By the end of December,
Ferenczi describes the mother as having happily devoted herself to making her daughter and Ferenczi happy. Subsequently,
the daughter is transferred to Freud for treatment. However,
Freud was not honest with her about Ferenczi and yet wrote
to Ferenczi about his patient, her diagnosis, and her treatment
(although Freud asked her not to tell anyone about her analysis). The treatment with Freud ended and the daughter returned to Ferenczi for treatment. For a long stretch of time,
Ferenczi simply could not decide permanently which woman
he wanted to marry. In March, 1912, he wrote that what he
had learned about the daughter through her analysis "significantly diminished her in my eyes, and . . . my eyes have again
focused on the qualities of Frau G." (p. 352). The next month
he wrote that he had told the daughter "that Frau G. is indis-
pensable to me . . . and that I have in her everything that I
need, except for the youth which I seek in her (Elma)" (p. 364).
He noted that "the pendulum swings in my inclination between
Frau G. and Elma" (p. 367). At one point he reported that he
was trying to "live together experimentally, in a threesome"

(p. 368). With no sense of irony, he noted that "the analysis with Elma is going very, very slowly" (p. 381). Ferenczi describes himself as in a painful dilemma. On one hand, he felt that he had learned much about the daughter through being her therapist and he was reluctant to "build my house on such a shaky foundation" (p. 381). On the other hand, there was "Frau G.'s age and the sexual intercourse with her that is not entirely satisfying physically" (p. 383). He repeatedly noted the pain that this circumstance caused him but found ways to address his limited options (e.g., between what he perceived to be shaky foundation and unsatisfying intercourse): "I decided to get relief by the normal way of prostitution" (p. 390). Finally giving up what he called his sexual overestimation of the daughter, he noted "she no longer attracts me personally" (p. 413), and eventually married her mother.

Four aspects of Freud's response to Elma, his patient who was sexually involved with his colleague, are particularly interesting. First, he agreed to withhold information from her. At one point he assured Ferenczi that "I will tell Elma nothing about your trip" (p. 348). Second, he interpreted any desire for revenge on her part as resistance to the therapy. Third, there was his description of her personality; in this he was in explicit agreement with Ferenczi: manifest narcissism. Finally, there was his formulation of the presenting problem of this woman who was the patient and sexual partner of Ferenczi who had also become the therapist and sexual partner of the woman's mother. It seemed clear to Freud: "She falls in love compulsively with doctors" (p. 327).

It is possible that all subsequent therapists may be, at least to some extent, vulnerable to prejudices that shift the professional responsibility for refraining from therapist–patient sex from the therapist to the patient. The specific features that elicit this prejudice are likely to differ for each subsequent therapist, although there are obviously some that are extremely common. It is crucial that subsequent therapists be aware of these potential prejudices that can block or distort appropriate clinical or forensic services.

Psychologist Lenore Walker (1994) constructed three fictional vignettes, each designed to elicit personal reactions from subsequent therapists and to foster professional collusion that relieves the perpetrator of responsibility and blames the patient. Each vignette describes a scene in which the therapist *did* sexually abuse the patient. Walker's skillful patterning of potentially prejudicial information, however, tends to bring many readers around to suspect that the therapist–patient sex was less unacceptable, less likely to be harmful for the patient, and more likely to be brought about and deserved by the patient.

> A senior and extremely prominent therapist, one who has contributed much to the field and is recognized for his humanitarian values, is going through a painful divorce. He becomes despondent, considers suicide, but continues to try to meet the pressing and legitimate needs of his many patients who rely on him for help. . . . A patient repeatedly tells him how attractive he is and how grateful she is. She wears extremely revealing tight lycra clothing and behaves in a skillfully seductive manner. During one session, suddenly and without the therapist's consent, she steps out of her clothes, unzips his pants . . . and performs fellatio on him. She then threatens to take her life unless he has sex with her each week. At a very low period in his life and extremely concerned for his patient's welfare, he gives in.

> A chronic and severe borderline patient has, in the course of her 41 years, engaged in numerous sexualized relationships with authority figures. In four previous courses of treatment, each one of her therapists labeled her exceptionally "promiscuous." She has held only three jobs in her life. Each time she seduced her boss. She has been married four times; in each instance, her husband filed for divorce after discovering that she was having affairs with friends. In addition to the borderline condition, she has been found, on the basis of psychological testing and formal assessment, to be his-

trionic, alcoholic, a chronic liar, and occasionally mildly psychotic. She has had three abortions (each time unable to identify the man who impregnated her) and suffered from a variety of venereal diseases.

The life history of Ms. X reveals her to be an exceptionally angry and litigious woman. She has initiated 11 separate lawsuits: 4 against medical doctors, 3 against therapists, 2 against stores ("slip and fall" cases alleging negligence of the store), 1 against a driver (whom she alleged ran a stop sign and hit her car), and 1 against an attorney who had represented her in one of the suits. Her current therapist maintains that, as he reviews the situation in retrospect, she did not seem to be seeking therapeutic services in good faith and had only sought his help in order to file a lawsuit against him. As a result, he felt that they had never really formed a therapeutic alliance or professional relationship, and thus the sexual relationship did not seem to produce any harm as it might have had it occurred in the context of a genuine therapeutic relationship. (Walker, 1994, pp. 210–211)

It is hard to overestimate the power and resilience of these prejudicial factors that can so overwhelm attempts to provide useful and appropriate clinical and forensic services. They are similar to the reflexive but fallacious assumptions that an individual who does not leave a job but claims to have been sexually harassed over a long period of time must have either fabricated or wanted the harassment and that a prostitute's claim that she has been raped must of course be false or exaggerated. Alertness to such common prejudices, like alertness to countertransference, can help clinicians avoid revictimizing patients and colluding with offenders.

Adequate knowledge and awareness of social, professional, and historical contexts (chapter 2) as well as the subsequent therapist's personal characteristics (discussed in this chapter) are essential aspects of providing clinical and forensic services to patients who have been sexually involved with a therapist. Attending carefully to these issues allows the subsequent therapist to create safe, appropriate, and helpful working conditions with a sexually exploited patient, the topic of the next chapter.

Chapter

4

Working Conditions

Whatever their theoretical orientation, clinicians working with sexually exploited patients must decide how to structure the work; how to initiate, maintain, and monitor essential processes (e.g., informed consent and assessment); and how to create conditions in which therapy may proceed. In some instances, a therapist makes decisions (e.g., no sexual behavior with the patient, no insurance fraud, no provision of services beyond the therapist's realm of competence). In some instances, therapist and patient collaborate in making decisions although either has a veto (e.g., establishing meeting times). And in some instances, the patient makes decisions (e.g., issues in the domain of informed consent). It is the therapist's responsibility to ensure that such decisions are accorded due attention, that their implications are adequately understood by the patient, and that responsibility for making the decisions is not inappropriately transferred (e.g., the therapist does not unilaterally decide that the patient will be subject to an intervention that places the patient at risk, and the patient does not unilaterally decide whether therapist and patient will have a sexual relationship).

The working conditions, which may evolve considerably after the first few sessions, can either support, protect, and empower therapist and patient in their work together or, in the extreme alternative, set the stage for disaster. This chapter focuses on seven crucial aspects or components of the working conditions that tend to be especially problematic in clinical and forensic work with sexually exploited patients.

Patient Knowledge and Consent

The patient who discloses sexual involvement with a prior therapist may not know that such involvement is unethical, that it places the patient at risk for serious harm, and the patient may seek to be "made whole" again through civil action. Any patient has a basic right to informed consent, but that right may have special meaning for the sexually exploited patient. The previous therapist took advantage of the patient's vulnerability and engaged in an act for which the patient's consent is meaningless (see chapter 1) but for which the patient (see chapter 5) and often society (see chapter 2) may blame the patient. Thus the patient may struggle within a catch-22—deprived of genuine consent but treated as if he or she not only consented to but was responsible for the abuse—and be unable to take seriously the idea of giving or withholding informed consent.

Perhaps the first task in addressing informed consent with a sexually exploited patient is to help ensure that the patient recognizes that the process of consent (or refusal to consent) is crucial and complex. For example, simply signing a form or passively agreeing with what the clinician says is in the patient's best interests does *not* constitute consent. The patient must know the options (including the option to decline assessment or therapy, even though such refusal may have complex consequences), have relevant information to understand the options, and arrive at a voluntary decision about what to do.

Second, the information must be understandable and useful. Approaches to informed consent should not be rote and oppressive but rather helpful, respectful, and, to use the concept developed by Seattle psychologist Laura Brown (in press), "empowered consent." Brown provided a detailed discussion of empowered consent that may be useful to any clinician working with sexually exploited patients. All too often, however, the notion of the patient's right to consent as a valuable and empowering resource gives way to an indifferent, resentful, or defensive approach.

> Nothing blocks a patient's access to help with such cruel efficiency as a bungled attempt at informed consent. . . . The doors to our offices and clinics are open wide. The resources are all in place. But not even the most persistent patients can make their way past our intimidating forms (which clerks may shove at patients when they first arrive), our set speeches full of noninformative information, and our nervous attempts to meet externally imposed legalistic requirements. A first step in remedying the situation is to recognize that informed consent is not a static ritual but a useful process. (Pope & Vasquez, 1991, p. 74)

Using forms as part of the process can produce numerous benefits and is especially important in forensic evaluations. Putting the most important issues into written form helps ensure that none is overlooked, minimizes the chances of miscommunication, and guards against memory's distortions. It also gives the patient something that can be taken home and studied at leisure. A written explanation can help the patient secure consultation or advice from others about what may be an exceptionally important set of decisions. It is equally important, however, to avoid the potential pitfalls of using forms. As Harvard psychiatrist Tom Gutheil and his colleagues wrote,

> The overriding danger of the form is that it tempts the clinician to treat the transaction as a discrete task that is accomplished, and thus terminated, once the patient has signed the form. This unfortunate misuse of the form defeats the very purpose of informed consent, which is to foster and sustain an ongoing dialogue. . . . At any point along the way, the patient should feel free to ask questions about the impact of the treatment, the impact of medication, the effects of the procedure, and so on. (Gutheil, Bursztajn, Brodsky, & Alexander, 1991, p. 79)

Third, the process of informed consent must address the central issues that could influence whether a person decides to participate in assessment or therapy. Appendixes B and C present a range of these issues relevant to sexually exploited patients.

Boundaries

Establishing safe, reliable, and useful boundaries is one of the most fundamental responsibilities of the therapist. The boundaries must create a context in which therapist and patient can do the work of therapy. They must form an environment in which the patient may experience and give voice to the most intense, unexpected, and powerful feelings, impulses, images, fantasies, and longings in the presence of another person, yet never be at undue risk for exploitation. They must accord reasonable privacy so that the patient is free to discuss what seems most embarrassing, undesirable, disgusting, frightening, or taboo.

Fees

One of the first boundary issues that therapist and patient confront concerns fees. Gutheil and Gabbard (1993) observed, "Money is a boundary issue in the sense of defining the business nature of the therapeutic relationship. This is not love, it's work" (p. 192). They noted that letting a debt accumulate by not attending to unpaid therapy bills may be viewed with great suspicion by those evaluating the therapist's work. "In the minds of fact finders, this raises a question: 'The clinician seems curiously indifferent to making a living; could the patient be paying in some other currency?'—a line of speculation one does not wish to foster" (p. 192).

Gutheil and Gabbard have raised one of the most significant and profound fee questions, one important for any therapist but especially for the therapist working with sexually abused patients. Therapists must ask themselves, "Why am I doing this? What do I want or expect to get out of it, what do I *actually* get out of it, and what happens (to me, to therapy, to the patient) when what I actually get out of it doesn't match up with what I want or expect?" Another set of questions focuses directly on the therapist–patient relationship: "Would I have any motivation to provide services to this particular person if I were not being paid a salary (by the mental health center, clinic, hospital, etc.) or a fee (by the patient, an insurance company, a managed health care plan, etc.) for this work? If so, would the motivation be sufficient (i.e., for me to provide these services to the patient) if I were not receiving a fee or salary? Is money a necessary condition for my helping this person? If I received no salary or fee, would I refuse to help the person?"[21] This process of clarification can be acutely uncomfortable, surprise the therapist, and even lead to changes in the nature or direction of a career path. It allows the therapist to identify needs and wants that may have been obvious but overlooked, to confront sources of satisfaction that may seem questionable or potentially harmful, and to uncover motivations that tend to remain stubbornly hidden from awareness. It enables the therapist to anchor the financial boundaries in a realistic foundation, to refrain from extorting or stealing what Gutheil and Gabbard termed "other currency" from a patient, to clarify candidly the ways in which financial boundary issues may be influencing the patient and the therapy, and to avoid rejecting or punishing—sometimes through extremely subtle and indirect ways—the patient for the therapist's dissatisfaction with the rewards of the work.

One of the most astounding attempts to play off financial currency against what Gutheil and Gabbard termed other currency in the context of sexual boundary violations occurred in a letter that Carl Jung wrote to the mother of Sabrina Spielrein, one of his patients (see chapter 3). Addressing the nonpayment of fees, Jung wrote:

> I moved from being her doctor to being her friend when I ceased to push my own feelings into the background. I could

---

[21]In some instances, patients seem to be more aware than the therapist of how financial factors influence the therapist's motivation and the therapist–patient relationship; in other instances, patients may hold distorted attributions (e.g., that idealize or denigrate the therapist's motivation to meet with the patient). Too often, patients may believe that raising such issues in therapy is taboo, and therapists may believe that raising such issues in supervision or consultation is taboo.

drop my role as doctor more easily because I did not feel professionally obligated, for I never charged a fee. The latter clearly establishes the limits imposed upon a doctor. You understand, of course, that a man and a girl cannot possibly continue indefinitely to have friendly dealings with one another without the likelihood that something more may enter the relationship. For what would restrain the two from drawing the consequences of their love? A *doctor* and his *patient*, on the other hand, can talk of the most intimate matters for as long as they like, and the patient may expect her doctor to give her all the love and concern she requires. But the doctor knows his limits and will never cross them, for he is *paid* for his trouble. . . .

Therefore I would suggest that if you wish me to adhere strictly to my role as doctor, you should pay me a fee. . . . In that way you may be *absolutely certain* that I will respect my duty as doctor under all *circumstances*.

As a friend of your daughter, on the other hand, one would have to leave matters to Fate. For no one can prevent two friends from doing as they wish. . . . My fee is 10 francs per consultation. (cited in Bettleheim, 1983, p. 42)

Research suggests that about 20% of the sexually exploited patients who enter subsequent therapy are charged a reduced fee or no fee at all (Pope & Vetter, 1991). The importance of self-examination in regard to needs, wants, motives, and other factors influencing financial boundary decisions does not mean that providing free or low cost services should become inherently suspect. There are compelling reasons for professionals to provide services to those who have been harmed by the profession and who cannot afford to pay the going rate. Gutheil and Gabbard (1993), for example, noted that "most clinicians learned their trade by working with indigent patients and feel that some attempt should be made to pay back this debt by seeing some patients for free—a form of 'tithing,' if you will" (p. 192). What is crucial is that the financial (as well as other) boundaries reflect the therapist's honest and searching inventory of needs, wants, motives, and other factors. The most serious trouble tends to result when therapists remain unaware of impulses that are contrary to the explicit rationales for the boundaries, as when a therapist who wants to be paid ends up not only providing free therapy but also resenting and sometimes hating the patient as a result. Considering such issues, Freud (1913/1958a), while emphasizing instances of "unpaid treatment [that] does not meet with any obstacles that I have mentioned and [for] whom it leads to excellent results" (p. 133), observed that for many therapists the patient's fee is "a medium for self-preservation" (p. 131) and that it is "more respectable and ethically less objectionable to acknowledge one's actual claims and needs rather than . . . to act the part of the disinterested philanthropist" (p. 131).

Chapter 6 discusses additional considerations for fees in forensic work with sexually exploited patients.

Nonsexual Touch

Most—but not all—therapist–patient sexual activity involves therapist and patient sexually touching each other. Consequently, any form of physical contact with the subsequent therapist may assume great significance for sexually exploited patients. (It is important to recognize that in some cases of sexual exploitation, mutual sexual touching does not occur; for example, a therapist may sit across the room and only watch— perhaps while masturbating—as he tells a patient to undress, assume certain positions, and masturbate.)

Whereas some therapists engage in various forms of nonsexual physical contact (e.g., holding the patient's hand or hugging) with specific patients, others may believe that such contact is a precursor to sexual contact. To date, there are no research data published in peer-reviewed scientific or professional journals supporting the notion that therapists who engage in nonsexual physical contact with patients are more likely to become sexually involved with patients (Pope, Sonne, & Holroyd, 1993, p. 281). Psychologists Jean Holroyd and Annette Brodsky, who conducted the first national study of therapist– patient sexual contact, found that the research did suggest that sexual intercourse with patients was associated with *differential* touching.

Erotic contact not leading to intercourse is associated with older, more experienced therapists who do not otherwise typically touch their patients at a rate different from other therapists (except when mutually initiated). Sexual intercourse with patients is associated with the touching of opposite-sex patients but not same-sex patients. It is the differential application of touching—rather than touching per se—that is related to intercourse. (Holroyd & Brodsky, 1980, p. 810)

Even if therapists do not believe that nonsexual touching (i.e., touching that is not differential according to gender) places them at risk for engaging in sex with patients, they may fear that colleagues who are aware of the touching will suspect that they are engaging in or likely to engage in sexual activities with patients. They may fear that it places them under a cloud of doubt. Many therapists may be suffering from a *touch anxiety* that is similar to that experienced by many adults "in regard to increasing public acknowledgment of child sexual abuse: Adults may be reluctant to hold children and to engage in nonsexual touch that is a normal part of life" (Pope & Vasquez, 1991, p. 105). Therapists "may go to great lengths to ensure that [they] maintain physical distance from . . . [clients] and under no circumstances touch them for fear that this might be misconstrued" or that it may subject therapists "to an ethics complaint or malpractice suit" (p. 105). Both patient and therapist are badly served when decisions about treatment are based solely on avoidance of being sued. The ways in which normal, nonsexual human touch have been made to seem inherently dangerous, wrong, and harmful unfortunately represent one of the many ways in which "the small, atypical group of therapists who have violated the prohibition against therapist–client sexual intimacies have not only exploited their clients but also helped to create an atmosphere in which" even the most normal human experiences and acts "seem dangerous and daunting for the vast majority of therapists who, whatever their sexual feelings toward patients, would never seriously consider violating the prohibition and placing their patients at risk for great and lasting harm" (Pope, Sonne, & Holroyd, 1993, pp. 4–5).

A decision to avoid any patient contact (or even proximity) that is based on touch anxiety must be clearly distinguished from a decision to avoid patient contact for other reasons. There is a substantial literature supporting the use of nonsexual touch with certain patients in certain situations (see, e.g., Bosanquet, 1970; Geller, 1978; Hopkins, 1987; Kohrman, Fineberg, Gelman, & Weiss, 1971; Mitchum, 1987; Pope, Sonne, & Holroyd, 1993; van der Kolk, 1993). However, there are a variety of conditions under which therapists may decide to ensure that nonsexual contact does not occur. For example, nonsexual contact is incompatible with certain theoretical orientations. Some (but by no means all) classical Freudian psychoanalysts avoid physical contact with patients on a theoretical basis. As another example, some patients may find physical contact with a therapist frightening, intrusive, unpleasant, and unwanted (see, e.g., Brown, 1989). As still another example, a therapist may find that some forms of touch are incompatible with the therapist's personal style and approach. Gartrell (1994), for example, discussed her experiences as a both client and therapist and concluded, "From my experiences as a client, from my understanding of the dynamics of sexual exploitation, and from my work with survivors of sexual abuse, I believe that a general policy of 'NO HUGS' for clients fits most comfortably with who I am" (p. 106).

If nonsexual physical contact between therapist and patient is not inherently incompatible with the therapist's approach, the following steps may be useful in creating appropriate and therapeutic boundaries.

First, the therapist can find out whether the nonsexual physical contact is unwanted by the patient. This is an aspect of informed consent. It is important to recognize that some patients may be ambivalent. For example, one patient who had been sexually involved with her previous therapist made it clear to her subsequent therapist that she would find any physical contact terrifying and invasive. She and her therapist agreed at the outset that no physical contact would occur and that even routine contact (e.g., a handshake) would be avoided. During the third year of therapy, however, the woman began to beg to be held and comforted by her therapist. She focused on increasingly vivid memories of how her mother had virtually never held her and seemed always to reject her. Session after session she lay on the couch and sobbed, pleading with her therapist to hold her as the only way that she might be comforted and healed. During this period, the therapist said something along the lines of "It hurts to see you in so much pain. I would hold you if I believed that it would help rather than harm you. But I believe strongly that holding you would not help you with this pain and that it would probably make things worse. There are other ways that we can work together. I believe that part of you knows and understands this because when we started our work together you asked me to make sure that no physical touching occurred no matter what happened." As time passed, the woman felt terrified (at the intensity of her desire for contact), enraged (at the therapist for maintaining the boundary), despairing (that she would always suffer and never find the comfort and healing that she longed for), ashamed (at her neediness), and embarrassed (at the fantasies that eventually evolved in which she imagined being held and comforted by her therapist and then using the physical closeness to stimulate herself sexually). Later, once she had made great progress in working through these issues, she reflected on something she had never previously disclosed: Even when she longed most intensely to be held and comforted in the therapist's lap, she had been terrified that her therapist might permit such contact despite their initial agreement that such contact would never occur.

Second, the therapist can determine whether nonphysical contact might be consistent with, and play a therapeutic role in, the treatment plan. Again, any prospects for physical contact as well as specific permission should be discussed with the patient as part of informed consent. Obviously, these considerations and the decisions should be adequately documented in the chart notes.

Third, the therapist can explore with the patient the meaning that nonsexual physical contact has for the patient. For some patients, for example, needs for recognition, validation, tenderness, nurturing, appreciation, or respect may have become confusingly blended with needs for physical (either sexual or nonsexual) contact.

Fourth, therapist and patient can explore the patient's account of the exploitive therapist's use, if any, of nonsexual touch. This history of touch is likely to be an important part of the background against which touch (or the absence of touch) in the subsequent therapy may be experienced and understood.

Fifth, the therapist can, as with other issues, be alert to ways in which the approach to physical contact issues in work with a sexually exploited patient serves the personal needs of the therapist rather than the clinical needs of the patient.

Roles and Relationships

When deciding whether to offer clinical or forensic services to any person, the therapist must determine whether there are roles or relationships that constitute an actual or apparent conflict of interest or otherwise threaten the boundaries and integrity of the professional relationship. Competent therapists are scrupulous to avoid entering into harmful dual or multiple relationships with their patients. Providing services to patients who have been sexually involved with a therapist requires the subsequent clinician be free of ties to the exploitive therapist. For example, assume that Mr. X seeks therapy from Dr. Y, telling her that he has been sexually involved with a former therapist, Dr. Z. If Drs. Y and Z are co-chairing their professional association's new "Let's Create a Better Public Image for Therapists" committee, Dr. Y's working relationship with Dr. Z creates an apparent (and probably actual) conflict of interest. Similarly, if Drs. Y and Z were business partners or co-workers in the same mental health clinic (so that the client's decision to file formal complaints would be likely to result in bad publicity for Dr. Z and financial and other penalties for the business or clinic), good friends, or otherwise shared a history of significant relationship, Dr. Y would, if she were to provide assessment, therapeutic, or forensic services to Mr. X, be entering into an apparent and probably actual conflict of interest. Any act or failure to act (during assessment, therapy, or forensics) by Dr. Y that might seem to dissuade Mr. X from filing a complaint, to bring Mr. X's veracity into question, to minimize Mr. X's distress, and so on would raise reasonable questions—in Mr.

X's mind when he later discovered and reflected on the special relationship between Drs. Y and Z, or in the minds of others whose perspective would not be subject to distortion by the special relationship—about Dr. Y's perspective, decisions, professional opinions, and interventions being slanted, however unintentionally, toward protecting Dr. Z at the expense of Mr. X. In such instances, a revictimization occurs: In the subsequent therapy as well as in the original, Mr. X's legitimate rights and interests are subverted and exploited to meet the needs of Dr. Z.

Session Length and Place

Decisions about whether to adjust the boundaries of time (e.g., by providing extended or frequent sessions) or place (e.g., a therapist meeting a patient outside the office) most often arise in work with sexually exploited patients when risk of suicide or self-injury such as mutilation increases. These issues are discussed in the section "Increased Suicidal Risk" in chapter 5.

Information

One of the most important boundaries for sexually abused patients is the boundary protecting what the patient talks about as part of the subsequent therapy. As is emphasized elsewhere (see, e.g., appendixes A and B), patients must understand any exceptions to confidentiality or privilege that are related to any formal complaints they may file against the offender. They must also understand other factors that may allow or require the subsequent therapist to disclose—in response to a valid subpoena,[22] through filing of a mandated report, during a deposition, and so forth—confidential information to third parties.

---

[22]Because wrongful disclosure of confidential information can be so damaging and because clinicians generally do not have appropriate training, authorization, and experience to make legal determinations, it is *strongly* recommended that any clinician who receives a subpoena for records or other information always consult first with his or her own attorney *before* taking any other action in response to the subpoena.

Patients can, of course, authorize the therapist to disclose information to other people. It is important that such authorization be written to ensure that rights to informed consent for waiver of confidentiality be respected. The *General Guidelines for Providers of Psychological Services* (APA, 1987), for example, stresses that unless otherwise authorized by law,

> Psychologists do not release confidential information, except with the written consent of the user involved, or of his or her legal representative, guardian, or other holder of the privilege on behalf of the user, and only after the user has been assisted to understand the implications of the release. (p. 21)

One of the most common disclosures to third parties is reporting information—from basic information about presenting problems and diagnosis to comprehensive accounts—to insurance companies or other organizations that pay for or authorize the provision of clinical services. Both therapist and patient may make false assumptions about the degree to which the information sent to such organizations remains private. Despite financial and other incentives to avoid spending much time and attention on this topic, therapists have a significant responsibility to determine that patients' consent to waiving confidentiality is genuinely informed. Keith-Spiegel and Koocher (1985) presented a hypothetical example of a therapist's routine statement to patients reflecting the uncertainty about what happens to information once it is submitted to an insurance company:

> If you choose to use your coverage, I shall have to file a form with the company telling them when our appointments were and what services I performed (i.e., psychotherapy, consultation, or evaluation). I will also have to formulate a diagnosis and advise the company of that. The company claims to keep this information confidential, although I have no control over the information once it leaves this office. If you have questions about this you may wish to check with the company providing coverage. You may certainly choose to pay for my services out-of-pocket and avoid the use of insurance altogether, if you wish. (p. 76)

In a regrettable number of instances, the negligence of the therapist leads to disclosure of confidential information to those who have no legitimate rights to the information. More than half (61.9%) of the therapists in one national study reported *unintentionally* violating their patients' confidences (Pope et al., 1987). Therapists must be scrupulous to avoid

- □ discussing confidential information on cordless or cellular phones or other transmitting devices whose signals might be intercepted by unauthorized receivers
- □ consulting with fellow professionals "on the run" in places where confidential information might be over-heard
- □ leaving confidential messages for patients on telephone answering machines that other people besides the patient may have access to
- □ playing back answering machine messages from patients while other people are in the room and can hear the messages
- □ leaving patients' charts or other documents out on one's desk or elsewhere so that colleagues or others can see the names of patients or other confidential information to which they have no legitimate rights of access (when the therapist or other custodian of the chart is not present, a secure lock should stand between a chart and those not authorized to see the chart)
- □ faxing confidential information to an unsecured machine so that one is unsure who will see, read, and perhaps take the documents
- □ sending confidential information via electronic mail that might be intercepted or read by unauthorized parties
- □ gossiping about their patients.

The therapist may violate the patient's trust and reliance on the boundaries around confidential information if the therapist does not ensure that the patient clearly understands who will have access to the chart in the absence of the patient's written authorization for release of information. For example, a patient seeing a hospital-based therapist may assume that only the therapist and the medical records clerk will have access to the chart; despite the patient's assumption, the chart may be available to all staff clinicians, one or two of whom may be social acquaintances of the patient. As another example, a patient receiving services through an employee health care plan from a large managed health care organization may believe that mental health records will be kept separate; confidential communications to the therapist, however, may become part of a general medical record and, depending on the employee contract for health services, may be available in some form to the employer. The therapist bears the responsibility to provide adequate information about access and management of the patient's chart to the patient so that the patient's decisions about how to proceed can be informed.

Clinicians must avoid carelessness when recording information in the chart. It is impossible to know how many people in health care, forensic, or other settings may eventually read a chart. Imagine, for example, a sexually exploited patient who tells his therapist a dream in which the previous therapist was embezzling money from a hospital. The dream has symbolic meaning for the patient, but the patient knows that the previous therapist never embezzled funds. The subsequent therapist jots down the previous therapist's name in the chart alongside the phrase "embezzled money from the hospital." The subsequent therapist is sure that he will remember the meaning of these notes. Two disastrous consequences follow. First, the medical record librarian and other people authorized to see the chart see the chart notation, assume that they have made a fascinating discovery, and start passing along the secret to their friends and colleagues. Soon virtually everyone in the small community "knows" that the previous therapist has embezzled money. Second, when the patient's malpractice case against the previous therapist comes to trial, the defense attorney highlights that chart entry and makes it appear that the patient is a liar. The claim that the chart notation referred to a dream is discounted because there is no mention of any dream. Clinicians must remain aware that whatever is recorded in the chart may be read by other mental health professionals (and sometimes lay people) and may become the focus of intense examination in a trial.

Finally, the case of *Dr. K v. State Board of Physician Quality Assurance* (1993) can serve as a reminder of situations in which patients appear to lose control over the privacy of their treatment records.

> After receiving formal written complaints[23] that psychiatrist and his former patient were having a romantic relationship, and the psychiatrist was depressed and abusing alcohol, State Board of Physical Quality Assurance initiated investigation and subpoenaed psychiatrist's records relating to patient's treatment. Psychiatrist filed motion to quash subpoena [which was denied]. Patient filed motion for reconsideration which was denied. . . . The Court of Special Appeals . . . held that: (1) Board had authority to begin investigation on basis of complaints, notwithstanding contention that matter was beyond the scope of Board's authority because personal relationship between psychiatrist and patient began after doctor-patient relationship terminated; (2) fact that patient had not complained about psychiatrist's behavior did not preclude disciplinary investigation; and (3) patient could not assert her constitutional right to privacy to bar disclosure to Board of records of her treatment by psychiatrist, as right to privacy was outweighed by state's compelling interest. (p. 453)

---

[23]"The complaints to the Board resulted from a visit to the complainants, both of whom are physicians and colleagues of Dr. K, by Dr. K's estranged wife. She alleged that Dr. K was having a romantic relationship with a former patient and that he was depressed and drinking heavily. The complainants then visited Dr. K personally and discussed his wife's charges. After listening to Dr. K's explanation of the events, which included an admission by the doctor that he was then maintaining a romantic relationship with patient A, they informed him that they would be filing a complaint with the Board because they felt that his relationship with a former patient violated professional ethical standards for a psychiatrist" (p. 455).

Revising the Boundaries of Therapy

At times a therapist working with a sexually exploited patient may reach an impasse in trying to decide whether to create, maintain, change, or cross a particular boundary. When stuck, the therapist may find it useful to consider the following 10 questions, which are abstracted from a much more detailed presentation by Pope, Sonne, and Holroyd (1993, pp. 179–190):

☐ No consideration is more fundamental than this: Is the contemplated action consistent with the prohibition against therapist–patient sexual involvement?

☐ Is the contemplated course of action likely to lead to (by way of a slippery slope) or create a risk for sexual involvement with the patient?

☐ Has the therapist clearly and consistently communicated to the patient that sexual involvement cannot and will not occur, and is the contemplated action consistent with that communication?

☐ Should taking the contemplated action be deferred until sexual and related issues have been clarified?

☐ Is the contemplated action consistent with the welfare of the patient?

☐ Is the contemplated action consistent with the basic informed consent of the patient?

☐ How is the patient likely to understand and respond to the contemplated action?

☐ Is the therapist competent to carry out the contemplated intervention?

☐ Does the contemplated action fall substantially outside the range of the therapist's usual behaviors? [That the contemplated action is unusual does not necessarily suggest that something is wrong with it. The creative therapist will probably try creative interventions. The typical therapist—if there is such a person—will probably engage in atypical behaviors from time to time. But possible actions that seem considerably outside the therapist's general approaches probably warrant special consideration.]

☐ Is there a compelling reason for not discussing the contemplated action with a colleague, consultant, or supervisor? One red flag to the possibility that a course of action is inappropriate is the therapist's reluctance to disclose it to others.

Evoking the Previous Therapy Sessions

No matter how carefully boundaries are created and maintained, the meetings with the subsequent therapist may be startlingly evocative, for the patient, of meetings with the previous therapist. The structural similarities of two treatment situations have the potential to cue memories that the patient experiences as painful, frightening, and overwhelming. The similarities may elicit or intensify flashbacks, startle responses (with the associated fight-or-flight impulses—perhaps prompting the patient to flee the consulting room during a session or flee the subsequent therapy altogether), and other reactions. The similarities may deepen and complicate the transference.

The potential of the subsequent therapy sessions to stir up memories of a previous abusive therapy is similar to the potential of therapy sessions to evoke traumatic memories in victims of torture.

> The dyadic therapeutic situation itself may be evocative of certain aspects of the torture experience: for example, two people, one of whom is licensed by or a representative of the state or larger society and the other of whom is vulnerable and in need, meeting privately in a room; the questioning of extremely personal matters, a process often experienced as intrusive; the character of the regular sessions being explicitly subject to privacy; the discrepancy in power; and the intensity of emotion usually evoked by the process. It is crucial that the therapist monitor and maintain safe, appropriate, and therapeutic boundaries so that the therapeutic relationship does not unconsciously recreate or act out the destructive relationship between torturer and victim. . . . Moreover, the setting itself as well as certain procedures (e.g., an institutionalized bureaucracy, even spending time in the waiting room) may evoke traumatic memories. An awareness of these potential similarities can enable clinicians

to minimize the extraneous points of similarity and the likelihood that the treatment situation itself will elicit flashbacks
and other traumatic recreations. As Primo Levi (1988) wrote,
"the memory of a trauma suffered or inflicted is itself traumatic because recalling it is painful or at least disturbing"
(p. 24). (Pope & Garcia-Peltoniemi, 1991, pp. 271–272)

Alertness to the possibility that a patient may be experiencing
intensely painful memories—even within the first few moments of the first session—evoked by the similarities of current
treatment sessions to the previous, abusive treatment sessions
is an important responsibility of the subsequent therapist.

Reacting to Patients' Allegations

A clinician is meeting with the patient, perhaps for the first
time, perhaps after months or even years of working together.
Without warning, the patient says, "There is something that I
need to tell you. My last therapist and I once had sex at the
end of a session." How does the clinician go about considering
this allegation? One of the most fundamental and inviolable
principles is to avoid making reflexive assumptions. The clinician must never, for example, reflexively assume that allegations of therapist–patient sex are always true. The results of
one national study of 1,000 instances in which patients told
subsequent therapists that they had been sexually involved
with a prior therapist suggested that about 4% of the allegations
were false (Pope & Vetter, 1991). Just as a therapist must never
reflexively assume that an allegation, even if extremely plausible, is necessarily valid, a therapist must also never reflexively
assume that an allegation, even if extremely implausible, is
necessarily false.

The clinician who is familiar with the topic of therapist–patient sex, well-prepared, and competent to consider the prospect that a patient may have been sexually involved with a prior
therapist is knowledgeable about the most common scenarios
of therapist–patient sexual involvement. Pope and Bouhoutsos

(1986, p. 4) presented 10 of the most common scenarios as follows:

1. **Role Trading:** Therapist becomes the "patient" and the wants and needs of the therapist become the focus.

2. **Sex Therapy:** Therapist fraudulently presents therapist–patient sex as valid treatment for sexual or related difficulties.

3. **As If . . . :** Therapist treats positive transference as if it were not the result of the therapeutic situation.

4. **Svengali:** Therapist creates and exploits an exaggerated dependence on the part of the patient.

5. **Drugs:** Therapist uses cocaine, alcohol, or other drugs as part of the seduction.

6. **Rape:** Therapist uses physical force, threats, and/or intimidation.

7. **True Love:** Therapist uses rationalizations that attempt to discount the clinical/professional nature of the professional relationship and its duties (see also Twemlow & Gabbard, 1989).

8. **It Just Got Out of Hand:** Therapist fails to treat the emotional closeness that develops in therapy with sufficient attention, care, and respect.

9. **Time Out:** Therapist fails to acknowledge and take account of the fact that the therapeutic relationship does not cease to exist between scheduled sessions or outside the therapist's office.

10. **Hold Me:** Therapist exploits patient's desire for nonerotic physical contact and possible confusion between erotic and nonerotic contact.

The clinician must also be aware of the myths, misconceptions, false assumptions, rationalizations, and other factors that may lead subsequent therapists to reflexively dismiss, disbelieve, or discount a patient's allegations about sex with a previous therapist. The following 10 cases illustrate some of those factors.

Case 1

A psychiatrist who was the immediate past president of a state psychiatric association, chief psychiatrist at a prominent psychiatric hospital, and former chief psychiatrist at a state correctional facility, and who was described by a presiding judge as "a respected psychiatrist and community figure," was charged with engaging in sexual involvements with seven male and female patients (Matheson, 1984, 1985). The legal actions resulted in a revocation of his license and a five-year prison sentence. According to court records, the psychiatrist attempted to persuade the patients "that sexual activity with their psychiatrist was part of their therapy and that he trusted that if they reported the incidents, their stories wouldn't be believed" (Matheson, 1984, p. 2).

□ Case 1 highlights through contradiction a common misconception about therapists who become sexually involved with patients: that they are inevitably the least well-trained, the least prestigious or respected, the least successful, and the least influential therapists. Unfortunately, therapists found to have sexually exploited their patients have served in capacities such as president of state professional associations, chair of state ethics committees, member of state licensing boards, university professor, prominent media psychologist, nationally known researcher, and so on. These public reports are consistent with a national study of state ethics chairs and similarly prominent therapists, which showed that of the majority who acknowledged *intentionally* violating laws or ethical standards that they believed conflicted with their patient's welfare, 9% specified sexual involvement with the patient as the prohibited action they took to help the patient (Pope & Bajt, 1988). Such prominence places offenders in positions in which they can have great potential influence over the professional response to the issue of therapist–patient sexual involvement, the procedures for handling complaints, and the actual processing of complaints against abusers. To the extent that victim/ survivors become aware, through newspaper accounts and similar public sources of information, that perpetrators may be among those involved in reviewing their complaints, victim/survivors may be less likely to file with licensing boards, ethics committees, hospital and clinic administrative boards, university administrations, and so on.

☐ Case 1 likewise illustrates some therapists' attempts to portray sexual involvement as a legitimate part of treatment. It is similar to the distortion put forth by child molesters that the sexual abuse was actually sex education. Because the ethics codes of all major mental health professions now explicitly prohibit such involvement, it has become relatively rare that therapists use this defense in licensing hearings, malpractice suits, criminal prosecutions, and so forth. However, patients may be unaware of this prohibition (see, e.g., Vinson, 1987) or believe a therapist's declaration that this one instance is the exception to the general prohibition.

☐ Case 1 also illustrates the falseness of the common reflexive assumption that a therapist who engages in sexual relationships with patients of one sex is consequently not at risk for engaging in sexual relationships with patients of the other sex. Unfortunately, when licensing boards (or hospital administrators, etc.) attempt to deal with sexually exploitive therapists by limiting their practice to patients of one gender, the assumption underlying this intervention may not be justified (see chapter 2).

☐ Finally, case 1 illustrates the attempt of some sexually abusive therapists (as well as of some rapists and child molesters) to ensure secrecy by convincing the victim/survivor that he or she would never be believed.

Case 2

A 71-year-old therapist "admitted sexually assaulting a 17-year-old boy . . . by whipping him on the buttocks, hands and feet while the boy was naked." The therapist had maintained that such whippings were part of an innovative treatment "to help [the patient] overcome a drinking problem" ("Therapist Sentenced for Whipping Patient," 1987, p. 3B).

☐ Case 2 is another illustration of an attempt to portray sexual involvement with a patient as a pioneering, trailblazing, startlingly original treatment approach.

☐ Case 2 also illustrates sexual involvement with a minor patient, although this topic is often absent—as if it did not occur—from much of the writing in this area (see chapter 4).

Case 3

A female patient was awarded $4.6 million by a Superior Court jury on the basis of her charge that her therapist "had intercourse with her during more than two years of therapy." The therapist "contended that he hadn't rejected her demands for sexual intercourse because such rejection was followed by her threat of suicide" (Shearer, 1981, p. 8).

□ Case 3 is a variation of the "legitimate treatment" defense of therapist–patient sexual involvement. The involvement is portrayed not as treatment per se but rather as a therapist's desperate attempt (often taken at great sacrifice) to prevent harm to a patient (see Eyman & Gabbard, 1991).

□ Case 3 also illustrates the frequent attempt to portray sexually exploitive therapists as helpless victims of powerful patients, as having no alternative but to engage in sex with a patient. The patient is portrayed as "in control"; the therapist in this distortion is defenseless. This distortion is similar to that put forth by many rapists and child molesters: that they are the real victims and that the sexual abuse was the responsibility of the child who was sexually abused or the individual who was raped (see chapter 2).

Case 4

A prominent media psychologist had his license revoked on the basis of accusations that he had had sex twice a week with a female patient 15 years younger for a one-year period. The psychologist maintained that "he was in love with the woman, to the point of considering divorcing his wife and marrying the patient. But he maintained he didn't have sexual relations with her . . . until . . . after she had stopped going to him for treatment. Also, he said he was having impotency problems at the time, and was far too busy to have had an affair with her" (Bloom, 1989, p. B-1).

□ Case 4 illustrates the frequently used justification that termination legitimizes sexual involvement with a patient. For discussion of this issue, see Appelbaum and

Jorgenson (1991); Brown (1988); Gabbard (1989a, 1992, in press); Gottlieb, Sell, and Schoenfield (1988); Herman et al. (1987); Schoener et al. (1989); Sell, Gottlieb, and Schoenfield (1986); Shopland and VandeCreek (1991), and Vasquez (1991). In one national study of 958 cases of therapist–patient sexual involvement, harm occurred in at least 80% of the cases in which the sexual involvement did not begin until after termination (Pope & Vetter, 1991).

☐ Case 4 also illustrates the attempt to cloak sexual abuse under the all-purpose protection of love and marriage (see Gabbard, in press). This misconception seems to be deeply rooted in American culture, which has tended to accept, excuse, deny, or discount a wide variety of sexual and physical abuse occurring in the context of marriage. Walker (1979; see also 1994), for example, has documented the degree to which physically battering another person has tended to be viewed historically as unacceptable and reprehensible unless it occurs in the context of marriage (or of two partners living together), in which case it has tended to be viewed as an acceptable way to resolve disputes. Similarly, Estrich (1987), while a professor of law at Harvard, documented the degree to which our society had appeared to either legitimize or increase its toleration for rape that occurs in the context of marriage. States have formalized and institutionalized "marital immunity":

> As of 1985, only ten states had completely eliminated the marital exception. Nine states provide an absolute exemption so that even the most brutal rape by a husband is not a crime. The rest protect husbands in most situations; there are only limited exceptions, for example, if the spouses are living apart pursuant to court order or separation agreement. (Estrich, 1987, p. 74)

This distorted idea that love and marriage redefine, neutralize, or somehow legitimize any form of sexual abuse is often publicly expressed by prominent individuals. Estrich (1987) quoted a California legislator who proclaimed, in resisting attempts to eliminate the marital exemption: "If you can't rape your wife, who can you rape?" (p. 74).

Case 5

The Ethics Committee of the American Psychiatric Association reported expelling a psychiatrist for sexual involvement despite the therapist's demonstrating that the involvement commenced a considerable period after termination. The association asserted "that the precise timing of the sexual relationship was not relevant. Even if the sexual activity did not start until after the termination of therapy, the psychiatrist's sexual involvement with the patient constituted exploitation of the 'knowledge, power and unique position that [the doctor] held in the patient's mental life' " ("Recent Ethics Cases," 1982, pp. 8–9).

- □ Case 5, like case 4, illustrates the attempt to use termination as a justification for a sexual relationship with a patient.

Case 6

A psychologist was found to have sexually assaulted a female patient 44 years younger. The psychologist testified that "he remembered clearly that all he did was sit next to her and drape his arm around her shoulder. 'It was a reassurance and kind of reinforcement of what she had been accomplishing.' " He emphasized, "I meant if my hand inadvertently got in the area of her breast, I was unaware of it" ("Therapist Guilty in Sexual Assault," 1988, p. 28).

- □ Case 6 illustrates one of the most curious conceptions: the notion of unintentional and inadvertent sexual assault in the course of psychotherapy (see chapter 2).

Case 7

A psychiatrist responded to an opposing attorney's questions about engaging in sex with a patient.

Q. Did there ever come a time that she . . . performed fellatio on you?

A. . . . .Whether there was oral-genital contact in the course of therapy, I am not certain.

Q. In what respect are you uncertain?

A. I am not certain that it did occur.
Q. Were there ever any instances in which you took your clothes off in front of this patient?
A. I don't recall.
Q. Did you ever lie on top of her?
A. I don't recall.
Q. Did you ever penetrate her?
A. I don't recall.
Q. Did she ever manually stimulate you sexually?
A. I don't recall. (Plaisil, 1985, p. 190)

□ Case 7 might be understood as a variation of case 6's notion of unintentional and inadvertent sexual assault in the course of psychotherapy. Case 7 seems to introduce the notion that a therapist may be uncertain about whether a patient's mouth has touched his penis, whether the patient has touched his penis with her hand, and whether the therapist himself has taken off his clothes, lain down on, and sexually penetrated a patient.

Case 8

A prominent researcher and professor at a prestigious university lost a suit against the American Psychiatric Association, which he had sued to protest action taken against him on the basis of his treatment of a patient suffering from recurrent depression. The association had acted on their investigation into charges

> that [the therapist] gave her several gifts during the course of therapy including a book on female sexual fantasies; she received letters from him signed "with deep care, concern, and loving feelings" and "with love"; during therapy [the therapist] and the patient discussed their feelings of mutual attraction, with [the therapist] admitting that he was sexually attracted to her; [the therapist] often put his arm around the patient's shoulders, and at one point she told him that "she had experienced an orgasm during a hug while rubbing his thigh"; and [the therapist] revealed intimate facts to the patient about his marital difficulties and an affair he said he

was having with another woman. ("APA's Ethics Procedures Upheld As Fair," 1985, p. 1)

□ Case 8 illustrates the misconceived notion that the unethical handling of sexualized transference necessarily involves intercourse.

Case 9

The *Los Angeles Times* described the disciplinary action taken by the licensing board against a "psychologist [and professor at a local university] who once headed the ethics committee of the California State Psychological Association." One aspect of the case involved "sexual relations [with a patient] while she was in therapy with [the psychologist] from 1979 until 1982. . . . [The psychologist] also violated his profession's ethics by going into business with his patient and revealing to her confidential information about other patients, including a fellow psychologist and a child molester" (Jalon, 1985, p. II-6).

□ Case 9 is similar to some of the prior cases in illustrating that sexually exploitive therapists can be among the most prominent, successful, and influential clinicians.
□ Case 9 also illustrates the frequent linking of sexual and nonsexual dual relationships (American Psychological Association, Ethics Committee, 1988; Epstein & Simon, 1990; Simon, 1992b). Reviewing her research findings, Borys (1988) discovered "a clear relationship between sexual and nonsexual dual role behaviors" (p. 181). One subset of nonsexual dual relationships alone "accurately predicted" the "erotic practitioners" in 78.3% of the cases. Borys concluded,

> As with familial incest, sexual involvement between therapist and client may be the culmination of a more general breakdown in roles and relationship boundaries which begin on a non-sexual level. This link was predicted by the systems perspective, which views disparate roles and behaviors within a relational system as interrelated. Changes in one arena are expected to affect those in other realms of behavior. The results of the current study suggest that the role boundaries and norms in the therapeutic relationship, just as those in

the family, serve a protective function that serves to prevent exploitation. (p. 182)

Benowitz (1991) found a similar theme when she examined the experiences of women who had been sexually involved with a female therapist. "A major theme in the participants' experiences with the sexualized therapy was that it occurred in a general context of blurred or inappropriate boundaries, the most common of which was the blending of therapeutic and social contacts, both in and out of sessions" (p. 85). (See also Borys, 1992; Borys & Pope, 1989; Epstein & Simon, 1990; Mann & Winer, 1991; Simon & Sadoff, 1992.)

Case 10

Another psychologist who served on the state licensing board subsequently had his license revoked by the same board after he was "accused of having a sexual relationship with a patient [and] maintaining outside business relations with patients" (Pugh, 1988, p. 3; see also Colorado State Board of Psychology Examiners, 1988).

☐ Case 10 illustrates again the fact that respected and influential therapists can engage in sexual relationships with clients and that sexual and nonsexual dual relationships often seem interrelated, as was discussed in regard to the previous case, in both theory and practice.

Finally, when the topic arises, the clinician must not only be open to considering the possibilities but also communicate to the patient that the topic is not out of bounds but will be carefully explored.

Hearing complaints about a colleague is likely to elicit uncomfortable feelings of shock, anxiety, dismay, or disbelief. Such feelings may lead a subsequent therapist to screen out further information. The patient may discern, on the basis of the therapist's questions, comments, facial expressions, or body language, that this topic is taboo. The phenomenon is similar to that of some parents who are reluctant to listen to their children reveal that a kindly uncle has made sexual advances. It is also similar to the dynamics that make some therapists seemingly insensitive to their patients' tacit messages of suicidal intent. Therapists must convey their openness and attentiveness to anything the patient has to say. (Pope & Bouhoutsos, 1986, p. 82)

The therapist's care to avoid reflexive assumptions and to communicate to the patient that the topic will be carefully, sensitively, and respectfully explored is essential for creating conditions in which therapist and patient can work together.

Assessment Issues

Few tasks are more pivotal in providing appropriate therapeutic and forensic services than assessment. Careful assessment helps guide the selection of interventions that not only address the patient's clinical needs but also make sense in light of the patient's strengths and weaknesses. Assessment is not a brief, discrete examination limited to the first session or two; it is a continuing part of therapy. It is a process through which the therapist remains alert to changes in the patient, to the positive or negative effects of the treatment plan, to the need for changes in direction or alternative methods of treatment. Adequate assessment of a patient is an essential foundation for providing forensic testimony about the psychological status of the patient.

Purpose and Planning

No assessment should ever begin without the clinician clearly understanding the purpose and ensuring that the patient also understands. Only if the clinician clearly understands the purpose can he or she make useful decisions about matters such as whether standardized psychological tests would be helpful and, if so, which ones. The purpose enables the clinician to decide what background documents will be useful and perhaps necessary. In forensic cases, for example, the clinician may be asked to review all available clinical documents, including the case notes of the previous therapist (see appendix D). The purpose of the assessment will be an important factor in planning *in advance* how feedback will be provided, by whom, to whom, when, and under what circumstances. An assessment may also be conducted (by the therapist who is providing the treatment or by another clinician) as part of a formal review of the subsequent treatment and treatment plan for sexually exploited patients (appendix E); such assessments can focus in more detail on whether the interventions seem to be benefiting the patient, whether other interventions might be more helpful, and whether there are potentially important issues that have not yet been addressed.

Patient History

Any adequate assessment of a patient who has been sexually involved with a prior therapist must include a comprehensive history. Current information about the person's states, traits, abilities, functioning, and so on must not be taken out of context but rather be understood in relation to the person's development, experiences, and background. Failure to take an adequate history can lead to invalid assessment results and inaccurate or misleading characterizations of the patient.

Understanding other abusive experiences (in addition to the sexual involvement with the therapist) and other sources of distress or difficulty can be crucial. About a third of the patients whose characteristics are summarized in Table 4 suffered incest or other forms of child sex abuse prior to experiencing therapist–patient sex, and about one tenth had been raped. These prior events may mask or complicate the dynamics associated with therapist–patient sex.[24] For example, Washington, DC,

---

[24]*Dillon v. Callaway*, 1993, provides an example of a case in which a therapist became sexually involved with a patient who was an incest victim/survivor. *McNicholes [appellee] v. Subotnik [appellee] v. St. Paul Fire & Marine Insurance Co. [appellant]*, 1993, provides an example of an even more complex situation. According to the opinion, a patient "filed an action against Subotnik in the District Court claiming severe psychological injuries resulting from her sexual relationship with him." Her reason for beginning treatment was "because she recently had been raped and was also a victim of childhood incest" (p. 106).

Table 4

Characteristics of Patients Who Had Been Sexually Involved With a Therapist (N = 958)

Characteristics of Patients	n	%
Was a minor at the time of the involvement	47	5
Married the therapist	37	3
Had experienced incest or other child sex abuse	309	32
Had experienced rape prior to involvement	92	10
Required hospitalization at least partially as a result of the involvement	105	11
Attempted suicide	134	14
Committed suicide	7	1
Achieved complete recovery from any harmful effects of the involvement	143	17[a]
Was seen pro bono or for reduced fee	187	20
Filed a formal (e.g., licensing or malpractice) complaint	112	12

Note. Adapted from Pope and Vetter, 1991, p. 431, by permission.
[a]17% of the 866 patients who experienced harm

psychologist Christine Courtois, clinical director of the Center for Abuse Recovery & Empowerment, emphasized that

> Therapists in general, and abusive and subsequent therapists must understand the special vulnerability and the dynamic patterns of adults sexually abused as children (especially when the abuse was incest and especially nuclear family incest of long duration). These patients may present as highly sexualized and/or may develop sexualized attachments especially in relationships in which they are dependent. Therapists who don't understand this dynamic or know how to handle it or those who prey on vulnerable patients may easily exploit this interaction pattern. This is nothing short of professional incest and does great additional damage to the sexually abused client. (C. Courtois, personal communication, January 18, 1994)

In forensic cases, the defense may attempt to establish that any current distress or difficulties experienced by the patient are due exclusively to rape, incest, or other similar experiences rather than to sexual involvement with a therapist. Controlled research[25] conducted by Seattle psychologists Shirley Feldman-Summers and Gwyndolyn Jones (1984; see also Feldman-Summers, 1989), however, suggested that greater distress or difficulty from prior conditions was significantly associated with *increased* harm from therapist–patient sex. What had happened earlier in the patient's life seemed to intensify the destructive effects of sexual involvement with a therapist. If relevant to the findings of a specific forensic assessment, this research-based concept can be easily communicated in common-sense terms to a jury through analogy. Being hit by a car going 40 miles per hour tends to cause damage to a pedestrian. If the pedestrian is suffering and healing from a prior injury (e.g., internal organs are still mending, previously broken bones have not yet solidly knit together), being hit by a car going 40 miles per hour would tend to cause greater damage. The prior condition creates an increased vulnerability to harm. When the patient's history reveals abuse, trauma, or a similar event, the event may have created a special vulnerability (or predisposition) to harm from therapist–patient sex or a preexisting condition that is aggravated by therapist–patient sex, or both. It is important that the clinician clearly differentiate between these two concepts, which are discussed in chapter 6.

Conducting an assessment that excludes adequate examination of a comprehensive history can, when patients have experienced abuse, trauma, or similar events, make it likely that the emerging description of the patient will be false and misleading. Herman, Perry, and van der Kolk (1989), for example, found that what appear to be borderline characteristics, symptoms, or features can—if the clinician fails to take, and

---

[25]A sample of patients who had experienced sex with a therapist was compared to a matched group of patients who had been sexually involved with a nontherapist physician and to a matched group of patients who had not been sexually involved with a therapist or physician.

take into account, a detailed and accurate history—mask a trauma and cause a diagnosis such as posttraumatic stress disorder (PTSD) to be prematurely and misleadingly ruled out:

> It appeared that memories of the abuse had become essentially ego syntonic. The subjects generally did not perceive a direct connection between their current symptoms and abusive experiences in childhood. This finding is compatible with observations from follow-up studies of trauma victims . . . which indicate that fragments of the trauma may be transformed over time and relived in a variety of disguised forms, e.g., as somatic sensations, affect states, visual images, behavioral reenactments, or even dissociated personality fragments. (p. 494)

In some instances, a clinician's failure to take a history and tendency to select current characteristics out of context (i.e., the context of the patient's developmental and personal history) may represent more general trends in the misuse of the borderline and similar diagnostic labels (see, e.g., Reiser & Levenson, 1984).

Arriving at a diagnosis or descriptive evaluation of a patient that is grounded in a comprehensive history can be crucial in forensic contexts. Therapists often misuse the authority of their profession to dismiss allegations of sexual or nonsexual dual relationships as merely a symptom of severe pathology. Psychologists Judith Hall and Rachel Hare-Mustin (1983) reported one ethics case in which a psychologist found by the APA Ethics Committee to have engaged in a prohibited dual relationship attempted to invalidate the complaint as a product of hysteria. *Betrayal* (Freeman & Roy, 1976) described a therapist's attempt to discredit the patient's complaint as a product of paranoia associated with schizophrenia. Psychologists Joseph Sanders and Patricia Keith-Spiegel (1980) reported a dual relationship case considered by the APA Ethics Committee: "The psychologist flatly and indignantly denied the charges. He then painted the profile of a highly disturbed woman with considerable anger and sexual problems. Within days, however, he contacted . . . the ethics committee . . . , confessed that his letter was a fabrication, and admitted that the charges were true" (p. 1102). These examples illustrate a common pattern in ethics and legal cases: When the evidence has shown or will show that a dual relationship occurred, one of the first lines of defense is often an ad hominem (or ad feminam) form of argument (denigrating the motives, character, etc., of the complainant), dismissing the claim as a product of hysteria, of schizophrenic paranoia, of a highly disturbed and angry individual, and so on. In such hearings, patients may come to feel that the central question—"Did a dual relationship occur and, if so, what were its consequences?"—is ignored, that the patients themselves are put on trial as the probable offenders, and that the central question has become "Is the patient angry?" or "Does the patient suffer from a mental, emotional, or behavioral disorder?" Like many rape victims who have tried to press charges, patients who make valid claims of sexual abuse by a therapist may feel that they themselves are put on trial by illegitimate tactics—falsifying diagnoses, lying about the patient's history, and so on—that are far outside the bounds of fairness or even fundamental human decency.

A comprehensive history is also essential for assessments using standardized psychological tests (a topic discussed in a subsequent section). Psychologist Lynne Rosewater (1985, 1987), for example, conducted research demonstrating that if actual abuse histories are either unknown or not taken into account in efforts to interpret the Minnesota Multiphasic Personality Inventory (MMPI), invalid or misleading interpretations are the likely result, especially with a diagnosis of borderline personality disorder or schizophrenia (see also Pope, Butcher, & Seelen, 1993). Careful consideration of a potential borderline diagnosis may be crucial when a plaintiff contends that allegations of therapist–patient sex are reality-based, whereas a defendant contends that they are the manifestation of a psychotic transference associated with borderline disorder (see, e.g., *Goldberg v. Davis*, 1992).

The research-based concept of an ahistorical or antihistorical assessment as incomplete, invalid, and misleading can, if relevant to a forensic assessment, be communicated to a jury on a common-sense basis. Consider, for example, a scenario in which a woman in a clinic waiting room constantly asks the receptionist if the receptionist thinks that she is OK (constantly demanding reassurance), keeps demanding to be seen immediately although she does not have an appointment (self-centered, cannot delay gratification), goes from laughter to tears (rapid shifts of emotion), often sobs loudly (exaggerated emotion), and cannot give a clear reason for why she wants to be seen so quickly (impressionistic style of communication that lacks detail). If the clinician observes these characteristics and does not inquire carefully about history, a variety of invalid or misleading diagnoses may emerge. For example, the clinician may use the parenthetical descriptions as a basis for tentatively concluding that the woman suffers from a hysterical or histrionic personality disorder. If the reader, however, assumes the role of the hypothetical clinician and takes sufficient history to learn that the woman had been raped earlier in the day, the process of assessment and inference may be quite different from that of the ahistorical clinician who views current characteristics out of historical or developmental context.

It is crucial that subsequent therapists never reflexively assume that a sexually exploited patient is functioning at a developmental level indicated by an assessment conducted at an earlier point in the patient's life. Such assumptions do not take adequate account of the potential effects of the patient's involvement with the exploitive therapist. An appropriate therapy has the potential to help a patient achieve new developmental levels. Each theoretical approach has its own understanding of and vocabulary for this process. Alexander (1961), for example, referred to therapy as offering a "corrective emotional experience" (p. 329). However, a sexually exploitive therapy can inflict a "corrosive emotional experience" that weakens and sometimes destroys the patient's developmental foundations. From another perspective, Orlinsky and Geller (1993; see also Geller, Cooley, & Hartley, 1981) reviewed research from developmental cognitive psychology and other approaches to explore how patients internalize (through schemas, etc.) their therapists, and how therapist-representations affect outcome. Examining one specific form of internalization, they noted that "reflexive identification is perhaps the most important transformation in any successful treatment, because through this patients may develop a therapeutic self schema directly applicable to themselves. By acquiring a self-caring and self-analytic attitude, patients can become more attentive, patient, empathetic, and nonjudgmentally accepting toward themselves, as their therapists had been" (p. 437). If, however, therapists have been sexually intrusive, demanding, exploitive, and abusive, the patients' self schema may be brutally damaged, self analysis and even self awareness may be blocked or distorted, and what seems to patients to be self-caring may be severely self-destructive. Assessment and therapy must take account of the possibility that the patient may be functioning at a less advanced developmental level.

The Therapeutic Context

Imagine a smart, articulate business executive. Four days a week she goes to her analyst, reclines on the couch, and free associates. Sometimes she seems to be speaking a chaotic gibberish, unable to keep up with the stream of images in her mind's eye. Sometimes she becomes so engrossed in her thoughts that she ignores the analyst's comments. Sometimes she is so caught up in the transference that she misinterprets the analyst's statements, sometimes responding in a childish voice as if she were desperately trying to please her father.

Imagine also that an industrial psychologist prepares to conduct an assessment of Ms. A for a possible promotion. Seeking to understand her personality style, he asks her to describe her analysis. She does so in great detail and with impressive accuracy. He asks her to describe what happens during some typical analytic session, and she does.

The psychologist concludes that she should be fired rather than promoted. The summary of his assessment report states, "Ms. A lacks even fundamental verbal skills. She often talks in incomprehensible gibberish. She is self-centered and doesn't seem able to carry on a conversation, often failing to acknowledge another person in the room, even if he makes comments repeatedly. She doesn't understand language well, misunderstanding and misinterpreting the most basic statements. She speaks in a childish, inappropriate voice that is extremely annoying. In my professional opinion, Ms. A would not be an asset but rather a severe liability to this or any business."

The psychologist in this scenario makes a serious error and reaches invalid conclusions. Although he focuses on Ms. A's accurate description of her behavior, the psychologist views it out of context. He treats behavior that occurs in the therapeutic setting—with its special rules, relationships, and dynamics—as if it were occurring in a nontherapeutic (e.g., business or social) setting. Those who conduct clinical or forensic assessments make a comparable error—leading to comparably invalid results—when they view a sexually exploited patient's behavior with the abusive therapist as if it occurred outside the therapeutic setting. The therapist, as Freud emphasized, must never view a patient's sexual responses to the therapist as if they were due to the therapist's own charms or characteristics. Similarly, those conducting assessments must never view a sexually exploited patient's sexual responses to an abusive therapist as if they accurately characterized the patient's sexual impulses, feelings, or actions in nontherapeutic settings. A patient's sexual behavior with an exploitive therapist can no more be assumed to reflect his or her sexual behavior in nontherapeutic settings than Ms. A's verbal responses and behavior can be assumed to reflect her verbal capacity, tendencies, and behavior in nontherapeutic settings.

Time

It is crucial that an adequate number of sessions be allocated to any formal assessment. Discussing the nature and purpose of the assessment and obtaining the patient's informed consent, allowing the patient to tell—in an unforced, unhurried manner—the story of how the sexual involvement occurred, conducting a mental status examination and otherwise assessing the patient's functioning at the time of the assessment, obtaining an adequately detailed history, administering standardized psychological tests, and performing other components of a formal assessment take time. Rushing a patient through these phases is never good practice, is unlikely to produce a valid assessment, and may be experienced by the patient as, in the words of one patient, a "drive-by assessment."

Issues of trust (see chapter 5) are likely to make assessments more difficult. To the extent that clinicians can allocate enough time for the patient to adjust to a strange and perhaps frightening or disorienting situation and to form, if possible, at least a tentative or provisional trust in the clinician conducting the assessment, the more an assessment is likely to yield detailed personal information, an adequate sampling of indicants of the person's dynamics and functioning, and some sense of who the person is *as a person* (and not just as a collection of attributes, symptoms, or test scores).

Delayed Appearance of Consequences

Some aspects of harm associated with therapist–patient sex may not appear concurrent with the sexual activities themselves but only after a significant delay. Any assessment must take account of this possibility. The courts at the appellate level have recognized that some destructive consequences may not emerge until a substantial period after the sexual behavior:

> Indeed what evidence there is in the record suggests [plaintiff's] injury *did not* occur at the time of the alleged sexual relations. . . . [Plaintiff's] description of delayed symptoms is consistent with the view of clinicians who have described the injury caused by the patient-therapist sexual relations as "post-traumatic stress." (*Mason v. Marriage and Family Center*, 1991, pp. 543–544)

Therapist–Patient Sex Involving Minors

So much of the literature on therapist–patient sex focuses on adult patients that it is easy for clinicians to overlook the possibility that a minor patient may have been sexually exploited by a therapist, that an adult patient may have been involved in therapist–patient sex as a minor, or that there are special considerations (e.g., legal or developmental) when minors are sexually abused by a therapist. For example, one anonymous national survey found 81 reports of sex between therapists and their minor patients (Bajt & Pope, 1989). Most (56%) of these minors were female, with an average age of 13, ranging from 17 down to 3. The average age of the male minor patients was 12, ranging from 16 down to 7. Another national study showed that about 5% of 958 cases of therapist–patient sexual interactions involved minor patients (see Table 4). It is particularly important to keep in mind the potential difficulty or ambiguity in a child's—particularly a very young child's—attempts to communicate what may have been an extremely bizarre, frightening, and harmful experience, especially in light of a "child's limited linguistic and other cognitive abilities, which are not fully developed and which draw upon a smaller base of experience than the adult's, [and which] tend to make the trauma much more difficult to work through" (Pope & Gabbard, 1989, p. 92). Although most jurisdictions do not currently hold therapist–patient sex to form a basis for mandatory or discretionary reporting or disclosure by a subsequent clinician (i.e., required or optional reporting in the absence of the informed consent of the patient or the patient's legal representative), child abuse reporting laws generally (but, again, depending on the facts and jurisdiction) *do* require a report. Such laws require child abuse reports *regardless* of who the alleged perpetrator is.

When a therapist engages in sex with a patient who is a minor, not only the patient but also the patient's parents may suffer. In *Marlene F.* (1989; see also *Bro v. Glaser*, 1994, for an extended discussion of these issues in other professional contexts), the California Supreme Court considered whether "the mother of a minor child [can] state a claim for the negligent infliction of emotional distress against the psychotherapist who, consulted to treat both mother and son, sexually molested the boy. . . ." The court responded: "We hold she can" (p. 585). The court reasoned that "the counseling was not directed simply at each mother and son as individuals,[26] but to both in the context of the family relationship. And the complaint alleged

---

[26]The complaint involved allegations from more than one mother about more than one son.

that the discovery by the mothers of the therapist's sexual misconduct caused them serious emotional distress, further disrupting that family relationship" (p. 590). Justice Arguelles, author of the majority opinion, expressed in a separate concurring opinion that the therapist's actions could be construed as the intentional infliction of emotional distress. "I believe that what we have before us is a case of outrageous conduct, atrocious and offensive acts committed within a relationship of trust, that might permit the imposition of liability for the intentional infliction of emotional distress, in addition to other theories available" (p. 592).

It is easy also for clinicians to overlook complex situations in which a child's therapist engaged in sex with the child's mother or father. As Harvard psychologist Gerald Koocher noted, "The parents are necessarily a part of the therapy and therapeutic context. For the therapist to satisfy sexual impulses with the parent of a child patient is unethical under any circumstances" (G. Koocher, personal communication, January 18, 1994; see also Koocher & Keith-Spiegel, 1990).[27]

Use of Standardized Tests

Whenever standardized psychological tests are used as part of an assessment, it is essential that the tests be adequately

---

[27]For discussion of situations in which the spouse of a patient files suit, see *Homer v. Long* (1992), *Richard F. H. v. Larry H. D.* (1988), and *Smith v. Pust* (1993). Over two decades ago, a court adjudicated a case in which both husband and wife had been clients of a psychologist. After a period of time had elapsed following termination of services to both clients, the psychologist had an affair with the wife. The husband sued, alleging that the psychologist had failed in his responsibilities. The psychologist maintained that there was no professional relationship at the time of the affair. The court held for the husband, awarding both general and punitive damages (*Whitesell v. Green*, 1973). For cases in which the court addressed the claims of a husband that a social worker (1985 case) or psychiatrist (1988 case) had been providing professional services to him and his wife regarding marital problems but had also engaged in sexual relations with the wife, see *Horak v. Biris* (1985) and *Richard F. H. v. Larry H. D.* (1988). For a case in which "a domestic abuse counselor . . . was discharged for having sexual intercourse with a client's girlfriend" (p. *1), see *Bolden v. Phyllis Wheatley Community Center, Inc.* (1994).

normed for the relevant population and adequately validated for the task to which they are put. Unfortunately, standardized tests may often be misused in the area of sexual abuse. Especially in forensic assessments but also in other contexts, a test or test battery may be put forth as showing that a person did experience a certain instance of abuse or did not experience a certain form of abuse or that another person did not engage in a certain form of abuse, did engage in a certain form of abuse, or has been rehabilitated and thus will not engage in abuse ever again—all in the complete absence of any successful attempt to validate the test or test battery for that purpose. As professor Irving Weiner stated,

> A psychologist commenting on the assessment of alleged sexual abuse was heard to identify a "certain sign": If a girl sees Card IV on the Rorschach as a tree upside down, then she has been a victim of sexual abuse. Whatever tortuous rationale might be advanced on behalf of such an influence, there is not a shred of empirical evidence to support it. Indeed, there is precious little evidence to support any isomorphic relationship between specific Rorschach responses and specific behavioral events. Psychologists who nevertheless use Rorschach responses in this way are behaving unethically, by virtue of being incompetent. (1989, pp. 829–830)

Fundamental cross-examination questions designed for use in therapist–patient sex cases may be useful in identifying the misuse of tests in this way (Pope, Butcher, & Seelen, 1993, pp. 169–186).

One example of the need for caution in attempts to use findings from standardized tests without reference to this particular population emerged from the UCLA Post Therapy Support Program, formed in the early 1980s to provide services to sexually exploited patients. Many of the traditional MMPI indicators that a patient is not suited for group therapy were invalid with this population. Furthermore, as was noted previously, interpretation of test results must be made in the context of the individual's history.

> The Minnesota Multiphasic Personality Inventory (MMPI) profiles may show extreme distress and dysfunction. It is

not unusual to see signs that would contraindicate admission into group treatment. . . . In such cases, a valid interpretation of the results of the MMPI and other psychological tests such as the Rorschach, Thematic Apperception Test (TAT), and Millon Clinical Multiaxial Inventory (MCMI), can be made only in light of the individual's history by a psychologist trained and experienced in diagnosis and treatment and for whom the assessment of patients who have been sexually intimate with a previous therapist is an area of authentic expertise. (Pope & Bouhoutsos, 1986, p. 64)

Sexually Transmitted Disease

To the extent that therapist and patient engaged in sexual contact with each other, there is the possibility that a sexually transmitted disease such as the human immunodeficiency virus has been transmitted. Addressing this possibility—and any concerns, fear, anxiety, or similar responses that the patient may experience in regard to the possibility or actuality—is an important aspect of a formal assessment.

How The Sexual Involvement Affected the Patient

An assessment of a patient who has been sexually involved with a therapist must address a fundamental question: What consequences did this involvement have for the patient? Chapter 5 discusses 10 of the most common consequences and their implications for the subsequent therapy. These reactions, to the extent that they emerge for a specific patient, occur in the context of the patient's experience and understanding of the exploitive therapist and the therapist–patient relationship. A comprehensive assessment will address the patient's attributions about how the involvement occurred (see, e.g., the previous list of 10 common scenarios), about the characteristics and behavior of the exploitive therapist (see, e.g., Pope, Sonne, & Holroyd, 1993, pp. 256–257), about how and why—if this has come about—the relationship ended, and about any more recent behaviors of the therapist that the patient may experience as positive or negative. Examples of therapists' behaviors that may tend to promote the recovery or intensify the suffering of a patient are provided in chapter 5, in the section "Guilt." The therapist's behavior in this regard may have significant implications. Professor Patricia Keith-Spiegel (1977), one of the earliest to address this issue, noted evidence "that intimidation by the psychologist, at the point when the client who is knowledgeable about ethics committees declares an intention to contact one, occurs with some frequency" (p. 5). In summary, an assessment of a sexually exploited patient seeks an account of the events and of the consequences, but it must also include an assessment of the patient's understanding of these behaviors and consequences.

Evaluating Clinics, Hospitals, and Staff

Studies suggest that over 10% of patients who have been sexually involved with a therapist require subsequent hospitalization (Bouhoutsos et al., 1983; Pope & Vetter, 1991; see also Table 4). Therapists providing services to sexually exploited patients must address issues of potential hospitalization carefully (see appendix F). Is there a hospital that is appropriate, affordable, and accessible for the patient?

One issue that must not be overlooked is the patient's safety from further abuse: Do both patient and therapist have sufficient reason to believe that the patient will not be at undue or avoidable risk for sexual exploitation while in the hospital? Perpetrators of the sexual exploitation may be therapists but also may be other hospital personnel, as reports by Bell (1983); Collins (1989); Collins, Mebed, and Mortimer (1978); Kirstein (1978); and Stone (1975) illustrate. A recent study found that although 94% of the respondents reported believing that nurse–patient sexual contact was inappropriate, 17% of the male nurses and 10% of the female nurses of a psychiatric hospital reported having engaged in sex with the patients (Bachmann, Bossi, & Moggi, manuscript submitted for publication; see also Bachmann, Bossi, Brenner, Moggi, & Pope, manuscript submitted for publication). *Fox v. Anonymous* (1993) discussed a situation in which a person who was an inpatient in a psychiatric hospital was sexually assaulted by one of the hospital's employees, an AIDS-infected counselor. Hospitalized patients, even those who receive close staff attention, may also be sexually assaulted by those who are not therapists or hospital personnel, as the events described in *Rogers v. Alabama Department of Mental Health and Mental Retardation* (1993) illustrate.

Extensive checklists (verifying education, supervision, licensure, employment, history of licensing or ethics complaints, etc.) for screening potential hospital personnel, for establishing and monitoring policies prohibiting sex with patients, and so on, have long been advocated as being important for minimizing the risk that hospital personnel will sexually exploit patients or fail to take reasonable steps to ensure that patients are not sexually abused by others (see, e.g., Pope & Bouhoutsos, 1986). More recently, however, the usefulness of such checklists that operationally define screening procedures and policy implementation has been recognized as an important component of malpractice risk management not only in hospitals but also in clinics, group practices, and similar settings. As defense attorney Brandt Caudill (1993) stated, "Given the current state of the law, it seems clear that psychologists must assume that they may be sued if a partner, employee, or supervisee engages in a sexual relationship with a patient, because it appears that the courts are moving to the position that a sexual relationship between a therapist and a patient is a recognizable risk of employment which would be within the scope of the employer–employee relationship" (p. 17). It may be very difficult for supervisors or employers to argue that the sexual relationship involving a supervisee or employee was not within the scope of employment. As one court held,

> We believe that the nature of the work performed by a psychotherapist is substantially different than that of a day-care teacher as in *Randi F.* or a security guard as in *Webb* or a medical doctor as in *Hoover* so that a psychotherapist who engages in sexual relations with a patient could not be said, as a matter of law, to have acted outside the scope of his employment. (*St. Paul Fire & Marine Insurance Company v. Downs*, 1993, p. 344; see *Snyder v. Major*, 1992, 1993, for Judge

Kimba Wood's analysis of malpractice insurance coverage for psychiatrists vs. nonpsychiatric physicians; see also *New Mexico Physicians Mutual Liability Company v. LaMure*, 1993.)

Illinois is an example of a state that enacted legislation making an employer liable when it knows or should reasonably know that a psychotherapist-employee engaged in sexual contact with a patient (*Ill. Rev. Stat.* §70–803, 1991).

The vice president of claims of the American Professional Agency (a company offering malpractice coverage) recommended, as part of an approach to risk management, an abbreviated list of steps for employers to take in screening potential employees in hospitals or other settings:

1. Develop a questionnaire that takes the individual back to the time of graduation from college. Make sure there are no gaps in employment that are not explained in writing.

2. Make sure your questionnaire contains a release for you to check the information provided on the form. . . .

3. Check with each state that has issued a license to practice to the individual. Make sure there are no skeletons in the closet that can be held against you for not finding them.

4. Verify all listed degrees and certifications with the issuing institution or organization. Because it is on paper does not make it so. Obtain a copy of all special certifications for your file.

5. Have the questionnaire include the name and address of all prior supervisors. Check with them for any problems.

6. Get a copy of their c.v. and review it for any discrepancies with the questionnaire. Keep the c.v. in your file. Yet, do not accept the c.v. as a substitute for the completion of the questionnaire.

7. Develop and implement a policy statement that specifically says "Sexual misconduct with a patient, former patient or anyone associated with either is grounds for immediate termination." Have each employee sign this statement and keep it in their personnel file. (Marine, 1994, p. 6)

Regardless of the degree to which malpractice risk management is or is not a concern or focus for individual clinicians and institutions, the basic responsibility to the individual patient must not be obscured. Attention to such issues in evaluating hospital personnel and practices may be an important part of managing the risk of being sued (see, e.g., Wasson, 1991), but a more fundamental responsibility is carefully minimizing the risk that a sexually exploited patient will be hospitalized in an institution that negligently allows additional instances of sexual exploitation. In the two examples that follow, it seems clear that attention to the steps in appendix E would have prevented sexual exploitation of patients by either clinician, because taking those steps would have meant that neither clinician would have been hired.

> In one prominent hospital, an inebriated former patient returned to shout wild accusations at a senior clinician with considerable supervisory responsibilities. The administrative and clinical staff quickly dismissed her charges—which included a variety of sexual and nonsexual dual relationships with patients—as clearly too bizarre to be credible, a function of the woman's hostility and pathology, and a slur on one of the hospital's most respected employees. However, the hospital was eventually forced to abandon its position during the course of a malpractice suit when other patients reported that they had complained more quietly about the therapist but that their complaints had not been investigated; when the clinician acknowledged the accuracy of documentation (credit card receipts) showing that his "clinical work" included visits to a local motel; when the employment record he submitted on his application form was found to have been fabricated; when it was discovered that he had spent both penitentiary and jail time during past decades for charges including rape and aggravated assault of women and child abuse involving young boys and girls. In another hospital, a clinician was granted admitting privileges and enjoyed a good reputation among his colleagues. Later it was discovered that not only was he not licensed, he had never earned an advanced degree. (Pope, 1990a, p. 1066)

Although the steps in appendix E have been presented and discussed primarily in terms of evaluating a hospital, they are useful for virtually any setting, including outpatient. The clinician can use the checklist to evaluate not only hospitals and other potential resources for sexually exploited patients but also the clinician's own work or training setting.

The Therapist's Personal Responses to the Patient and to the Work

Working with patients who have been sexually involved with a therapist can stir up intense feelings in subsequent therapists. If not promptly recognized and addressed, these feelings can lead to errors in providing services to patients. Table 5 summarizes a 1991 article setting forth 10 sources of errors in working with sexually exploited patients, each source representing a different kind or set of personal responses by the therapist. Reviewing this list periodically may help clinicians avoid some of the most common errors in working with sexually exploited patients.

These responses are similar in many respects to the sexual attraction that therapists feel for their patients (see Pope, Sonne, & Holroyd, 1993)[28]: They are *common* responses. There is noth-

---

[28]A national study of psychologists (87% of whom reported sexual attraction to a client; Pope et al., 1986) and a follow-up study of social workers (81% of whom reported attraction; Bernsen et al., in press; related research based on a national sample of social workers was reported by Grodney [1990] and on a national sample of certified counselors was reported by Gibson & Pope [1993]) provided detailed information about characteristics of patients to whom therapists were attracted and the nature of, implications of, and responses to the attraction. The Bernsen et al. study found, for example, that 22% reported having sexual fantasies about a client while engaging in sex with someone else; there were significant differences between social workers who were and those who were not in private practice; and most reported an absence of formal training on the topic of sexual attraction to clients in their graduate programs or internships.

Although studies of psychiatrists and psychologists suggest that higher *general* education and status are associated with higher likelihood of offending (i.e., those with more general education are statistically more likely to offend; see Pope, 1990c, for review of the research), loglinear analysis of these two national studies of sexual attraction to patients indicates that increased education specifically focusing on sexual attraction to patients is associated with a lower likelihood of offending for the *first* time, although the effects, while

ing wrong with a response per se—it is normal and understandable. The response becomes problematic only if it goes unrecognized and unaddressed, distorting the therapist's interventions. For example, the tendency to make the patient fit the textbook—if unrecognized and unaddressed—may lead the therapist to assume the role of mind reader, seeming to know what the patient thinks, feels, and decides without bothering to ask or listen to the patient. Unrecognized and unaddressed, the sense of vicarious helplessness can stir the therapist to become a protecting and avenging angel, overidentifying almost to the point of merging with the patient, going to seemingly unlimited lengths to make up for the abuse suffered at the hands of the prior therapist, and acting ostensibly on behalf of the patient (regardless of the patient's wishes) to pursue complaints against the offending therapist. Unrecognized and unaddressed, the feeling that the therapist is serving only as a target for rage or neediness can cause him or her to react viciously against the patient (using clinical rather than physical violence in response to the perceived attack) or to turn away,

---

statistically significant, are quite small, amounting to only a few percentage points (Bernsen et al., in press); it is important to note that there is no comparable research showing any effectiveness of education in preventing those who have already offended from reoffending.

An analysis of data from all 8 national studies in Table 2 (pp. 16–17) found—although any interpretation or discussion of the relationship of the findings among these studies must take into account the qualifications and information presented in the footnotes to Table 2 and in articles by Pope (1990) and Bernsen et al. (in press)—significant gender (i.e., offenders were about four times more likely to be male than female) and year (i.e., there was about a 10% decrease in reported incidence each year) effects but no significant profession effect (i.e., no difference in reported rates among psychiatrists, psychologists, and social workers; year had significantly more predictive power once effects due to profession had been accounted for than the predictive power of profession once effects due to year had been accounted for; once year of study is taken into account, significant differences between professions disappear). When data from the 8 national studies are pooled, there are 5,148 participants, with each of the three professions (psychiatry, psychology, and social work) represented by at least two studies conducted in different years. Across the 8 studies, about 6.8% of the male therapists and 1.6% of the female therapists reported having engaged in sex with a client; overall about 4.4% of the therapists reported having become sexually involved with a client.

Table 5

Ten Common Responses of Therapists to Victims of Therapist–Patient Sexual Involvement

Therapist's Response	Description
1. **Disbelief and Denial**	The tendency to reject reflexively—without adequate data gathering—allegations about therapist–patient sex (because, e.g., the activities described seem outlandish or improbable)
2. **Minimization of Harm**	The tendency to assume reflexively—without adequate data gathering—that harm did not occur, or that, if it did, the consequences were minimally, if at all, harmful
3. **Making the Patient Fit the Textbook**	The tendency to assume reflexively—without adequate data gathering and examination—that the patient *must* inevitably fit a particular schema
4. **Blaming the Victim**	The tendency to attempt to make the patient responsible for enforcing the therapist's professional responsibility to refrain from engaging in sex with a patient and holding the patient responsible for the therapist's offense
5. **Sexual Reaction to the Victim**	The therapist's sexual attraction to or feelings about the patient; such feelings are normal but must not become a source of distortion in the assessment process
6. **Discomfort at the Lack of Privacy**	The therapist's (and sometimes patient's) emotional response to the possibility that under certain conditions (e.g., malpractice, licensing, or similar formal actions against the offending therapist or a formal review of assessment and other services by the insurance company providing coverage for the services) the raw data and the results of the assessment may not remain private

(continued)

Table 5   (continued)

Therapist's Response	Description
7. **Difficulty "Keeping the Secret"**	The therapist's possible discomfort (and other emotional reactions) when he or she has knowledge that an offender continues to practice and to victimize other patients but cannot, in light of confidentiality or other constraints, take steps to intervene
8. **Intrusive Advocacy**	The tendency to want to guide, direct, or determine a patient's decisions about what steps to take or what steps not to take in regard to a perpetrator
9. **Vicarious Helplessness**	The therapist's discomfort when a patient who has filed a formal complaint seems to encounter unjustifiable obstacles, indifference, lack of fair hearing, and other responses that seem to ignore or trivialize the complaint and fail to protect the public from offenders
10. **Discomfort with Strong Feelings**	The therapist's discomfort when experiencing strong feelings (e.g., rage, neediness, or ambivalence) expressed by the patient and focused on the therapist

Note. Adapted from Sonne and Pope, 1991, pp. 174–187, by permission; see also Pope, Sonne, and Holroyd, 1993, pp. 241–261.

perhaps keeping the patient at an extreme emotional distance or thinking up a plausible pretext for termination. These 10 sources of error (see Sonne & Pope, 1991, for a detailed discussion) tend to constitute the therapist's personal responses to the most common consequences (for the patient) of therapist–patient sex, and it is these common consequences that are the focus of chapter 5.

Chapter

5

Consequences and Interventions

This chapter explores common reactions experienced by sexually exploited patients, how these consequences can affect the subsequent therapy, and useful therapeutic approaches to these reactions. These consequences often seem to cluster into a distinct syndrome with both acute and chronic phases. (See, e.g., Hare-Mustin, 1992; Mann & Winer, 1991; Pope, 1985, 1986, 1988, 1989c, in press; Pope, Sonne, & Holroyd, 1993, appendix C; and Sonne, 1989.)

Therapist–patient sex syndrome, as a descriptive model, can serve four major purposes. First, this common pattern can help guide assessment. The clinician can inquire carefully about the most frequent consequences and dynamics. Not all sexually involved patients will manifest all aspects of the syndrome, but a comprehensive assessment needs to address carefully each aspect. Therapist–patient sex syndrome is similar in this respect to battered woman syndrome (Walker, 1979, 1984, 1994): A comprehensive assessment of a woman who has been in a battering relationship addresses carefully each area of battered woman syndrome even though not every women who has been persistently battered by a partner manifests the syndrome.

Second, it can help prevent the careless and invalid attribution of the patient's reactions to other syndromes, profiles, or models that can appear quite similar. It would make life much simpler if each syndrome had its own unique set of descriptors. Psychometrically there would be no overlap, and possible confusion would be eliminated. Clinically, however, extremely different syndromes may appear extremely similar in certain circumstances, and in some instances, when the available information is incomplete, may be virtually indistinguishable. Assume, for example, that a patient arrives at a therapist's office for an intake appointment. When the therapist invites the patient to enter the consulting room, the patient walks unsteadily toward a chair, begins talking incoherently, and then slumps over, apparently unconscious. There are numerous syndromes whose descriptive patterns are consistent with this scenario. The patient might have suffered a stroke, lapsed into a drug or alcohol-induced stupor, fallen into a diabetic coma, manifested a conversion reaction, or malingered. If the therapist in this scenario carelessly or reflexively assumes that the patient's characteristics could fit one and only one profile (e.g., malingering), great harm can result. Giving specific names to different syndromes, even though there may be considerable overlap, helps prevent unjustifiably lumping together as completely equivalent syndromes that, while similar, reflect different causation, process, or clinically indicated intervention. Just as the therapist in the scenario must consider a variety of possible syndromes, profiles, or models that may help in understanding the nature, meaning, and causes of the patient's characteristics, clinicians working with patients who describe sexual involvement with a previous therapist must consider a variety of syndromes, profiles, or models that may be helpful but may, in certain circumstances, be difficult to distinguish from each other. Pope, Keith-Spiegel, and Tabachnick (1986), for example, noted that therapist–patient sex syndrome "appears to bear similarities to various aspects of borderline (and histrionic) personality disorder, posttraumatic stress disorder, rape response syndrome, reaction to incest, and reaction to child or spouse battering" (p. 148). (Therapist–patient sex syndrome is consistent with a prototypal model and employs polythetic diagnostic criteria [see, e.g., Clarkin, Widiger, Frances, Hurt, & Gilmore, 1983; Spitzer, Endicott, & Gibbon, 1979; Widiger, 1982; Widiger, Frances, Spitzer, & Williams, 1988; Widiger, Sanderson, & Warner, 1986]; thus the similarity to, e.g., borderline personality disorder is not surprising. As Widiger and his colleagues [1986] noted, "polythetic and multiple diagnoses are an improvement over monothetic and mutually exclusive diagnoses by more accurately representing individual differences. . . , but the overlap and heterogeneity can be problematic for research" [pp. 551–552].)

Third, it can help guide consideration of possible interventions and the creation and evaluation of the treatment plan. Psychologist Janet Sonne of Loma Linda University Medical School, for example, in evaluating the outcome of the UCLA Post Therapy Support Program for patients who had been sexually involved with a therapist (Sonne, 1989; see also Sonne, Meyer, Borys, & Marshall, 1985), reported,

> All of the clients acknowledged that they had benefited from the group therapy. The group experience appeared specifically helpful for all clients in alleviating 5 of the 10 major aspects of . . . therapist–patient sex syndrome . . . : emptiness and isolation, guilt, emotional lability or dyscontrol, increased suicidal risk, and cognitive dysfunction (i.e., flashbacks, intrusive thoughts, nightmares). Improvement in the 5 other aspects (impaired ability to trust, ambivalence, suppressed rage, sexual confusion, and identity and role reversal) tended to be more dependent on the specific dynamics of the individual client.
>
> Clients who struggled with continuing and intense issues of mistrust and ambivalence were least likely to benefit from the group and tended to be most disruptive of effective group process. (p. 113)

Fourth, it can help a juror or other lay person understand special consequences of therapist–patient sex that otherwise might seem counterintuitive. For example, jurors and other lay people might believe that a patient is clearly not credible in describing damage from therapist–patient sex or in attributing the cause of the damage to a sexual relationship with a therapist because

□ even after termination the patient occasionally met with the therapist, participated in sexual activities with the therapist, and told friends that the sex made her feel as if she were the most special person in the universe;

□ the patient had made several prior statements (some in writing to the therapist) that she herself had seduced the therapist because her sexuality was out of control and that the responsibility for the sex was clearly hers;

□ although the patient now claims to have been harmed by the sex, she refused to seek help from any other therapist; and

□ she delayed filing suit until after the statute of limitations had run out (and is now asking for an extension).

Like rape trauma syndrome (Burgess & Holmstrom, 1974) and battered woman syndrome (Walker, 1979, 1984, 1994), therapist–patient sex syndrome can help triers of fact to understand that certain common behaviors—however much they may suggest to a lay person that a patient is obviously lying, exaggerating, or malingering—are not incompatible with credibility, are not improbable in the context of therapist–patient sex, and are not inconsistent with the harm that can follow from therapist–patient sex. For a discussion of the presentation of therapist–patient sex syndrome in legal cases, see Mann and Winer (1991).

There are crucial considerations in regard to therapist–patient sex syndrome. First, the earliest descriptions of this pattern (e.g., Pope, 1985) have emphasized that—just as not every person who is raped develops rape trauma syndrome and not every woman who is repeatedly beaten develops battered woman syndrome—not every patient who has been sexually involved with a therapist will experience all or even any of these consequences associated with therapist–patient sex syndrome. It is a common but by no means inevitable pattern. An adequate assessment must never fail to evaluate whether each of the common responses is present but also must never reflexively assume that any particular response is inevitably present. Each patient is unique and experiences "this destructive event in his or her own way in the context of his or her unique life" (Pope & Bouhoutsos, 1986, p. 21).

Second, the presence of therapist–patient sex syndrome does not, of course, preclude the presence of other consequences, responses, or sequelae to the involvement with the therapist (e.g., a therapist may have administered drugs to the patient as a prelude to sexual activity—see the list of 10 common scenarios in chapter 4—and the patient may have become addicted to or harmed by the drug) or conditions not associated with the involvement (e.g., a patient may have suffered and continue to suffer from an organic disorder). Third, forensic testimony about therapist–patient sex syndrome should *never* be introduced to prove that a patient was sexually involved with a therapist. Like rape trauma syndrome or battered woman syndrome, therapist–patient sex syndrome is a descriptive and explanatory construct, the usefulness and legitimate uses of which have been previously described. The following sections discuss common consequences for patients who have been sexually involved with a therapist, their implications for subsequent therapy, and approaches or interventions that may be useful.

Guilt

Irrational guilt plagues many sexually exploited patients. The guilt is irrational because it is always and without exception the therapist's responsibility to refrain from engaging in sexual involvement with a patient. The contexts described in chapter 2 can be useful in helping both patient and subsequent therapist to understand this guilt and its implications for therapy. It is a reaction similar to that experienced by many who have encountered rape or incest. Even though the responsibility for refraining from rape always falls on the rapist and never on the one who is being raped, women, men, and children who have been raped may feel extremely and chronically guilty. They may berate themselves with accusative and blaming interrogations: Why didn't I have a weapon so I could protect myself? Why didn't I struggle more? Why didn't I scream louder? Why didn't I dress so that I covered all my skin and hid my shape? Why didn't I talk the rapist out of it? Why did I ever go into an area where I could be raped? Adults who, as children, were sexually molested by a parent may misleadingly see in their own personality and behavior confirmation that they feel guilty for good reason: They secretly wanted the parent's attention, approval, and love. They were too sexual and provocative. They enjoyed and sought hugs and affection. They thought "naughty" thoughts. Their bodies sometimes responded while being bathed or toweled dry in ways that elicited or justified the parent's incestuous behavior.

Patients may feel guilty not only about the sexual activity but also about breaking the silence, speaking about "secret" events that the therapist wanted to conceal from others, and loosening the bond with which the previous therapist had drawn the patient into the abuse. "Many patients who are sexually exploited by their therapists refuse to reveal the unethical behavior, often explaining that it would be a betrayal of their intimacy with the therapist. One wonders if access to a patient in an exploitive way is often gained by therapists through appeal to the patient's longing for intimacy" (Lebe & Namir, 1993, p. 18).

As with any feeling the patient may experience, the first step is to acknowledge and accept that the patient has the feeling. Both therapist and patient may find some feelings so uncomfortable that one or both deny, discount, or distort the patient's experience. Patients may need considerable reassurance that it is safe and permissible to feel or discuss certain feelings. Therapists likewise may need support—from a supervisor or consultant—when a patient's expression of feeling seems threatening to the therapist, stirs up intensely uncomfortable reactions, or otherwise makes it difficult for the therapist to continue being helpful (see The Therapist's Personal Responses to the Patient and to the Work, in chapter 4).

Beyond acknowledgment and acceptance, patients tend to find it useful when the therapist provides relevant information and helps the patient to consider the nature, causes, and implications of the feeling. Although patients feeling irrational guilt often find it helpful for the therapist to say clearly that therapist–patient sex abuse is not the fault of the patient, the sense of irrational guilt tends to persist and to respond only to the patient's own exploration of and working through the issues (aided by the therapist or others), a process that often takes considerable time. As with all aspects of patients' responses to therapist–patient sex, it is crucial that subsequent therapists take adequate account of contexts (see chapter 2). The context formed by gender factors, for example, can be vital in understanding the irrational guilt that seems to plague so many female patients who have been sexually involved with their therapists. Melanie Carr, MD, of the Department of Psychiatry of the University of Toronto, and Gail Robinson, MD, director of the Program in Women's Health at The Toronto Hospital, wrote,

> [W]omen are often programmed to take responsibility for and feel guilty about relationships and their problems. The almost universal expression of guilt and shame expressed by women who have been sexually involved with their therapists is a testament to the power of this conditioning. (Carr & Robinson, 1990, p. 126)

Taking account of contexts can be helpful in understanding not only the guilt itself but also the ways in which reactions to the patient may tend to confirm the irrational guilt and in which the guilt may influence the patient's behavior (e.g., in declining to file a complaint). Comparing therapist–patient sex to rape, Davidson (1977) wrote,

> Women victims in both instances experience considerable guilt, risk loss of love and self-esteem, and often feel that they may have done something to "cause" the seduction. As with rape victims, women patients can expect to be blamed for the event and will have difficulty finding a sympathetic audience for their complaint. Added to these difficulties is the reality that each woman has consulted a therapist, thereby giving some evidence of psychological disequilibrium prior to the seduction. How the therapist may use this information after the woman decides to discuss the situation with someone else can surely dissuade many women from revealing these experiences. (p. 48)

In addition to *attending carefully to context*, therapists may find it useful to consider the following interventions when irrational guilt becomes a focus of therapy:

☐ *Talking With Another Patient*. Talking with someone who has been there can play a major role in resolving guilt issues and may be particularly useful when therapists and patients have reached an impasse. First, patients may find it easier to disclose and discuss certain thoughts, feelings, behaviors, or reactions to another person who has had similar experiences. Patients may feel less ashamed (and that the other person will be less likely to respond in a critical, accusative, and blaming manner) when talking about something that the listener has also experienced. Second, patients who have not worked through these issues may readily and severely blame themselves for the exploitation. However, when they listen to someone else describe such experiences—even when the other person's experiences are strikingly similar to their own—they may clearly see that the other person does not rightly bear guilt. As they recognize (sometimes with the help of the other person or the therapist) this discordance between the standards they use to evaluate their own experience of abuse and the experiences of others, they can begin to reevaluate their feelings of guilt.

☐ *Reading.* Seeing in black and white the prohibition against therapists engaging in sex with their patients, reading about the responsibility that therapists bear for refraining from sexually exploiting patients, and finding this information repeated in a variety of printed sources may help patients to believe more deeply that these are accepted professional standards and not simply a personal opinion of the subsequent therapist.

☐ *Exploring elaborations and complications of guilty feelings.* The irrational guilty feelings associated with the previous therapy may not be limited to guilt at the perceived responsibility for causing and participating in the sexual involvement. Patients may feel guilty about breaking the secret and disclosing to another that the sexual acts occurred. They may feel guilty because the previous therapist was critical of what they would or would not do sexually, of how they participated in the sex, or the degree to which they failed to please or satisfy the therapist. They may begin to recognize and express their anger at the abuse and may feel guilty about what they perceive to be negative, unjustifiable, or socially unacceptable feelings.

☐ *Exploring protective processes.* As patients talk about the irrational guilt associated with the previous therapy, it may begin to seem as if the guilt were serving a protective function. In some instances the guilt may signify to them that they were responsible and in control during the abuse (i.e., the guilt flowing from their perceived failure as patients to set and enforce appropriate limits for the therapist). If they, in fact, are responsible for causing the abuse, then *they* are in control and will be able to avoid future abuse. The abuse may have made the world seem an unpredictable, dangerous place; the guilty assumption of responsibility places patients in charge because they are responsible and in control; the world becomes predictable and nonthreatening. Patients feel invulnerable to abuse because they can cause (or prevent) it. This protective aspect of guilt and self-blame has been extensively studied among rape survivors and can, depending on the circumstances, be a significant barrier to recovery (Janoff-Bulman, 1992; Janoff-Bulman & Lang-Gun, 1988; Meyer & Taylor, 1986; Taylor, 1990; Walker, 1994). In other instances, irrational guilt may represent patients' attempts to gain control over what they see as their destructive, evil, or dangerous sexuality. Exploited patients and exploitive therapists may attribute the abuse to patients' rampant, irresistible, or out-of-control sexuality; the irrational sense of guilt may represent patients' acceptance of this attribution and attempt to control the cause of the abuse. In still other instances, the irrational guilt may represent patients' attempts to protect abusing therapists from accountability for their exploitive behavior. Patients may have learned to place the abusing therapist's wants and needs before their own welfare; the assumption of irrational guilt (saying in effect, "This is my fault") may strive toward exonerating, pleasing, and avoiding the wrath of the abusing therapist.

☐ *Exploring the previous therapist's words and behavior*. It may be useful for some patients to explore in detail what the exploitive therapist said, did, or implied to transfer the therapist's responsibility to the patient, to blame the patient for the involvement, and to foster the sense of irrational guilt. As is discussed in chapter 6, legal defenses in therapist–patient sex cases are often similar to those in rape cases. The defense focuses on three propositions: (a) the victim was a "slut" (i.e., a person with such an unsavory background that whatever happened could not, against that background, be considered "abuse" and/or the person "deserved" what happened), (b) the victim "asked for it," and (c) the victim "enjoyed it." Obviously, therapists who have sexually abused their patients can intensify and prolong the harm by encouraging patients to accept responsibility for the abuse. Conversely, exploited patients may find it exceptionally useful, as they struggle with self-blame and irrational guilt, to receive (perhaps through their subsequent therapist) a statement from the previous therapist, such as "I greatly regret what I have done to you. It was my responsibility to avoid sexually exploiting you, and I chose not to fulfill that responsibility. I now accept responsibility for what I did to you, and am willing at this moment, without any coercion or conditions, to assume the financial costs of what I've done to you. What I provided was not therapy but exploitation. The exploitation was not your fault." The potential healing power of such a statement coming from an abusing therapist can be comparable to that of a similar statement from the rapist or the incest perpetrator to the victim/survivor.

☐ *Exploring how the guilt affects the relationship with the subsequent therapist.* Attending carefully to the ways in which the guilt affects the therapist–patient relationship can be an important aspect of the subsequent therapy. Some patients feel so guilty that they believe that they do not deserve recovery and thus find it difficult to work with the subsequent therapist toward healing. Some blame themselves so relentlessly that they resist any process of empowerment: They believe that they have managed so terribly what they could control that increased control would be disastrous. Some find themselves viewing the exploitive therapist as "all good" while they, as patients consumed with irrational guilt, are "all bad"; this leaves them wondering if the subsequent therapist is more like the patient (and therefore bad) or more like the previous therapist (and therefore exploitive).[29] Some look to the

---

[29]Harvard psychiatrist Bessel van der Kolk (1993) noted that fear often fosters idealization: When patients are most afraid, they may be most likely

subsequent therapist to confirm their guilt by responding with criticism, blame, and accusations. (When the subsequent therapist fails to confirm their irrational guilt, patients may wonder if the therapist is incompetent or simply does not understand how bad the patients are.) Some, believing that they caused the abuse in the prior therapy, fear that their power and nature will cause abuse to occur in the subsequent therapy.

Impaired Ability to Trust

The work that therapists and patients do often rests on and draws its strength from patients' deep and profound trust. Patients may walk into the office of a perfect stranger and begin disclosing personal information about themselves that no one else will be permitted to hear. Therapists may ask questions that would be unwarranted, intrusive, and offensive if asked by someone else. Recognizing the powerful nature of the "secrets" that patients tell their therapists, all states recognize some form of professional confidentiality and therapist–patient privilege: With a relatively few defined exceptions, therapists are prevented from disclosing to third parties what patients say during the course of therapy.

In some respects the therapeutic process is similar to surgery. In surgery, patients allow themselves to be physically opened up in the hope that their condition will improve. They must trust that surgeons will not take advantage of their vulnerable state to cause harm or exploit. Similarly, therapy patients undergo a process of psychological opening up in the hope that their condition will improve. They must trust that therapists will not take advantage, harm, or exploit.

---

to idealize a therapist. He described a sexually exploited patient who consulted him while still in treatment with the sexually exploitive therapist. Van der Kolk stated that he would work with the patient only if the patient ceased the relationship with the previous therapist. So great was the patient's idealization of the exploitive therapist, however, that bringing the prior relationship to an end was not possible, and the patient ceased working with van der Kolk.

Freud (1924/1952) originally drew this analogy. He observed that the newly developed "talking therapy" was "comparable to a surgical operation" (p. 467) and emphasized that "the transference especially . . . is a dangerous instrument. . . . [I]f a knife will not cut, neither will it serve a surgeon" (p. 471). To acknowledge the potential harm that could result from psychotherapy was, according to Freud, fundamental:

> [I]t is grossly to undervalue both the origins and the practical significance of the psychoneuroses to suppose that these disorders are to be removed by pottering about with a few harmless remedies. . . . [P]sychoanalysis . . . is not afraid to handle the most dangerous forces in the mind and set them to work for the benefit of the patient. (Freud, 1915/1963, p. 179)

Psychologist Sidney Smith (1984) was the first to apply this surgical analogy to a therapist's decision to engage in sex with his or her patients.

> The specifics of these sexual engagements . . . clearly indicate the therapist's sadistic impulses. The rationalizations . . . are in truth based on efforts to disguise this hidden sadistic meaning. These rationalizations are not unlike some surgeons who discover exactly the same indications for surgery over and over again. . . . As Karl Menninger (1938) has indicated, some doctors are obsessed with cutting out thyroid glands, others with excising ovaries, others go after pieces of intestine, but it is the compulsion of cutting that drives them, not the objective realities of the patient's condition. The same repetition-compulsion can be found in the sexually abusing therapist, and it is the element of sadism that seems to stand at the forefront of the therapist's behavior. (pp. 93–94)

These analyses clarify the trust that vulnerable patients accord to professionals—therapists or surgeons. Patients must be able to trust that a therapist will do nothing that knowingly and needlessly places them at risk for deep, pervasive, and lasting harm.

When therapists decide to use patients' trust not to help but to sexually exploit, the betrayal of trust alone can cause pervasive and lasting damage. Mann and Winer, discussing the ways that exploitation of trust can harm patients, quoted Adrienne Rich:

> When we discover that someone we trusted can be trusted no longer, it forces us to reexamine the whole instinct and concept of trust. For a while, we are thrust back into some bleak, jutting ledge . . . in a world before kinship, or naming, or tenderness exist; we are brought close to formlessness. (cited in Mann & Winer, 1991, p. 325)

Among the approaches that may be most useful in addressing issues of trust in the subsequent therapy are the following:

1. *Paying scrupulous attention to fulfilling trust.* Therapists bear a significant responsibility to avoid violating the trust that is essential to therapy. It can be exceptionally useful for therapists to review their procedures and behaviors to determine whether issues of trust are being adequately respected and fulfilled. For example, patients may be quite concerned about intentional or unintentional breeches of confidentiality, about whether the therapist is adequately competent to address certain issues, or about whether the therapist has leveled with them (e.g., about the diagnosis or prognosis). Ensuring that none of these issues has been neglected or mishandled because of inattention, fatigue, countertransference, or other factors can help ensure that the clinical realm is trustworthy for the patient.

2. *Being explicitly open to expressions of mistrust.* Sexually exploited patients may be afraid, embarrassed, ashamed, or otherwise reluctant to say to the subsequent therapist, "I don't trust you." By communicating clearly that mistrusting a subsequent therapist is a frequent but not inevitable experience of sexually exploited patients, therapists enable expression of mistrust.[30]

---

[30]Patients may mistrust not only the subsequent therapist but also the health care profession more generally. The trustworthiness of the profession can form an important context for the subsequent therapy (see chapter 2). For example, exploited patients may discover news accounts suggesting that

3. *Focusing on words and actions that embody trust.* Therapists may be uncomfortable hearing that patients mistrust them and may cope by changing the topic. It is often useful, however, to invite patients to explore the words and behaviors that, in their experience, reflect or embody issues of trust. Patients may note a pattern while focusing on their experiences with the previous therapist. For example, perhaps whenever the patient wore certain clothes, sat in a particular way, or brought up a certain topic, the exploitive therapist would react in a certain way (e.g., by leering, by suggesting that the patient must want sex, or by talking about the therapist's sexual reactions) that *to the patient* constituted a violation of trust. By discussing and exploring patients' understandings of such patterns, subsequent therapists and patients may begin to develop a shared vocabulary about elusive aspects of trust, to think together about how trust may best be given a safe environment in which

---

licensing boards may have gone far beyond due process to provide professionals with undue protection from accountability at the expense of public welfare or justice. In one instance, an infant died in 1982 related to a physician's actions; a second-degree murder conviction followed. The next year, the physician's actions were related to two additional infant deaths. The licensing board found merits in complaints against the doctor but allowed him to continue to practice. In the following three years there were six additional deaths. In 1989 the doctor was convicted on nine counts of second-degree murder. The following year a newspaper reported, "Even now, while serving a 56-year sentence . . . the physician retains his board-issued medical license . . ." ("How the System Protected a Bad Doctor," 1990, p. 12; see also Pope, Sonne, & Holroyd, 1993, pp. 253–260). In another instance, a law enforcement investigation report showed, according to newspaper accounts, that a medical licensing board had "ordered the dismissal or destruction of hundreds of complaints against doctors," that "the wholesale dismissal of cases was part of a pattern," and that "medical Board officials had lied to the legislature . . . and had ordered that patients not be told that their complaints had been dismissed" (Ellis, 1993, p. A1). Despite such undue protection for professionals, exploited patients may encounter the attempts to make procedures even more favorable to professionals (e.g., that professionals should be able to personally choose or appoint the individual or individuals who will review licensing complaints against them). To the degree that the professions fail to ensure that their policies and procedures are trustworthy (e.g., do not mistake undue protection from accountability for due process), abused patients may respond by turning away from both subsequent therapy and formal complaint systems.

to grow, and to be alert to words or acts that may intensify the patients' mistrust.

4. *Emphasizing self-trust.* Patients may intellectually believe that subsequent therapists are trustworthy, but the feeling of mistrust may persist. In fostering the recovery and empowerment of patients, it is particularly important to avoid urging patients to block out, override, or ignore mistrustful feelings. Encouraging patients to trust themselves and their own feelings (even when those feelings involve a mistrust of the subsequent therapist) tends to be one of the most helpful interventions. It is very likely that this is contrary to the approach taken by the abusive therapist who may have pressured or manipulated the patient to blot out or ignore any misgivings. The feeling of trust cannot be imposed, commanded, or willed into existence. It must be allowed to develop, a process that may take considerable time.

5. *Attending to issues of trust in understanding behavior.* It is not uncommon for patients who have been sexually involved with a therapist to seek consultation from one therapist after another. To an uninformed observer, a patient who has sought treatment from a succession of 10, 20, or 30 therapists over the course of a few years may seem to lack seriousness, to be bored or lonely (thus seeking one or more hours of conversation from each clinician), or to be without the desire or conscientiousness to make use of therapy. However, the frequent pattern of seeking help from a succession of therapists is often related to issues of trust. In some instances, patients may find it all but impossible to develop trust in a subsequent therapist in light of their abuse experience. In other instances, abrupt termination before the completion of treatment is triggered by the beginnings of trust. The emergence of even the most tentative trust sets off alarm bells. The experiences with the abusive therapist have created in the patient the belief that trust is intolerably dangerous—sure to lead to another betrayal.

Ambivalence

Patients who have been sexually exploited by a therapist may find themselves either suspended or careening between two opposing sets of impulses: (a) to escape from the abuse and the lingering effects of the abuse, to seek justice and restitution for the offense, and to move on with life, recovered and empowered, and (b) to deny the abuse or to redefine it or fantasize it as not abusive, to cling to and protect the offender, and to minimize any inconvenience to the offender. Therapists who have worked with survivors of incest or battering will be likely to recognize this form of ambivalent attachment. A sexually molested daughter, for example, may want to keep the secret, to affirm that she provoked or at least must share blame for the sex, to make sure that daddy is not forced to leave the home, and to see that nothing happens that might make her father mad or unhappy; she may at other times (or even simultaneously) seek relief, safety, reassurance, recovery, and so on. Similarly, a battered partner may try to cling to, pacify, shield, and please the batterer, even though these impulses compete with efforts to seek help, recovery, restitution, and justice.

Ambivalence can be one of the most paralyzing, painful consequences of therapist–patient sex. The patient can find no stability in the world: When things finally seem settled, the opposite pole of the ambivalence asserts itself, and the world turns inside out again. The patient cannot find a way to make sense of the world. No description of the unfolding of events seems to fit. The exploitive therapist, for example, may seem to offer the tenderness, concern, and validation that the patient has always sought while also—as the patient reflects upon the developing events—robbing the patient not only of tenderness, concern, and validation but also of the chance that they will ever enter the patient's life.

When ambivalence creates an unstable world that the patient cannot bring into focus, one of the most useful initial steps is for the therapist to provide explicit reassurance that it is acceptable to feel and express the ambivalence. In the absence of such assurances, patients who have been working for a year or more on understanding and recovering from abuse may hesitate to tell the subsequent therapist something along the lines of, "I've been having these fantasies lately and wonder if maybe it wouldn't make sense for me to see if my previous therapist might be willing to get together with me again and give it another try. I think I might be able to do some things differently and please him more this time, so maybe it might work out and he really would leave his wife like he said," only to be followed soon after with fear, dismay, and self-criticism for thinking thoughts that now seem crazy.

A second useful step is to help the patient begin developing a narrative—the story of what happened—that takes full account of the ambivalence. Telling a story in words when the patient is ambivalent can be so disconcerting that the narrative will often remain stunted and incomplete, representing only one side of the ambivalence, generally the side that seems "safest" and that the patient believes the therapist most wishes to hear. The therapist can gently help the patient begin adding some of the discordant aspects to descriptions of events.

A third step—particularly useful for the many patients who have trouble developing or even beginning a narrative—is to attend to nonverbal forms that can represent the abuse experience. Horowitz (1978a) noted that "modes available for the conscious expression of meanings include enactive, image, and lexical representations" (p. 38). Visual images may capture the experience with much more immediacy. Some patients find it easier, at least initially, to express the experience through drawings. Art therapy can be valuable either as a component of or adjunct to individual psychotherapy. Some patients find their attention focused more on enactive representations and bodily sensations. Physical feelings, posture, or movements may be the primary vocabulary through which the patient has access to and can try to understand the abuse experience. Dance and movement therapies as well as other interventions that focus on bodily awareness may be helpful. Obviously in light of the patient's history of sexual abuse, there must be careful attention to issues of therapeutic boundaries so that the body work does not recreate the abuse.

A fourth step is to work with the patient to consider how meanings that emerge in the image or enactive modes may be translated into the verbal or lexical mode (see, e.g., Geller, 1978; Horowitz, 1978a, 1978b, 1986; see also Geller, Cooley, & Hartley, 1981; Orlinsky & Geller, 1993). British psychotherapist

Adam Phillips (1993) of London's Charing Cross Hospital (The Wolverton Center) described a sequence of events in therapy illustrating the important interplay of the image, enacted, and verbal modes. A 12-year-old girl was plagued with abandonment and other issues and attending public school 300 miles from her home. The presenting problem was a severe school phobia.

> The only thing that struck me as genuinely off about her was her attitude to my holiday breaks. When I told her of the dates of my holidays or made comments to prepare her, she treated all these remarks as a kind of hiatus in the conversation; I felt quite suddenly as though I was talking in her sleep. She was oblivious but in no way puzzled. Very politely she would let me have my say, as though I was someone with an intrusive obsession who every so often needed to blurt something out about the difficulties of separation. If I got irritated and asked her if she had heard what I was saying, she was mildly bemused but it made no difference. She would treat the sessions before the holiday as quite ordinary and would carry on the next session as though nothing had come between us. I found her absolute refusal to take me seriously as someone who went away rather endearing. I was aware that she had intrigued me with this, which, in another context, or in someone else, might have given me serious cause for concern.
>
> And then in the session before the third holiday break she arrived with an atlas. I had told her, and had been telling her for some time, that I was going away for two weeks to America. In what sense she had heard this I had no way of knowing. But in this session she went straight to the table and traced maps of America and Britain. She then reproduced them on a piece of paper and said to me, "While you're *there* [pointing to America], I'll be *here* [pointing to Britain] making the tea." I said, "That's amazing! T is the difference between here and there"; and she grinned and said, "So I'll be making the difference." (pp. 79–80)

Patients often find it helpful if the therapist will say something along the lines of, "Can you put that image [or bodily sensation] into words?" It is not uncommon for one pole of the ambivalence to gain expression in one of the three modes, and the other pole to emerge in the language of another mode. As the patient works to combine meanings from all three modes into a narrative, the ambivalence itself may be identified and explored. Events that may have been shut out of awareness can be gradually acknowledged and integrated into the sequence of words with which the patient tries to give shape to his or her own experience.

It is crucial that the therapist recognize the potentially powerful—sometimes overwhelming—effects of putting a traumatic experience into words. Patients may recount the events as if they were happening in the present. Transference may intensify. Yet as long as patients have moved at their own pace in giving voice to the abusive experience (and are free of intrusive pushing from therapists), simply describing the sequence of events tends to be an exceptionally healing and empowering process. The literature suggests that recounting disturbing experiences can produce a variety of beneficial interpersonal (e.g., Agger & Jensen, 1990; Cienfuegos & Monelli, 1983; Pope & Garcia-Peltoniemi, 1991; Weschler, 1990) and somatic (e.g., Berry & Pennebaker, 1993; Pennebaker, 1993; Pennebaker, Kiecolt-Glaser, & Glaser, 1988) implications.

Emptiness and Isolation

Many sexually abused patients report feeling both emptiness and isolation. The emptiness was expressed by one patient as follows: "It is as if I don't really exist without him. I'm not there, not myself. He's the only one who can fill me up, not sexually but in terms of who I am." The emptiness is associated with isolation. It is as if what has happened to sexually exploited patients has changed them to the extent that they do not feel that they can rejoin the world of humans, that their identity has been degraded, shredded, or altered to such an extent that they cannot communicate with others.

Some talk about this sense of isolation in terms of the experience of the abuse: Even though they may intellectually know that others have been through similar experiences, it feels as if they alone have been selected. Such descriptions are similar to those of some incest and rape survivors: However much they may know with their minds that others have been molested or raped, it *feels* as if they were singled out. Others focus more on how they experience their lives in the aftermath. They may feel as if the abuse has made them "dead" or eternally numb and hollow, and that there is no fullness, fulfillment, or "life" to their experience. They may be waiting for death, convinced that there is no way for them to reenter the world of other people. For some, separation from the therapist with whom they were sexually involved is terrifying. In 1912, Elma Pálos wrote to Sándor Ferenczi, who had been her analyst and sexual partner (as well as the analyst and sexual partner of her mother), "This being alone that now awaits me will be stronger than I; I feel almost as if everything will freeze inside me. . . . If I am alone, I will cease to exist" (cited in Brabent et al., 1993, pp. 383–384). In a preliminary report (based on the first 60 patients) of a questionnaire study undertaken at the Institut für Psychotraumatologie and sponsored by the German government, psychologists Monika Becker-Fischer and Gottfried Fischer emphasize "isolation and loneliness" among a pattern of other consequences of therapist–patient sex that "correspond to a great extent with the 'therapist–patient sex syndrome' " (personal communication, March 3, 1994).

To some extent, the sense of emptiness and isolation may be related to the abuse of trust discussed previously. Patients may understandably believe (or be led to believe) that therapy is a safe environment in which they can invest themselves into a deeply trusting relationship. When that relationship is violated, they may feel that they have lost the self that they placed within the supposedly safe environment (emptiness) and lack the ability to be recognized, respected, and taken seriously by another person (isolation). The previous therapist may have encouraged—through commands, threats, "prescriptions," or subtle manipulation—the patient's social isolation to help reinforce the patient's dependency, the therapist's power, and the likelihood that the secret of the abuse would not be disclosed to others (Pope & Bouhoutsos, 1986).

One of the healing acts that therapists may provide for patients lost in this sense of emptiness and isolation is to listen carefully, patiently, and respectfully to patients' expressions of the horror, panic, lostness, and numbness that can accompany feelings of emptiness and isolation. Gentle reassurance (e.g., that the person is not doomed to eternal emptiness and isolation) tends to be helpful, but *only after* patients are convinced that therapists have heard and understood (or at least attempted to understand) the agonizing, disempowering, and disorienting effects of the sense of emptiness and isolation. If reassurance is offered *before* patients believe that therapists have taken the time and trouble to learn about the acutely uncomfortable feelings, they may feel more empty and alone than ever. They may become convinced that therapists just do not understand and are incapable or unwilling to learn.

The more horrifying, pervasive, and overwhelming the sense of emptiness and isolation, the more threatening it may be to the therapist. Virtually all therapists have felt the temptation to avoid such troubling feelings altogether or to keep them safely confined through intellectualization. For many exploited patients, the healing process can begin only when they have reason to believe that the therapist is open to their experience through feeling as well as intellectualization.

Patients may also find it useful to read first-person accounts of other patients who have experienced therapist–patient sex. Among the volumes that patients have found useful, specifically in addressing the experience of emptiness and isolation and more generally in recovery and empowerment, are *Betrayal* (Freeman & Roy, 1976), *A Killing Cure* (Walker & Young, 1986), *Sex in the Therapy Hour: A Case of Professional Incest* (Bates & Brodsky, 1989), *Therapist* (Plaisil, 1985), *You Must Be Dreaming* (Noel & Watterson, 1992), and *Abus de Pouvoir* (Frenette, 1991). Evelyn Walker provided an intensely immediate account of an extreme sense of emptiness and isolation:

> By this time, of course, I had given up on the rest of my life. I lived the twenty-four hours of every day for the five- or ten-minute phone conversations with my Zane [the therapist

with whom she was sexually involved]. If it hadn't been for my appointments with him twice a week, I would never have gotten out of bed. . . .

I had withdrawn to the point where I spent all of my time, except for when I went to see Zane, in the bedroom with the shades drawn. I never knew when it was day or night, whether [my husband] was at work, or downstairs, or somewhere on a trip. I kept the television on because I couldn't stand the quiet. (Walker & Young, 1986, pp. 71–72)

Patients may find that reading such first-person accounts does much more to reduce their sense of emptiness and isolation than hearing a therapist attempt to reassure them that this is a typical reaction.

Patients may also find it especially useful, when addressing issues related to emptiness and isolation, to speak with other patients, either by informal contacts or in self-help or treatment groups. Being with another who has survived similar experiences is a direct and immediate way to reduce isolation and emptiness. They may find themselves forming a connection with the comparatively less threatening voice in one of these books before they are able to overcome isolation and feel a connection with someone who is physically present. They may be able to use a book's narrative to help find meaning in their own experience. Reading about someone who has survived and worked through sexual abuse may provide an empowering model that the reader may be able to draw strength and support from, perhaps through processes similar to vicarious learning and covert modeling (see, e.g., Bandura, 1969, 1977; Kazdin, 1978; Levenson & Pope, 1992). Research studies suggest that books can form a vital resource for people faced with desperate circumstances (Emery & Csikszentmihalyi, 1981a) and support the notion that

Books provide examples of previously successful responses to existential problems. . . . Persons who face particularly intense problems in their lives, such as poverty, oppression, marginality, homelessness, and so on, may learn to model their responses to these problems on successful examples provided by the cultural heritage transmitted in books. (Emery & Csikszentmihalyi, 1981b, p. 17)

Emotional Lability

Emotional lability can be one of the most disconcerting consequences of sexual involvement with a therapist. Emotions seem to lose their reliability and customary patterns. Changes in emotion can be sudden, swift, and without apparent reason. While discussing a seemingly neutral event, the person grows afraid. During the description of a pleasant event, the person's eyes well with tears. Emotional intensity may alternate with emotional numbness. The person may rarely experience what she or he would call a normal emotion.

One intervention that many patients find useful is for therapist and patient to allocate a part (or in some cases, all) of each session to attending to, focusing on, and being receptive to the patient's emotions. Depending upon the patient's level of distress and apprehension, the task may be as simple as inviting the patient to sit or lie comfortably, pay close attention to each emotional state as it emerges, and attempt to describe or name the emotion. Focusing on the emotions and emotional changes in the presence of a therapist who is attentive and reassuring can help the patient to become less afraid of, confused about, or avoidant of intense emotions and unpredictable emotional shifts. In a cognitive–behavioral framework, a process of systematic desensitization can occur in which the person finds internal stimuli (i.e., emotions) more approachable, less threatening and forbidding (see, e.g., Freeman & Dattilio, 1992; Levenson & Pope, 1992; Meichenbaum, 1977; Persons, 1989; Singer, 1974; Wolpe, 1958). As the person becomes more comfortable with emotions, however intense and suddenly shifting, the focus can widen from attending to, accepting, and describing emotional states to exploring patterns and associations.

This reconnecting with and reclaiming of emotions can be both healing and empowering. Emotional reactions, which prior to the sex abuse may have been both familiar parts of the individual's interior life and guides to understanding experience, may have subsequently become so frighteningly alien and seemingly unconnected with environmental events or internal processes that the person feels that both inner and outer life are out of control. In extreme instances, the person may feel helpless vis-à-vis his or her own emotions. Becoming able to tolerate then attend to, accept, and understand the causes, patterns, and implications of shifting emotions can help lessen feelings of being out of control with regard to one's interior life. Emotions become a familiar part of the self rather than alien forces attacking the self.

Suppressed Anger

Sexually abused patients are often—quite understandably—angry. The anger is often suppressed and may begin to emerge only months or years after all contact with the exploitive therapist has ended. The reasons why the anger is suppressed (or sometimes turned inward on the patient) are many. In some cases, the abusing therapist has been exceptionally careful to intimidate, manipulate, or coerce the patient into avoiding any expression (or even recognition) of anger. Therapists are trained to understand emotions and often skilled at modifying a vulnerable patient's reactions to his or her own emotions. However, the suppression may come about not so much through the therapist's subtle skills as through blunt force. One sexually abused patient described how her therapist would scream at her whenever she seemed angry or even irritated. Over a relatively long course, she became unable to recognize her own anger, which seemed to hide from her awareness. She grew terrified that those around her might become angry at her. Often she would come to a therapy session and sit silently for long periods of time, occasionally saying to the subsequent therapist, "You're mad at me, aren't you?" During the early phase of therapy, no words or behavior by the subsequent therapist would reassure her that the therapist was not angry at her. She lived in terror of her own anger and of the consequences should it ever emerge.

Some patients fear that their anger, should it emerge, would obliterate their sense of self or would destroy those around them. As psychologist Janet Sonne (1987) wrote, "Although the patient may occasionally acknowledge her intense rage, she will more often suppress her anger for fear of being overwhelmed by it, or of harming its object (the therapist) or others" (p. 119). When the anger surges into awareness, the intensity can be stunning. As one patient described it, "More often than not, I was on the edge of boiling over with rage, and I walked around barely contained" (Noel & Watterson, 1992, p. 211).

Kluft (1989) illuminated the key to assessment and intervention when sexually exploited patients are experiencing anger:

> Anger is quite common. The patient has been outraged both on the level of reality and on the level of whatever deeper hopes and fantasies were brought into and/or stimulated by the previous therapy and then dashed. It is important not, in a countertransferentially based diagnostic error, to conclude that the patient is simply a severe or narcissistic personality disorder with an excess of primitive rage. The therapist must be prepared to help the patient deal with very strong angry feelings for quite a while, aware that they may be turned against the therapist or, more commonly, against the patient's self. (p. 496)

The key, as Kluft pointed out, is to take adequate account of the context. It is not uncommon for unknowledgeable, careless, or countertransference-driven clinicians to refuse to identify, recognize, or take into account context. Seeming to view the patient in a vacuum lacking any interpersonal history, cultural framework, or environmental influences, clinicians can make the profoundly destructive error of noticing only the patient and the patient's anger and assuming that the anger must be solely a function of the patient's character and personality—unprovoked, irrational, or pathological. Clinicians who take account of context, however, are able to consider the potential relevance of a much more plausible possibility: that anger in response to sexual exploitation by a therapist is anger that has been provoked, anger that is a justified response to an unethical abuse of power, and, potentially (again, depending on the full context), a healthy and empowering rather than pathological reaction.

Whereas helping patients to recognize, accept, and respect their anger can be an important part of recovery and empowerment, interventions designed to rid the individual of anger or awareness of anger can be cruelly counterproductive. If the anger is a reasonable response to something that has been done to the patient by one of the subsequent therapist's colleagues, then attempts to make the anger disappear are not unlike addressing a fire alarm's warning by disconnecting the alarm rather than checking to see if there is a fire or addressing a string of neighborhood rapes by tearing up police reports of the rapes. Obviously there are many ways to attempt getting rid of patients' anger. Some medications decrease, mask, or dull responsiveness to anger. Some cognitive–behavioral approaches use reason to convince patients that they are not angry, or at least should not be angry, or if anger is completely unavoidable then they should not bring it up so often to the therapist. Other approaches may rely on a catharsis method that attempts to drain the patient of anger through oral (e.g., screaming) or physical (e.g., beating a pillow) exercises, a method that may in fact be counterproductive and cause complications (see, e.g., Tavris, 1989).

It must, of course, always and without exception be the patient's decision how to respond to the anger. A patient, for example, may be furious at a therapist who has sexually abused him or her. How to respond to that fury is up to the patient. The patient may want to file a licensing complaint, an ethics complaint, and a malpractice suit; or the patient may choose to do none of these. Recovery and empowerment are supported most effectively not when a therapist attempts to guide a patient to the "right" decisions but rather when a therapist acknowledges, attempts to understand, accepts, and respects both the patient's decisions and the process by which the patient arrived at the decisions. The therapist's respect for the patient's autonomy and independence will stand in stark contrast to the abusing therapist's attempts to manipulate, coerce, crowd, and take advantage of the patient's decisions.

Sexual Confusion

Sexually exploited patients may understandably wind up unsure of their sexuality. The therapist's sexual abuse convinces some that they are "only good for sex." It is as if they have become convinced that they will not "register" with anyone else and will have no value except in their ability to gratify the other person's sexual wants and needs. The experience with the sexually exploitive therapist seems to generalize to other relationships. Others engage in sex as reenactment of the relationship with the therapist. For those who feel empty and isolated, reenacting with others the sexual behaviors previously experienced with the exploitive therapist seems to represent an attempt to fill up the self and break through the isolation.

For still others, sex—and particularly casual sex or sex in which the patient derives little pleasure—becomes a way to express the feelings of irrational guilt. It is as if the sexual behavior were a way to say, "I am worthless and this is all I deserve." One patient was told by her male therapist that if she ever wanted to get well, she must repeatedly pull up her dress, take down her underpants, and masturbate while the therapist watched. She was told that she secretly wanted to do this and that it was necessary in order for her to overcome the sexual inhibitions that were making her miserable. Long after the repetitive sexual relationship with the therapist stopped, she reported a pattern that she seemed to follow almost against her will: As if in a trance, she would think of her therapist, go find a man she had never met before, and follow the commands of her therapist as if she were actually hearing them. Because she did not know these men, she was subjecting herself to danger and abuse. She was physically forced to perform sexual acts against her will and was threatened, beaten, and almost killed during some encounters. None of the men wore a condom; consequently, she suffered a sexually transmitted viral infection. As she later talked during a subsequent therapy about her confused behavior, she described how she had frequently hoped that she would die during one of the encounters. For one patient who had been sexually involved with a male therapist, her sexually confused behavior was described as follows:

> Once in a while, maybe every six months, she would feel the urge to have a glass of wine at dinner, then go out and pick up a strange man and spend the night with him at a hotel or motel. She wanted to be with men who didn't ask a lot of questions, who, like herself, were interested in being with someone just for the night, then separating. . . .
>
> Fortunately, in her few sexual forays, she did not meet a Jack the Ripper; neither the poet nor the drummer treated her with anything but respect. She had a dim awareness that her escapades, seldom though they occurred, showed how little she cared what she did with her life. (Freeman & Roy, 1976, pp. 115, 117)

Whereas some patients express their sexual confusion through sexual behavior, others avoid sexual activity with others or alone (e.g., they refrain from masturbation). One patient avoided any sexual activity with anyone else for five years while she worked through the trauma caused by sexual involvement with her therapist. During long periods of time, she expressed fear that she would "have a nervous breakdown" if anyone touched her sexually. Another patient was so mistrustful of other people that sexual closeness was impossible. Psychologist Janet Sonne observed that female patients who participated in the earliest therapy groups in 1982 and 1983 at the UCLA Post Therapy Support Program

> expressed a cautiousness or even disgust with their sexual impulses and behavior as a result of sexual involvement with their previous therapists. For some female clients who identified themselves as heterosexual before they were involved sexually with female therapists, there tended to be significant confusion over their "true" sexual orientation. (1989, pp. 106–107)

Many of the previous examples focus on either repetitive or avoidant sexual behaviors. The confusion about sexuality that results from therapist–patient sex can reach extremely deep levels.

> In some cases the trauma has been so profound that the patient has difficulty accurately distinguishing sexual impulses, sensations, or feelings from affects or other experiences. Thus a patient who becomes extremely angry or anxious may label the experience as "sexual arousal." Situational cues that seem to the patient to have nothing to do with sex may elicit sexual fantasies, impulses, arousal, or behavior. Such reactions may be part of the patient's more general feelings of being "out of control." (Pope & Bouhoutsos, 1986, p. 103)

Appelbaum (1987) described some of the difficulties that can occur in subsequent therapy when a patient is experiencing sexual confusion.

> [S]he had seen a number of therapists after she had terminated from the lesbian therapist. And she had attempted to engage all of the subsequent therapists in a sexual relationship with her because that was how therapy was "supposed to be done." She had been told by the therapist initially that in order for her to overcome the problems with incest in her family that she needed to have some sort of cathartic experience. So the therapist basically replicated exactly what her mother had done to her as a child and I sat back and sort of scratched my head when she explained the treatment plan that I was now supposed to follow with her, and looked at her and I said "Wait a minute. Your mother did this and it was called exploitation. When the first therapist did this to you, why don't we call that exploitation too." And then she had some real problems and didn't know whether . . . we could work together. She was not certain in terms of what her sexual preference was; she basically had formed a large friendship network with other clients that were being treated by her previous therapist, and so when she started realizing and started trying to deal with the issue of having been

exploited, all her friends left and she had virtually no support system for a long period of time. (pp. 5–6)

One of the most useful approaches that a subsequent therapist can take when sexual confusion is at issue is to seek to understand the degree to which sexual involvement with a previous therapist may have led sexuality itself to usurp, distort, or obliterate the patient's identity, frame of reference, and way of perceiving, understanding, and being in the world. The coin of this realm has two sides: (a) sexuality is the defining force in the patient's world, that which alone gives meaning to the patient's identity, represents the patient's only way of reaching other people, and constitutes the patient's sole sense of worth, or (b) sexuality is the destroying force in the patient's world, that which besmirches the patient's identity, seems to take over the patient's behavior with other people, and chokes off the patient's ability to feel good about him or herself.

In addition to seeking to understand the ways in which sexual exploitation by a therapist may have resulted in the patient's sense that sexuality is something alien, working preemptively to hollow out the self or to establish a fragile identity (based almost solely on the ability to satisfy the sexual needs and wants of powerful others), it is also important to seek understanding of the ways in which sexuality and eroticism may have become lost from the patient's life. This loss can be at once devastating, paralyzing, disempowering, and demoralizing. Cut off from this source of potential information, connection, and fulfillment, a patient may become less able to be open to and to integrate feelings. As Audre Lorde (1978) wrote,

We have often turned away from the exploration and consideration of the erotic as a source of power and information, confusing it with its opposite, the pornographic. But pornography is a direct denial of the power of the erotic, for it represents the suppression of true feeling. Pornography emphasizes sensation without feeling.

The erotic is a measure between the beginnings of our sense of self, and the chaos of our strongest feelings. It is an internal sense of satisfaction to which, once we have ex-

perienced it, we know we can aspire. For once having experienced the fullness of this depth of feeling and recognizing its power, in honor and self-respect we can require no
less of ourselves. (p. 3)

It is also crucial that the therapist attend carefully to the ways
in which the patient's sexual feelings may threaten the relationship with the subsequent therapist. As psychologist Laura
Brown (1988) wrote, "The fear that a therapist will not protect
them from their own regressed or transferential feelings can be
overwhelming, and may serve as a barrier to seeking out therapy for fear of encountering it in another therapist" (p. 253).

Increased Suicidal Risk

Research studies suggest that about one in every hundred patients who have been sexually involved with a therapist will
take his or her own life and that about 14% will make at least
one suicide attempt (Bouhoutsos et al., 1983; Pope & Vetter,
1991). Kluft (1989) wrote,

> Depression, suicidal concerns, and pressures toward self-
> mutilation and subtle mechanisms of self-harm are frequent
> issues. The exploited patient may have minimal self-esteem
> and be grieving not only the previous therapist but numerous
> other losses occasioned by the misadventure that took place.
> Guilt may intensify these issues, as may ongoing pressures
> from the previous therapist in some egregious instances. It
> is not uncommon for the majority of the early course of
> subsequent therapies to be dominated by such concerns.
> Many patients will need to rely on a supportive network of
> concerned others if hospitalization is to be averted; some will
> need hospital stays. The success of organic therapies for
> depressions in this group is mixed; responses to them are
> often incomplete. (p. 496)

One patient who had been sexually involved with her therapist described her sudden attempt to end her life:

> I do not remember clearly planning anything. I just went
> straight for the medicine cabinet as soon as I got home, and

I lined up all of the bottles of pills I had accumulated. For no reason that makes sense to me now, I removed all the labels first and flushed them down the toilet. I got a big glass of juice from the kitchen, because I knew I would need it to swallow pills, and then I emptied them into my hand and swallowed them a handful at a time.

After I had done it, I had the most marvelous feeling. Maybe it was the peace of mind I had originally sought through therapy. Whatever the source, I lay on my bed and felt light, peaceful, calm. I remember thinking that nobody would ever hurt me again. . . . (Walker & Young, 1986, pp. 51–52)

To evaluate and address concerns about suicide or other self-destructive behaviors, therapists may find it useful to consider the following steps:

☐ Clinicians must monitor the risk of suicide or other self-harming behaviors carefully. Some therapists find it useful to note in the chart for each session a phrase such as "no or minimal suicidal risk." Knowledge that they intend to write such a comment, if warranted, after each session serves as a reminder to evaluate carefully any change in risk for suicide or other self-destructive behavior.

☐ Therapists must ensure that a planned intervention matches the assessed risks in the context of the patient's needs and resources; the therapist's theoretical orientation, personal style of therapy, and resources; and the working relationship or therapeutic alliance between patient and therapist. It is important that therapists consider the full range of possible interventions in deciding which ones are consistent with their own theoretical orientation, personal style, and resources. For example, Bruce Danto, former president of the American Association of Suicidology, stated, "With these problems, you can't simply sit back in your chair, stroke your beard and say, 'All the work is done right here in my office with my magical ears and tongue.' There has to be a time when you shift gears and become an activist. Support may involve . . . making house calls" (Danto, cited in Colt, 1983, p. 50). Similarly, Davison and Neale (1982) wrote that "the clinician treating a suicidal person must be prepared to devote more energy and time than he or she usually does. . . . Late-night phone calls and visits to the patient's home may be frequent" (p. 268).

Obviously, even if a home visit is clinically warranted and consistent with the diverse criteria listed in the previous paragraph, the crossing of this boundary may echo for the patient the previous therapist's boundary violations and may greatly complicate the therapist–patient relationship and the subsequent therapy. Training in the consideration and use of such interventions is crucial (Pope, Sonne, & Holroyd, 1993). Norman Farberow, co-founder of the Los Angeles Suicide Prevention Center and one of the preeminent pioneers in working with suicidal patients, discussed boundary alterations such as the therapist providing very frequent or long (e.g., lasting all day) sessions to the acutely suicidal patient as

> examples of the extraordinary measures which are sometimes required to enable someone to live. Providing this degree of availability to the client gives the client evidence of caring when that caring is absolutely necessary to convince that client that life is worth living, and nothing less extreme would be effective in communicating the caring. In such circumstances, all other considerations—dependence, transference, countertransference, and so on—become secondary. The overwhelming priority is to help the client stay alive. The secondary issues—put "on hold" during the crisis—can be directly and effectively addressed once the client is in less danger. (Farberow, 1985, p. C9)

An example of one of these extraordinary measures to communicate caring involved a young woman hospitalized during a psychotic episode. She expressed nothing but disgust for her therapist, whom she said did not care about her. The patient escaped from the hospital.

> The therapist, upon hearing the news, got into her car and canvassed all the bars and social clubs in Greenwich Village which her patient was known to frequent. At about midnight, she found her patient and drove her back to the hospital. From that day forward, the

patient grew calmer, less impulsive, and made great progress in treatment. Later, after making substantial recovery, she told her therapist that all the interpretations during the first weeks in the hospital meant very little to her. But after the "midnight rescue mission" it was clear , even to her, how concerned and sincere her therapist had been from the beginning. (Stone, 1982, p. 171)

□ The field of suicidology is so complex and evolving so rapidly that therapists working with a suicidal patient may find it exceptionally useful to read on a frequent basis a recent book or review article or chapter focusing on assessment and intervention (e.g., Bongar, 1991; Bongar, Maris, Berman, & Litman, 1992; Simon, 1992a).

□ If the level of suicidal risk implies that outpatient treatment does not provide adequate safety for the patient's self-destructive impulses, it is important to consider carefully whether hospitalization might accord more safety. As was noted earlier, research suggests that about 14% of patients who have been sexually involved with a therapist require hospitalization that seems to be due, at least in part, to the sexual activities (Bouhoutsos et al., 1983; Pope & Vetter, 1991). Part of considering hospitalization for patients who are at risk for taking their own lives involves an adequate examination of the hospitals that are available to the patient (see appendix E); however, access to an adequate period of hospitalization may be severely curtailed. As Maltsberger (1993) stated in his Presidential Address to the American Association of Suicidology, "We joke in Boston that it is easier to get somebody into Harvard College than into the state hospital. The state system discharges patients like Mr. _____ quickly after the first symptomatic improvement, blinding itself to the fluctuating nature of such illnesses as his, taking no interest in the possibility of lasting therapeutic improvement a long stay might afford. They cannot: they are very overcrowded. Private hospitalization for long periods is impossible except for the fabulously rich; insurance companies and the health-maintenance organizations will not pay" (pp. 18–19). Another part involves assessing the patient's desires as well as needs, and the ways in which hospitalization is likely to affect the process of recovery and empowerment. As Larke Nahme Huang, a psychologist practicing in Washington, DC, noted, "Hospital management issues, power struggles, rivalries between professional disciplines, and so on can aggravate the client's crisis. Don't wait until the last minute, when you're in the midst of a crisis, to learn about these realities and to take steps to prevent them from adding to your client's misery" (Huang, cited in Pope & Vasquez, 1991, p. 166; see also Gabbard, 1989b; Pope, 1990a). Yet another part involves a candid evaluation of how effective hospitalization is likely to be in protecting the patient's life. Farberow offered this caution: "We tend to think we've solved the problem by getting the person into the hospital, but psychiatric hospitals have a suicide rate more than 35 percent greater than in the community" (cited in Colt, 1983, p. 58).

□ At times, working with a suicidal patient may be so frightening, stressful, or overwhelming that it can have a paralyzing effect on the therapist. It can be difficult to see, understand, and respond to the patient in adequate context. Out of context, the patient's self-destructiveness can appear as an unfortunate character flaw, a monument to the therapist's ineffectiveness, or a precursor to a malpractice suit. The narrowed range of the therapist's focus on self-destructiveness (narrowed because adequate context has been excluded) can block potentially helpful words and actions by the therapist. Yale psychologist Jesse Geller noted,

> One of the . . . problems in treating suicidal patients is our own anger and defensiveness when confronted by someone who does not respond positively—and perhaps appreciatively—to our therapeutic efforts. It can stir up primitive and childish feelings in us—we can start to feel vengeful, withholding, and spiteful. The key is to become aware of these potential reactions and not to act them out in relationship with the patient. (cited in Pope & Vasquez, 1991, p. 164)

One therapist described how she became aware early in her career of the ways in which working with a suicidal patient seemed to paralyze her emotionally.

I had a slasher my first year in the hospital. She kept cutting herself to ribbons—with glass, wire, anything she could get her hands on. Nobody could stop her. The nurses were getting very upset. So I went to the director, and in my best Harvard Medical School manner began in a very intellectual way to describe the case. To my horror, I couldn't go on, and I began to weep. I couldn't stop. He said, "I think if you showed the patient what you showed me, I think she'd know you cared." So I did. I told her that I cared, and that it was very distressing to me. She stopped. It was an important lesson. (Colt, 1983, p. 60).

Role Reversal and Boundary Disturbance

Many patients who have been sexually involved with a therapist appear to exchange roles: The therapist gradually turns the focus of the sessions from the patient to the therapist. The clinical needs of the patient recede in importance, and the personal needs of the therapist emerge as paramount. Often this transition begins with the therapist's gradually increasing self-disclosure. Whatever the supposed rationale for the personal disclosures, they serve to introduce the personal desires of the therapist into the therapy and to shove the clinical needs of the patient aside. Rather than the therapist working to address the patient's clinical needs, the patient begins working to meet the therapist's personal desires. To some degree, it is as if the therapist and patient change roles.

Clinicians who have worked with children who have been sexually molested by a parent will find this role reversal familiar. In incestuous families, the molested child may seem to change roles with the parent. Rather than the parent assuming responsibilities to meet the legitimate developmental and other needs of the child, the child becomes an instrument for meeting the needs (sexual but also emotional) of the parent. The child learns to ignore his or her own needs and to anticipate and meet the needs of someone else.

The therapeutic process tends to generalize to other aspects of the patient's life. Thus when therapy is positive, appropriate, and effective, the help that the patient receives tends to reach beyond the limited time that the patient spends with the therapist during a session and beyond the course of therapy itself (i.e., the benefits tend to last beyond termination; otherwise termination would mark the loss of all therapeutic gains). However, when therapists use the therapeutic process to express their sexual impulses at the expense of the patient, the negative effects likewise tend to generalize to the patient's experiences outside sessions and beyond termination of the meetings with the abusive therapist. Often the patient, through the violation and exploitation of the therapeutic process, learns to ignore or suppress personal needs and to strive to gratify the needs of others.

Such iatrogenically induced refusal to acknowledge, respect, or care for the self can disturb the patient's sense of boundaries. The customary boundaries that define, mediate, and protect the self may be broken, blurred, or dissolved in order to meet the needs of another (or others) more immediately and completely.

Legitimate therapy of any kind tends to be helpful in enabling patients to learn, develop, or reclaim clear roles and appropriate boundaries. In any legitimate therapy, the therapist refrains from using and abusing the patient to gratify personal needs. The therapist is there to help the patient, to help address the patient's clinical needs. The patient is there to get help, not to gratify the therapist. One of the specific interventions that promote recovery and empowerment in this area is modeling. Sonne (1989) described the use of modeling in the UCLA Post Therapy Support Program's therapy groups:

> The group therapist . . . was confronted with the complex task of helping clients determine and set appropriate interpersonal boundaries. Modeling by the therapists appeared to be very helpful. As the group leaders limited intrusions into the boundaries of the therapeutic relationship (e.g., declined a dinner invitation) and displayed and encouraged appropriate self-disclosure within the group process, group members typically expressed relief with the clarity of boundaries and began to negotiate more actively on their own. (p. 111)

Cognitive Dysfunction

Sexual involvement with a therapist frequently produces or aggravates cognitive dysfunction, particularly in the areas of attention and concentration. Intrusive thoughts, unbidden images, nightmares, and flashbacks may plague the patient and seem as if they were occurring in the present. In some cases, this constellation of cognitive reactions may be part of a posttraumatic stress disorder. Discussing treatment of patients sexually exploited by a previous therapist, Kluft (1989) noted that "cognitive dysfunctions are part of the presentation of the traumatized. . . . The treatment must be paced gently, may be assisted by the employment of many of the techniques of cognitive therapy, and may be facilitated by efforts to abreact and master the events that underlie disruptive phenomena" (p. 497).

As always, viewing such cognitive difficulties in adequate context is crucial. Superficial attempts to limit therapy to making the traumatic memories, images, or thoughts go away will not, of course, undo the exploitive acts that caused the difficulties or promote the patient's recovery and empowerment. As part of an integrated treatment plan, however, cognitive behavioral strategies designed to reduce cognitive dysfunction can help the patient to feel less a victim of his or her own cognitions. Beck (1970) and Cautella and McCullough (1978), for example, presented specific techniques for helping patients cope with unbidden images and intrusive thoughts. Psychiatrist Mardi Horowitz (1984) presented a more comprehensive approach:

> Post-traumatic stress disorder may itself modify the personality, so that in chronic cases that come to therapy there is much to be done after dealing with the reaction to the stressful event itself. . . . Psychotherapy should begin with reconstruction and review of the past, move on to present difficulties, and conclude when adaptive mechanisms for future use are in an adequate state of recovery. (pp. 374–375)

Some patients are continuously tormented and almost completely disabled by flashbacks, unbidden images, intrusive thoughts, nightmares, and other cognitions. To lessen the pain, anxiety, and persuasiveness of such cognitions, patients may find it useful to spend perhaps one hour a day attending to and working through the cognitions by recording them, either by using audiotape or by writing them down in a journal (Pope, 1985). Some patients bring these recordings to therapy sessions; others simply discuss the process and content with the therapist. This approach, which was originally suggested by a patient, offers several potential advantages:

- □ It helps patients to take a more active role in the recovery process and a more active (and less helpless) stance vis-à-vis the negative mental images.
- □ It enables patients to structure their time and activities.
- □ It helps patients to direct and control these cognitions (and alter their reactions to them).
- □ It helps patients to internalize the therapeutic process.
- □ It helps patients to learn the therapeutic process of translating images into words, a significant step toward understanding and integration (Horowitz, 1978a, 1978b, 1986; Meichenbaum, 1977, 1978; Singer & Pope, 1978; also see the earlier section, "Ambivalence").

Certain approaches such as eastern and western styles of meditation (e.g., Forte, Brown, & Dysart, 1988; Goleman, 1977; Taylor, 1978) that have shown great effectiveness in other situations should be used with great care and are probably contraindicated for most sexually exploited patients who are vulnerable to cognitive dysfunction. Attempts to "clear the mind," "assume an attitude of passive repose," "open up the attention," and so on often leave the patient more vulnerable to surges of unbidden images, intrusive thoughts, flashbacks, and so on, that overwhelm. One patient who had learned meditation when quite young decided to resume the practice to help relieve the turmoil she suffered as a result of sexual involvement with a therapist. Meditation, however, seemed to evoke a dissociative state during which she felt lost and made incomprehensible sounds. She emerged from her repeated attempts to meditate in a state of panic. Discussing this experience with her subsequent therapist, she discovered that the sounds were recreations of the noises that her previous therapist had made when he was having sex with her. That so seemingly gentle, safe, and effective a technique as meditation can, under certain circumstances, leave a patient more vulnerable to distress underscores the importance of matching carefully each potential intervention to the individual patient's needs and situation with alertness to unintended side effects. Imagery techniques and similar approaches that are more structured or offer more support from the therapist in comparison to the previously discussed meditation methods may, if carefully chosen and monitored, be more useful for sexually exploited patients who are vulnerable to cognitive dysfunction (see, e.g., Jaffe, 1980; Kazdin, 1978; Leuner, 1978; Levenson & Pope, 1992; Pope, 1982).

The research (e.g., Bouhoutsos et al., 1983; Pope & Vetter, 1991; Vinson, 1987) suggests that whatever the consequences that patients may experience from sexual involvement with a therapist, the probability is small that they will file a formal complaint. For some, filing a malpractice suit or similar action is a significant step in recovery and empowerment. Such actions, however, confront both patient and clinician with an array of special issues, the topic of the next chapter.

Chapter

6

Forensic Issues

Therapist–patient sexual involvement poses special forensic challenges to clinicians. The purpose of this chapter is to identify specific topics that warrant special attention. Clinicians seeking more general discussions of forensic responsibilities are referred to Blau (1984), Pope, Butcher, and Seelen (1993, pp. 47–83, 119–187), and Shapiro (1991); if the case involves a minor patient, additional relevant information can be found in Kalichman (1993) and Koocher and Keith-Spiegel (1990). Appendixes G and H present an outline and cross-examination questions that clinicians may find useful in preparing for depositions and courtroom testimony.

The Roles of the Witness

When providing forensic testimony, clinicians who have assessed or treated sexually exploited patients generally assume the role of expert witness, fact witness, or both.

The expert witness is recognized by the court as having special education, training, qualifications, or experience that can help the trier of fact (often the jury but sometimes the judge) to understand information that is considered outside the realm of common or lay knowledge. For example, triers of fact are not presumed to understand what psychological tests are, how they are used, and what their results mean; an expert witness might be called to explain the process of psychological testing to the jury.

The fact witness (sometimes called a percipient witness) is recognized by the court as able to testify about the relevant facts. For example, an attorney may want to establish that the plaintiff sought professional help for depression in 1990 before seeking help from the defendant in 1992. The attorney might call a therapist who would testify that (a) the plaintiff made and kept three appointments in 1990, and (b) the patient filled out and signed a screening form—a copy of which would be introduced into evidence—indicating that the reason she sought therapy was depression. Note that the therapist is not appearing as an expert witness but only providing testimony to establish that the plaintiff sought professional help for depression in 1990.

Expert witnesses in therapist–patient sex cases often assume both roles to some extent. Maintaining awareness of the distinction—and, sometimes, overlap—between expert and fact witness can help ensure that the clinician clarifies with the attorney the rules of evidence applicable for the relevant jurisdiction. It can also help the clinician clarify the nature of the relevant testimony; that is, what information is based solely on what the clinician has perceived, what is based on the expertise that the clinician brings to the case, and what is based on a combination of the two?

There are several important steps for a clinician to take in evaluating the prospects of assuming a forensic role. First, it is crucial for the clinician to clarify with the attorney who seeks his or her testimony whether the attorney intends to elicit expert or fact testimony, or both. For example, the attorney may misunderstand the clinician's areas of expertise (and thus seek expert testimony about an area in which the clinician is not an expert) or assume wrongly that the clinician knows and can testify about certain events.

Second, if a clinician has been asked to conduct a forensic assessment of a patient (who is not a therapy patient of the clinician) when therapist–patient sex is at issue, the clinician must candidly assess whether he or she possesses adequate expertise in the relevant areas (e.g., therapist–patient sex or psychological assessment). Reviewing the demonstrable bases of this expertise with the attorney is an important step in preventing misunderstandings and avoiding unpleasant surprises. Assuming adequate expertise, the next step is to ensure that the procedures for conducting and reporting the assessment are sufficiently clear to allow for adequate informed consent. Appendix B presents a sample consent form for forensic evaluation when therapist–patient sex is at issue.

Third, if the clinician has been asked (or subpoenaed) to testify about a plaintiff who is a current therapy patient, the clinician has the responsibility to help the patient understand how the clinician's direct involvement in the forensic process may affect the therapy. For example, how will it affect the patient and the therapist–patient relationship for the patient to sit in court and listen to the clinician testify about the patient's background, diagnosis, and prognosis? How will it affect the patient and the relationship for the patient to be present as the clinician is cross-examined? The clinician who has been asked or subpoenaed to testify must also ensure that both clinician and patient clearly understand how issues of confidentiality and privilege—reviewed with the patient at the beginning of therapy as part of the informed consent process—come into play in light of the impending testimony. When a patient files *any* formal complaint—even if sexual involvement is not part of the complaint—with a licensing board, civil court, or other authority, health care professionals who have provided services to the patient must take care to avoid violating confidentiality, privilege, and related rights on the reflexive and unexamined assumption that the patient has inevitably waived all rights of notification or challenge in regard to disclosure of his or her records. According to the published opinion in one case, a woman

> complained to the Board of Psychology of the State of California about . . . a licensed clinical psychologist. The Board initiated disciplinary action against [the psychologist] and a hearing was set before an administrative law judge. . . . In anticipation of the hearing, [the psychologist] served 17 or

more subpoenas duces tecum on [the woman's] past and present physicians and psychotherapists and her former attorneys. Copies of the subpoenas were served on the Board but no notice of any kind was given to [the woman]. The records were produced to the ALJ at a prehearing conference and the ALJ gave them to [the psychologist's] attorney.

When [the woman] discovered the disclosure, she filed a petition for a writ of mandate to compel the Department of General Services to quash the subpoenas and return the documents. The Board of Psychology (as one real party in interest) did not oppose the petition and disclaimed any interest in [the woman's] personal records. [The psychologist] (the other real party in interest) claimed the petition was moot because the disciplinary action had been settled but nevertheless insisted the records had been properly subpoenaed. . . .

The trial court granted the petition, finding service of the subpoenas without prior notice to [the woman] violated her rights of privacy, and ordered [the psychologist] to pay [the woman's] attorneys' fees of $70,830. (*Sehlmeyer v. Department of General Services*, 1993, p. 1075)

The appellate court noted that "Stempf contends his subpoenas comply with the literal letter of the law as expressed in the Government Code" (p. 1076). The appellate court further noted: "According to Stempf, the Legislature's failure to mention Code of Civil Procedure section 1985.3 in subdivision (a) of section 11510 of the Government Code demonstrates a specific intent to exclude administrative subpoenas from the operation of section 1985.3. We do not engage in the somewhat sticky statutory analysis required to resolve this point—because even if Stempf is correct, there still exists a constitutional and common law right to privacy which resolves the underlying issue against Stempf" (p. 1077). The appellate court affirmed the trial court's judgment and order, holding that "before confidential third-party records may be disclosed in the course of an administrative proceeding, the subpoenaing party must take reasonable steps to notify the third-party of the pendency and nature of the proceedings and to afford the third-party a fair opportunity to assert her interests by objecting to disclosure, by seeking an appropriate protective order from the administrative tribunal, or by instituting other legal proceedings to limit the scope or nature of the matters sought to be discovered" (pp. 1080–1081). Because this particular case focused solely on the issue of notice, the court stated, "We do not address [the woman's] rights, if any, against the healthcare providers who turned over records without her consent. (See also Evid. Code 995 [physician required to claim privilege] . . .)" (p. 1080). No matter how certain a clinician may be about an obligation to disclose records, the wisest course *always* includes consultation with the clinician's own attorney (not relying solely on advice provided by attorneys of other parties in the case) *before* responding to a subpoena for a patient's records.

Fourth, the clinician has presumably fulfilled the responsibility to avoid providing professional services to this patient if there is any other relationship that would create an actual or apparent conflict or problem (see chapter 4). However, it is worthwhile to recheck to see if there is any relationship that might hinder the clinician's ability to fulfill forensic responsibilities. Because the defendant is a fellow therapist, the possibility of such a relationship is somewhat increased (e.g., if the defendant has joined a group practice directed by the clinician's best friend, a judgment against the defendant is likely to have painful financial and public relations consequences for the friend's business). Any relationship about which the clinician has *any* doubts, questions, or concerns should be disclosed immediately to the attorney.

Fifth, appearing as a witness in a legal case in which therapist–patient sex is at issue *excludes* attempts to serve as the patient's lawyer, to offer legal counsel and guidance, or to manage trial strategy. Those who are conducting forensic assessments of or providing therapy to a sexually exploited patient must be constantly alert to the subtle ways in which the clinician may begin functioning as an attorney. The clinician conducting a forensic assessment may make comments such as "Why don't we take a break and go off the record here" (once the clinician is on the stand there will probably be no statutory basis for a refusal to testify about what happened during the break), "I think that it would be better for your case if you _____ ," or

"There are no right or wrong answers to the following test" (if how the patient responds has no relevance for or influence on the legal proceedings, then it is difficult to see why the clinician has included the test in a forensic battery; if how the patient responds is relevant to and may influence the outcome of the legal proceedings, the patient has a right not to be misled about this potential consequence). The clinician providing therapy may make comments such as "The sexual relationship you describe happened five years ago, so it is beyond the statute of limitations and you can't file a suit" (in some instances, the statute of limitations may be tolled or the case filed in such a way that a certain statute of limitations does not apply[31]), "What that therapist did to you was so outrageous, you're sure to win a lawsuit" (even an attorney, let alone a clinician, can never guarantee a legal victory), or "The facts you're telling me are so complicated that it just doesn't sound like you have a case" (an attorney is the one qualified by training and authorized by the state to provide legal guidance).

Payment

Clear payment arrangements with the patient and with the attorney should be established at the beginning of the work. The cross-examination questions that a skilled attorney can employ to raise doubt or even scorn in a juror's mind about payment issues are many (see, e.g., Pope, Butcher, & Seelen, 1993; Shapiro, 1991). Appellate decisions addressing the degree to

---

[31]Clinicians must take great care to avoid dismissing the legal prospects of an exploited patient. Discussing the case of *Riley v. Presnell* (1991), Jorgenson and Appelbaum (1991) emphasized that it is "only the latest of a growing number of cases in which courts are refusing to toss out claims against mental health professionals because they have been brought after the statute of limitations has expired. The discovery rule is particularly useful to plaintiffs in cases alleging sexual misconduct. Many experts believe that the conditions facilitating developments of the illicit relationship with the therapist, notably an idealizing transference, prevent patients from recognizing that they have been harmed. Indeed, the first application of the discovery rule to psychiatry occurred in such a case [*Greenberg v. McCabe*, 1979]" (p. 684).

which cross-examination may focus on an expert's fees and finances include *Mohn v. Hahnemann Medical College and Hospital* (1986) and *Trower v. Jones* (1988).

Any clinician who enters into a contingency fee arrangement (i.e., the attorney pays the clinician for services rendered, contingent on whether the attorney wins the case) may be in for a rough time on cross-examination. The opposing attorney can confront the clinician with numerous forensic texts that state clearly the ethical and professional prohibition against accepting contingency fees for testimony (e.g., Blau, 1984; Pope, Butcher, & Seelen, 1993; Shapiro, 1991). In some states, such contingency payments have been prohibited by legislation.

A clinician who allows the patient to run up a substantial unpaid bill is also likely to face detailed deposition and cross-examination questions. In some instances, the clinician may place a lien on the patient's future income. Sometimes the accumulating bill never arises as a topic of discussion between therapist and patient. Sometimes the therapist may assure the patient that no attempt will be made to collect the balance unless the patient comes into a sufficient amount of money, the patient often having no realistic prospects of such income unless he or she prevails in the malpractice suit. The following questions illustrate how an opposing attorney may seek to address the topic of unpaid bills:

- ☐ Isn't it true that if the patient wins this suit you stand to collect $_____ ?
- ☐ So if the jury were to award the plaintiff any money at all, you would be taking $_____ ?
- ☐ Is it your understanding that if your testimony were to be helpful to your patient in winning this case, you also would collect $_____ , but if your testimony were not helpful enough and your patient ended up losing this case, then you also would be unable to collect $_____ ?
- ☐ Do you believe that there is an ethical principle that patients have a right to understand the nature of the billing arrangements? If so, has your patient always been aware that the only way for you to get paid would be for him or her to persist with this lawsuit? So your patient knew that he or she could not drop the lawsuit without depriving you of your chance to collect $_____ ?

☐ Is it possible that much if not all of the possible distress that your patient alleges is actually due *not* to anything that the previous therapist did or failed to do but rather to the incredible pressure to follow through on this lawsuit in order to pay this debt to which you have subjected him or her?

☐ Is it possible that the guilt, depression, ambivalence, and so on that you say this patient experiences focus specifically on what might be considered by some to be a financial trap that you set for a vulnerable patient (i.e., guilty and depressed because the patient is unable to pay you; ambivalent about paying off this large amount)?

☐ As you thought about the testimony that you were going to provide today, were you aware that if your patient won the suit you would collect a substantial sum?

A professor of social work who has conducted research in the area of therapist–patient sex and provided therapy to sexually exploited clients described a cross-examination during one of her earliest forensic cases that focused on payment issues.

I was at the mercy of wherever [the defense attorney] was going and I hadn't a clue. He asked if my client had ever skipped appointments; had I charged her for missed appointments; had she paid me at the end of each and every session; did each and every check clear; had my office manager ever typed any document for my client; had he ever made a phone call on behalf of my client; was my fee for my client in perfect alignment with those I charged others.

All of these questions, I learned later, were to determine whether or not I was *in any way* profiting from this case. Of course, I was not and my answers clearly demonstrated that. However, if I had made *any* decisions other than those I just happened to make with her, he could have made it look like I was somehow in this case for my own financial sake. I was inexperienced in being examined and only thought of the issues as diagnostic, clinical and ethical. It taught me the importance of never going into a hearing without counsel. (K. Allen, personal communication, November, 1993)

Transference

Psychiatrist Glen Gabbard (in press) of the Menninger Clinic provided a concise description of transference in regard to the sexual involvement between therapist and patient: "Transference is usually defined as the displacement of feelings associated with past figures, such as parents, onto the therapist, rendering a sexual relationship with the therapist symbolically incestuous. Research strongly suggests that the transference, even in successfully concluded and carefully terminated cases, tends to persist after the formal sessions cease." When communicating to jurors who have not previously come across the term, it is important to emphasize that transference is not a patient's reporting or talking about the past or past figures. In intense transference, patients seem to reenact past relationships (and the associated feelings) as if they were occurring in the present (e.g., a woman might react to a therapist as if the therapist were the woman's father). Freud (1949) described how in the transference "the patient produces before us with plastic clarity an important part of his life history, of which he could otherwise have given us only an unsatisfactory account. It is as though he were acting it in front of us instead of reporting it to us" (p. 194).

The concept of transference arises so often in cases in which therapist–patient sex is at issue that it is important for expert witnesses providing testimony to possess a thorough knowledge of the concept *regardless of the expert's theoretical orientation.* In their comprehensive review of how therapist–patient sex cases are tried, Mann and Winer (1991) noted,

> The majority of court opinions explore . . . the importance of the phenomena of transference and countertransference. At all levels, opinions reveal that courts are highly informed about transference. In the majority of opinions, it is the distortion or mishandling of transference and the resulting countertransference that becomes the basis of malpractice charges. (pp. 330–331)

To help the trier of fact understand principles that are not commonly assumed to be within the realm of lay knowledge, expert witnesses must not only possess the knowledge but also be able to communicate it clearly and effectively to the jury or judge. The widely cited case of *Simmons v. United States* (1986) provided an example of an expert's discussion of the nature of transference that avoided unfamiliar technical terms. In its decision, the federal appeals court quoted at length from the testimony of Seattle psychologist Laura Brown, whose pioneering contributions to the study of therapist–patient sex have helped shape and define the field.

> What the notion of transference assumes is that as therapy develops, and if therapy is working the client comes to either consciously or unconsciously, or both, regard the therapist as a child might regard the parent. This is important because in order for a therapist to have positive powerful impact in helping the client to change and heal, the therapist has to have the same kind of authority power in a positive way with the client that the parents once had, or the parental figures once had in a negative way with the client while the client was growing up. And so what happens when therapy is working . . . is that this transference relationship grows so that the client comes to experience the therapist as a powerful, benevolent parent figure. And, what that means is that you've got a symbolic, sometimes conscious, sometimes not, parent-child relationship existing in the therapy setting, even though you have two adults there. (*Simmons v. United States*, 1986, p. 1365)

Once experts have helped the trier of fact to understand the nature of transference, they can explain how therapists can take advantage of the transference to exploit patients sexually. It is important to emphasize that "abuse of transference" and "therapist–patient sex," although related, are *not* identical concepts and cannot be used interchangeably. The landmark case of *Zipkin v. Freeman* (1968) provided a clear analysis of an important principle: The heart of the case was the abuse of transference—the sexual involvement reflected an abuse of transference—but the mishandled transference would have caused harm *even* if the therapist had stopped short of explicit sex. As Judge Seiler wrote for the majority,

> The gravamen of the petition is that the defendant did not treat Mrs. Zipkin properly and as a result she was injured. He mishandled the transference phenomenon, which is *a reaction that psychiatrists anticipate and which must be handled properly* [italics added]. . . .
> Once Dr. Freeman started to mishandle the transference phenomenon, with which he was plainly charged in the petition and which is overwhelmingly shown in the evidence, it was inevitable that the trouble was ahead. It is pretty clear from the medical evidence that the damage would have been done to Mrs. Zipkin even if the trips outside the state were carefully chaperoned, the swimming done with suits on, and if there had been ballroom dancing instead of sexual relations. (p. 761; see also *Landau v. Werner*, 1961)

Judge Eager, writing a concurring opinion, noted that, although the case was pled "under the *guise* of negligence," the abuse of the transference reflected "a vicious mind" on the part of the perpetrator. He noted that "one does not conduct an illicit adventure with a woman over a period of months through negligence, professional or otherwise" (p. 765; emphasis in the original).

Some defendants may attempt to argue that a sexual relationship between a therapist and patient is no different from a sexual relationship that occurs between any other two people who are not therapist and patient. It is important for the expert witness to be able to explain clearly that transference is one of the factors refuting the argument that the therapeutic relationship is no different from any other relationship and thus sexual activity within the therapeutic relationship is no different. Because of the special nature of transference (as described by Gabbard and by Brown earlier in this section), a patient's attraction to a therapist or desire for sexual activity can never be considered without taking adequate account of the transference. As Freud wrote in 1915, the therapist "must recognize that the patient's falling in love is induced by the analytic situation and is not to be ascribed to the charms of his person, that he has no reason whatsoever to be proud of such a 'conquest,' as it would be called outside analysis" (Freud, 1915/1963, p. 169). Transference is an important part of the context and cannot be excluded from consideration. As one court put it, "[A] sexual relationship between therapist and patient cannot be viewed separately from the therapeutic relationship that has developed between them. The transference phenomenon makes it impossible that the patient will have the same emotional response to sexual contact with the therapist that he or she would have to sexual contact with other persons" (*L. L. v. Medical Protective Co.*, 1984, p. 178). Finally, because there are so many theoretical orientations, expert witnesses should be aware of the ways in which transference, a term that emerged from the psychodynamic framework, has come to be understood within other theoretical frameworks (see, e.g., Singer, 1985).

Beyond Transference

Expert witnesses must be able to explain to a jury that transference is by no means the only basis of the prohibition against therapist–patient sex, the only means through which therapists can sexually exploit their patients, or the only mechanism through which therapist–patient sex harms patients. Two of the most important were discussed by Gabbard (in press): the internalized therapist and the power differential. As Gabbard noted, transference involves distortions: The patient reacts to the therapist with feelings transferred from earlier relationships with powerful or important figures (such as parents) in the patient's life. But a patient can also create and internalize representations of the therapist that involve little if any distortion. Gabbard reviewed the research supporting the idea that these representations are important to the ability of therapy to create positive change that extends beyond the individual therapy session or the course of therapy. Obviously, when the representation that is internalized is one of exploitation, the destructive effects of an abusive therapist can extend beyond the individual therapy session.

Gabbard also discussed the diverse ways in which the balance of power in the therapeutic relationship is never equal. For example,

> therapists may have access during the course of therapy to their patients' deepest secrets, hopes, fears, and fantasies. The potential for therapists to exploit this knowledge for purposes not originally intended needs to be recognized. . . . [Sexually-exploited patients] who wish to file a complaint face an implicit threat of blackmail. To file a complaint with the civil courts, a licensing board, or an ethics committee, patients must usually waive their rights to privilege and confidentiality. When they file a complaint, they explicitly (e.g., by signing a waiver for an ethics committee) or implicitly (e.g., by placing their mental or emotional state at issue before the courts) allow the . . . therapist to disclose to third parties the contents of their supposedly confidential communications to the therapist, as well as the therapist's professional opinions about their condition. Thus, in malpractice suits, a patient's deepest secrets may become a matter of public record and literally become front page news. (Gabbard, in press)

Thus the same therapist who abused the intimate knowledge of a patient by sexually abusing the patient is, in forensic settings, in a position to abuse that intimate knowledge—and the patient—once again by using the knowledge (with the therapist's embellishments and distortions) to discredit the patient's accusations. (For a discussion of the issues regarding limiting the disclosure of the plaintiff's name in a malpractice case—i.e., using initial rather than name in the title of the case—and similar information, see *R. W. v. Hampe*, 1993.) As Gabbard (in press) quoted psychologist Annette Brodsky, coauthor of the first national survey of psychologist–client sexual contact, "the imbalance of power of the initial interactions can never be erased."

Vulnerability and Preexisting Conditions

As was emphasized in chapter 4, it is important that the clinician differentiate between *vulnerability* (also called *predisposition*) and *aggravation of preexisting condition*. Denver attorney Joyce Seelen, a nationally recognized attorney emphasizing the litigation of therapist–patient sex cases, provided a concise discussion of the two concepts.

> Vulnerability is oftentimes called the "thin skulled plaintiff" concept. Wrongdoers take their victims as they find them. Jurisdictions generally agree that the fact that the harm suffered by one plaintiff exceeds harm that would reasonably have been expected does not defeat liability. Vulnerability is no defense (see, e.g., *Immekus v. Quigg* [1966], *Hoffman v. Schafer* [1993]). Sometimes this is a concept that juries don't like. Why should you unduly punish a landowner who allows a buildup of ice just because the person who slipped broke his back instead of twisting his ankle? However, therapist–patient sex cases are different. The therapist knows the vulnerability going in, which makes the instruction seem fair.
>
> Aggravation of preexisting condition is a separate concept. This is different from vulnerability. When the patient entered treatment, she had a preexisting condition (e.g., depression, PTSD), which caused her pain, discomfort, or impaired functioning. Defendant did something which aggravated that condition and, as a result, she suffers more pain, discomfort, or impaired functioning and her prognosis is worse. Unlike the vulnerability concept, which places liability for all loss on the wrongdoer, the jury is generally told that in cases of aggravation of preexisting condition it should apportion damages between the preexisting condition and the subsequent condition, if it can. If it cannot, the defendant is liable for the entire disability. (J. Seelen, personal communication, January 15, 1994)

The Patient's Sexuality

When patients take legal action against sexually abusive therapists, they may find that their own sexuality is the focus of the trial and under sharp attack. As Gabbard noted, the deepest and most private experiences, including the most personal sexual experiences, may become front-page news. Therapist–patient sex, which bears similarities to rape in so many other ways (chapter 2), also frequently encounters a similar legal defense: Defense attorneys for those accused of rape or therapist–patient sex often use a tripartite defense that is commonly, although crudely, known as "She's a slut, she asked for it, and she needed (or benefited from) it." One attorney skilled in trying therapist–patient sex cases (and who had previously defended people accused of rape) emphasized that in therapist–patient sex cases, like rape cases, the fundamental "defense includes trying to prove that the victims are promiscuous, trying to prove the clients were asking for it" (Terwilliger, 1989, p. D1). When the defense attempts to show that a person is of supposedly low moral character and to present otherwise private sexual experiences in sufficient public detail, the jury may find it difficult to identify with the person, conclude that the person has been through so many or such diverse sexual experiences that one more (i.e., with a therapist) could not possibly make any difference, or believe that the person got exactly what he or she deserved. Such attempts may be quite effective. Research suggests, for example, that jurors tend to accord more importance to a rape survivor's moral character in rape cases than to medical examinations or other evidence about the injury (Masnerus, 1989, p. 20).

Discussing their most private sexual experiences in a public setting while being forced to respond to a defense attorney's skilled follow-up questions may tax the psychological resources of even the most strong, determined, and resilient patients. During depositions, defense attorneys may probe relentlessly and in great detail the entire span (from earliest sexual awareness to any sexual acts that may have occurred immediately prior to the deposition) of sexual history, the list of all sexual partners (by name and most recent address so that they can be deposed by the defense in order to construct a baseline of the plaintiff's sexual partnerships and functioning), the inventory of the plaintiff's sexual acts and how the plaintiff responded during each one, the detailed array of plaintiff's sexual fantasies and impulses (whether or not acted upon), the range of the plaintiff's sexual desires, the occurrence of any sexual dysfunctions, and so on.

The reader need only imagine what it might be like to respond to detailed questions in each of those areas under oath, while a court reporter records every word and in the presence of numerous strangers and the media (e.g., Court TV), to gain some sense of how difficult it may be for patients who face deposition or courtroom testimony about their sexuality. Three examples may provide a clearer understanding of what plaintiffs may face. In the following passage, a plaintiff responds to a defense attorney's questions about her sexual experiences.

> "During the period of a year and a half that you were married, did you have satisfactory sexual relations with your husband?"
> "It was satisfactory in the beginning. It was not satisfactory at the end," she said.
> . . .
> "When did you start having the lesbian relationships?" he asked.
> "About 1963," she said.
> . . .
> He questioned her about sex with Dr. Hartogs, asking if she had engaged in cunnilingus, and she said, "That's correct."
> . . .
> "Were there days when you had sexual intercourse with him three times a day?"
> "There was an occasion, yes," she replied.
> . . .
> "You weren't forced into that, were you?"
> "I was not physically tied down, no."
> "But you enjoyed sex with him, didn't you?" (Freeman & Roy, 1976, pp. 146–150)

Another plaintiff encountered the following questions from the defense attorney:

> Could I mentally control vaginal lubrication? At what angle were my legs spread? Did I have orgasms? . . . Have you

ever had occasion to swap sexual partners with any-
body? . . . And when you engaged in sex, did you just have
intercourse with these people or would you have oral sex
with them, too? (Bates & Brodsky, 1989, p. 66)

The defense attorney also sought "a photograph of [the plain-
tiff] to circulate at local bars . . . in order to gather information
about [the plaintiff's] social life" (Bates & Brodsky, 1989, pp.
105–106).

Finally, five former patients of a therapist in a licensing disciplinary hearing faced questions about their sexual histories
and experiences.

Five of the [psychiatrist's] former patients testified that the
[psychiatrist] had used his role as their psychiatrist to influence them to engage in sexual relations with him. Over the
department's objections, the hearing officer allowed the [psy-
chiatrist] to present evidence of each of these women's sexual
histories, even to the extent of allowing testimony as to the
names and numbers of their sexual partners, their pregnancies outside marriage, their aborted pregnancies, and their
experiences as victims of incest and sexual abuse as children.
(*Department of Professional Regulation v. Wise*, 1991, p. 714)[32]

Under *no* circumstances should such questions come as a
surprise to a patient, once he or she has begun to testify. Subsequent therapists can play a crucial role in helping patients to
anticipate, endure, and, if necessary, recover from the psychological rigors of cross-examination focusing on the plaintiff's

---

[32]In this case, the appellate court held that, "as a general proposition,
evidence of a witness's sexual relations with a person other than an accused,
whether in a civil, criminal, or administrative context, is simply not relevant
to the question of the witness's credibility. There are exceptions to this proposition, not the least of which involves situations where proof of such a
relationship is necessary to establish a witness's bias against the accused or
motive to testify falsely. However, evidence of a witness's relationship with
a person other than the accused, standing alone, has no probative value in
the credibility determination" (*Department of Professional Regulation v. Wise*,
1991, p. 715).

sexual experiences. They may help patients ensure that they have adequately discussed their concerns about such cross-examination tactics with their own attorney. In some jurisdictions, plaintiff attorneys may have legal grounds for curtailing questioning about the plaintiff's sexual history.

The Subsequent Therapist as the Problem

The defense may attack the subsequent therapist rather than (or in addition to) the patient. Subsequent therapists who testify in therapist–patient sex cases should not be caught off guard by this approach. Considering how one might respond to the following kinds of questions will help the therapist avoid the surprise of personal attack during deposition or courtroom testimony:

- ☐ Isn't it true, doctor, that the patient never complained of any distress caused by the defendant until he or she became your patient?
- ☐ And is it not true that there is no record of any harm supposedly due to the defendant's actions until we come to your charts?
- ☐ Weren't you the first one to talk to this patient about filing a suit against the defendant?
- ☐ We've heard testimony about the power that therapists supposedly have over their patients. Do you have such power over this patient?
- ☐ Let me ask you this, doctor: If this patient is actually suffering because of what happened in her therapy, and if my client did not cause that suffering, and if you are the only other therapist she has ever had, then, by the process of elimination, wouldn't her therapy with you be the cause of her suffering?
- ☐ Have you supported this patient's filing of this lawsuit? [If not . . .] Do you believe that trying to do this without your support could cause problems for her in any way? [If so . . .] Is there any possibility that a patient might file such a suit in order to please her therapist?
- ☐ If your initial diagnosis and treatment plan for this patient were wrong, what sorts of problems might that have caused for her?

❑ Doctor, have you made any mistakes in your diagnosis or treatment of this patient?

❑ On what basis do you believe that you are competent to treat patients who say they have been sexually involved with a therapist? Please explain to the court the nature of your competence in this particular area of practice.

Hypnosis and Hypnotherapy

Whenever there is a question of whether therapist–patient sex may have occurred in the context of hypnosis or hypnotherapy, it is important, of course, that a subsequent therapist or expert witness be familiar with the relevant literature (e.g., Fromm & Pope, 1990; Perry, 1979; Venn, 1988).[33] The use of hypnotic techniques in the *subsequent* therapy, however, may have profound forensic implications. To the extent that a patient's testimony is based on memory, any factors that might distort the patient's memory are likely to emerge in deposition and cross-examination. Research has examined the tendency of hypnotic techniques to facilitate or inhibit the accurate recall of information (e.g., Lynn, Milano, & Weekes, 1991; Sheehan, Stratham, & Jamieson, 1991), and in some jurisdictions legislation or case law may address the admissibility or weight of testimony based on hypnotically elicited or refreshed memory. Subsequent therapists and those conducting forensic assessments who consider using hypnotic techniques bear a responsibility

---

[33]Perry (1979) discussed in detail a fascinating case in which a "hypnotist was found guilty of 3 sexual offenses against 2 female clients" (p. 187). According to Perry, the hypnotist "freely admitted that he had utilized hypnosis for sexual purposes; his defense was that it was impossible hypnotically to coerce a person into an unconsenting act. He believed that in such a situation, the person would immediately emerge from hypnosis. He did not know that other reactions are possible. The women involved insisted that they did not wish to have sexual relations with the hypnotist; that they were aware of being unwilling parties to a sexual act, but that because they were hypnotized, they were unable to prevent it from occurring" (1979, p. 190).

to know the forensic implications of such techniques. In his review of the research, McConkey (1992) concluded,

> If a decision is made nevertheless to proceed with the use of hypnosis [in forensic settings], it should be understood clearly that the experimental findings provide no guarantee that any benefits (e.g., increased accurate recall) will be obtained through its use, and that some costs (e.g., inaccurate recall, inappropriate confidence) may well be incurred through its use. This is the strongest inference that should be drawn from the experimental findings by those who are considering using forensic hypnosis. Given this, a balanced evaluation of the potential costs and benefits of the effects of hypnosis on memory should limit the use of forensic hypnosis in any substantial way. (p. 426)

On Being Duped

The judicial system of the United States is, of course, an adversarial system. Attorneys have become quite skilled at creating and exploiting a witness's anxiety through cross-examination. One attorney described with relish the signals that tell "the cross-examiner to uncoil and strike":

> Have you ever seen a "treed" witness? Have you ever had the experience of watching a witness's posterior involuntarily twitch? Have you ever seen them wiggle in their chairs? Have you ever seen their mouths go dry? Have your ever seen the beads of perspiration form on their foreheads? Have you ever been close enough to watch their ancestral eyes dilating the pupil so that they would have adequate tunnel vision of the target that was attacking? (Burgess, 1984, p. 252)

Attorneys may increase and capitalize on the anxiety and other discomfort that *any* witness may experience when providing important testimony in the face of vigorous, informed, planned, and surgically precise cross-examination questions. Anxiety and discomfort may have an almost paralyzing effect on the witness's ability to think clearly and respond promptly to questions. A common cross-examination approach is to keep the witness off balance as much as possible, introduce subtle (and then more profound) fallacies into the questions, and see if the witness—so anxious that he or she fails to notice the logical inconsistencies—will accept or agree to statements that will ultimately discredit the witness or the witness's testimony. When this tactic works, it is usually only after testimony has been completed that the expert witnesses realizes that he or she has been duped.

In the following example, the attorney conducting the cross-examination attempts a logical sleight of hand to dupe a nervous witness. The witness had previously testified about research indicating that female psychology graduate students who had had sex with their professors were, once they graduated and began conducting psychotherapy, at significantly higher risk to become sexually involved with their patients; the number of male participants in the study who had engaged in sex with professors was too small to allow a statistical test of the association (Pope et al., 1979).[34]

Q: Now, doctor, during your direct testimony did you not describe to the court research that supposedly found that psychology students who had sex with a professor were at increased risk, once they became therapists, to have sex with their patients?

A: Yes.

Q: Doctor, have you actually read that study?

A: Yes, at least the study was able to look at the link for women.

Q: Well, doctor, does the article state that more female students than male students had sex with their professors?

---

[34]The study by Pope et al. (1979) is not the only research finding a link between certain previous sexual events and mental health workers' probability subsequently to violate sexual boundaries in clinical settings. Kurt Bachmann, MD, Jeannette Bossi, PhD, and Franz Moggi, MS (manuscript submitted for publication) reported, on the basis of anonymous survey research at two Swiss psychiatric hospitals, that "Whereas 55.6% . . . of the male nurses who had been subjected to childhood sexual abuse committed sexual boundary violations with their patients, only 12.9% . . . of the men who did not evidence a history of abuse overstepped the boundaries of an appropriate nursing relationship (Fisher Test = 10.75, DF = 1, $p \leq 0.025$)."

A: Yes.

Q: And does the article state that more male therapists than female therapists had sex with patients?—

A: Yes.

Q: (moving in for the kill and speaking in a voice dripping with dismissive condescension) Is it not clear even to you, doctor, that these two findings are contradictory, that if sex with a professor is associated with later sex with patients and if more female students have sex with a professor then it *must* follow that more female therapists would later be having sex with patients, which is clearly not the case?

The expert witness in this example must not only avoid accepting the attorney's use of fallacy but also the attorney's attempt to take advantage of the jury's probable lack of knowledge about basic research methodology, fundamental statistics, and logical inference. The witness must help the jury to understand why the contradiction that the attorney is trying to establish is, of course, no contradiction at all but rather, as the attorney acknowledges after the trial, a misinterpretation of the type that beginning graduate students are taught to recognize and avoid.

The attorney's seeming contradiction is based on a denial of demonstrably significant effects associated with demographic variables (in this case, gender). The attorney talks as if sex with a professor were the *sole* factor influencing whether an individual later, as a therapist, has sex with patients. Simply pointing out the logical errors in the attorney's assumptions is likely to be less effective than providing examples—either as part of the response to cross-examination questions or later during redirect testimony—that show why the attorney's conclusion is wrong. For example,

□   In a certain factory in which all workers have the same job description and all workers work at the same task, greater productivity by a worker is positively statistically associated with higher pay. On average, women are more productive than the men but, also on average, women earn about 60%–80% of what the men earn. Is this impossible? Of course not: Productivity tends to be associated with higher pay for both men and women at the factory, but it is only *one* of the factors influencing how much an individual is paid. Another factor associated with determining how much each worker is paid is gender (and this factory may have a significant problem with gender discrimination in its pay structure).

□ Assume that there is a city with two areas: a high-crime area and a low-crime area. Living in the high-crime area increases a person's risk of being raped by 300% (compared to what it would be if the individual were living in the low-crime area). Far more men than women live in the high-crime area but far more women than men living in the high-crime area are raped. Again, this pattern is by no means a contradiction. Residing in the high-crime area significantly increases anyone's chances of being raped, but residence is only one factor; another is gender: Women are much more likely to be raped than are men.

Confronted with the cross-examination questions about the research outlined above, one clinician responded with an example that did not rely on gender:

I do not agree with your conclusion that it is "impossible." To accept that reasoning would be like stating that because height is significantly associated with success in basketball, the team with the tallest players would always win the championship. Height is significantly associated with success in basketball but the team with the tallest players does not necessarily win the championship because height is not the *only* factor associated with success.

Part of the work of the expert witness is maintaining expertise in the areas in which he or she testifies. The current understanding of the area of therapist–patient sex (e.g., how it occurs and its consequences) is based on a large and expanding body of research. The expert must be familiar with this research, understand the principles by which data are collected and interpreted, be alert to ways in which information can be distorted and used to mislead, and be able to communicate this content clearly to a jury.

A Final Word on Context

This book has emphasized throughout the importance of context, which chapter 2 discussed in some detail. The most fundamental research findings, well-validated assessment procedures, and carefully thought out professional opinions can, if they emerge out of context, tragically mislead the trier of fact and undermine the forensic practitioner's responsibilities. Clinicians who have served as therapists or conducted forensic assessments bear a crucial responsibility when they provide testimony about sexually exploited patients: They must take careful account of context.

Testimony about sexually exploited patients must always take account of the context of therapy within which their relationship with the offender developed. As was noted previously in the section "Transference," Freud emphasized that a therapist could never view or understand a patient's sexual attraction as if it occurred outside the context of therapy. Induced by the therapeutic situation, the sexual feelings mean something distinctly different than if they were to occur outside of the therapeutic context. The offender makes a false claim if he or she attributes the patient's attraction to the "charms" of the therapist. Those who provide forensic testimony about sexually exploited patients can make similar false claims if they attempt to portray patients' sexual attraction to (or fantasies about, or behavior with, etc.) the perpetrator as if it were attraction that developed outside the therapeutic context. To deny the therapeutic context and its influences is one of the most fundamental errors that forensic practitioners offering testimony about sexually exploited patients can make.

Those who provide testimony in therapist–patient sex cases must also take account of the forensic context. The witness takes an oath to tell the truth, the whole truth, and nothing but the truth. Whether as an expert or fact witness, the professional who provides testimony has the responsibility to help the trier of fact understand what happened, or why it happened, or what it means. The witness does this by responding fully, accurately, and honestly to questions asked by the attorneys and sometimes by the judge.

It is understandable, perhaps, why some witnesses seem to ignore this context of crucial professional responsibility. Those who have been retained by plaintiff or defense attorneys to conduct forensic assessments of sexually exploited patients may see their highest loyalty as belonging to "their side." Their forensic reports are carefully filtered to exclude any information that might be of use to an opposing attorney. Test results and other data that might offer some vague advantage for the retaining attorney are nurtured, enhanced, and spotlighted so that they appear decisive. Others may seek to be the center of attention, the one whose testimony decides the trial, the expert of all experts, the one who is most quoted in media accounts of the trial, and the one whom attorneys are most likely to call in the future. The highest loyalty is to self. And still others, especially those who have worked as subsequent therapists for sexually exploited patients, may become avenging angels (see chapter 4), overidentifying with the patient and going to any lengths to "make whole" and compensate for the patient's history of hurt.

When witnesses deny the context of their forensic responsibilities and their oath, harm results: harm to the principal parties of the legal dispute who are deprived of the justice that can result only when the roles and rules are not corrupted, harm to the triers of fact who are deprived of an honest presentation of information, harm to the public confidence in the witnesses' profession, and harm to the witness's integrity. Ironically, ignoring the context of forensic responsibilities in order to accomplish the kind of goals listed in the previous paragraph is likely to be self-defeating. The subsequent therapist, for example, who fights vigorously against the defense attorney, avoiding answering questions directly, trying to make every response to a cross-examination question an opening for a speech on behalf of the patient, and so on, may in fact thwart the defense attorney's efforts to obtain clear answers that might benefit the defense but also may come across to the jury as hopelessly biased, lacking in honesty, and not to be trusted (a suspicion that may attach itself in jurors' minds to the subsequent therapist's patient as well).

Sexually exploited patients originally entered therapy and

found that offending therapists failed to acknowledge, respect, or maintain the therapeutic context of trust and safety. All too often, responses to exploited patients are shaped by contexts that obscure the offense, mask patterns of harm, and distort attributions of responsibility. Those who provide assessment, therapy, and forensic services to such patients bear a significant responsibility to remain aware of these contexts and their effects. By fulfilling that responsibility, they justify the trust that exploited patients, colleagues, the courts, and society place in them.

References

Agger, I., & Jensen, S. B. (1990). Testimony as ritual and evidence in psychotherapy for political refugees. *Journal of Traumatic Stress, 3,* 115–130.

Akamatsu, T. J. (1988). Intimate relationships with former clients: National survey of attitudes and behavior among practitioners. *Professional Psychology: Research and Practice, 19,* 454–458.

Alexander, F. (1961). *The scope of psychoanalysis.* New York: Basic Books.

American Home Assurance Co. v. Cohen, 815 F. Supp. 365 (W. D. Wash. 1993).

American Psychiatric Association. (1987). *Diagnostic and statistical manual of mental disorders* (3rd ed., rev.). Washington, DC: Author.

American Psychiatric Association (1994). *Diagnostic and statistical manual of mental disorders* (4th ed.). Washington, DC: Author.

American Psychological Association. (1963). Ethical standards of psychologists. *American Psychologist, 18,* 56–60.

American Psychological Association, Board of Professional Affairs, Committee on Professional Standards. (1987). General guidelines for providers of psychological services. *American Psychologist, 42,* 712–723.

American Psychological Association, Ethics Committee. (1988). Trends in ethics cases, common pitfalls, and published resources. *American Psychologist, 43,* 564–572.

American Psychological Association Insurance Trust. (1990). *Bulletin: Sexual misconduct and professional liability claims.* Washington, DC: Author.

Amir, M. (1971). *Patterns of forcible rape.* Chicago: University of Chicago Press.

APA's ethics procedures upheld as fair in federal court. (1985, May 3). *Psychiatric News,* p. 11.

Applebaum, G. (1987, January). Consequences of sexual exploitation of clients. Panel presentation at "Boundary Dilemmas in the Client-Therapist Relationship: A Working Conference for Lesbian Therapists." Los Angeles.

Appelbaum, P. S., & Jorgenson, L. (1991). Psychotherapist–patient sexual contact after termination of treatment: An analysis and a proposal. *American Journal of Psychiatry, 148,* 1466–1473.

Bachmann, K. M., Bossi, J., Brenner, H. D., Moggi, F., & Pope, K. S. *Nurse–patient sexual contact in somatic hospitals.* Manuscript submitted for publication.

Bachmann, K. M., Bossi, J., & Moggi, F. *Nurse–patient contact in psychiatric hospitals in Switzerland.* Manuscript submitted for publication.

Bailey, K. G. (1978). Psychotherapy or massage parlor technology. *Journal of Consulting and Clinical Psychology, 46,* 1502–1506.

Bajt, T. R., & Pope, K. S. (1989). Therapist–patient sexual intimacy involving children and adolescents. *American Psychologist, 44,* 455.

Bandura, A. (1969). *Principles of behavior modification.* New York: Holt, Rinehart & Winston.

Bandura, A. (1977). *Social learning theory.* New York: Prentice-Hall.

Barnhouse, R. T. (1978). Sex between therapist and patient. *Journal of the American Academy of Psychoanalysis, 6,* 533–546.

Bash v. Board of Medical Practice. 579 S. Ct. 1145 (1989).

Bates, C. M., & Brodsky, A. M. (1989). *Sex in the therapy hour: A case of professional incest.* New York: Guilford Press.

Beck, A. T. (1970). Role of fantasies in psychotherapy and psychopathology. *Journal of Nervous and Mental Disease, 150,* 3–17.

Bell, C. C. (1983). On sex and the psychiatric patient. *American Journal of Psychiatry, 140,* 1269.

Belli, M. M., & Carlova, J. (1986). *Belli for your malpractice defense.* Oradell, NJ: Medical Economics Books.

Bennett, B. E., Bryant, B. K., VandenBos, G. R., & Greenwood, A. (1990). *Professional liability and risk management.* Washington, DC: American Psychological Association.

Benowitz, M. S. (1991). *Sexual exploitation of female clients by female psychotherapists: Interviews with clients and a comparison to women exploited by male psychotherapists.* Unpublished doctoral dissertation, University of Minnesota, Minneapolis.

Bernsen, A., Tabachnick, B. G., & Pope, K. S. (in press). National survey of social workers' sexual attraction to their clients: Results, implications, and comparison to psychologists. *Ethics & Behavior.*

Berry, D. S., & Pennebaker, J. W. (1993). Nonverbal and verbal emotional expression and health. *Psychotherapy & Psychosomatics, 59,* 11–19.

Bettelheim, B. (1983, June 30). Scandal in the family. *New York Review of Books,* pp. 39–44.

Blau, T. H. (1984). *The psychologist as expert witness.* New York: Wiley-Interscience.

Bloom, D. (1989, March 22). Psychologist's license revoked after sex with patient. *Riverside [California] Press Enterprise,* p. B-1.

Bolden v. Phyllis Wheatley Community Center, Inc. WL 71376 (Minn. App. 1994).

Bongar, B. (1991). *The suicidal patient: Clinical and legal standards of care.* Washington, DC: American Psychological Association.

Bongar, B., Maris, R. W., Berman, A. L., & Litman, R. E. (1992). Outpatient standards of care and the suicidal patient. *Suicide and Life-Threatening Behavior, 22,* 453–478.

Borys, D. S. (1988). *Dual relationships between therapist and client: A national survey of clinicians' attitudes and practices.* Unpublished doctoral dissertation, University of California, Los Angeles.

Borys, D. S. (1992). Nonsexual dual relationships. In L. VandeCreek, S. Knapp, & T. L. Jackson (Eds.), *Innovations in clinical practice: A source book* (Vol. 11, pp. 443–454). Sarasota, FL: Professional Resource Press.

Borys, D. S., & Pope, K. S. (1989). Dual relationships between therapist and client: A national study of psychologists, psychiatrists, and social workers. *Professional Psychology: Research and Practice, 20,* 283–293.

Bosanquet, C. (1970). Getting in touch. *Journal of Analytical Psychology, 15,* 42–55.

Bouhoutsos, J. C. (1985, August). Patient–therapist sex: Search for solution to a systems problem. Symposium at the annual meeting of the American Psychological Association, Anaheim, CA.

Bouhoutsos, J. C., Holroyd, J., Lerman, H., Forer, B., & Greenberg, M. (1983). Sexual intimacy between psychotherapists and patients. *Professional Psychology: Research and Practice, 14,* 185–196.

Brabent, E., Falzeder, E., & Giampieri-Deutsch, P., under supervision of A. Haynal (1993). *The correspondence of Sigmund Freud and Sándor Ferenczi: Vol. 1. 1908–1914* (P. T. Hoffer, Trans.). Cambridge, MA: Harvard University Press.

Bro v. Glaser. Cal. App. LEXIS 175 (1994).

Brodsky, A. (1989). Sex between patient and therapist: Psychology's data and response. In G. O. Gabbard (Ed.), *Sexual exploitation in professional relationships* (pp. 15–25). Washington, DC: American Psychiatric Press.

Brooten, K. E., & Chapman, S. (1987). *Malpractice.* New York: Grune & Stratton.

Brown, L. S. (1984). The lesbian feminist therapist in private practice and her community. *Psychotherapy in Private Practice, 2,* 9–16.

Brown, L. S. (1988). Harmful effects of posttermination sexual and romantic relationships between therapists and their former clients. *Psychotherapy, 25,* 249–255.

Brown, L. S. (1989). Beyond thou shalt not: Thinking about ethics in the lesbian therapy community. *Women & Therapy, 8,* 13–25.

Brown, L. S. (in press). *Subversive dialogues.* New York: Basic Books.

Brownfain, J. J. (1971). The APA professional liability insurance program. *American Psychologist, 26,* 648–652.

Burgess, A. W. (1981). Physician sexual misconduct and patients' responses. *American Journal of Psychiatry, 136,* 1335–1342.

Burgess, A. W., & Holmstrom, L. L. (1974). Rape trauma syndrome. *American Journal of Psychiatry, 131,* 981–986.

Burgess, J. A. (1984). Principles and techniques of cross-examination. In B. G. Warschaw (Ed.), *The trial masters: A handbook of strategies and tactics that win cases* (pp. 249–255). Englewood Cliffs, NJ: Prentice-Hall.

Bursztajn, H. J., & Gutheil, T. G. (1992). Protecting patients from clinician–patient sexual contact. *American Journal of Psychiatry, 149,* 1276.

California Department of Consumer Affairs. (1990). *Professional therapy never includes sex.* (Available from Board of Psychology, 1430 Howe Avenue, Sacramento, CA 95825)

Callanan, K., & O'Connor, T. (1988). *Staff comments and recommendations regarding the report of the Senate Task Force on Psychotherapist and Patients Sexual Relations.* Sacramento: Board of Behavioral Science Examiners and Psychology Examining Committee.

Carotenuto, A. (1982). *A secret symmetry: Sabina Spielrein between Jung and Freud* (A. Pomerans, J. Shepley, & K. Winston, Trans.). New York: Pantheon.

Carotenuto, A. (1992). *The difficult art: A critical discourse on psychotherapy* (J. Tambureno, Trans.). Wilmette, IL: Chiron.

Carr, M., & Robinson, G. E. (1990). Fatal attraction: The ethical and clinical dilemma of patient–therapist sex. *Canadian Journal of Psychiatry, 35,* 122–127.

Carr, M. L., Robinson, G. E., Stewart, D. E., & Kussin, D. (1991). A survey of Canadian psychiatric residents regarding resident–educator sexual contact. *American Journal of Psychiatry, 148,* 216–220.

Caudill, O. B. (1993, Winter). Can psychologists be vicariously liable for sexual misconduct? *Advance,* pp. 5, 17–18.

Cautella, J. R., & McCullough, L. (1978). Covert conditioning: A learning-theory perspective on imagery. In J. L. Singer & K. S. Pope (Eds.), *The power of human imagination: New methods of psychotherapy* (pp. 227–254). New York: Plenum Press.

Center must pay $5.7 million over abuse by priest it treated. (1994, January 22). *Los Angeles Times,* p. B13.

Cheatham v. Rogers. 824 S. W. 2d 231 (1992).

Chesler, P. (1972). *Women and madness.* New York: Avon Books.

Chicago Insurance Co. v. Griffin. 817 F.Supp. 861 (D. Hawaii 1993).

Cienfuegos, J., & Monelli, C. (1983). The testimony of political repression as a therapeutic instrument. *American Journal of Orthopsychiatry, 53,* 43–51.

Clarkin, J., Widiger, T. A., Frances, A., Hurt, S., & Gilmore, M. (1983). Prototype typology and the borderline personality disorder. *Journal of Abnormal Psychology, 89,* 181–193.

Coleman, P. G. (1988). Sexual relationships between therapist and patient—different countries, different treatment. *Journal of Psychiatry & Law, 16,* 577–623.

Collins, D. T. (1989). Sexual involvement between psychiatric hospital staff and their patients. In G. O. Gabbard (Ed.), *Sexual exploitation in professional relationships* (pp. 151–162). Washington, DC: American Psychiatric Press.

Collins, D. T., Mebed, A. K., & Mortimer, R. L. (1978). Patient–therapist sex: Consequences for subsequent treatment. *McLean Hospital Journal, 3,* 24–36.

Colorado State Board of Psychology Examiners Case No. PY88-01. (1988, October 3).

Colt, G. H. (1983). The enigma of suicide. *Harvard Magazine, 86,* 47–66.

Committee on Women in Psychology. (1989). If sex enters into the psychotherapy relationship. *Professional Psychology: Research and Practice, 20,* 112–115.

Connel, N., & Wilson, C. (Eds.). (1974). *Rape: The first sourcebook for women.* New York: New American Library.

Courtois, C. A. (1988). *Healing the incest wound.* New York: Norton.

Cummings, N. A., & Sobel, S. B. (1985). Malpractice insurance: Update on sex claims. *Psychotherapy, 22,* 186–188.

Dahlberg, C. C. (1970). Sexual contact between patient and therapist. *Contemporary Psychoanalysis, 5,* 107–124.

Davidson, V. (1977). Psychiatry's problem with no name. *American Journal of Psychoanalysis, 37,* 43–50.

Davison, G. C., & Neale, J. M. (1982). *Abnormal psychology: An experimental clinical approach.* New York: Wiley.

Debose v. Wolfe. Denver District Court Case 91CV4346; under appeal State of Colorado 92CA1929 (1994).

Department of Professional Regulation v. Wise. 575 So.2d 713 (Fla.App. 1 Dist. 1991). Rehearing denied March 13, 1991.

Dillon v. Callaway. 609 N.E.2d 424 (Ind. App. 2 Dist. 1993). Transfer denied May 12, 1993.

Dr. K. v. State Board of Physician Quality Assurance. 98 Md. App. 103, 632, A.2d 453 (1993).

Durré, L. (1980). Comparing romantic and therapeutic relationships. In K. S. Pope (Ed.), *On love and loving: Psychological perspectives on the nature and experience of romantic love* (pp. 228–243). San Francisco: Jossey-Bass.

Ellis, V. (1993, January 21). Hundreds of medical complaints destroyed: Agency facing loss of state funding ordered cases to be dismissed or shredded in 1990, inquiry shows. *Los Angeles Times,* pp. A1, A29.

Emery, O. B., & Csikszentmihalyi, M. (1981a). An epistemological approach to psychiatry: On the psychology/psychopathology of knowledge. *Journal of Mind and Behavior, 2,* 375–396.

Emery, O. B., & Csikszentmihalyi, M. (1981b). The specialization effects of cultural role models in ontogenetic development in upward mobility. *Child Psychiatry and Human Development, 12,* 3–18.

English, B. (1992, December 16). Medical men get a message. *Boston Globe,* p. 41.

Epstein, R. S., & Simon, R. I. (1990). The exploitation index: An early warning indicator of boundary violations in psychotherapy. *Bulletin of the Menninger Clinic, 54,* 450–465.

Estrich, S. (1987). *Real rape.* Cambridge, MA: Harvard University Press.

Eyman, J. R., & Gabbard, G. O. (1991). Will therapist–patient sex prevent suicide? *Psychiatric Annals, 21,* 669–674.

Farberow, N. (1985, May 12). How to tell if someone is thinking of suicide. *Los Angeles Herald Examiner,* p. C9.

Feldman-Summers, S. (1989). Sexual contact in fiduciary relationships. In G. O. Gabbard (Ed.), *Sexual exploitation in professional relationships* (pp. 193–209). Washington, DC: American Psychiatric Press.

Feldman-Summers, S., & Jones, G. (1984). Psychological impacts of sexual contact between therapists or other health care professionals and their clients. *Journal of Consulting and Clinical Psychology, 52,* 1054–1061.

Feldman-Summers, S., & Pope, K. S. (1994). The experience of "forgetting" childhood abuse: A national survey of psychologists. *Journal of Consulting and Clinical Psychology, 62,* 636–639.

Ferguson v. People of the State of Colorado. 824 P.2d 803 (Colo. 1992). Rehearing denied February 24, 1992.

Finkelhor, D. (1984). *Child sexual abuse: New theory and research.* New York: Free Press.

Forte, M., Brown, D., & Dysart, M. (1988). Differences in experience among mindful meditators. *Imagination, Cognition and Personality, 7,* 47–60.

Fox v. Anonymous. 869 S. W. 2d 499 (1993). Rehearing denied January 10, 1994.

Freeman, A., & Dattilio, F. M. (Eds.). (1992). *Comprehensive casebook of cognitive therapy.* New York: Plenum Press.

Freeman, L., & Roy, J. (1976). *Betrayal.* New York: Stein & Day.

Frenette, L. (1991). *Abus de pouvoir: Récit d'une intimité sexualle thérapeutie-cliente.* Montreal, Canada: Les Presses d'Amérique.

Freud, S. (1949). *An outline of psychoanalysis.* New York: Norton.

Freud, S. (1952). *A general introduction to psychoanalysis* (rev. ed.; J. Riviere, Trans.). New York: Washington Square. (Original work published 1924)

Freud, S. (1958a). Further recommendations in the technique of psychoanalysis: On beginning the treatment. In J. Strachey (Ed. and Trans.), *The standard edition of the complete psychological works of Sigmund Freud* (Vol. 12, pp. 121–144). London: Hogarth Press. (Original work published 1913)

Freud, S. (1958b). Observations on the transference-love. In J. Strachey (Ed. and Trans.), *The standard edition of the complete psychological works of Sigmund Freud* (Vol. 12, pp. 157–173). London: Hogarth Press. (Original work published 1915)

Freud, S. (1963). Further recommendations in the technique of psychoanalysis: Observations on transference-love. In P. Rieff (Ed.), *Freud: Therapy and technique* (pp. 167–179). [Authorized English translation of the Revised edition by J. Riviere.] New York: Collier Books. (Original work published 1915)

Fromm, E., & Pope, K. S. (1990). Countertransference in hypnotherapy and hypnoanalysis. *Independent Practitioner, 10,* 48–50.

Gabbard, G. O. (Ed.) (1989a). *Sexual exploitation in professional relationships.* Washington, DC: American Psychiatric Press.

Gabbard, G. O. (1989b). Splitting in hospital treatment. *American Journal of Psychiatry, 146,* 444–451.

Gabbard, G. O. (1992). An overview of countertransference with borderline patients. *American Psychoanalyst, 26,* 6–7.

Gabbard, G. O. (in press). Reconsidering the American Psychological Association's policy on sex with former patients: Is it justifiable? *Professional Psychology: Research and Practice.*

Gartrell, N. K. (1994). Boundaries in lesbian therapist–client relationships. In B. Greene & G. M. Herek (Eds.), *Lesbian and gay psychology: Theory, research, and clinical applications* (pp. 98–117). Thousand Oaks, CA: Sage.

Gartrell, N. K., Herman, J. L., Olarte, S., Feldstein, M. & Localio, R. (1986). Psychiatrist–patient sexual contact: Results of a national survey, I: Prevalence. *American Journal of Psychiatry, 143,* 1126–1131.

Gartrell, N., Herman, J., Olarte, S., Feldstein, M., & Localio, R. (1987). Reporting practices of psychiatrists who knew of sexual misconduct by colleagues. *American Journal of Orthopsychiatry, 57,* 287–295.

Gartrell, N. K., Herman, J. L., Olarte, S., Feldstein, M., & Localio, R. (1989). Prevalence of psychiatrist–patient sexual contact. In G. O. Gabbard (Ed.), *Sexual exploitation in professional relationships* (pp. 3–14). Washington, DC: American Psychiatric Press.

Gartrell, N. K., Milliken, N., Goodson, W. H., Thiemann, S., & Lo, B. (1992). Physician–patient sexual contact: Prevalence and problems. *Western Journal of Medicine, 157,* 139–143.

Geller, J. D. (1978). The body, expressive movement, and physical contact in psychotherapy. In J. L. Singer & K. S. Pope (Eds.), *The power of human imagination: New methods in psychotherapy* (pp. 347–378). New York: Plenum Press.

Geller, J. D., Cooley, R. S., & Hartley, D. (1981). Images of the psychotherapist. *Imagination, Cognition and Personality, 1,* 123–146.

Gibson, W., & Pope, K. S. (1993). The ethics of counseling: A national survey of certified counselors. *Journal of Counseling and Development, 71,* 330–336.

Gilbert, L. A., & Scher, M. (1989). The power of an unconscious belief. *Professional Practice of Psychology, 8,* 94–108.

Glaser, R., & Thorpe, J. (1986). Unethical intimacy: A survey of sexual contact and advances between psychology educators and female graduate students. *American Psychologist, 41,* 43–51.

Goldberg v. Davis. 602 N.E.2d 812 (Supreme Court of Illinois 1992).

Goleman, D. (1977). *The varieties of meditative experience.* New York: Dutton.

Gottlieb, M. C., Sell, J. M., & Schoenfeld, L. S. (1988). Social/romantic relationships with present and former clients: State licensing board actions. *Professional Psychology: Research and Practice, 19,* 459–462.

Greenberg v. McCabe. 453 F Supp 765 (ED Pa 1978), affd 594 F 2d 854 (3d cir 1979), cert denied, 444 US 840. (1979).

Grodney, D. (1990). *Ethical and unethical practices in clinical social work: A survey of practitioners' attitudes.* Unpublished doctoral dissertation. New York University School of Social Work.

Gutheil, T. G., Bursztajn, H. J., Brodsky, A., & Alexander, V. (1991). Managing uncertainty: The therapeutic alliance, informed consent, and liability. In T. G. Gutheil, H. J. Bursztajn, A. Brodsky, & V. Alexander (Eds.), *Decision making in psychiatry and the law* (pp. 69–86). Baltimore: Williams & Wilkins.

Gutheil, T. G., & Gabbard, G. O. (1992). Obstacles to the dynamic understanding of therapist–patient sexual relations. *American Journal of Psychotherapy, 46,* 515–525.

Gutheil, T. G., & Gabbard, G. O. (1993). Concept of boundaries in clinical practice: Theoretical and risk-management dimensions. *American Journal of Psychiatry, 150,* 188–196.

Hall, J. E., & Hare-Mustin, R. T. (1983). Sanctions and the diversity of complaints against psychologists. *American Psychologist, 38,* 714–729.

Hare-Mustin, R. T. (1974). Ethical considerations in the use of sexual contact in psychotherapy. *Psychotherapy: Theory, Research and Practice, 11*, 308–310.

Hare-Mustin, R. T. (1992). Cries and whispers: The psychotherapy of Anne Sexton. *Psychotherapy, 29*, 406–409.

Hatcher, E. R. (1993, June 4). Firm boundaries: No exceptions. *Psychiatric News*, p. 23.

Henderson, D. J. (1975). Incest. In A. M. Freedman, H. I. Kaplan, & B. J. Sadock (Eds.), *Comprehensive textbook of psychiatry* (pp. 1530–1539). Baltimore: Williams & Wilkins.

Herman, J. L. (1981). *Father–daughter incest*. Cambridge, MA: Harvard University Press.

Herman, J. L. (1992). *Trauma and recovery*. New York: Basic Books.

Herman, J. L., Gartrell, N., Olarte, S., Feldstein, M., & Localio, R. (1987). Psychiatrist–patient sexual contact: Results of a national survey, II: Psychiatrists' Attitudes. *American Journal of Psychiatry, 144*, 164–169.

Herman, J. L., Perry, J. C., & van der Kolk, B. A. (1989). Childhood trauma in borderline personality disorder. *American Journal of Psychiatry, 146*, 490–495.

Hoffman v. Schafer. 815 P.2d 971 (Colo. App. 1991), affd. 831 P.2d 897 (Colo. 1993).

Holroyd, J. (1983). Erotic contact as an instance of sex-biased therapy. In J. Murray & P. R. Abramson (Eds.), *Bias in psychotherapy* (pp. 285–308). New York: Praeger.

Holroyd, J. C., & Bouhoutsos, J. C. (1985). Sources of bias in reporting effects of sexual contact with patients. *Professional psychology: Research and Practice, 16*, 701–709.

Holroyd, J., & Brodsky, A. (1977). Psychologists' attitudes and practices regarding erotic and nonerotic physical contact with clients. *American Psychologist, 32*, 843–849.

Holroyd, J. C., & Brodsky, A. M. (1980). Does touching patients lead to sexual intercourse? *Professional Psychology, 11*, 807–811.

Homer v. Long. 599 A.2d 1193 (Md. App. 1992).

Hopkins, J. (1987). Failure of the holding relationship: Some effects of physical rejection on the child's attachment and on his inner experience. *Journal of Child Psychotherapy, 13*, 5–17.

Horak v. Biris. 474 N. E. 2d 13 (1985).

Horowitz, M. J. (1978a). Controls of visual imagery and therapist intervention. In J. L. Singer & K. S. Pope (Eds.), *The power of human imagination: New methods in psychotherapy* (pp. 37–49). New York: Plenum Press.

Horowitz, M. J. (1978b). *Image formation and cognition* (2nd ed.). New York: Appleton-Century-Crofts.

Horowitz, M. J. (1984). Stress and the mechanisms of defense. In H. H. Goldman (Ed.), *Review of general psychiatry* (pp. 362–375). Los Altos, CA: Lange Medical Publications.

Horowitz, M. J. (1986). *Stress response syndromes* (2nd ed.). Northvale, NJ: Aronson, Inc.

How the system protected a bad doctor. (1990, May 20). *Los Angeles Daily News*, p. 12.

Ill. Rev. Stat. §70–803 (1991).

Immekus v. Quigg. 406 S.W.2d 298 (Mo. Ct. App. 1966).

In re Howland. (1980). Before the Psychology Examining Committee, Board of Medical Quality Assurance, State of California, No. D-2212. Reporters' Transcript, Volume 3.

Ivins, M. (1993). *Nothin' but good times ahead*. New York: Random House.

Jaffe, D. T. (1980). *Healing from within*. New York: Knopf.

Jalon, A. (1985, September 4). Psychologist repentant for having sex with a patient. *Los Angeles Times (Valley Edition)*, Part II, p. 6.

Janoff-Bulman, R. (1992). *Shattered assumptions: Toward a new psychology of trauma*. New York: Free Press.

Janoff-Bulman, R., & Lang-Gun, L. (1988). Coping with disease, crime, and accidents: The role of self-blame attributions. In L. Y. Abramson (Ed.), *Social cognition and clinical psychology* (pp. 116–147). New York: Guilford Press.

Jorgenson, L., & Appelbaum, P. S. (1991). For whom the statute tolls: Extending the time during which patients can sue. *Hospital and Community Psychiatry, 42*, 683–684.

Judge urged to resign after child rape decision. (1985, July 18). *Los Angeles Herald Examiner*, p. A6.

Kalichman, S. C. (1993). *Mandated reporting of suspected child abuse: Ethics, law, & policy*. Washington, DC: American Psychological Association.

Kardener, S. H. (1974). Sex and the physician–patient relationship. *American Journal of Psychiatry, 131*, 1134–1136.

Kavoussi, R. J., & Becker, J. V. (1987). Psychiatrist–patient sexual contact. *American Journal of Psychiatry, 144*, 1249–1250.

Kazdin, A. E. (1978). Covert modeling: The therapeutic application of imagined rehearsal. In J. L. Singer & K. S. Pope (Eds.), *The power of human imagination: New methods in psychotherapy* (pp. 255–278). New York: Plenum.

Keith-Spiegel, P. (1977, August). *Sex with clients*. Paper presented at the annual meeting of the American Psychological Association, Washington, DC.

Keith-Spiegel, P. C., & Koocher, G. (1985). *Ethics in psychology*. New York: Random House.

Kirstein, L. (1978). Sexual involvement with patients. *Journal of Clinical Psychiatry, 39*, 366–368.

Kluft, R. (1989). Treating the patient who has been sexually exploited by a previous therapist. *The Psychiatric Clinics of North America, 12*, 483–500.

Kohrman, R., Fineberg, H., Gelman, R., & Weiss, S. (1971). Technique of child analysis: Problems of countertransference. *International Journal of Psychoanalysis, 52*, 487–497.

Koocher, G. P., & Keith-Spiegel, P. (1990). *Children, ethics, and the law: Professional issues and cases*. Lincoln: University of Nebraska Press.

Kottler, J. A. (1993). *On being a therapist* (rev. ed.). San Francisco: Jossey-Bass.

Ladner v. American Assurance Company. N.Y. App. Div. LEXIS 1038 (1994).

Landau v. Werner. 105 Sol. J. 257 (1961).

Lebe, D., & Namir, S. (1993, December). *Boundary dilemmas posed by contemporary psychoanalytic theories.* Paper presented at the meeting of the American Academy of Psychoanalysis, New York.

Leuner, H. (1978). Basic principles and therapeutic efficacy of guided affective imagery (GAI). In J. L. Singer & K. S. Pope (Eds.), *The power of human imagination: New methods in psychotherapy* (pp. 125–166). New York: Plenum.

Levenson, H., & Pope, K. S. (1992). Behavior therapy and cognitive therapy. In H. H. Goldman (Ed.), *Review of general psychiatry* (3rd ed., pp. 408–416). Norwalk, CT: Appleton & Lange.

L. L. v. Medical Protective Co. 122 Wis.2d 455, 362 NW2d 174 (1984).

Lorde, A. (1978). *Uses of the erotic: The erotic as power.* Trumansburg, NY: The Crossing Press.

Lynn, S. J., Milano, M., & Weekes, J. R. (1991). Hypnosis and pseudomemories: The effects of prehypnotic expectancies. *Journal of Personality and Social Psychology, 60,* 318–326.

Maltz, W, & Holman, B. (1984). *Incest and sexuality.* Lexington, MA: Lexington Books.

Maltsberger, J. T. (1993, April). *A career plundered.* Presidential Address at the meeting of the American Association of Suicidology, San Francisco.

Mann, C. K., & Winer, J. D. (1991). Psychotherapist's sexual contact with client. *American Jurisprudence Proof of Facts* (3rd series, Vol. 14, pp. 319–431). Rochester, NY: Lawyers Cooperative Publishing.

Marine, E. (1994, January/February). Knew or should have known. *Los Angeles County Psychological Association News,* p. 6.

Marlene F. 48 Cal. 3d 583 (1989).

Marmor, J. (1972). Sexual acting out in psychotherapy. *American Journal of Psychoanalysis, 32,* 327–335.

Maruani, G., Pope, K. S., & de Verbizier, J. (1989). Ethics and psychotherapy in France. *Imagination, Cognition, and Personality, 9,* 355–357.

Masnerus, L. (1989, February 19). The rape laws change faster than perceptions. *New York Times,* p. 20.

Mason v. Marriage and Family Center. 228 Cal. App. 3d; 279 Cal.Rptr. 51 (1991). Petition for review denied May 30, 1991.

Masters, W. H., & Johnson, V. E. (1976). Principles of the new sex therapy. *American Journal of Psychiatry, 110,* 3370–3373.

Matheson, J. (1984, December). AMI member "whistle-blower" in successful prosecution of Eau Claire psychiatrist. *AMI of Wisconsin Newsletter,* p. 2.

Matheson, J. (1985, July 20). Psychiatrist sentenced to prison for five years. *The Milwaukee Journal,* p. 9.

McConkey, K. M. (1992). The effects of hypnotic procedures on remembering: The experimental findings and their implications for forensic hypnosis.

In E. Fromm & M. R. Nash (Eds.), *Contemporary hypnosis research* (pp. 405–426). Washington, DC: American Psychological Association.

McNicholes [appellee] v. Subotnik [appellee] v. St. Paul Fire & Marine Insurance Co. [appellant]. 12 F.3d 105 (1993).

Meichenbaum, D. (1977). *Cognitive-behavior modification: An integrative approach.* New York: Plenum Press.

Meichenbaum, D. (1978). Why does using imagery in psychotherapy lead to change? In J. L. Singer & K. S. Pope (Eds.), *The power of human imagination: New methods in psychotherapy* (pp. 381–394). New York: Plenum.

Meyer, C., & Taylor, S. (1986). Adjustment to rape. *Journal of Personality and Social Psychology, 50,* 1226–1234.

Mitchum, N. T. (1987). Developmental play therapy: A treatment approach for child victims of sexual molestation. *Journal of Counseling and Development, 65,* 320–321.

Mohn v. Hahnemann Medical College and Hospital. 515 A2d 920 (PA Sp. Ct. 1986).

New Mexico Physicians Mutual Liability Company v. LaMure. 860 Pacific Reporter, 2d, 734 (1993).

Noel, B., & Watterson, K. (1992). *You must be dreaming.* New York: Poseidon.

O'Connor, T. (1992). Diverting justice: Unanswered questions on diverting licensees from discipline. *California Regulatory Law Reporter,* pp. 4–5.

Orlinsky, D. E., & Geller, J. D. (1993). Patients' representations of their therapists and therapy: New measures. In N. E. Miller, L. Luborsky, J. Barber, & J. P. Docherty (Eds.), *Psychodynamic treatment research: A handbook for clinical practice* (pp. 423–466). New York: Basic Books.

Osborn v. Board of Regents of the State of New York et al. 606 N. Y. S. 2d 361 (1993).

Pennebaker, J. W. (1993). Putting stress into words: Health, linguistic, and therapeutic implications. *Behavior Research & Therapy, 31,* 539–548.

Pennebaker, J. W., Kiecolt-Glaser, J. K., & Glaser, R. (1988). Disclosure of traumas and immune function: Health implications for psychotherapy. *Journal of Consulting & Clinical Psychology, 56,* 239–245.

Perr, I. N. (1989). Medicolegal aspects of professional sexual exploitation. In G. O. Gabbard (Ed.), *Sexual exploitation in professional relationships* (pp. 211–228). Washington, DC: American Psychiatric Press.

Perry, C. (1979). Hypnotic coercion and compliance to it: A review of evidence presented in a legal case. *International Journal of Clinical and Experimental Hypnosis, 27,* 187–218.

Persons, J. B. (1989). *Cognitive therapy in practice: A case formulation approach.* New York: Norton.

Perspectives. (1990, April 23). *Newsweek,* p. 17.

Phillips, A. (1993). *On kissing, tickling, and being bored: Psychoanalytic essays on the unexamined life.* Cambridge, MA: Harvard University Press.

Plaisil, E. (1985). *Therapist.* New York: St. Martin's/Marek.

Pope, K. S. (1982). *Implications of fantasy and imagination for mental health: Theory, research, and interventions* (Contract no. 82M024784505D). Bethesda, MD: National Institute of Mental Health.

Pope, K. S. (1985, August). *Diagnosis and treatment of therapist–patient sex syndrome.* Paper presented at the meeting of the American Psychological Association, Los Angeles.

Pope, K. S. (1986, May). *Therapist–patient sex syndrome: Research findings.* Paper presented at the meeting of the American Psychiatric Association, Washington, DC.

Pope, K. S. (1988). How clients are harmed by sexual contact with mental health professionals. *Journal of Counseling and Development, 67,* 222–226.

Pope, K. S. (1989a). Rehabilitation of therapists who have been sexually intimate with a patient. In G. O. Gabbard (Ed.), *Sexual exploitation in professional relationships* (pp. 129–136). Washington, DC: American Psychiatric Press.

Pope, K. S. (1989b). Student–teacher sexual intimacy. In G. O. Gabbard (Ed.), *Sexual exploitation within professional relationships* (pp. 163–176). Washington, DC: American Psychiatric Press.

Pope, K. S. (1989c). Therapist–patient sex syndrome: A guide for attorneys and subsequent therapists to assessing damage. In G. O. Gabbard (Ed.), *Sexual exploitation in professional relationships* (pp. 39–56). Washington, DC: American Psychiatric Press.

Pope, K. S. (1990a). Ethical and malpractice issues in hospital practice. *American Psychologist, 45,* 1066–1070.

Pope, K. S. (1990b). Therapist–patient sex as sex abuse: Six scientific, professional, and practical dilemmas in addressing victimization and rehabilitation. *Professional Psychology: Research and Practice, 21,* 227–239.

Pope, K. S. (1990c). Therapist–patient sexual involvement: A review of the research. *Clinical Psychology Review, 10,* 477–490.

Pope, K. S. (1991). Rehabilitation plans and expert testimony for therapists who have been sexually involved with a patient. *Independent Practitioner, 22,* 44–52.

Pope, K. S. (1993). Licensing disciplinary actions for psychologists who have been sexually involved with a client: Some information about offenders. *Professional Psychology: Research and Practice, 24,* 374–377.

Pope, K. S. (in press). Assessing patients and therapists who have been involved in therapist–patient sexual intimacies: Evaluating harm, recovery, and rehabilitation. In J. N. Butcher (Ed.), *Practical considerations in clinical personality assessment.* New York: Oxford University Press.

Pope, K. S., & Bajt, T. R. (1988). When laws and values conflict: A dilemma for psychologists. *American Psychologist, 43,* 828.

Pope, K. S., & Bouhoutsos, J. C. (1986). *Sexual intimacies between therapists and patients.* New York: Praeger/Greenwood.

Pope, K. S., Butcher, J. N., & Seelen, J. (1993). *The MMPI, MMPI-2, & MMPI-A in court: A practical guide for expert witnesses and attorneys.* Washington, DC: American Psychological Association.

Pope, K. S., & Feldman-Summers, S. (1992). National survey of psychologists' sexual and physical abuse history and their evaluation of training and competence in these areas. *Professional Psychology: Research and Practice, 23*, 353–361.

Pope, K. S., & Gabbard, G. O. (1989). Individual psychotherapy for victims of therapist–patient sexual intimacy. In G. O. Gabbard (Ed.), *Sexual exploitation in professional relationships* (pp. 89–100). Washington, DC: American Psychiatric Press.

Pope, K. S., & Garcia-Peltoniemi, R. E. (1991). Responding to victims of torture: Clinical issues, professional responsibilities, and useful resources. *Professional Psychology: Research and Practice, 22*, 269–276.

Pope, K. S., Keith-Spiegel, P., & Tabachnick, B. G. (1986). Sexual attraction to patients: The human therapist and the (sometimes) inhuman training system. *American Psychologist, 41*, 147–158.

Pope, K. S., Levenson, H., & Schover, L. R. (1979). Sexual intimacy in psychology training: Results and implications of a national survey. *American Psychologist, 34*, 682–689.

Pope, K. S., Sonne, J. L., & Holroyd, J. (1993). *Sexual feelings in psychotherapy: Explorations for therapists and therapists-in-training*. Washington, DC: American Psychological Association.

Pope, K. S., & Tabachnick, B. G. (1993). Therapists' anger, hate, fear, and sexual feelings: National survey of therapists' responses, client characteristics, critical events, formal complaints, and training. *Professional Psychology: Research and Practice, 24*, 142–152.

Pope, K. S., & Tabachnick, B. G. (in press). Therapists as patients: A national survey of psychologists' experiences, problems, and beliefs. *Professional Psychology: Research and Practice*.

Pope, K. S., Tabachnick, B. G., & Keith-Spiegel, P. (1987). Ethics of practice: The beliefs and behaviors of psychologists as therapists. *American Psychologist, 42*, 993–1006.

Pope, K. S., & Vasquez, M. J. T. (1991). *Ethics in psychotherapy and counseling: A practical guide for psychologists*. San Francisco: Jossey-Bass.

Pope, K. S., & Vetter, V. A. (1991). Prior therapist–patient sexual involvement among patients seen by psychologists. *Psychotherapy, 28*, 429–438.

Pope, K. S., & Vetter, V. A. (1992). Ethical dilemmas encountered by members of the American Psychological Association: A national survey. *American Psychologist, 47*, 397–411.

Prejean, H. (1993). *Dead man walking*. New York: Random House.

Pugh, T. (1988, March 23). State charges psychologist with numerous violations. *Rocky Mountain News*, p. 3.

Rapp, M. S. (1987). Sexual misconduct. *Canadian Medical Association Journal, 137*, 193–194.

Recent ethics cases. (1982, April 16). *Psychiatric News*, pp. 8–9, 38.

Redlich, F. C. (1977). The ethics of sex therapy. In W. H. Masters, V. E. Johnson, & R. D. Kolodny (Eds.), *Ethical issues in sex therapy* (pp. 143–157). Boston: Little, Brown.

Reiser, D. E., & Levenson, H. (1984). Abuses of the borderline diagnosis: A clinical problem with teaching opportunities. *American Journal of Psychiatry, 141*, 1528–1532.

Richard F. H. v. Larry H. D. 198 Cal. App. 3d 591 (1988).

Riley v. Presnell. 565 NE2d 780 (Mass 1991).

Robinson, W. L., & Reid, P. T. (1985). Sexual intimacies in psychology revisited. *Professional Psychology: Research and Practice, 16*, 512–520.

Rogers v. Alabama Department of Mental Health and Mental Retardation. 825 F. Supp. 986 (1993).

Rosewater, L. B. (1985). Schizophrenic, borderline or battered? In L. B. Rosewater & L. E. Walker (Eds.), *Handbook on feminist therapy: Psychotherapy for women* (pp. 215–225). New York: Springer.

Rosewater, L. B. (1987). The clinical and courtroom application of battered women's personality assessments. In D. J. Sonkin (Ed.), *Domestic violence on trial* (pp. 86–94). New York: Springer.

Roy v. Hartogs. 381 N.Y.S. 2d 587; 85 Misc.2d 891 (1976).

Russell, D. E. H. (1986). *The secret trauma: Incest in the lives of girls and women.* New York: Basic Books.

R. W. v. Hampe. 626 A.2d 218 (PA Sp. Ct. 1993).

Sanders, J. R., & Keith-Spiegel, P. (1980). Formal and informal adjudication of ethics complaints against psychologists. *American Psychologist, 35*, 1096–1105.

Saul, L. J. (1962). The erotic transference. *Psychoanalytic Quarterly, 31*, 54–61.

Schoener, G. R., Milgrom, J. H., Gonsiorek, J. C., Luepker, E. T., & Conroe, R. M. (1989). *Psychotherapists' sexual involvement with clients: Intervention and prevention.* Minneapolis: Walk-In Counseling Center.

Searles, H. F. (1959). Oedipal love in the countertransference. *International Journal of Psychoanalysis, 40*, 180–190.

Sehlmeyer v. Department of General Services. 17 Cal. App. 4 1072 (1993).

Sell, J. M., Gottlieb, M. C., & Schoenfeld, L. S. (1986). Ethical considerations of social/romantic relationships with present and former clients. *Professional Psychology: Research and Practice, 17*, 504–508.

Shapiro, D. L. (1991). *Forensic psychological assessment: An integrative approach.* Boston: Allyn & Bacon.

Sharfstein, S. S. (1993). Report of the secretary: Summary of actions of the Board of Trustees, May 1992–March 1993. *American Journal of Psychiatry, 150*, 1573–1588.

Shearer, L. (1981, August 23). Sex between patient and physician. *Los Angeles Times Parade*, p. 8.

Sheehan, P. W., Stratham, D., & Jamieson, G. A. (1991). Pseudomemory effects and their relationship to level of susceptibility to hypnosis and state instruction. *Journal of Personality and Social Psychology, 60*, 130–137.

Shopland, S. N., & VandeCreek, L. (1991). Sex with ex-clients: Theoretical rationales for prohibition. *Ethics & Behavior, 1*, 35–44.

Siassi, I., & Thomas, M. (1973). Physicians and the new sexual freedom. *American Journal of Psychiatry, 130*, 1256–1257.

Simmons v. United States. 805 F2d 1363, (9th Cir 1986).

Simon, R. I. (1992a). Clinical risk management of suicidal patients. In R. I. Simon (Ed.), *Review of clinical psychiatry and the law* (Vol. 3, pp. 3–66). Washington, DC: American Psychiatric Press.

Simon, R. I. (1992b). Treatment of boundary violations: Clinical, ethical, and legal considerations. *Bulletin of the American Academy of Psychiatry and Law*, 20, 269–288.

Simon, R. I., & Sadoff, R. L. (1992). *Psychiatric malpractice: Cases and comments for clinicians*. Washington, DC: American Psychiatric Press.

Singer, J. L. (1974). *Imagery and daydream methods in psychotherapy and behavior modification*. New York: Academic Press.

Singer, J. L. (1985). Transference and the human condition: A cognitive-affective perspective. *Psychoanalytic Psychology*, 2, 189–219.

Singer, J. L., & Pope, K. S. (1978). The use of imagery and fantasy techniques in psychotherapy. In J. L. Singer & K. S. Pope (Eds.), *The power of human imagination: New methods in psychotherapy* (pp. 3–34). New York: Plenum Press.

Smith, S. (1984). The sexually abused patient and the abusing therapist. *Psychoanalytic Psychology*, 1, 89–98.

Smith v. Pust. 19 Cal. App. 4th 263 (1993).

Snyder v. Major. 789 F. Supp. 646 (S.D.N.Y. 1992).

Snyder v. Major. 818 F. Supp. 68 (S.D.N.Y. 1993).

Sonne, J. L. (1987). Proscribed sex: Counseling the patient subjected to sexual intimacy by a therapist. *Medical Aspects of Human Sexuality*, 16, 18–23.

Sonne, J. L. (1989). An example of group therapy for victims of therapist–client sexual intimacy. In G. O.. Gabbard (Ed.), *Sexual exploitation in professional relationships* (pp. 101–127). Washington, DC: American Psychiatric Press.

Sonne, J. L., Meyer, C. B., Borys, D., & Marshall, V. (1985). Clients' reaction to sexual intimacy in therapy. *American Journal of Orthopsychiatry*, 55, 183–189.

Sonne, J. L., & Pope, K. S. (1991). Treating victims of therapist–patient sexual involvement. *Psychotherapy*, 28, 174–187.

Spitzer, R. L., Endicott, J., & Gibbon, M. (1979). Crossing the border into borderline personality and borderline schizophrenia. *Archives of General Psychiatry*, 36, 17–24.

St. Paul Fire & Marine Insurance Company v. Downs. 617 N.E.2d 338 (Ill. App. 1 Dist. 1993).

Stake, J. E., & Oliver, J. (1991). Sexual contact and touching between therapist and client: A survey of psychologists' attitudes and behavior. *Professional Psychology: Research and Practice*, 22, 297–307.

Stone, A. A. (1990, March). No good deed goes unpunished. *The Psychiatric Times*, pp. 24–27.

Stone, L. G. (1980). *A study of the relationship among anxious attachment, ego functioning, and female patients' vulnerability to sexual involvement with their male psychotherapists*. Unpublished doctoral dissertation, California School of Professional Psychology, Los Angeles.

Stone, M. (1976). Boundary violations between therapist and patient. *Psychiatric Annals, 6,* 670–677.

Stone, M. (1982). Turning points in therapy. In S. Slipp (Ed.), *Curative factors in dynamic psychotherapy* (pp. 259–279). New York: McGraw-Hill.

Stone, M. H. (1975). Management of unethical behavior in a hospital staff. *American Journal of Psychotherapy, 29,* 391–401.

Stromberg, C. D., Haggarty, R. F., Leibenluft, McMillian, M. H., Mishkin, B., Rubin, B. L., & Trilling, H. R. (1988). *The psychologist's legal handbook.* Washington, DC: Council for the National Register of Health Service Providers in Psychology.

Tavris, C. (1989). *Anger: The misunderstood emotion* (2nd ed.). New York: Simon & Schuster.

Taylor, E. (1978). Asian interpretations: Transcending the stream of consciousness. In K. S. Pope & J. L. Singer (Eds.), *The stream of consciousness: Scientific investigations into the flow of human experience* (pp. 31–54). New York: Plenum Press.

Taylor, S. E. (1990). *Positive illusions: Creative self-deception and the healthy mind.* New York: Basic Books.

Terwilliger, C. (1989, October 16). Client says she sued doctor to save herself and others. *Cedar Springs [Colorado] Gazette Telegraph,* p. D1–D2.

Therapist guilty in sexual assault. (1988, April 8). *Rocky Mountain News,* p. 28.

Therapist sentenced for whipping patient. (1987, September 1). *Minneapolis Star and Tribune,* p. 3B.

Trower v. Jones. 520 N.E.2d 297 (1988).

Twemlow, S. W., & Gabbard, G. O. (1989). The lovesick therapist. In G. O. Gabbard (Ed.), *Sexual exploitation in professional relationships* (pp. 71–87). Washington, DC: American Psychiatric Press.

Unbelievable. (1983, January 24). *Los Angeles Herald Examiner,* p. F2.

Unger, R. K. (1979). *Female and male: Psychological perspectives.* New York: Harper & Row.

van der Kolk, B. A. (1993, October 24). *The assessment and treatment of psychological trauma: A developmental perspective.* Pre-meeting institute at the annual meeting of the International Society for Traumatic Stress Studies, San Antonio, TX.

Vasquez, M. J. T. (1991). Sexual intimacies with clients after termination: Should a prohibition be explicit? *Ethics & Behavior, 1,* 45–61.

Venn, J. (1988). Misuse of hypnosis in sexual contexts: Two case reports. *International Journal of Clinical and Experimental Hypnosis, 34,* 12–18.

Vinson, J. S. (1987). Use of complaint procedures in cases of therapist–patient sexual contact. *Professional Psychology: Research and Practice, 18,* 159–164.

Walker, C. E., Bonner, B. L., & Kaufman, K. L. (1988). *The physically and sexually abused child.* New York: Pergamon Press.

Walker, E., & Young, T. D. (1986). *A killing cure.* New York: Holt, Rinehart & Winston.

Walker, L. E. A. (1979). *The battered woman.* New York: Harper & Row.
Walker, L. E. A. (1984). *Battered woman syndrome.* New York: Springer.
Walker, L. E. A. (1989). Psychology and violence against women. *American Psychologist, 44,* 695–702.
Walker, L. E. A. (1994). *Abused women and survivor therapy: A practical guide for the psychotherapist.* Washington, DC: American Psychological Association.
Walker v. Parzen. Superior Court of the State of California, County of San Diego, Case #437641 (1981).
Wasson, G. M. (1991). Hospital liability for negligent selection of staff physician. *American Jurisprudence Proof of Facts* (3d series, Vol. 14, pp. 433–525). Rochester, NY: Lawyers Cooperative Publishing.
Weinberg, K. (1955). *Incest behavior.* New York: Citadel.
Weiner, I. B. (1989). On competence and ethicality in psychodiagnostic assessment. *Journal of Personality Assessment, 53,* 827–831.
Weschler, L. (1990). *A miracle, a universe.* New York: Pantheon Books.
Whitesell v. Green. No. 38745 (Hawaii Dist. Ct. 1973).
Widiger, T. A. (1982). Prototype typology and borderline diagnosis. *Clinical Psychology Review, 2,* 115–135.
Widiger, T. A., Frances, A., Spitzer, R. L., & Williams, J. B. (1988). The DSM-III-R personality disorders: An overview. *American Journal of Psychiatry, 145,* 786–795.
Widiger, T. A., Sanderson, C., & Warner, L. (1986). The MMPI, protypal typology, and borderline personality disorder. *Journal of Personality Assessment, 50,* 540–553.
Wigmore, J. H. (1970). *Evidence in trials at common law.* Boston: Little, Brown. (Original work published 1934)
Wolpe, J. (1958). *Psychotherapy by reciprocal inhibition.* Stanford, CA: Stanford University Press.
A woman's a sex object. (1977, May 27). *San Francisco Examiner,* p. 2.
Zipkin v. Freeman. 436 S.W. 2d 753 Mo. (1968).

Appendix A

Research Findings About Therapists' Behaviors and Experiences (see chapter 3)

Therapist's Behavior or Feeling	% of Therapists Reporting Behavior or Feeling		
	Study 1[a]	Study 2[b]	Study 3[c]
Using self-disclosure as a therapy technique	93.3%		
Disclosing details of current personal stresses to a client		38.9%	
Telling a client that you care about him or her			77.9%
Crying in the presence of a client	56.5%		
Having clients address you by your first name	96.2%		
Holding a client's hand			60.4%
Hugging a client	86.2%		81.1%
Kissing a client	28.5%		5.6%
Lying down next to a client			0.4%
Lying on top of or underneath a client			0.4%
Cradling or otherwise holding a client in your lap			
Giving a massage to a client			2.8%
Reassuring a client that having sexual feelings about a therapist is not uncommon			77.9%
Noticing that a client is physically attractive			95.8%

Therapist's Behavior or Feeling	% of Therapists Reporting Behavior or Feeling		
	Study 1[a]	Study 2[b]	Study 3[c]
Telling a client that you find him or her physically attractive			38.9%
Suggesting that a client tell you about his or her sexual fantasies			68.1%
Telling a sexual fantasy to a client			6.0%
Engaging in a sexual fantasy about a client	71.8%		
Flirting with a client			19.6%
Feeling sexually attracted to a client	89.5%		87.3%
Telling a client, "I am sexually attracted to you"	20.1%		
Having a client tell you that he or she is sexually attracted to you			73.3%
Feeling sexually aroused while in the presence of a client			57.8%
Having a client seem to become sexually aroused in your presence			18.2%
Having a client seem to have an orgasm in your presence			3.2%
Talking with a current client about sharing a sexual relationship after termination			2.0%
Becoming friends with a client after termination	57.3%	30.2%	
Telling a client that you are angry at him or her	89.7%		77.9%
Raising your voice at a client because you are angry at him or her			57.2%
Having fantasies that reflect your anger at a client			50.9%
Feeling hatred toward a client			31.2%
Telling a client that you are disappointed in him or her	51.9%		
Feeling afraid that a client may commit suicide			97.2%
Feeling afraid that a client may need clinical resources that are unavailable			86.0%
Terminating therapy if a client cannot pay	62.0%		
Lending money to a client	25.4%		
Inviting a client to a party or social event	15.8%	7.2%	
Accepting a gift worth over $50	21.9%	6.5%	
Feeling afraid because a client's condition gets suddenly or seriously worse			90.9%

Therapist's Behavior or Feeling	% of Therapists Reporting Behavior or Feeling		
	Study 1[a]	Study 2[b]	Study 3[c]
Feeling afraid that your colleagues may be critical of your work with a client	88.1%		
Feeling afraid that a client may file a formal complaint against you	66.0%		

[a]A national survey of 1,000 psychologists with a 46% return rate (Pope, Tabachnick, & Keith-Spiegel, 1987)

Many of the items from Pope et al. (1987) were translated and a small, interdisciplinary survey was conducted using a sample of mental health workers in France (Maruani, Pope, & de Verbizier, 1989). Among the findings of the French study were that 70% reported that they had never told a client: "I'm sexually attracted to you"; 75% reported that they had never formed a friendship or social relationship with a former client; 75% reported that they had never cried in the presence of a client; 70% reported that they had never hugged a client; 70% reported that they had never accepted a client's gift that was worth more than 250 Francs; 5% reported that they had never accepted a client's gift that was worth less than 50 Francs; and 20% reported that they had never told a client that they were angry at him or her.

[b]A national survey of 4,800 psychologists, psychiatrists, and social workers with a 49% return rate (Borys & Pope, 1989)

[c]A national survey of 600 psychologists with a 48% return rate (Pope & Tabachnick, 1993)

Appendix B

Sample Informed Consent Form for Forensic Assessment When Therapist–Patient Sex Is at Issue

This appendix presents one possible example of a form for obtaining written informed consent for a forensic assessment when therapist–patient sex is at issue. The sample form "Informed Consent For Forensic Assessment (With Special Attention to Therapist–Patient Involvement)" and discussion that appear below have been adapted and amended from a more general "Sample Informed Consent Form for Conducting Forensic Assessments" (Pope, Butcher, & Seelen, 1993, pp. 197–199) and were greatly influenced by consent forms previously created by both Laura Brown and the late Alan Malyon.

Although there are many possible approaches to informed consent for forensic assessment in this area, any consent form must be adapted to the purposes and procedures of a specific assessment, to the needs of the patient who is raising the issue of sexual involvement, to the theoretical orientation or approach of the clinician conducting the assessment, to any unique circumstances of the assessment, and to the array of relevant legislation, case law, administrative regulations, and professional standards. To meet these requirements, clinicians conducting such assessments may find it useful to have a comprehensive form in their computer's database. The form could have numerous statements relevant to the clinician's most common assessment situations as well as reminders of other topics that may, however rarely, need to be addressed. When planning each forensic assessment, the clinician could duplicate the computer file containing this comprehensive form and then edit the duplicate so that it best addresses the elements of the next assessment.

It is essential that the clinician review such forms with his or her own attorney *before using the form* to ensure that it is consistent with all applicable ethical, legal, administrative, and professional standards as well as the approach and needs of the clinician planning the forensic assessments. It is also essential that the clinician take adequate time to review an informed consent form with the patient who is to be assessed so that the patient understands all aspects of the planned assessments that might substantially affect the patient's decision regarding whether to proceed with the evaluation (see chapters 4 and 6).

Finally, such forms may play an essential role in the process of informed consent, but neither the clinician nor any one else should ever assume that the mere presence of the form constitutes or completes the process of consent.

> Providing information in written form can be vital in ensuring that clients have the information they need. But the form cannot be a substitute for an adequate process of informed consent. At a minimum, the clinician must discuss the information with the client and arrive at a professional judgment that the client has adequate understanding of the relevant information.
>
> Clinicians using consent forms must ensure that their clients have the requisite reading skills. Illiteracy is a major problem in the United States; clinicians cannot simply assume that all of their clients can read. Moreover, some clients may not be well versed in English, perhaps having only rudimentary skills in spoken English as a second or third language. (Pope & Vasquez, 1991, p. 85)

Informed Consent for Forensic Assessment (With Special Attention to Issues of Therapist– Patient Sexual Involvement)

Your attorney has asked that I conduct a psychological assessment in connection with your court case, which involves issues related to sexual involvement with a therapist. This form was written to give you information about the assessment process. The assessment will contain three main parts.

In the first part, which may take more than one session, I will be giving you several standardized psychological tests. [Add a brief description of the tests.] We will discuss the instructions in detail when I give you the tests. It will be important that you understand the instructions for each test. If you do not understand the instructions for a test, it will be important for you to let me know immediately so that we can ensure that you understand.

In the second part, I will interview you. During the interview, I will ask you questions about yourself and ask you to talk about yourself. Some of the questions will be about your relationship with your former therapist. There may, of course, be areas that you are reluctant to talk about. If so, please be sure to tell me that the questions are making you uncomfortable or that you have reasons for not providing the information. We can then talk about your concerns.

In the third part, I will describe my conclusions to you and will review with you the information from the interview and tests. You will have an opportunity to discuss any of the opinions or information that I review with you. I will invite you to comment on the information and on my opinions. This will give you an opportunity to call my attention to any errors in fact or conclusion that you believe I have made and any aspects that you believe are incomplete or misleading. (It is possible, of course, that we may disagree about certain conclusions or other aspects of this assessment.)

It is important that you be as honest as possible when responding to the items on the standardized tests, providing information during the interview, and writing your response to the assessment. Information that is withheld, incomplete, wrong, or misleading may be far more damaging than if I am able to find out about it now and put it in context in my report or testimony. It is important for us to discuss any concerns you have in this area.

Although I will try to be thorough when I interview you, I may not ask about some areas or information that you believe are important. If so, please tell me so that we can discuss it.

I am a [psychologist, psychiatrist, or other professional title] licensed by the state of [name of state]. If you have reason to believe that I am behaving unethically or unprofessionally during the course of this assessment, I urge you to let me know at once so that we can discuss it. If you believe that I have not adequately addressed your complaints in this area, there are several agencies that you may consult, and, if you believe it appropriate, you may file a formal complaint against me. One agency is the state governmental board that licenses me to practice: [name, address, and phone number of the licensing board]. Other agencies are the ethics committees of my state professional association, [name, address, and phone number], and national professional association, [name, address, and phone number]. However, you have my assurance that I will conduct this assessment in an ethical and professional manner and will be open to discussing any complaints that you have in this area.

Please check each item below to indicate that you have read it carefully and understand it.

- ☐ I understand that Dr. _____ has been hired by my attorney, [fill in attorney's name], to conduct a psychological assessment for a case in which sexual involvement with a previous therapist is an issue.
- ☐ I understand that I will be asked to talk about the sexual involvement with a previous therapist, and I agree to do so.
- ☐ I understand that it is important for me to be honest and accurate when answering questions or providing information during this assessment.

☐ I understand that Dr. _____ may write a formal report about me based on the results of this assessment.

☐ I authorize Dr. _____ to send a copy of this formal report to my attorney and to discuss the report with him or her.

☐ I understand that Dr. _____ will not provide me with this written report but that I may, if I choose, schedule an additional appointment with Dr. _____ to discuss the results of this assessment.

☐ I authorize Dr. _____ to testify about me and this assessment in depositions and trial(s) related to my legal case.

☐ I understand that I may interrupt or discontinue this assessment at any time.

☐ I understand that even if I interrupt the assessment and it is not resumed or if I discontinue the assessment, it is possible (depending on the applicable laws, on rulings by the court, and/or on decisions by the attorneys in this case) that Dr. _____ may be called to submit a report or testify about the assessment, even if the assessment is incomplete.

☐ I understand that if I disclose certain types of special information to Dr. _____ , he/she may be required or permitted to communicate this information to other people. As previously discussed with Dr. _____ , examples of such special information include reports of child or elder abuse and threats to kill or violently attack a specific person.

☐ I understand that the assessment will be audiotaped.

☐ I understand that the audiotaped record of the assessment will be given to my attorney and may become evidence in the deposition or trial(s).

If you have read, understood, and checked off each of the prior sections, please read carefully the following statement and, if you are in agreement, please sign the statement. Do *not* sign if you have any questions that remain unanswered after our discussion of them or if there are any aspects that you don't understand or agree to; contact your attorney for guidance concerning how to proceed so that you fully understand the process and can decide whether you wish to continue.

Consent Agreement: I have read, agreed to, and checked off each of the previous sections. I have asked questions about any parts that I did not understand fully. I have also asked questions about any parts that I was concerned about. By signing below, I indicate that I understand and agree to the nature and purpose of this assessment, to the way(s) in which it will be reported, and to each of the points listed above.

_____

Signature

_____

Name (please print)

_____

Date

Appendix C

Informed Consent Issues for Providing Therapy to a Patient Who Has Been Sexually Involved With a Prior Therapist

As was discussed in chapter 4, informed consent is best viewed as a process rather than a static formality. The process is likely to occur differently and to possess different content according to whether the therapy is, say, cognitive–behavioral, psychodynamic, feminist, existential, systems, or gestalt. Aside from differences of theoretical orientation and technique, each therapist, patient, and situation is unique, and the process of informed consent must be shaped to respect and take account of that uniqueness.

Although the process, both oral and written, will vary significantly from therapist to therapist, patient to patient, and setting to setting, certain issues seem central to this process. What follows is a list of some of the most significant issues that tend to be a part of the informed consent process. It may be useful for the therapist to review this list periodically, considering the degree to which each issue may be essential to a particular patient's providing or withholding informed consent. Because both informed consent and therapy itself are processes, the list may be useful not only at the beginning of therapy but also in subsequent stages as the patient's situation, therapeutic needs, and treatment plan change.

☐ Is there any evidence that the person is not fully capable of understanding the information and issues relevant to giving or withholding informed consent?

☐ Are there any factors that would prevent this person from arriving at decisions that are truly voluntary?

☐ Does the person adequately understand the type and nature of the services that the therapist is offering?

☐ Are there other ways (that might replace or supplement the therapy that you provide) that the person might effectively address the relevant issues of concern? If so, is the person adequately aware of them?

☐ If the degree of the therapist's education, training, or experience in the area of providing clinical or forensic services to sexually exploited patients would be relevant to the person's decision about whether to begin or continue work with the therapist, does the person have the relevant information?

☐ To the extent that the person has identified the previous therapist and other relevant individuals, groups, or organizations, has the subsequent therapist not only ensured that there is no dual relationship, apparent conflict of interest, role conflict, or other complication that might adversely affect the therapy or forensic services but also disclosed any former or concurrent relationships that might affect the person's decisions about whether to pursue or continue therapy with the subsequent therapist?

☐ Does the person understand that the therapist is not an attorney and cannot provide legal counsel or representation?

☐ Does the person understand whether the therapist is licensed (or is, e.g., an unlicensed intern), the nature of that license (e.g., psychology, psychiatry, or social work), and how the license status may affect issues such as types of services provided (e.g., medications), confidentiality, privilege, and so forth?

☐ If any information about the person or the treatment will be communicated to or will be in any way accessible to others in your setting (e.g., administrative staff, utilization review committees, quality control personnel, or clinical supervisors) either orally (e.g., through supervision or case conferences) or in writing (e.g., through chart notes, treatment summaries, or treatment reports), is the person adequately aware of these communications and modes of access and of their implications?

☐ If information about the person or the treatment will be

communicated to any payment source (e.g., an insurance company or a government agency), is the person adequately aware of the nature, content, and implications of these communications?

☐ Have any potential limitations in the number of sessions (e.g., a managed care plan's limitation of 10 therapy sessions or an insurance plan's limitation of payments for mental health services to a specific dollar amount) or length of treatment (e.g., if the therapist is an intern whose internship will conclude within 3 months, after which the therapist will no longer be available) been adequately disclosed to the person and the potential implications been adequately discussed?

☐ Does the person adequately understand the therapist's policy regarding missed or canceled appointments?

☐ Has any information about the therapist that might significantly affect the person's decision to begin or continue work with the therapist been adequately disclosed and discussed? For example, a patient who has decided to begin therapy and file a formal complaint to address sexual exploitation by a previous therapist may later feel betrayed if he or she learns only after a year of therapy and on the eve of trial (during which her subsequent therapist is expected to be a key witness) that the subsequent witness has frequently expressed the opinion that therapist–patient sexual involvement tends to benefit patients, has been sanctioned by an ethics committee, and has two licensing complaints pending.

☐ Does the person adequately understand limits to accessibility to the therapist (e.g., will the therapist be available to receive or return phone calls during the day, during evening, on nights, weekends, or holidays)? Does the person adequately understand limits to the extent of such accessibility between regularly scheduled sessions (e.g., will phone contacts be limited to brief periods of 5 or at most 10 minutes, or will the therapist allow longer phone consultation)?

☐ Does the person adequately understand what steps to take and what resources are (and are not) available in case of a crisis, emergency, or severe need?

☐ If the person or the treatment are to be used for teaching or related purposes, does the person adequately understand the nature, extent, and implications of such arrangements?

☐ Does the person adequately understand limitations to privacy, confidentiality, and privilege, particularly those related to discretionary or mandatory reports by the therapist and to any legal actions that the person may initiate in regard to the therapist–patient sexual involvement?

☐ Does the person adequately understand the degree to which treatment notes and any other documents in the chart will be made available to the patient and/or to the patient's attorney?

☐ Does the person have information or access to information about options for filing formal complaints (e.g., licensing, malpractice, ethics, or criminal)?

☐ If the person has filed or is considering filing a lawsuit or other formal complaint against the previous therapist, is the person aware of how the procedures associated with such complaints may affect the process of therapy?

☐ Because, as is often emphasized throughout this book, each patient, therapist, and therapy are unique and no list can enumerate the relevant issues for all therapies, the therapist might consider what important issues the prior items in this list have missed as follows. As the therapist tries to identify empathically with the person seeking treatment, what would the therapist wish to know if he or she were in the patient's position? What information would the person wish to know that might significantly affect a decision about beginning therapy?

Appendix D

Guidelines for Reviewing a Prior Therapist's Treatment Notes and Chart Materials

Clinicians providing therapy to or conducting forensic assessments of patients when therapist–patient sex is at issue typically review, unless they are withheld or otherwise unavailable, records made by the previous therapist. The following questions may be useful in providing a careful review of these documents.

☐ Do the records specify the referral source? Was the referral source contacted again?
☐ Do the records specify the presenting complaint or the reason that the individual sought therapy?
☐ Was a mental status examination conducted?
☐ Were any psychological tests or standardized assessment instruments used? If so, are the raw data, scoring sheets, and interpretations (including computerized scorings or interpretations) available?
☐ Is the patient's physical or medical condition mentioned? Is there any indication that the individual was suffering from any physical or medical condition?
☐ Was an adequate history taken? What significant aspects of the history, if any, are omitted?
☐ Are there any records of prior assessment, treatment, hospitalization, and so forth?
☐ Is there any record of a diagnosis? If so, at what point does it first appear? If it is a diagnosis from the *Diagnostic and Statistical Manual of Mental Disorders* (American Psy-

chiatric Association, 1987, 1994), how is the patient's condition assessed in terms of each axis? Is the diagnosis ever revised?

☐ Is there any indication of hallucinations, delusions, or similar conditions? If so, when are they first noted, what additional assessment of such conditions is conducted, and how are they addressed? (Note: Defense attorneys frequently assert that claims of sexual involvement are false and the result of delusions or of the conditions noted in the questions that immediately follow.)

☐ Is there any indication of an actual or potential psychosis?

☐ Is there any indication of a factitious disorder?

☐ Is there any indication of malingering?

☐ Is there any indication that the patient is not truthful or reliable?

☐ Do the notes provide any indication that there was a treatment plan? If so, is there any indication that the effectiveness of the treatment plan was carefully monitored? In what ways was the treatment plan effective, ineffective, or harmful? Is there any indication that the treatment plan was ever revised in light of progress in therapy, new information, or other factors?

☐ Is there any documentation that the patient freely gave informed content for treatment? If so, to what, specifically, did the patient consent?

☐ Is there any indication that the therapist referred the patient to any other professionals, facilities, or organizations for consultation, assessment, adjunctive treatment, or other purposes? If so, is there any record of the results of the referral?

☐ Is there any indication that the therapist consulted with any other professionals, facilities, or organizations in regard to this patient? If so, is there any record of the results of the consultation?

☐ Is there any indication that the therapist issued or received requests for information from other professionals, facilities, or organizations in regard to this patient? If so, are the requests accompanied by an appropriate waiver of confidentiality from the patient? Is it clear what information was sent to or received from others?

☐ Do the billing records appear to be clear and complete? Does the fee ever change? If so, do the records indicate the reason for the change?

☐ When all records (e.g., therapy notes, billing records, and treatment logs) are taken together, does it appear that there are therapy notes for all sessions? Was every session billed appropriately (e.g., were there some sessions for which the patient was not billed)?

☐ Was there any third-party payment source (e.g., private insurance or governmental plan)? What diagnosis (or diagnoses), session dates, and so forth, were provided to the payment source, and is this information in accord with information elsewhere in the chart materials?

☐ Is there any indication of sexual feelings, discussion, or behavior on the part of patient or therapist?

☐ Is there any indication of physical contact between therapist and patient?

☐ Did meetings between therapist and patient ever occur outside the clinical consulting room? If so, what were the conditions?

☐ Are any of the behaviors or experiences mentioned in Appendix A referred to directly or indirectly?

☐ Is there any mention of transference or countertransference?

☐ To what extent was there a formal termination process? Why did therapist and patient cease meeting? What factors mentioned in the documentation seem relevant to the ending of formal sessions or informal meetings between therapist and patient?

Appendix E

Therapist's Outline for Frequent Review of Treatment and Treatment Plan for a Patient Who Has Been Sexually Involved With a Prior Therapist

☐ Does the patient seem to be benefiting from the services that have been provided so far? What issues have been effectively addressed? What significant issues have not yet been addressed?

☐ Have the patient's strengths, abilities, and resources (personal or environmental) been adequately assessed? Does the current treatment plan adequately take account of these strengths, abilities, and resources?

☐ Have issues of informed consent been adequately addressed, particularly with regard to any recent changes in assessment strategy or treatment planning?

☐ Do the patient's descriptions of sexual involvement with a therapist (or other matters) raise any issues of either mandatory or discretionary reporting? If so, have these issues been adequately addressed?

☐ Are there other mandated actions, aside from reporting, that need to be considered? For example, California requires subsequent therapists to provide a pamphlet, *Professional Therapy Never Includes Sex* (California Department of Consumer Affairs, 1990), to patients who report sexual involvement with a prior therapist and to discuss the pamphlet with them. (Even if not required, pamphlets such as *If Sex Enters the Psychotherapy Relationship* [Committee on Women in Psychology, 1989] may be helpful.)

☐ Have potential risks, if any, for violence, abuse, or life-threatening behaviors in regard to this patient been adequately assessed?

☐ To what degree, if at all, does the patient seem to be experiencing any of the following:

- impaired ability to trust (often focused on conflicts about dependence, control, and power)
- guilt
- ambivalence
- feelings of emptiness and isolation
- identity and boundary disturbances
- sexual confusion
- lability of mood (particularly involving depression)
- suppressed rage
- increased suicidal risk
- cognitive dysfunction (especially in the areas of attention and concentration, frequently involving intrusive thoughts, unbidden images, flashbacks, and nightmares)

If so, are these issues adequately addressed in the treatment plan?

☐ Is there any evidence that the patient has medical needs that are not being met? Are there any issues or concerns about the possibility of infection by the human immunodeficiency virus that need to be addressed?

☐ If other professionals (e.g., an attorney handling a malpractice suit against the previous therapist) are also providing services to the patient, is there any evidence that any relevant issues related to coordination of services, miscommunications, turf issues, lines of responsibility, and so on have not been adequately addressed?

☐ Do the chart notes and documentation adequately reflect the current state of assessment, treatment, and treatment planning?

☐ Have any treatment issues emerged for which the therapist is not adequately competent or prepared? If so, have these issues been adequately addressed through options such as supervision by, consultation with, or referral to a colleague who possesses expertise in the relevant areas?

☐ Is the therapist experiencing, for whatever reasons, the type of reactions (e.g., boredom and disinterest in the case, an overwhelming urge to control the patient, a wish or tendency to avoid contact with the patient, or extreme discomfort at the prospect that he or she might be called to testify in a malpractice suit against a fellow therapist) that might constitute countertransference or some other phenomenon that might distort, block, or otherwise interfere with providing professional services? If so, have these reactions been adequately addressed (e.g., through consultation with a colleague)?

Appendix F

Review of Hospitalization Issues

☐ Do any of the institution's programs specialize in helping patients who have been sexually involved with a prior therapist (see Pope, Sonne, & Holroyd, 1993, p.261)?

☐ Do any of the clinical staff possess special expertise in working with patients who have been sexually involved with a prior therapist?

☐ What written policies does the institution have regarding sexual involvement between clinicians and patients? For example, is there any policy that addresses any of the following scenarios:

- A staff therapist on the unit has no clinical contact with the patient. However, the staff therapist greets the patient, spends time talking with the patient, offers the patient a ride home upon discharge, and has sex with the patient.

- A staff therapist on the unit has no clinical contact with the patient and does not speak to the patient during the course of hospitalization. After discharge, the therapist runs into the patient at a market, makes an introduction, and begins dating the patient.

- A staff therapist works in another unit of the institution and has no responsibilities on the unit where the patient is hospitalized. The therapist meets the patient in the hospital cafeteria, strikes up a conversation, and begins dating the patient after discharge (see, e.g., Hatcher, 1993).

☐ What written policies does the institution have regarding sexual involvement between nonclinical staff and patients? For example, do written policies address the possibility that a staff receptionist, safety officer, medical records librarian, or maintenance worker who works on the unit becomes sexually involved with a patient before or after termination?

☐ What written policies does the institution have regarding sexual involvement between unpaid volunteers who work at the institution and patients?

☐ To what extent are these policies made known to people whom they do or could affect?

☐ How are violations of the policy handled?

☐ Does the institution employ clinical or nonclinical workers who are known to have engaged in sex with a patient (whether the incident or incidents occurred at the institution or at another setting)?

☐ Does the institution adequately screen potential employees?

• Do the employment application form and application documents cover an adequate range of information?

• Are any educational degrees verified?

• Are any licenses or certifications verified?

• Is the previous employment history verified?

• Are there letters of evaluation from those in a position to know the individual (e.g., clinical supervisors or administrators)? Do these letters carry an appropriate date? (A copy of a "To whom it may concern" letter dated a decade prior to the individual applying for the current job may be out of date, lack relevant information, and no longer represent the views of the person who wrote the letter.)

• Are there records of phone calls to relevant individuals (e.g., clinical supervisors or administrators) to obtain information?

• What procedures did the institution follow to determine whether the applicant had ever been subject to a licensing complaint and, if so, what the outcome was?

- What procedures did the institution follow to determine whether the applicant had ever been subject to an ethics complaint and, if so, what the outcome was?
- What procedures did the institution follow to determine whether the applicant had ever been subject to a malpractice suit and, if so, what the outcome was?
- What procedures did the institution follow to determine whether the applicant had ever been subject to a criminal complaint and, if so, what the outcome was?
- What procedures did the institution follow to determine whether the applicant had ever been fired for cause and, if so, what the circumstances were?

□ How many, if any, instances have there been in which someone alleged that the institution was the setting for or was otherwise involved in therapist–patient sex? How were these allegations evaluated? What was the outcome?

□ To what extent have topics relevant to therapist–patient sex been the focus of the institution's inservice training programs over the past 5 years?

Appendix G

Therapist's Outline for Review Prior to Deposition and Cross-Examination

☐ Will the patient be present during the therapist's testimony? If so, have issues relating to the patient's encountering the therapist in a new setting and listening to testimony about the patient been addressed, as appropriate, with the patient?

☐ Have relevant published works presenting research, theory, and so forth in the area of therapist–patient sex (see, e.g., Tables 1 and 2) been reviewed?

☐ Is the therapist's curriculum vitae complete and up-to-date?

☐ Does the curriculum vitae clearly reflect adequate education, training, and experience in providing assessment, therapeutic, and forensic services in this area (i.e., to patients who have been sexually involved with a previous therapist) to constitute demonstrable competence or expertise? If not, can the therapist address this issue of competence or expertise?

☐ Have all chart notes and related documents been reviewed?

☐ If a subpoena has been issued, has it been reviewed carefully to determine whether it directs the therapist to bring certain materials to the deposition or trial? If so, have all relevant issues regarding whether these materials should be made available been appropriately examined and resolved (e.g., in certain instances subpoenaed material may be protected by privilege)? If the therapist intends to bring the materials to the deposition or trial, have the materials been located and secured?

☐ Have possible time conflicts regarding testimony been discussed? For example, the therapist may be scheduled to testify Wednesday morning. The attorney calling the therapist to testify may have stressed that the direct examination will begin at 9:00 a.m. and should take no more than an hour. The attorney estimates that the cross-examination will also take no more than an hour. Accordingly, the therapist plans to complete testimony no later than noon and to see patients beginning at 1:30 in the afternoon. However, it is possible that there may be long delays before the court is called to order Wednesday morning. Numerous objections, unexpected (by the attorney calling the therapist) rulings, and several recesses may stretch the direct examination to two or three times the estimated length. The attorney conducting the cross-examination may decide to question the therapist for—literally—two or three days. The possibility that the therapist may not have completed testifying in time to see patients Wednesday afternoon needs to be adequately discussed and contingency plans created.

☐ Have all payment arrangements regarding the therapist's deposition or trial testimony been clarified and agreed to by the relevant parties? Are all relevant parties complying with these arrangements?

☐ Is there any need for (or benefit from) the therapist consulting with his or her own attorney? In many instances, therapists let themselves be guided by the attorney who calls them to testify. However, because the attorney is representing the interests of another person, it may be appropriate for a therapist preparing to appear as a witness in a case involving his or her patient to consult with independent counsel.

☐ Is the therapist aware of any bias, countertransference, or other personal reactions that might interfere with the ability to provide clear, truthful, and undistorted testimony? If so, how can these be effectively addressed?

Appendix H

Cross-Examination Questions for Therapists Who Testify About a Patient's Sexual Involvement With a Therapist

Therapists providing clinical services to patients who allege sexual involvement with a therapist are likely to face an extensive and probing deposition and a challenging cross-examination. This appendix presents questions that are commonly asked.

Reviewing these questions may help therapists to prepare for deposition and cross-examination. The questions will not come as a surprise (as they would if a therapist were encountering them for the first time while testifying), and the witness can have time to reflect on their meaning, to review relevant information (e.g., treatment records and relevant publications), and to consider them from various perspectives prior to providing responses under oath. The witness can ensure that the answers to these questions are as informed, accurate, and clearly expressed as possible.

Reviewing these questions can not only help therapists to prepare to testify in a specific case but also provide opportunities to rethink and reevaluate the therapists' work more generally. Thinking about these questions and their implications may help therapists to identify weaknesses in their ways of practicing and to improve their resources and procedures for providing services to any sexually exploited patient.

Although these questions are phrased for the subsequent therapist, they may also be helpful to other mental health witnesses (expert or fact), regardless of whether they are called by the patient's attorney, the previous therapist's (i.e., the therapist alleged to have engaged in therapist–patient sexual activity) attorney, attorneys for other parties to the case (e.g., the previous therapist's supervisor or the hospital or managed care facility for which the previous therapist was working when the sexual involvement was alleged to have occurred), or by the court itself (e.g., when the court appoints a clinician to conduct an independent psychological assessment of the patient).

Therapist's Previous Work With Patients Who Allege Sexual Involvement

☐ How many patients have you seen clinically who have alleged that they were sexually involved with a previous therapist?

☐ When you consider all the instances in which patients have alleged to you that they have been sexually involved with a previous therapist, how many instances were there in which you finally concluded that the allegations were valid? In how many instances did you conclude that the allegations were invalid? Were there any instances in which you were unable to reach a final conclusion about the validity of the allegations?

☐ On what basis do you decide whether a patient's allegations are true or false? That is to say, what does it take for you to conclude that allegations are true? . . . are false? Please list each type of evidence you take into account and each element of your reasoning.

Therapist's Knowledge of Relevant Research, Theory, and Current Practice

☐ Do you believe that a therapist working with a patient who is alleging therapist–patient sexual involvement needs to be adequately aware of the current research, theory, and practice relevant to therapist–patient sex? (This question is a foundation for the questions that follow. If the therapist answers "no," it is likely that the attorney will elicit extensive testimony about the rationale and implications for this belief.)

☐ Are you adequately aware of the current research, theory, and practice relevant to therapist–patient sex?

☐ What are the most recent research studies in this area that you are familiar with?

☐ What are the most recent publications regarding theory in this area that you have read and are familiar with?

☐ What are the most recent publications regarding practice in this area that you have read and are familiar with?

Therapist's Sources of Knowledge About the Patient

☐ How many hours have you spent with the patient?

☐ Have you reviewed all relevant background documents? Please list those documents that you have reviewed. Would these include
  • prior medical records?
  • prior records of psychological assessment or treatment?
  • records of any hospitalizations?
  • school records?
  • prior records of employment?
  • depositions and other legal documents?

☐ In conducting your assessment of this patient, providing therapy to this patient, preparing to testify, or at any other time, have you ever made an effort to contact or interview any family member, friend, or acquaintance of this patient?

☐ Have you ever made an effort to contact or interview any teachers, employers, coworkers, or others involved in this patient's education or work?

☐ Have you ever made any effort to contact or interview the previous therapist with whom the patient alleges she or he had sex?

☐ Have you made any effort to contact or interview any health care or mental health care professional who has provided assessment, treatment, consultation, or other services to the patient?

☐ Aside from those individuals previously mentioned, have you made any effort to contact or interview anyone else who might have information that would be relevant to your assessment of the patient, the therapy you provided to the patient, or to your testimony here today?

Therapist's Use of or Reliance on Standardized Psychological Tests

☐ Was your therapy with this patient guided by an assessment that included use of standardized psychological tests, regardless of whether you personally administered, scored, or interpreted the tests?

☐ For each test, what are the reliability and validity *when the test is used with this population* (i.e., people who allege sexual involvement with a prior therapist)?

☐ Are you aware of any standardized test that can reliably indicate whether a patient has been sexually involved with a prior therapist?

☐ Are you aware of any research indicating that psychological test results can be misleading if interpreted in the absence of an adequate history?

☐ What aspects of this patient's characteristics and personal history were relevant to proper interpretation of the psychological tests?

Financial Issues

☐ How much are you charging for your testimony in this case?

☐ When did you first discuss financial arrangements (e.g., how much the patient would pay per session) with the patient? What was the nature of those original arrangements? Were those arrangements part of the informed consent?

☐ Have the financial arrangements been changed in any way? If so, how?

☐ Have the financial arrangements, including changes, been fully documented?

- ☐ Did you, the patient, or any other relevant person ever depart in any way from these financial arrangements?
- ☐ Under these financial arrangements, how much money have you earned—whether or not the money has actually been paid to you—for your time and work in regard to this patient?
- ☐ Up to now, how much money, if any, has actually been paid to you?
- ☐ Currently, how much is owed to you? Significant amounts will probably form the basis of numerous subsequent questions addressing issues such as the therapist's allowing a substantial debt to accumulate and the ways in which the likelihood of payment of this debt might hinge on the outcome of the trial, which in turn might be affected by the therapist's testimony. In the latter instance, the therapist's possible bias is explored; the cross-examining attorney's questions may make clear that the therapist's testimony may significantly influence whether the therapist receives payment of moneys owed to him or her.
- ☐ Have you ever sought a lien for any money that the patient owes to you?
- ☐ Have any of the attorneys in this case or those acting on the attorney's behalf offered you any money for your services or for other reasons?

Compliance With Subpoena Duces Tecum

The three sets of questions in this section are taken verbatim from Pope, Butcher, & Seelen (1993, pp. 140–142).

- ☐ Have you complied fully with each and every element of the subpoena to produce? Are there any items that you did not make available?
- ☐ Were any of these documents altered in any way? Were any of them recopied, erased, written over, enhanced, edited, or added to in any way since the time each was originally created? Are the photocopies made available true and exact replicas of the original documents without any revision?
- ☐ Have any documents falling within the scope of the sub-

poena or otherwise relevant to the case been lost, stolen, misplaced, destroyed, or thrown away? Are any documents you made, collected, handled, or received that are within the scope of this subpoena or otherwise relevant to the case absent from the documents made available to me?

The Therapist's Forensic Experience When Therapist–Patient Sex Was at Issue

☐ Have you ever participated in civil, criminal, licensing, or any other forums in which allegations of therapist–patient sex were at issue?

☐ How many such cases involved patients to whom you had personally provided professional services?

☐ In how many such cases did you appear as a witness called by the plaintiff?

☐ In how many such cases did you appear as a witness called by the defense?

☐ In how many such cases did you appear in some other capacity than as a witness called by the plaintiff or defense?

☐ In how many such cases have you been allowed to testify as an expert witness (rather than in some other capacity such as a percipient or fact witness)?

Index

Callanan, K., 44
Carlova, J., 39
Carotenuto, A., 61
Carr, M. L., 18n, 123
Catharsis method, 142
Caudill, Brandt, 110
Cautella, J. R., 154
Chapman, S., 39
Cheatham v. Rogers, 58
Chesler, P., 4, 20, 21
Chicago Insurance Co. v. Griffin, 30n
Child abuse. *See also* Incest; Minors
  ambivalence and, 132
  claims that victim contributed to,
    38–39
  disclosure of therapist–patient sex
    and, 105
  as prior event, 96–97
  role reversal and, 152
  therapist–patient sex compared
    with, 7
Cienfuegos, J., 135
Clarkin, J., 118
Client. *See* Patient, sexually
  exploited
Clinical profiles
  patient uniqueness and, 2–3
  therapist–patient sex syndrome
    model and, 117–119
Clinician. *See* Therapist, exploitive;
  Therapist, subsequent
Cognitive dysfunction, 154–156, 220
Coleman, P. G., 7n
Colley, Justice (appellate court), 59
Collins, D. T., 109
Colt, G. H., 148, 151, 152
Complaint
  confidentiality issues and, 159–
    161
  false. *See* False allegations
  fear of, 47, 203
  probability of filing of, 43n, 87,
    156
  refusal to file, 122
Confidentiality. *See also* Reporting
  subsequent therapy and, 78–82

trust and, 127
unintentional disclosure and, 80,
  159–161
Conflicts of interest, 77–78, 161
Connel, N., 21
Conroe, R. M., 21
"Conspiracy of silence," 39, 60
Context. *See also* Boundaries;
  Therapeutic context
  cognitive dysfunction and, 154
  gender factors and, 14–20, 122–
    123
  importance of awareness of, 13–
    14
  patient anger and, 141–142
  scope issues and, 24–34
  therapist's beliefs and, 47–48
  witness responsibilities and, 180–
    182
Contingency fees, 163
Contributory negligence, 10
Cooley, R. S., 101, 133
"Corrective emotional experience,"
  101
"Corrosive emotional experience,"
  101
Courtois, C. A., 25, 97
Cross-examination
  attacks on plaintiffs in, 170–174
  attorney tactics and, 162–164,
    174–175, 176–179
  commonly asked questions in,
    229–234
  fees and, 162–164
  misuse of standardized tests and,
    107
  preparation of patient for, 170–
    174
  review prior to, 227–228
Csikszentmihalyi, M., 138–139
Cummings, N. A., 29, 30

Dahlberg, C. C., 21
Danto, B., 148
Dattilio, F. M., 139
Davidson, V., 21, 28, 123

NATIONAL UNIVERSITY
LIBRARY ·FRESNO

About the Author

Kenneth S. Pope, PhD, received graduate degrees from Harvard and Yale, is a Diplomate in Clinical Psychology, and is a Fellow of the American Psychological Association (APA) and the American Psychological Society (APS). Having previously served as clinical director and psychology director in both private hospital and community mental health center settings, he is currently in independent practice. He taught courses in abnormal psychology, psychological and neuropsychological assessment, and related areas at the University of California, Los Angeles (UCLA), where he served as psychotherapy supervisor in the UCLA Psychology Clinic. A recipient of the Frances Mosseker Award for Fiction, the Belle Meyer Bromberg Award for Literature, the California Psychological Association's Silver Psi Award and Distinguished Contributions to Psychology as a Profession Award, and the APA Division of Clinical Psychology (12) Award for Distinguished Professional Contributions to Clinical Psychology, he served as chair of the Ethics Committees of the APA and of the American Board of Professional Psychology. He has authored or coauthored over 100 scientific and professional articles; his books include *Sexual Intimacies Between Therapists and Patients* (with J. C. Bouhoutsos), *Sexual Feelings in Psychotherapy: Explorations for Therapists and Therapists-in-Training* (with J. L. Sonne and J. Holroyd), *The MMPI, MMPI-2, and MMPI-A in Court: A Practical Guide for Expert Witnesses and Attorneys* (with J. N. Butcher and J. Seelen), *Ethics in Psychotherapy and Counseling* (with M. J. T. Vasquez), *Law & Mental Health Professionals: California* (with B. Caudill), *On Love and Loving, The Stream of Consciousness: Scientific Investigations into the Flow of Human Experience*, and *The Power of Human Imagination: New Methods of Psychotherapy* (the latter two with J. L. Singer).

NATIONAL UNIVERSITY
LIBRARY FRESNO

1095